PRAGMATISM IN ISLAMIC LAW

Middle East Studies Beyond Dominant Paradigms
Peter Gran, *Series Editor*

Select titles from Middle East Studies beyond Dominant Paradigms

Artisan Entrepreneurs in Cairo and Early-Modern Capitalism (1600–1800)
Nelly Hanna

Gender and Class in the Egyptian Women's Movement, 1925–1939: Changing Perspectives
Cathlyn Mariscotti

The Large Landowning Class and the Peasantry in Egypt, 1837–1952
Raouf Abbas and Assem El-Dessouky;
Amer Mohsen and Mona Zikri, trans.; Peter Gran, ed.

Militant Women of a Fragile Nation
Malek Abisaab

Minorities and the Modern Arab World: New Perspectives
Laura Robson, ed.

Native Tongue, Stranger Talk: The Arabic and French Literary Landscapes of Lebanon
Michelle Hartman

The Shi'ites of Lebanon: Modernism, Communism, and Hizbullah's Islamists
Rula Jurdi Abisaab and Malek Abisaab

Unveiling the Harem: Elite Women and the Paradox of Seclusion in Eighteenth-Century Cairo
Mary Ann Fay

Pragmatism *in* Islamic Law

Ahmed Fekry Ibrahim

Syracuse University Press

First Paperback Edition 2017
17 18 19 20 21 22 6 5 4 3 2 1

∞ The paper used in this publication meets the minimum requirements of the American National Standard for Information Sciences—Permanence of Paper for Printed Library Materials, ANSI Z39.48-1992.

For a listing of books published and distributed by Syracuse University Press, visit www.SyracuseUniversityPress.syr.edu.

ISBN: 978-0-8156-3517-8 (paperback) 978-0-8156-3394-5 (cloth) 978-0-8156-5319-6 (ebook)

Library of Congress has cataloged the hardcover edition as follows:
Ibrahim, Ahmed Fekry.
Pragmatism in Islamic law : a social and intellectual history / Ahmed Fekry Ibrahim.
pages cm. — (Middle East studies beyond dominant paradigms)
Includes bibliographical references and index.
ISBN 978-0-8156-3394-5 (cloth : alk. paper) — ISBN 978-0-8156-5319-6 (e-book)
1. Jurisdiction (Islamic law) 2. Jurisdiction (Islamic law)—Egypt. 3. Procedure (Islamic law) 4. Islamic law—History. I. Title.
KBP1664.I27 2015
340.5'92—dc23 2014047345

Manufactured in the United States of America

In loving memory of my father,

Fekry M. Ibrahim Masud (1945–2005)

Ahmed Fekry Ibrahim is an assistant professor of Islamic law at the McGill Institute of Islamic Studies in Montreal. He holds a BA from al-Azhar University and an MA degree from the American University in Cairo. He completed his PhD in Islamic Studies at Georgetown University in 2011. His dissertation, entitled "School Boundaries and Social Utility in Islamic Law: The Theory and Practice of *Talfīq* and *Tatabbuʿ al-Rukhaṣ* in Egypt," traced the pragmatic utilization of Sunnī legal pluralism in twentieth-century Egypt to developments that took place in the Mamluk and Ottoman periods in court practice and juristic discourse. In 2011–12, he received a EUME postdoctoral fellowship with the Berlin research program "Europe in the Middle East—The Middle East in Europe," organized by Berlin-Brandenburgische Akademie der Wissenschaften, Fritz Thyssen Stiftung, and Wissenschaftskolleg zu Berlin. His teaching and research interests include Islamic legal practice in Ottoman courts, Islamic law from below, the impact of socioeconomic and cultural changes on juristic discourse and court practice, and the formation of Islamic law. He is currently working on two monograph-length studies of child custody in Islamic law and Islamic legal hermeneutics, two research projects for which he has recently won two major three-year research grants (2014–17) from the Fonds de recherche du Québec—Société et Culture (FRQSC) and the Social Sciences and Humanities Research Council of Canada (SSHRC).

Contents

Illustrations

Preface

Pragmatic Adjudication and Pragmatic Eclecticism

I HAVE COINED THE TERM *pragmatic eclecticism*, the subject of this study, to make a link between certain concepts of Islamic law such as *tatabbuʿ al-rukhaṣ*, *talfīq*, and *takhayyur* (see pp. 3–5) and general discussions of *pragmatism* in other legal traditions such as the common law.[1] My objective is to demystify and deghettoize Islamic law, placing it squarely within the legal traditions of the world by emphasizing the *law* aspect, which often gets lost in sensationalist discussions of the *Islamic*. To understand the term pragmatic eclecticism, one must delve into the broader concept of *pragmatic adjudication*. Pragmatic adjudication, or legal pragmatism, is a notion drawn from philosophical pragmatism, a movement that originated in the United States in the second half of the nineteenth century. Philosophical pragmatism's main principle is that we can only have reflective clarity about propositions when we identify their practical consequences.[2] Legal pragmatism draws on the anti-formalism and anti-foundationalism of philosophical pragmatism, viewing law as a practice that depends on context and instrumentality rather than on secure formal foundations.[3]

As such, legal pragmatists emphasize (1) contextualism, (2) anti-foundationalism, and (3) consequentialism. Legal pragmatism has a *descriptive* element, because legal decisions have historically been informed by contexts that can be unmasked to show the fallacies of formalist determinacy, as well as a *normative* aspect, according to which legal pragmatists assume that instrumentalist jurisprudence is the only way to bring about *substantive* justice, that is, doing what is right in a particular case even if that goes against legal rules. Pragmatists do not completely reject formal rules but rather consider them as one set of many factors that a judge should consider when deciding a case.[4] Yet their notion of justice has been criticized for its subjectivism and violation of the rule of law, which requires certainty, stability, and predictability.[5]

According to pragmatists, empirically and scientifically relevant data should have an impact on legal decisions,[6] for, in Dewey's words, the logic of judicial decisions should be "*relative to consequences rather than to antecedents.*"[7] In his critique of adherence to old formal rules, Dewey admonishes:

> Here is where the great practical evil of the doctrine of immutable and necessary antecedent rules comes in. It sanctifies the old; adherence to it in practise [*sic*] constantly widens the gap between current social conditions and the principles used by the courts. The effect is to breed irritation, disrespect for law, together with virtual alliance between the judiciary and entrenched interests that correspond most nearly to the conditions under which the rules of law were previously laid down.[8]

The rigidity of the doctrine of immutable antecedent in Dewey's critique of common law formalism is reminiscent of criticisms of the rigidity of *taqlīd* in Islamic legal historiography.[9] According to this analysis, such formalism creates a gap between social conditions and legal principles, leading to a tension between law and society. The main objective of this book is to explore how jurists dealt with the *relative* rigidity of the formalist rules of *taqlīd*. I contend that the Ottoman Egyptian judiciary exercised pragmatic adjudication and jurisprudence in the courtroom and in legal treatises by focusing on the legal result through the permission of forum and doctrinal shopping (pragmatic eclecticism), rather than relying on the formalist rules of each school. In other words, they were more concerned with the consequences of their adjudication, which they navigated through legal procedure, than with the positive law and methodology of each school.

Pragmatic eclecticism, whereby legal actors selected doctrines to accommodate specific social needs, is a type of pragmatic adjudication achieved through legal procedure. One important difference between American pragmatic adjudication and pragmatic eclecticism is that the former is tied to the individual judge and her or his legal reasoning in a given case. Certainly, the judge's pragmatic adjudication is informed by her or his situatedness in society and especially in the judiciary, but they can in theory devise unpredictable novel solutions. This is not the case with pragmatic eclecticism in the Ottoman Egyptian context, because it was designed by the judiciary (the state's representative) as an overarching procedure, granting judges and subjects of the law a certain level of discretion in the choice of forum, while restricting them to existing school rules. Judges encountered formalist constraints, for instance, in cases in which there was no legal pluralism, such as the existence of a consensus on a given issue, making adjudication a hybrid of pragmatic and formalist decisions. This hybrid allowed a host of legal players such as judges, legal subjects, and muftis to engage in maneuvers to deal with specific social and economic issues. Importantly, such licenses were sanctioned by the state through its judicial bureaucracy.

This book is a longitudinal study of juristic discourse on pragmatic eclecticism and of the practice in seventeenth- and eighteenth-century Ottoman Egypt. Although the sample shows that pragmatic adjudication qua pragmatic eclecticism was widely utilized—so much so that it led to a high level of predictability that would have been absent from a more individualistic form of pragmatic adjudication—one should not overlook other factors such as school affiliation, the absence of a judge, or the vacancy of a deputyship that may have played a role in the choice of judges.[10] The sample also suggests that most judges adjudicated on the basis of their own schools in accordance with the ideal doctrine of Islamic law of the postclassical period. Yet we find instances in which a Ḥanafī judge, for instance, would adjudicate according to Ḥanbalī law rather than refer the case to a Ḥanbalī judge.[11] One, therefore, should not expect that the findings of this study would necessarily be consistent across different regions or other periods of the Ottoman Empire. Rather, one should assume that the picture of pragmatic eclecticism drawn from our sample represents a strong tendency within Islamic law that was both valorized in juristic discourse and widely practiced in Ottoman Egyptian courts.

Montreal, August 2016

Acknowledgments

IN THE COURSE of the many years it has taken for this project to come to life, I have incurred many debts to family, friends, and colleagues. Throughout the journey of the conception, labor, and fruition of this project, I have come to benefit from the intellectual companionship and help of many people. I am grateful to Felicitas Opwis, Ahmad Dallal, Judith Tucker, and John Voll from Georgetown University for their intellectual and moral support in the first stage of the project. The American Research Center in Egypt (ARCE) provided funding for the earliest stage of this project in 2009–10. This funding enabled me to examine unpublished manuscripts and archival material without which this project would not have been possible. I am grateful to the staff at Egypt's National Archives (Dār al-Wathā'iq al-Qawmiyya), Egypt's National Library (Dār al-Kutub), the British Library, Georgetown University Library, the Library of the Free University of Berlin, and the Institute of Islamic Studies Library at McGill University. For their editorial and research help, I am grateful to Steve Millier as well as my research assistants and students, Omar Edaibat, Margaret Gilligan, Ahmad Munir, and Segolene Lapeyre of McGill University.

Georgetown University-Qatar provided a generous fellowship in 2010–11 that helped me conduct more research for this project. To write this book, Europe in the Middle East—The Middle East in Europe (EUME) of the Berlin-based Forum Transregionale Studien provided postdoctoral funding that enabled me to expand my research and write the first full book draft in 2011–12. For their critical engagement with my research, I am particularly grateful to Georges Khalil, EUME fellows, and Zukunftsphilologie fellows, as well as to Gudrun Krämer and Birgit Krawietz from the Institut für Islamwissenschaft at Freie Universität Berlin, who also provided me with the resources available at the Berlin Graduate School of Muslim Cultures and Societies to continue my research in the summer of 2013.

Throughout the last stages of the development of this project, I have benefited from discussions with Amira Sonbol, Peter Gran, Nelly Hanna, Sara Nimis, David Powers, Christopher Melchert, Khaled Fahmy, Khaled al-Rouyahib, Behnam Sadeghi, Emad Helal, Junaid Quadri, Ahmed El Shamsy, Pascale Ghazaleh, Amina Elbendary, Craig French, Manan Ahmed, Mohammad Fadel, Walter Edward Young, Islam Dayeh, Jonathan Brown, Edward Kolla, Kasia Nadine Rada, Henri Lauzière, Nora Lafi, Nadjma Yassari, Kenneth Cuno, Lena-Maria Möller, Sarah Albrecht, Adam Sabra, Julie Billaud, Mireille Fournier, Zeinab Abul-Magd, Alexandra Kemmerer, Aishah Nofal, and the anonymous reviewers of *Islamic Law and Society*. I have also benefited from discussions at conferences and seminars at, in roughly chronological order, the American University in Cairo, the American Research Center in Egypt (ARCE), the Middle East Studies Association (MESA), Georgetown University-Qatar Faculty Seminar, the Institut für Islamwissenschaft at the Free University of Berlin, and Europe in the Middle East—The Middle East in Europe (EUME). Last but not least, I would like to thank my colleagues at the Institute of Islamic Studies at McGill University for their intellectual companionship and friendship.

PRAGMATISM IN ISLAMIC LAW

Introduction

IN MAY 2011, ʿAbd al-Munʿim Abū al-Futūḥ, an Egyptian presidential candidate and former member of the Muslim Brotherhood (MB), surprised many Egyptians when he unequivocally rejected the Islamic legal punishment for apostasy.[1] Although Abū al-Futūḥ is seen as a progressive figure within the MB, many of his supporters and opponents were shocked at his disregard for premodern Islamic substantive law. Almost simultaneously with Abū al-Futūḥ's announcement, a recorded sermon by a Muslim preacher associated with the purist Salafī movement in which he called for jihad as a solution to the country's economic problems, went viral on the Internet.[2] According to this famous and controversial preacher, the booty taken from enemies, including prisoners of war, could give a boost to Egypt's economy although it would entail legalizing slavery again to bring back this lucrative trade.[3] Despite the sensationalism and politicization with which the media covered the circulating video, these episodes highlight the points of tension between general conceptions of modernity and notions of cultural purism.

Such oscillation between the embracement of modernity and its discourses, on the one hand, and a purist rejection of such discourses, on the other, has characterized the debates among different factions seeking to define Islam in a post–Arab Spring Egypt. The fall of the Mubarak regime in 2011 heralded a new era, which gave momentum to the debate about the reinstatement of Islamic law. Modern purists (known as Salafīs) called for a million-person demonstration in Cairo's Tahrir Square to demand the restoration of Sharīʿa. According to them, Egypt's 2011 Revolution presented a golden opportunity to end the centuries of persecution that had started with Mehmed Ali's reign (r. 1805–48).[4] The demonstration sent shock waves through liberal circles and even within al-Azhar, which views purist legal interpretations with scorn. Despite the toppling of the Muslim Brotherhood's President Mohamed Morsi and the heavy crackdown on the Islamist (and non-Islamist for that matter) opposition to the new order, Islamic law remains an important point of contention in post-Morsi Egypt.[5]

I use "Islamic law" to refer to *furūʿ* (substantive law), *uṣūl al-fiqh* (legal methodology), and *fiqh* (jurisprudence), but with the caveat that the subject matter of "Islamic law" includes doctrines related to ethical values and ritual practice that do not fall within the purview of law in the strict sense in British or Continental European legal systems. My use of "Islamic law" should therefore be understood to refer to ethical, ritual, and legal doctrines, as well as to legal methodology and the link between the two in which legal methodology is applied to gain an understanding (*fiqh*) of substantive law. The word *Sharīʿa* is most often used in the primary sources to mean simply substantive law, but sometimes (especially in the modern period) a clear distinction is drawn between Sharīʿa, which is divine law as lodged in the mind of God, and *fiqh*, human approximations and understanding of the divine ideal.[6] Owing to the complexity of the term *Sharīʿa* and its little understood evolutionary path into modernity, I will generally avoid using the Arabic word unless I am citing the primary or secondary sources.

In the early twentieth century, the efforts made to codify personal status laws across the region were largely aimed at accommodating modern notions of equal citizenship and the nuclear family. Some reformers viewed Islamic legal doctrines, juristic interpretations, and laws as discriminatory toward women and minorities. Their project aimed to create laws that were "modern" while maintaining Islamic authenticity by remaining committed to the Islamic scriptural sources. The modern architects of reform used both *ijtihād* (individual legal reasoning), which refers to "the interpretation of scripture directly with no intermediate authorities standing between the sources and the individual jurist," and doctrinal eclecticism to achieve these objectives.[7] This eclecticism was a process in which the doctrines of the four Sunnī schools were drawn upon to select the least stringent juristic opinion (known in the primary sources as *tatabbuʿ al-rukhaṣ* or *takhayyur*), or where two juristic opinions were combined in the same legal transaction (known in the primary sources as *talfīq*). I place the three terms (more on them below) associated with this phenomenon under my conceptual category *pragmatic eclecticism*, for they all denote the eclectic utilization of legal pluralism to achieve pragmatic objectives.[8] The term *pragmatic* and its derivatives such as *pragmatists* or *ḍarūra-pragmatists* are not intended to refer to an author's *weltanschauung*, but simply to his position on this particular issue. In other words, al-Subkī (d. 683/1284) and al-Zarkashī (d. 794/1392) might be seen as taking a pragmatic approach on legal pluralism, but a nonpragmatic approach on another issue. A case in point is al-Ghazālī (d. 505/1111) and al-Shāṭibī (d. 790/1388), who, despite their famous opposition to pragmatic eclecticism, were the champions of the theory of public weal (*maṣlaḥa*).[9]

The distinction I draw between choice of legal opinions based on the assessment of evidence or for pragmatic reasons was clearly articulated by jurists such as al-Juwaynī (d. 478/1085) and al-Suyūṭī (d. 911/1505). The terms *tatabbuʿ al-rukhaṣ* and *tarjīḥ* were often presented in the primary sources as binaries, with the former referring to the pragmatic selection of less stringent juristic views and the latter to choices based on the assessment of evidence underpinning each view. This binary was clearly stated by Jalāl al-Dīn al-Suyūṭī (d. 911/1505), who drew a distinction between crossing school boundaries for a religious reason (*amr dīnī*), for a worldly reason (*amr dunyawī*), or arbitrarily (*mujaraddan ʿan al-qaṣd*).[10]

When the choice of juristic opinions is based on the strength of evidence or on the number of authorities supporting a given view, this is usually called "preponderance" (*tarjīḥ* or *taṣḥīḥ*).[11] *Tarjīḥ* generally implies that the different opinions fall within the boundaries of valid disagreement (*khilāf*), and therefore a view that contradicts the opinion perceived to be "preponderant" (*rājiḥ*) cannot be regarded as false.[12] This evidentiary departure from one's school doctrine, whether performed by jurists or the laity, was permitted by most jurists, as it was considered to be supported by the sources of Islamic law and the authority vested in jurists to interpret them. Choosing juristic opinions based on the legal result, rather than the process of substantiation of evidence, generated a controversy throughout Islamic history. One would assume that, given the choice, rational legal authorities and subjects would attempt to engage in forum and doctrinal shopping to facilitate their transactions.[13] Three terms are used in the primary sources to refer to this process, *talfīq, tatabbuʿ al-rukhaṣ*, and, in the modern period, *takhayyur* to refer to *tatabbuʿ al-rukhaṣ*. These terms, which I combine under my conceptual category "pragmatic eclecticism," refer to selections of juristic opinions both within the same school and across school boundaries. Pragmatic eclecticism can be utilized by four legal actors, namely subjects of the law, judges (*qāḍīs*), jurisconsults (muftis), and author-jurists (jurists who compile law books, creating, justifying, modifying, and codifying legal doctrine).

It was also owing to the negative connotations of *tatabbuʿ al-rukhaṣ* that jurists, especially its proponents, sometimes avoided using the term, and instead described a process in which the choice of juristic opinion is motivated by the legal result as opposed to evidentiary grounds. To avoid this terminological indeterminacy in the primary sources, which is compounded by the occasional absence of any terms in the Arabic sources, as well as the use of different terms diachronically to refer to the same phenomenon (as is the case with *tatabbuʿ al-rukhaṣ* and *takhayyur*), I use the term *pragmatic eclecticism* to refer to *tatabbuʿ al-rukhaṣ* and *talfīq* in a general sense. When a distinction between *tatabbuʿ al-rukhaṣ* and *talfīq* is required, I maintain the Arabic terms or use the phrase "complex pragmatic eclecticism" to refer specifically to *talfīq* and "simple pragmatic eclecticism" to refer to *tatabbuʿ al-rukhaṣ*.

The English phrase "forum selection" or "forum shopping" would not be sufficient to cover the entire spectrum of meaning of the terms used in the primary sources (*talfīq, tatabbuʿ al-rukhaṣ*, and *takhayyur*). While pragmatic eclecticism refers simply to "forum shopping," when performed by the parties to legal transactions inside a court, it also includes eclecticism with regard to doctrines, rather than forums such as the case of an author-jurist who selects a weak juristic view from within his own school owing to its utility. This type of eclecticism does not fall under the English category of "forum selection," since there is no change of forum (or school in this case), but rather doctrinal eclecticism. In addition, "forum selection" would not be sufficient as a translation of *talfīq*, in which two juristic views (possibly belonging to two different schools) are combined in the same transaction. The Arabic terms, for which I use the term "pragmatic eclecticism," also include doctrinal selections made by a jurisconsult (a legal authority who issues nonbinding legal opinions on matters of law and rituals), when he chooses a legal doctrine from a school other than his own in order to facilitate people's transactions. The same is true for the doctrinal selections made by author-jurists in their fatwa collections, which are a form of doctrinal, legislative pragmatism akin to that exercised in the modern period by legislators in twentieth-century Egypt, as we shall see in chapter 6.

On the issue of apostasy, Abū al-Futūḥ, who was never trained as a jurist, exercised such eclecticism when he selected from a range of juristic opinions a position that he deemed more appropriate for modern times. However, this approach is usually rejected by purists whose stance on modernity is generally not one of accommodation.[14] The struggle between modernists and purists over the definition of law has become a central point of contention among different players in post-Mubarak and post-Morsi Egypt. As we will see in our discussion of Egypt after the Arab Spring in chapter 6, different players come to the debate with competing methodologies informed by both premodern debates of Islamic law and modern contingencies.[15]

In the modern period, European laws infiltrated Islamic societies. Personal status laws became virtually the only realm of Islamic law, whereby legislators endeavored to design a legal system inspired by Islamic law yet respectful of modern discourses of women's rights and equal citizenship.[16] As we shall see, this eclecticism was utilized in twentieth-century Egypt, where the official school of law was and still is Ḥanafism, drawing upon the other Sunnī schools (Mālikī, Shāfiʿī, Ḥanbalī) to accommodate modern needs in Egypt's partial codification of personal status laws. For instance, modern Egyptian legislators drew upon the Mālikī school in order to provide women with more divorce rights. The secularization of the other fields of law (for example, criminal, commercial, maritime, procedural) was never fully accepted by many Muslims, giving rise to attempts at devising an "Islamic state" where all the laws are based on Islamic law. In framing different conceptions of the place of Islamic law in Islamic governance, pragmatic eclecticism was utilized by some jurists and activists to provide a vision of what an "Islamic state"—with Islamic law being central to that state—should look like. In this vein, the views of some Muslim scholars and activists such as the Tunisian Rāshid al-Ghannūshī and the Egyptian Yūsuf al-Qaraḍāwī represent pragmatic eclectic projects that treat the entire Sunnī legal tradition with its immense diversity as one open code that they can draw upon to accommodate their communities' evolving needs. They treat the four schools that survived into the postformative period of Islamic law, as well as previous scholars that emerged before the schools stabilized or even Companions of the Prophet, as possessing potentially useful legal opinions for their projects.[17]

By embracing this approach, these reformers were oblivious to the methodological and hermeneutic coherence of the resulting system of law, especially as these different schools and legal authorities utilized exceedingly different methodological and hermeneutic approaches that are incompatible at best or contradictory at worst. Was overlooking methodological coherence through a focus on the utilitarian functions of legal pluralism a novel development in Islamic law in the modern period? Was this type of pragmatic eclecticism debated prior to the nineteenth century?

Modern legal reform and, by extension, other more contemporary attempts that draw upon the same legal strategies have been dismissed as inauthentic by some legal historians. They have argued that what remains of the traditional system is nothing more than a veneer.[18] There is also a perception among some historians that there was an intimate connection between Islamic legal methodology and substantive law prior to the nineteenth century. This link was upset by the utilization of *takhayyur* and *talfīq* in the modern period. Thus, juxtaposing the modern period with pre-nineteenth-century Sharīʿa, Nathan Brown holds that, in the modern period, "the divorcing of the sharīʿa and training in a specific school of law has also progressed, and objections to eclecticism in choosing among schools of law (*takhayyur*) have consequently declined."[19]

Wael B. Hallaq contrasts this link with the inherent arbitrariness of *takhayyur* and *talfīq*, which, in his estimation,[20] leads to an incoherent methodology, thus severing the organic connection with traditional law and society.[21] Such arbitrariness is a characteristic of the modern period, since both *takhayyur* and *talfīq,* according to this view, were forbidden in Islamic law for both the jurists and state authorities. Hallaq cautions, however, that "[i]n pre-modern Sharīʿa, the individual Muslim had the freedom to choose among the schools, in whole or in part, but he or she was bound to whichever school chosen for a transaction."[22] This situation was compounded by the demise of the institutions of Sharīʿa such as the endowment (*waqf*) and school (*madrasa*),[23] which guaranteed jurists their independence from the state.[24]

Undergirding this discourse is the assumption that both *talfīq* and *takhayyur*—the underlying foundations of Islamic modernist discourse—were by-products of modernity, an assumption that I challenge in this book. The general premises of contemporary historians can thus be summarized as follows:

1. *Takhayyur* and *talfīq* are largely modern phenomena (although some recognize the existence of *takhayyur* prior to the nineteenth century).

2. In traditional Islamic law, there was always a connection between substantive law (*furūʿ*) and legal methodology (*uṣūl*), that is, the legal hermeneutic and reasoning underpinning legal opinions. This connection was lost in the modern period.

3. The arbitrary reformist methodology, which is solely motivated by expediency, contrasts with the more methodologically coherent, traditional approach that was based on the consistent methodology of each school.

This study seeks to show that pragmatic eclecticism (whether in the form of *takhayyur, tatabbuʿ al-rukhaṣ*, or *talfīq*) was hardly novel. My intention is not to claim apologetically that the modern partial codification of Islamic law has brought nothing new to Muslim nation-states. To be sure, the very act of codification—certainly not a neutral tool—has created an utterly new legal dynamic. There are clear ruptures, including the loss of endowments and the creation of a new class of legists, trained in Western legal systems, who drastically challenged the authority of jurists. No less challenging to their status is the transformation of legal authority from a jurists' law to legislation. While acknowledging these ruptures, I wish, nevertheless, to argue that (1) reformist strategies were largely "traditional," as pragmatic eclecticism was indeed practiced throughout Islamic history; and (2) substantive legal rules were often epistemically and logically divorced from the school structure in the premodern period through the utilization of pragmatic eclecticism.

I will challenge the idealist prism through which some historians have viewed premodern Islamic law by showing that (1) the severance of the link between the methodology of each school and positive law through pragmatic eclecticism was a characteristic of Islamic law (and most legal systems for that matter as evidenced by the prevalence of legal transplants in most legal systems) both in the premodern and modern periods; and (2) the legal reasoning utilized by jurists to justify pragmatic eclecticism departed significantly from the rules of legal methodology (*uṣūl*), as jurists resorted to "ad hoc reasoning" (to use Behnam Sadeghi's term) in which the rules of legal methodology were not observed;[25] for example, terms such as "necessity" (*ḍarūra*) and "need" (*ḥāja*) were utilized, not as neatly outlined in handbooks of legal methodology but in a way that resembles a form of "name-dropping" in order to justify pragmatic eclecticism without engaging the *uṣūl* theory from which these terms are drawn. A similar phenomenon has recently been observed by Sadeghi, who shows that the term *abrogation* was used by jurists to counter the contrary evidence of the canon (the Qur'an and hadith) without satisfying the requirements of abrogation outlined in handbooks of legal methodology.[26] Jurists resorted to these departures when a commitment to legal methodology could not achieve the desired legal outcome, to wit, the permission of pragmatic eclecticism.

Perhaps part of the reason for the view of pragmatic eclecticism as "arbitrary" is motivated by the fact that the differences among the legal schools reflect geographical, historical, and methodological variations and origins. Such differences, it may follow, will lead to situations in which the legal "transplants" resulting from school boundary-crossing will no longer represent the values of the juristic class or the society into which these laws are imported. Such a phenomenon of transplantation of legal rules through pragmatic eclecticism, as well as its concomitant "arbitrariness" and "inconsistency," is not a peculiarity of Islamic law, but it is rather part and parcel of most legal systems.[27]

In order to make these larger theoretical points, I examine pragmatic eclecticism (both in its simple and complex forms of *tatabbuʿ al-rukhaṣ* and *talfīq* respectively) in juristic discourse, as well as conduct a praxeological examination of the manifestations of law as a living organism in the court context. I show that pragmatic eclecticism was permitted by many jurists starting around the thirteenth century, and was widely practiced in Egyptian courts prior to the nineteenth century. I conclude that the strategies used in the codification of Islamic law in twentieth-century Egypt were mostly traditional in their approach, mirroring Ottoman juristic attitudes for the most part. Finally, I explore the place of Islamic law in Egypt after the Arab Spring and the role of pragmatic eclecticism in this new context.

Incredibly, no thorough study of forum shopping (from within the Sunnī schools) among Muslims prior to the nineteenth century has been conducted. Ron Shaham, for instance, studied legal forum shopping among Egyptian Christians within the pluralistic legal system of the nineteenth century. He showed that Christians regularly maneuvered between their own family laws and those of the Islamic majority and suggested that a similar study should be conducted for the four Sunnī schools of law among Muslims.[28] Neither is there a study that diachronically traces attitudes among jurists toward eclecticism in juristic discourse. There is, however, evidence that people chose judges based on the desired legal outcome, rather than on strict adherence to a specific school. Judith E. Tucker, for example, discusses a fatwa (a nonbinding legal opinion issued by a mufti) by the seventeenth-century Ḥanafī jurist Khayr al-Dīn al-Ramlī, in which the fatwa-seeker has previously chosen a Shāfiʿī judge to obtain a divorce according to Shāfiʿī law.[29] Similarly, in her study of seventeenth- and eighteenth-century court records from Jerusalem and Damascus, she shows that the court system made use of legal diversity, granting women a divorce in situations in which Ḥanafī doctrine would not have achieved the desired results.[30] This process corresponds to what Mamluk and Ottoman jurists dubbed *tatabbuʿ al-rukhaṣ*, the pre-nineteenth-century equivalent of *takhayyur.*

I demonstrate that pragmatic eclecticism, which was forbidden in juristic discourse in the formative period, became increasingly subject to debate in the Mamluk and Ottoman periods. The result of these debates was that its status changed from being forbidden by consensus to its gradual permissibility within the more fluid *ikhtilāf* paradigm.[31] In addition to shedding light on the nature of juristic discourse and court practice of pragmatic eclecticism, I seek to answer some questions related to the administration of the Ottoman judiciary. These questions include: Did the legal pluralism of the Mamluk period come into conflict with early Ottoman attempts at homogenization and codification? If there was a division of labor among the four Sunnī schools of law, how consistent was it? Was the choice of forum (Sunnī school of law) not circumscribed at all by the Ottoman authorities? Answering these questions will not only illuminate the history of Islamic law, but it will also make a contribution to our understanding of the Ottoman authorities' approach to Egyptian legal pluralism. During this discussion, I will also address the tension between the Ottoman authorities and local Egyptian-Mamluk society over Mamluk legal pluralism and Ottoman attempts at Ḥanafization, that is, transforming Egyptian legal pluralism into a uniform Ḥanafī system. This examination of the practice of pragmatic eclecticism will also shed light on how the Ottoman authorities, having given up on their earlier policies of Ḥanafization, resorted to Sunnī legal pluralism to solve economic problems,[32] and, in some cases, to protect women's financial rights.

Legal Stability, Flexibility, and Pragmatic Eclecticism

One need not think of the two extremes of flexibility and stability, namely *ijtihād* (individual legal reasoning) and *taqlīd* (legal conformism) in a strictly binary fashion but rather as two points on a continuum. "Absolute" or "independent" *ijtihād*, in which the scholar, in theory, applies himself directly to the textual sources often through analogical reasoning (*qiyās*), unencumbered by legal precedent, is at one end of the continuum.[33] The *mujtahid* (the jurist exercising *ijtihād*) surveys the entire corpus of scriptural sources (the Qur'an and hadith) on a particular issue, theoretically unhindered by any previous juristic opinions or a specific hermeneutic. Thus in theory he or she may articulate a novel juristic view that contradicts existing legal doctrine. At the other end lies "absolute *taqlīd*" (legal conformism) of the lowest rank of jurists who, like the laity, are required to rely on the established precedent of the legal authorities. This is also where one may place pragmatic eclectic *taqlīd*, in which there is no direct engagement of the authority of the textual sources of the law, but simply a choice of juristic opinions owing to pragmatic considerations.

Somewhat close to the middle of the continuum lies "intra-school *ijtihād*," (known in the primary sources as *ijtihād fi'l-madhhab*) in which a jurist examines the scriptural sources directly, but within the methodological and substantive legal parameters of a school.[34] This type of *ijtihād* was often drawn upon in novel cases that the leading authorities of a given school did not address. After the maturation of the Sunnī schools, "intra-school *ijtihād*" was rarely utilized to offer completely novel solutions to old problems, although that certainly did happen. Also subsumed under this large category of "intra-school *ijtihād*" is the evidentiary assessment of different opinions with reference to the sources of the law known as the exercise of "preponderance" (*tarjīḥ*).[35] Although there is some appeal to the textual sources and legal reasoning, the jurist is restricted by the interpretive choices and hermeneutic of his school. The jurist exercising *tarjīḥ* is not expected to depart, in any significant way, from the largely predetermined juristic options established by the schools' leading authorities. Another term that overlaps greatly with *tarjīḥ* is *tashhīr* (not to be confused with "punitive parading"), which refers to declaring a legal doctrine "famous" (*mashhūr*). Despite its frequent use interchangeably with *tarjīḥ*, sometimes a distinction can be sensed whereby *tashhīr* is a collective description of majoritarian school doctrine, whereas *tarjīḥ* refers to a jurist's subjective judgment based on his own scrutiny of the sources of law.[36] Also under the category of "intra-school *ijtihād*," one can place ad hoc reasoning close to the absolute *taqlīd* side since legal reasoning is not conducted on the basis of legal methodology. I will also include under "ad hoc reasoning" juristic justifications based on social realities, vague and unregulated general conceptions of necessity (*ḍarūra*), moral decline (*fasād ahl al-zamān*),[37] or actual practice (*'umūm al-balwā*). Actual practice is sometimes referenced to justify legal doctrines since challenging such practice would constitute great hardship, and therefore the reasoning overlaps with the reasoning of *ḍarūra* and *ḥāja*.[38]

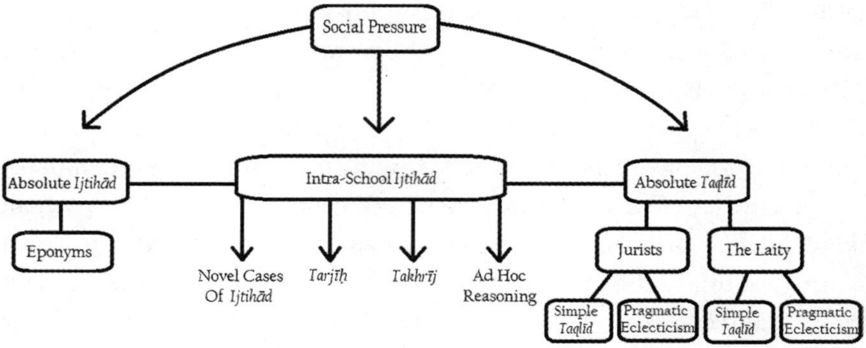

1. *Ijtihād-taqlīd* continuum. Courtesy of Margaret Gilligan, 2014.

Once there was enough pressure from nonlegal historical realities, pragmatic eclecticism, which is on the absolute *taqlīd* end of the continuum, was utilized to make adjustments to school doctrines. If this adjustment could not achieve the desired outcomes, jurists resorted to both ad hoc reasoning and *tarjīḥ* as can be seen from figure 1. With the stabilization of the four Sunnī schools and the dominance of *taqlīd*, working with the scriptural sources unhindered by the methodology of any school all but disappeared. Change was achieved mostly through the exercise of pragmatic eclecticism and preponderance (*tarjīḥ*), with the latter often containing ad hoc reasoning designed to privilege the result that a given jurist desired. While *tarjīḥ* is located toward the middle of the *ijtihād-taqlīd* continuum, pragmatic eclecticism is decidedly on the "absolute *taqlīd*" end simply because juristic views are selected based on their utility.

Influenced by the general tendency in the primary sources to present an image of decline of juristic aptitude after the "golden age" of the formative period, early scholarship in European languages on Islamic law assigned a sense of rigidity and lack of creativity to the regime of *taqlīd*.[39] The equation of *taqlīd* with rigidity, expressed implicitly and explicitly in the debate over the closure of the gate of *ijtihād*, was challenged by Sherman A. Jackson, who pointed out that the creative energies of jurists were not depleted despite the rise of *taqlīd*. He used Alan Watson's notion of "legal scaffolding," which refers to adjustments made through new divisions, exceptions, and distinctions, with the aim of expanding or restricting the scope of existing laws, to argue that such creative adjustments were taking place in Islamic law despite the closure of the gate of absolute *ijtihād*. Jackson placed "legal scaffolding" within "intra-school *ijtihād*," which was the main avenue of legal change within the Sunnī school system.[40]

Thanks to the work of contemporary scholars, who challenged the rigidity narrative, there is hardly a historian of Islamic law today who would disagree with the proposition that Islamic law, like any other legal system, has experienced throughout its long history instances of change motivated by the realia of law on the ground.[41] Rather than argue that Islamic law stagnated under the regime of *taqlīd* or claim that jurists had an unlimited prerogative to depart from school doctrines, a more plausible account should not overlook the essential relationship between the two legal ideals of stability and flexibility, understood through the *ijtihād-taqlīd* continuum. A mature legal system develops mechanisms to manage these two legal principles to minimize ruptures while ensuring that laws deemed unacceptable to jurists can be modified, with the caveat that change is the exception and that the rule is continuity. Legal systems whether in the common law or civil law traditions are characterized by what Alan Watson calls "legal inertia" or "inaction," terms that refer to an aversion to legal innovation and a need to maintain the stability of legal rules.[42] This ethos of legal continuity is expressed succinctly by Jean-Étienne-Marie Portalis (d. 1807 CE), the most prominent of four jurists who drafted the French Code Napoléon in 1804 CE: "la doctrine des rédacteurs est qu'il *faut conserver tout ce qu'il n'est pas nécessaire de détruire*, et qu'il ne faut se permettre des changements, que *lorsque la plus grande des innovations serait de ne pas innover*."[43]

Despite the revolutionary spirit engulfing the drafting of the Code Napoléon, legal continuity remained an essential ideal. Under the mature regime of *taqlīd*, most jurists, who were, in theory, not allowed to depart from their school doctrine,[44] represent the ideal of legal inertia. As such, to claim that Islamic law was not characterized by legal inertia (epitomized by *taqlīd*) is to argue for Islamic legal exceptionalism. The inertia ethos was a main characteristic of most genres of Islamic legal writing such as the legal compendia genre (*mukhtaṣar*), the legal disagreement genre (*ikhtilāf*), and legal commentary (*ḥāshiya*), but the possibility of legal change was always there, especially in the genres dealing with novel cases (*masā'il*) and legal responsa (fatwas).[45]

It takes a considerable amount of pressure from shifting social realities and the evolving values of the juristic class for legal inertia to give way to legal change. In his recent case study of women's prayers in the Ḥanafī tradition, Behnam Sadeghi postulates that legal inertia was the main catalyst for juristic justifications of existing laws. He argues that in the Ḥanafī context, the continuity of certain laws regarding women's prayer, as well as ruptures and modifications to some of these laws, was not motivated by changes in the canon of scriptural sources (Qur'an and hadith), but rather by legal inertia. The main catalyst for continuity and change was related to the interaction between social realities and legal inertia, rather than the interaction between the canon and the jurists' hermeneutic methodology. This is not to say that the canon played no role in the creation of law, but rather that its role was minimal in the postformative period.[46] Any account of the development of Islamic law that attempts to assign unlimited power to *ijtihād* or incorrigible rigidity to *taqlīd* misses the point that every mature legal system has to strike a balance between stability and flexibility.[47]

When legal inertia is overcome by overwhelming social, political, and economic realities, how is change allowed to modify the legal order? Many historians would argue that it was through *ijtihād* as outlined in handbooks of legal methodology (*uṣūl*), whereby the jurist engages in a direct examination of the textual sources, that such change was brought about. This belief is so deeply rooted in Islamic legal historiography that much intellectual energy has been expended on the issue of *ijtihād* by both sides of the debate over the closure of the gate of *ijtihād*, when in fact the two sides of the debate were not talking about the same thing. While Joseph Schacht referred to the far end of the *ijtihād-taqlīd* continuum, to wit, "absolute *ijtihād*," wherein a given jurist is not restricted in his examination of the textual sources by the methodological and positive legal restrictions of a school, Hallaq's challenge largely focused on modifications of doctrine subsumed under "intra-school *ijtihād*."[48] The views of Schacht and Hallaq are therefore not as different from each other as seems at first sight, since most instances of change came from both the middle (intra-school *ijtihād*, mostly *tarjīḥ*) and "absolute *taqlīd*" end of the continuum, with jurists generally veering away from "absolute *ijtihād*," that is, new interpretations of the sources.

What motivated the shift from *ijtihād* to *taqlīd*? To answer this question, we have to return to the institutional, structural questions of Islamic law's navigation of the two legal ideals of stability and flexibility. In the formative period of absolute *ijtihād*, jurists navigated these two legal ideals through the common law model, in which judges made laws but their law-making power was restricted through a form of legal precedent in the early regional schools, what Schacht calls "the living tradition." This common law model was replaced by what I elsewhere call the "codification episteme" in the classical period of Islamic law. As Mohammad Fadel observed, the dominance of *taqlīd* reflected the triumph of the "rule of law" over judicial discretion.[49] This shift from the common law to the codification episteme, a shift that took place during the course of the eleventh through thirteenth centuries, created a relative emphasis on legal inertia over legal flexibility (more on this in chapter 1). It was in this context that there was a pressing institutional need to relax avenues of legal change through pragmatic eclecticism. With the dominance of the codification episteme, which emphasized legal stability and determinacy of rules over flexibility and centralization over local contingencies, there was an institutional need for more flexibility to accommodate the evolving needs of society and empire. This need explains both the institutionalization of pragmatic eclecticism in the Mamluk Empire and the radical transformations in juristic attitudes toward its practice in the early thirteenth century.

There are two types of school boundary-crossing: the holistic adoption of a new school for pragmatic reasons such as salaried positions endowed to a different school from one's own, and crossing school boundaries in a single transaction because the other school's doctrine is less stringent.[50] The change of school, whether atomistically or holistically, can be motivated by pragmatic considerations related to the content of the opinion in question, rather than to the process of reasoning. Such changes, however, can also be motivated by an assessment of the evidence and reasoning of a juristic opinion or school methodology. Most jurists, both of the formative and postformative periods, accepted the choice of juristic views based on a hermeneutic engagement with competing proofs. In the late eighth century and early ninth century, this process was practiced by al-Shaybānī, al-Shāfiʿī, and other early jurists to determine the view with the strongest evidence. Save for a minority that supported strict "school loyalty" (*tamadhhub*), weighing different school opinions hermeneutically was also permitted after the stabilization of the schools in the age of legal conformism. This process was known as the exercise of "preponderance" (*tarjīḥ*).

Islamic legal subjects have always practiced pragmatic eclecticism despite the almost unanimous opposition of jurists of the first four centuries of Islam, when interpretive freedom was the norm inside the courtroom. The practice of pragmatic eclecticism in the age of judicial interpretive freedom was restricted almost exclusively to the activities of jurisconsults (muftis). Since the decisions issued by jurisconsults were not binding, it was conceivable that one could shop for a legal answer relating to marriage, divorce, and rituals, even in the absence of legal determinacy. Although a jurisconsult's opinion could not be predicted with a high level of accuracy, the layperson was not obligated to follow it and could conceivably shop for another opinion. Such practice was widely discussed, itself evidence of the practice, and strictly forbidden almost unanimously by jurists until the end of the twelfth century.

Conversely, owing to the binding nature of a judge's decision, pragmatic eclecticism in the courtroom assumes the existence of clear bodies of law with a high level of determinacy. In the age of interpretive freedom (*ijtihād*), legal indeterminacy, compounded with the laity's inability to seek a different forum of adjudication once a judicial decision was made, rendered the practice of forum shopping impracticable. In other words, once the judge issued a decision, the layperson, who could not predict the decision before its issuance with a high level of accuracy, had no choice but to follow it. Unrestricted interpretive freedom allowed judges to accommodate legal needs by devising new solutions for old problems without having to rely on pragmatic eclecticism (whether in the form of forum shopping or doctrinal eclecticism). The context of legal conformism (*taqlīd*), where there is a corpus of law that can be examined and strategically mobilized to serve different commercial and social needs, is, therefore, a prerequisite for judicial pragmatic eclecticism. Jurists were aware of this institutional prerequisite. One jurist argues, for instance, that the codification (*tadwīn*) of school doctrine was essential to the rise of pragmatic eclecticism.[51] In the age of legal conformism, pragmatic eclecticism could be practiced not only in the activities of jurisconsults outside the courtroom, but also in judicial practice. It was also after the dominance of legal conformism that divisions emerged among jurists over the validity of this practice, as we shall see in chapters 2 and 3.

Pragmatic eclecticism was not only utilized across school boundaries, but also drawn upon to adapt internal school doctrines to social needs. Within a school corpus, one sometimes finds tension between the preponderant view, which is the most evidentially sound, and the pragmatic view, which is the most practically expedient. Jurists were aware that they were engaging in doctrinal eclecticism to redefine the dominant legal rule within a school (known as the *madhhab*-opinion) owing to pragmatic considerations rather than evidential reasoning. In fact, there were situations in which the preponderant rule, which enjoyed the strongest evidence, was replaced by a self-consciously less evidentially sound view owing to pragmatic considerations.[52] In some cases, it was out of necessity (*ḍarūra*)—itself an ambiguous term used in an ad hoc manner to justify all sorts of laws deemed less stringent—that the preponderant view would be replaced by a weaker doctrine,[53] and the school's new rule was, in this case, a description of existing juridical practice.[54] When the school's position did not serve social needs, legal subjects—in cases of litigation, notarization, and ritual practice—were able to transcend all school boundaries in their search for less stringent rules from the other Sunnī schools. This is how social needs were accommodated by the legal system vertically, that is, within the school and without the need to cross school boundaries. Most discussions of pragmatic eclecticism in the primary sources, however, refer to school boundary-crossing, rather than to vertical adjustment of legal doctrine within a given school.

The practice of pragmatic eclecticism led to opposition from a group of jurists who, emphasizing the evidentiary aspect of the law over its pragmatism, obliged the laity to follow one school in all legal transactions (known as *tamadhhub*).[55] The few supporters of school loyalty, such as the Shāfiʿī jurists al-Juwaynī (d. 478/1085) and Abū al-Ḥasan al-Kiyā (d.

504/1110), imposed school loyalty on the laity in order to stop the practice of forum shopping.[56] According to Abū al-Ḥasan al-Kiyā, school loyalty was not practiced in the first generation of Muslims because the schools had not been written down (*qabla tadwīn al-madhāhib*), and, therefore, there was no concern that people would purposefully pick and choose from different schools. But since the establishment of the schools, people had no choice but to strictly abide by a single school in all transactions as a precaution against pragmatic eclecticism (*tatabbuʿ al-rukhaṣ*). Given that laypeople were incapable of weighing one school against another on the basis of legal evidence, some argued that they should never change their mufti. Any such change could only be based on bias, not knowledge.[57] School loyalty was also associated with a belief in the superiority of one school or eponym. Such strict school loyalty was censured by some scholars who feared that such practice is tantamount to elevating the eponyms of those schools to the status of prophets.[58]

While most jurists did not require strict school loyalty, they did not challenge its practice by the laity, as evidenced by the existence of towns and whole regions that continued to be dominated by one school with very limited juristic opposition. This was particularly the case in North Africa, where the Mālikī school has overwhelmingly dominated to the present day. What most jurists opposed was strict school loyalty, in the sense of obligating people to follow one school in all transactions. As long as the legal outcome was not the motivation, most jurists argued that changing schools both holistically and in a single transaction is permissible for jurists, who alone are qualified to compare the evidence of competing legal opinions and choose the one that appeals most to their reason. By the same token, laypeople were permitted to change muftis, so long as the change was not motivated by pragmatic considerations.[59]

The Case of Egypt

In this study, I focus on Egypt because it is a good representative of both juristic discourse and legal modernization in the nineteenth and twentieth centuries, especially as it was an important Ottoman province with a vibrant juristic community. Because of its geographical location and history, three of the four Sunnī schools of law enjoyed considerable following among the population. Mālikism had a large presence in Egypt, where much of the school's later doctrine was developed. The situation is similar to that of Shāfiʿism, as the eponym of the school spent the later part of his life in Egypt, where he developed his more authoritative doctrine. Ḥanafism also saw a rapid expansion in Egypt after the Ottoman conquest in 1517, gaining the status of official school, thus depriving Shāfiʿism of the leading role it had enjoyed in the Mamluk period. Of the four Sunnī schools, Ḥanbalism had the least following in Egypt. However, as we will see in chapter 4, its utilization to facilitate certain transactions was disproportionately high compared to the number of its adherents.

In my attempt to chart the attitudinal transformations in juristic discourse toward pragmatic eclecticism, I do not focus exclusively on Egyptian jurists. It is often difficult to map juristic attitudes geographically because scholars were highly mobile in their pursuit of knowledge. Many spent most of their formative years away from where they were born, often in major centers of scholarship such as Cairo and Damascus. Geography is less useful in any attempt to outline group doctrine than the legal school unit, which transcends borders. Jurists engaged with each other across vast expanses of territory, such that their works were utilized by members of the same school regardless of geographical origin, as was dictated by local needs and values.

It is, therefore, appropriate to discuss the juristic literature within the schools as a discourse produced for and by a well-connected network of scholars. When geographical school differences occurred, jurists usually pointed them out. In such instances, the school may have had two or more competing doctrines that were geographically contingent. This is the situation with the issue of *talfīq* among the Mālikīs. As we shall see in chapter 3, one Egyptian Mālikī, for instance, referred to the fact that North African Mālikīs permitted *talfīq* while Egyptian Mālikīs did not. He then proceeded to specify that he preferred the North African view.[60]

Research Scheme and Sources

In this study, I explore the roles played by participants in the legal process, namely through examination of the following questions: How much power did legal subjects have in choosing the forum of adjudication in the courtroom? What roles did muftis and legal practitioners play in navigating legal pluralism? With these questions in mind, I attempt to show that juristic discourse did not stand aloof from the practice of the laity in the courts. The way people approached the law and understood it, as well as the knowledge that was disseminated to laypeople through muftis and minor religious scholars, served to create a legal practice that contradicted the putative juristic consensus of the formative period. The tension between practice and theory was felt in legal discourse, with some jurists rejecting the practices of the laity as anomalies that needed to be corrected and others trying to bridge the gap between theory and practice in accordance with a less prescriptive approach. It is in the discussion and practice of the pragmatic utilization of Sunnī legal pluralism that we see how participants in the legal process managed to transform the contents of substantive law.

In laying the groundwork for this investigation, I studied the indices of the Dār al-Kutub al-Qawmiyya and al-Azhar libraries in Cairo, which contain large collections of manuscripts of legal methodology (*uṣūl al-fiqh*) and substantive law (*furūʿ*). Out of a total of approximately two thousand manuscripts, I located about fifty titles with discussions relevant to the legal strategies under examination. I used these unpublished sources along with published works to gauge the prevailing attitudes toward these legal strategies diachronically. I then selected a representative sample from the Ottoman courts of Cairo and Bulaq in the seventeenth and eighteenth centuries to provide illustrative examples of these legal strategies in practice.

In chapter 1, I offer a historical account of the social and political background of the legal transformations discussed in this book, particularly under the Mamluks and the Ottomans. I also broach the important theological debate over the unity or multiplicity of truth on legal matters, which is essential to any discussion of legal pluralism. In chapters 2 and 3, I show that attitudes toward pragmatic eclecticism in juristic discourse started to change around the end of the twelfth century and the beginning of the thirteenth century, despite the claim that there was a consensus against pragmatic eclecticism. Jurists were aware that such practices were taking place in the courts, and, over time, they grew more accepting of them. In the late Ottoman period, jurists were regularly engaged in this discussion, so much so that treatises for and against such practices were written, sometimes causing discord within the juristic community.

In chapter 4, I show, through the study of three courts in Cairo and Bulaq, that the change of school for pragmatic purposes was practiced in the Ottoman period in ways that correspond to both *tatabbuʿ al-rukhaṣ* and *talfīq*. This practice helped jurists establish a more flexible *taqlīd* system by drawing on the diversity of legal opinions within the four schools. In chapter 5, I discuss attitudes toward pragmatic eclecticism from the nineteenth century until the contemporary period. I show that modern juristic attitudes represent a discursive continuity with the pre-nineteenth-century period. I also discuss the ways in which the terms have come to be understood by modern jurists and academics, as well as the approaches devised by reformers, who call for a second wave of codification of Islamic law.

In chapter 6, I cover the evolution of the Egyptian legal system in the nineteenth and early twentieth centuries and the utilization of pragmatic eclecticism in the modern codification of Islamic law in Egypt. I conclude in chapter 6 with a discussion of more recent approaches to legal pluralism, especially in the context of the resurgence of political Islam in several countries in the wake of the Arab Spring.

Note on Periodization

There are many ways to periodize the various radical transformations that took place in the long history of Islamic law. My periodization scheme will consist of (1) the formative period, which starts with the birth of Islam and ends with the rise of schools roughly around the early tenth century;[61] (2) the classical period, extending from the rise of schools, which marked the early stages of the shift to the codification episteme, until the full maturation and institutionalization of *taqlīd* by the end of the twelfth century and early thirteenth century; (3) the postclassical period, extending from the early thirteenth century until 1500; (4) the early modern period, extending from the 1500s CE to modernity; (5) the modern period, which is marked by the establishment of the Egyptian army and the institutions of administrative, economic, and social control put into its service in the 1820s CE.

The "formative period" refers to the early centuries when substantive law and legal methodology were being developed in the course of the struggle between rationalists (*ahl al-ra'y*) and traditionalists (*ahl al-ḥadīth*). The latter group, which arose in opposition to the utilization of unrestricted rational human reasoning in law making, believed that the textual sources, including Prophetic reports along with the injunctions of the Qur'an, should be the main sources of the law. Al-Shāfi'ī (d. 204/820) achieved a synthesis, according to which Prophetic reports occupied an important place in the derivation of legal rules, and so did rational methods of deriving law such as analogy.[62] The emergence of schools out of this synthesis in the late ninth and early tenth centuries could serve as a shift from the formative to the classical period.[63]

The emergence of schools and the creation of clear boundaries among them, where members defended collective doctrines and engaged in processes of authority construction,[64] marked the beginning of a long process of transformation from judicial discretion to the codification episteme, or from *ijtihād* to *taqlīd*. Needless to say, determining the shift of emphasis from *ijtihād* to *taqlīd* and the maturation of *taqlīd* cannot escape being somewhat arbitrary. It is hard to pinpoint the specific date or even the decade wherein *taqlīd* reached its full maturity, as the process of change was gradual and fluid.

According to Jackson, *ijtihād* and *taqlīd* should be viewed as competing hegemonies, with *ijtihād* dominating until around the twelfth century and *taqlīd* dominating until the nineteenth century.[65] Jackson's remarks are insightful since there was no period in all of Islamic legal history in which one side of the continuum, whether absolute *ijtihād* or absolute *taqlīd*, dominated unopposed by the other layers of the continuum. The rise of Islamic law itself was a site of both *taqlīd*, as evidenced by the continuity of many customary laws predating Islam, and legal change.[66] Even at the end of the full maturation of *taqlīd*, when legal truth was thought by most jurists to be restricted to the views of the four schools, we still find some scholars arguing for *ijtihād* beyond the confines of school opinions. To reconcile their views on *ijtihād* with the dominant doctrine, some jurists argued that the four schools contained the "truth" on most matters, but that there remained some issues about which new *ijtihād* was necessary, even if it contradicted the four schools.[67]

Owing to the complexity of the transformation from *ijtihād* to *taqlīd* and its cumulative nature, which took centuries to fully mature, it is essential to think of the rise of *taqlīd* as a process rather than as a singular event. This *longue durée* perspective can offer a more nuanced understanding of the many institutional changes that transformed Islamic law from a judge's law to a collective enterprise articulated, standardized, canonized, and, one may even say, semicodified by author-jurists. By the end of this process, which consisted of several cumulative institutional changes, Islamic law ceased to be made by judges who were unencumbered, at least in theory, by precedent. It was transformed into a socio-intellectual enterprise that was articulated by author-jurists outside the courtroom but in dialogic interaction with court practice.[68]

Building on Jackson's insights, I hold that the eleventh and twelfth centuries were essential to the final maturation of *taqlīd* and the marginalization of both absolute and intra-school *ijtihād*. According to the primary sources, by the eleventh century schools had matured and stabilized. The expression "the stabilization of the schools" (*istiqrār al-madhāhib*) appears in al-Māwardī's *Adab al-Qāḍī*' (d. 450/1058), a book written in Baghdad between 1045 and 1058 CE, as the Seljuks were capturing the city in 1055 CE.[69] It is also the time when the last follower of the Ẓāhirī school, Ibn Ḥazm (d. 456/1064), died in Umayyad Spain, marking the restriction of Sunnī schools to the four that we know today.

The institutional ascent of *taqlīd* accelerated during the course of the eleventh and twelfth centuries. It was during the late eleventh and early twelfth centuries that a new discussion over the absence of *mujtahids* emerged. Al-Ghazālī (d. 505/1111), for instance, accepted the appointment of intra-school *mujtahids*, since, according to him, independent *mujtahids* were extinct. Abū al-Wafā' b. 'Aqīl (d. 513/1119) also reported a debate that took place in the Niẓāmiyya Madrasa between a Ḥanafī and his Ḥanbalī opponent, in which the Ḥanafī's position that *mujtahids* became extinct was refuted by his Ḥanbalī interlocutor.[70] During the twelfth century jurists also began to argue that there was a hierarchy of authority within the Ḥanafī school.[71] This hierarchy came to represent the preponderant (*rājiḥ*) views of the school.

The full maturation of the institutionalization of the *taqlīd* episteme was completed when judges and muftis were no longer required to exercise their individual reasoning. Permitting judges to be *muqallids* took place after al-Māwardī's (d. 450/1058) time, as he assumed that judges must interpret the scripture and deduce rules for themselves. According to Jackson, it was clear by the thirteenth century in the work of the Shāfiʿī Ibn Abī al-Damm (d. 622/1244) that judges were simply required to "apply" an existing and determinate body of law, rather than deduce legal rules from the sources.[72] Jackson's observations are confirmed by Hallaq's, who notes that while the words *iftā'* (giving a fatwa) and *ijtihād* were used interchangeably in the eleventh century, which meant that the mufti had to be a *mujtahid*, by the thirteenth century muftis were allowed to be *muqallids*,[73] suggesting that *taqlīd* had stabilized.

By the thirteenth century, jurists assumed not only that absolute *mujtahids* were extinct, but also that the higher levels of intra-school *mujtahids* were either rare or extinct. The intra-school *mujtahids* known as *aṣḥāb al-wujūh*, for example, were said to have disappeared by the end of the eleventh century. Save for a few and far between, judges and muftis were thought to be memorizers of legal doctrines, who had to follow the dominant positions of their schools. Despite the dominance of *taqlīd*, legal change continued to take place but only when there were pressing sociocultural and economic pressures to necessitate making amendments to school doctrines.[74]

The postclassical perception of the decline of knowledge and the absence of *mujtahids* was nicely illustrated by Tāj al-Dīn al-Subkī (d. 771/1370), who argued that jurists who lived in the first three centuries of Islam (*mutaqaddimīn*) were not interested in exercising preponderance (*tarjīḥ*) with regard to issues of juristic disagreement (*khilāf*) because knowledge was widespread and every jurisconsult (mufti) followed his own reasoning. According to him, every jurisconsult was able to issue legal edicts based on his own reasoning (*yuftī bi-mā yu'addī ilayhi naẓaruh*). However, the scarcity of knowledge that rendered *taqlīd* necessary caused jurists to take an interest in discovering the *rājiḥ* opinions so that less knowledgeable muftis could follow those with greater knowledge.[75]

By the time *taqlīd* had fully matured, an element of flexibility was later introduced by institutionalizing pragmatic eclecticism. I was able to locate the earliest justification of pragmatic eclecticism in juristic discourse in the early years of the thirteenth century, in Ibn 'Arabī's magnum opus *al-Futūḥāt al-Makkiyya*, which he started while living in Mecca in 599/1201 and finished in 629/1231 in Damascus under the Ayyubids. The thirteenth century also witnessed the rise of the *mukhtaṣar* genre, which was, as one scholar of Islamic law put it, "code-like."[76] Since this book deals with pragmatic eclecticism, itself the final mechanism of the institutionalization of *taqlīd*, the end of the classical period will be linked to the final stages of this process of institutional transformation, rather than to its beginning at the formation or "stabilization" of schools. I will use the end of the twelfth century and beginning of the thirteenth century as the period when Islamic law shifted to the postclassical period.

I will use the term "early modern" to refer to the period between the sixteenth and early nineteenth centuries,[77] when radical transformations in world trade and technology transformed the Ottoman Empire. These transformations prepared the ground for further evolutions in the nineteenth century. Several dates are given for the Middle East's rise from early modernity into modernity, including the Napoleonic invasion of Egypt (1798), the career of Mehmed Ali (r. 1805–48), the Egyptian invasion of the Levant (1831), and the Western-inspired Ottoman reforms known as the Tanzimat (1839–76). The Eurocentric Napoleonic periodization, which places Europe at the forefront of all changes in the Middle East, has been challenged by Peter Gran, who proposes 1760 as an alternative watershed, characterized by the capitalist accumulation that began in Egypt in the second half of the eighteenth century during the reign of 'Alī Bey al-Kabīr (r. 1760–72). Gran also proposes the period between 1815 and 1837 as representing a "precapitalist formation" that was essential to Egypt's integration into the world market, owing to the rise of a new state with aggressive agricultural and commercial policies.[78] Timothy Mitchell offers an even later date, as he sees something particular about the second half of the nineteenth century. During this time, the very nature of control characteristic of the Egyptian state under Mehmed Ali was transformed through institutions such as the army, which allowed for long-term institutional continuity. From 1822, Egyptians were taken in tens of thousands and turned into soldiers in the Egyptian army, an event that Mitchell considers the beginning of the country's new regimentation. Following the fall of the First French Empire in 1815, Egypt was to receive many officers and engineers from the defeated French armies, which made Egypt the first province in the Ottoman Empire to create a modern army.[79] Although Mitchell considers the establishment of the Egyptian army to be the beginning of the country's new regimentation, he links the appearance of the politics of the new modern state to the new order of the army and the model village, both, according to him, emerging between 1860s and the First World War.[80]

According to Khaled Fahmy, the Egyptian army, whose foundations were laid by Mehmed Ali in 1820, was instrumental in founding the Egyptian nation through novel practices of surveillance and control. The Egyptian nation was brought into being through a multiplicity of practices and discourses of control such as the issuing of identity cards, regularly checking the bodies of conscripts for diseases, and subjecting their bodies to strict regimes. These practices led to changes in the very nature of the government and its management of the Egyptian population. The Egyptian army, which was based on conscription, was the raison d'être of many other institutions in the emerging state apparatus such as factories producing commodities for the army, schools graduating its officers, and hospitals treating its soldiers.[81] The disciplinary and coercive power of the army maintained the economic order established by Mehmed Ali.

In addition to the creation of the army in 1820, Mehmed Ali began to cultivate long-staple cotton in 1821, two events that Fahmy considers to be the twin pillars of Mehmed Ali's regime. These two events, while not causally linked, later became codependent as the profits from the sale of cotton grew exponentially in the 1820s through the monopolies put in place over its sale. These profits were the lifeline that was used to build a formidable army.[82] Egypt's entry into the long-staple cotton industry was linked to the international textile boom and its rising profits owing in part to advances in textile technology.[83] These international economic developments transformed Egypt from a commercial export hub to a country whose economy was dominated by the production of cotton for European manufacturers, increasing Egypt's incorporation into the European economy.[84] It was also in the 1820s that Mehmed Ali started his modernization of Egypt's education by sending students to study at the Joseph Lancaster's Central School in London.[85]

It was not long after the establishment of an Egyptian army fashioned after European militaries that Mehmed Ali introduced a major penal code in 1829, which provided for the imposition of fixed penalties. This criminal law assumed, for example, that in cases of murder and highway robbery, the accused would be tried by the Islamic judge (*qāḍī*), and then, if acquitted, by al-Majlis al-Mulkī al-ʿĀlī, a secular court acting as the High Court between 1825 and 1829. This criminal law was followed by another criminal code in 1830, addressing crimes connected with agriculture and village life, known as *Qanūn al-Filāḥa*. Peters wonders whether Mehmed Ali's criminal legislation represents a continuation of traditional Ottoman criminal legislation or a form of legal modernization. He finds elements of discontinuity including some articles emphasizing equality before the law, as well as others based on social class differentiation. Although these legislative acts offered some protection against arbitrary behavior of state officials, they did not subject the khedive to the same rules. Peters concludes that these criminal codes were a continuation of traditional Ottoman criminal legislation.[86] It is hard to imagine that the criminal laws of 1829–30 were not influenced by the huge statist project undertaken by Mehmed Ali, and the attendant bureaucracy and methods of control. Despite his judgment that the criminal laws of 1829–30 were continuous with the Ottoman period, Peters confirms that the period between 1829 and 1882 was more important to legal modernization in Egypt than the colonial period,[87] implying that the foundations of legal modernization were laid during these five decades.

No specific event by itself can satisfactorily capture the assumptions and transformations inherent in the term "modernity." According to Peter Gran, the most realistic choices for the beginning of Egyptian modernity are 1805, marking the rise of Mehmed Ali, and 1863, when Ismail came to power (r. 1863–79). Gran explains the difficulty of accepting 1805, to wit, that Mehmed Ali's project collapsed and had to be recreated decades later, whereas the difficulty of accepting 1863 is partly owing to the fact that "many of the crucial issues stem from long-term trends that cannot be precisely dated."[88] Nonetheless, Gran considers 1863 to be the better of the two options. While I agree with Gran on the difficulty of pinpointing a date at which modernity started, my periodization will be placed somewhere between the two dates, in a way that ties it not to the general project of a ruler but to institutional and structural transformations in the way the state and its institutions viewed themselves vis-à-vis the citizenry. The 1820s will therefore serve as my starting point of Egyptian modernity. It was in the 1820s that the army, the single most important institution of surveillance and control, was created. The founding of the army, the foundational bedrock of Egyptian modernity, was simultaneous with the successful cultivation of long-staple cotton, systematic educational missions to Europe, and Egypt's greater incorporation into European-dominated capitalism. Despite the failure of Mehmed Ali's project and Ismail's attempts to reinvent it in the 1860s and 1870s, the state structures and institutions created to service the army engraved a modern institutional ethos in the Egyptian state that did not vanish and was later reinvigorated by Ismail.

Note on Dates, Places, Terms, and Gender Neutrality

Most dates in this book will be provided in the Islamic calendar followed by the Common Era date, separated by a slash. For specialists, personal names are generally transliterated—unless the person in question is known with a particular spelling—whereas place names and names of dynasties are not. I do not correct the gender bias in the primary sources, but when speaking in my own voice, I try to use gender-neutral language as much as possible. Nevertheless, this work is a representation of juristic discourse that is not gender neutral.

PART ONE

Setting and Context

1

The Codification Episteme and the Multiplicity of Truth

IN THIS CHAPTER, I will set the context for the book in two parts. The first addresses the institutional context that prepared the ground for the rise of pragmatic eclecticism, dealing with the relationship between the rise of "legal conformism" (*taqlīd*) and the institutional needs for legal stability. The second part deals with early theological debates over the nature and permissibility of legal pluralism, an essential discussion that frames the jurists' conceptualization of the tension between the divine nature and unicity of Islamic law, on the one hand, and legal pluralism, on the other. I will begin with the tension between legal flexibility and stability, which is essential to understanding the institutional preconditions that paved the way for the rise of pragmatic eclecticism.

The Institutional Logic of Codification

The Common Law and Civil Law Epistemes

Let us now discuss the distinction between common law and civil law epistemes in order to situate Islamic law within this paradigm. This discussion goes to the heart of the institutional transformations that took place in Islamic law throughout its long history because of the changing needs of empire. The distinction between common law and civil law models is one of degree, since legislation and judicial decisions have their place in both systems. Common law systems rely partially on legislation, whereas judges in civil law systems, far from simply "applying" the law, engage in interpretations that can lead to extending the scope of the law considerably beyond that originally contemplated by legislators. Such interpretive maneuvering defies any claim to the absolute clarity and comprehensiveness of legislation. Such a claim is captured nicely in the words of the French revolutionary Jean-Louis Carra, whose ideal code is "invariable." It is a code in which "everyone can find the laws without much exertion."[1]

Common law and civil law jurisdictions are not binaries, where the presence of one means the negation of the other, but rather continuums with varying and evolving emphases on different characteristics of the two epistemes. There are legal systems that contain characteristics of both systems. South Africa is the major remaining jurisdiction of a primarily civil law system that contains some common law features, especially in the realm of private law. While the South African case belongs to the civil law episteme, Scots law is the reverse. It contains more features of common law than of civil law.[2] In addition to the difficulty of parsing the differences between common law and civil law systems, there is the issue that no taxonomy across legal cultures, each with its own episteme, can satisfactorily juxtapose all the characteristics of a legal system against another. With this caveat in mind, I should emphasize that any taxonomy of Islamic law, as Lawrence Rosen argues, should be treated as a heuristic device rather than a positivistic exercise.[3]

According to Rosen, any taxonomy of legal systems must address two main criteria: the place occupied by the law in the overall distribution of power and the extent to which the legal system takes cultural conceptualizations into consideration.[4] Common law systems address the power-local culture dialectic by dispensing power to the local level through mechanisms of indirect control, while letting local cultural conceptualizations fill up much of the content of the law.[5] The dispersion of power to the local level is achieved through analogical reasoning, which operates without a comprehensive theory that accounts for the particular outcomes it yields. It is through analogical reasoning that judges are able to accommodate new circumstances.[6]

Alan Watson warns against treating codification as the main distinctive features of a civil law tradition and proposes a much narrower definition of what constitutes a civil law tradition: "a system in which parts or the whole of Justinian's *Corpus iuris civilis* have been in the past or are at present treated as the law of the land or, at the very least, are of direct and highly persuasive force; or else it derives from any such system."[7] Be that as it may, we can situate Islamic law within a *codification episteme* (regardless of whether codification is an essential part of civil law traditions or not) in the age of *taqlīd*. The difficulties of definition aside, let us return to the tension between stability and flexibility to explore how the common law and civil law epistemes in the European context balanced these two legal ideals. Stability was achieved in English common law, for example, by placing some restrictions on the judge's ability to make law through the notion of "precedent," whereby once a decision is made, later judges are obliged to follow it. Flexibility was also built into the notion of precedent itself, since English law distinguishes between *ratio decidendi*, an essential point of law, which is indispensable and necessary to reach a legal decision, and nonessential points *obiter dicta*. The rule of precedent is applied only to essential points of law and judges are not obliged to follow precedent in nonessential points, whose determination itself requires a fair amount of interpretation. When a new situation resembles but is not identical with a previous case, the judge can either follow precedent or draw a distinction between the two cases to justify his departure from precedent. An element of flexibility can also be found in extreme cases in common law, in which judges can consider a previous judgment erroneous and overrule it, thereby providing a new precedent. However, in a common law system, the balance between stability and flexibility involves a relative privileging of flexibility over stability since it was the judge who created law. Unlike a king or a legislature imposing legal uniformity top-down from a metro-pole across vast territories, a judge is directly involved in the local practice of law and therefore is arguably capable of being more responsive to local needs and socioeconomic contingencies.[8]

Codification, an important feature of the civil law model at least in the modern period, is often associated with the emergence of a crisis of determinacy of legal rules owing to orality or the massive accumulation of legal rules to such an extent that a need arises for "legal security" (*sécurité juridique*). Such security is achieved by reducing the complexity of laws and increasing the level of legal determinacy, comprehensiveness, and predictability.[9] This concept of legal security overlaps with the "rule of law" in common law traditions. Codification often takes place when the law reaches a degree of dispersion and contradictions that is no longer bearable, especially for an empire engaging in a centralization drive. The evolution of canon law geographically and temporally, for instance, produced a need for codification once a constellation of social and political forces were in need of legal security. Such a need often leads to early forms of codification, which are usually private efforts in which magistrates, lawyers, and other legal authorities collect legal doctrines that are later made into law by a sovereign. These private compilations can also be found in the Jewish legal tradition in the work of the Spanish Jewish philosopher Maimonides, the leader of the Jewish community in Egypt, where he died in 1204 CE. His codification of medieval Jewish law was a classic attempt to create legal security. From an empire's perspective, codification is a way to unify its territories and diverse populations under one uniform system.[10]

Where does Islamic law fit into this discussion in light of the shift of emphasis from *ijtihād* to *taqlīd*? Noel James Coulson did not draw a distinction between the two hegemonies of legal conformism (*taqlīd*) and interpretive freedom (*ijtihād*), placing Islamic law squarely in the common law category. He argued that in the formative period, judges assumed the function of lawmakers before the establishment of the authority of schools. It was through their activities that customary practices were often incorporated into Islamic law. Owing to legal pluralism, Coulson contended, one judge based his ruling on one opinion, while another judge decided differently on a similar case. This indeterminacy gave judges who opposed the notion of binding judicial precedent considerable freedom in making law.[11] In a similar fashion, Schacht held that Islamic law was foremost a methodology, rather than a set of substantive rules, and therefore any codification of Islamic law is by definition a distortion.[12]

In Rosen's view, Islamic law functions in similar ways to common law systems because of the role played by judges in utilizing locally situated relationships, especially in their determination of the probity of witnesses.[13] He explained that the Islamic rules of evidence and expert witnessing propel matters to the local level. The muftis' frequent articulation of the principle of a case regularizes concepts and modes of reasoning, much like Anglo-American courts of appeal. The gates of *ijtihād*, he noted, were never closed, and Muslim judges continuously exercised their own reasoning to reach new decisions.[14]

The Hegemony of the Codification Episteme

Contrary to the above views, I contend that the shift to the *taqlīd* hegemony is essential to our characterization of Islamic law as fitting a common law or a codification model owing to the attendant radical transformations in the roles assigned to various legal authorities. Under the regime of *ijtihād*, Islamic law was similar to common law systems in that judges and muftis had much freedom in exercising hermeneutic and analogical reasoning by mobilizing a mix of precedents, texts, and social welfare as part of their process of legal reasoning. Because of the flexibility of the legal hermeneutic adopted by jurists of the formative period and the sheer ambiguity and contradictions within the corpus of textual sources (Qur'an and hadith), such engagement could yield exceedingly diverse results.[15] The immense interpretive possibilities offered by the interaction between a flexible hermeneutic and the scriptures gave Islamic law under the regime of *ijtihād* the flexibility typical of common law jurisdictions.

The rising hegemony of legal conformism and the marginalization of interpretive freedom represented a shift of emphasis from a common law to a codification episteme, with a concomitant centralizing ethos. Judges no longer made law, nor did they stand among the most learned in the law. Jurisconsults (muftis) played a role very similar to that of the Roman jurist in providing opinions to courts.[16] The rise of *taqlīd* was likened to Byzantine *florilegium*, the copying of previous forms of text.[17] This shift was motivated by two main objectives: achieving legal stability and the routinization of law across large expanses of land, elements that are essential to imperial centralization. In the Islamic tradition, an attempt at such centralization and codification can be found as early as the Abbasid period, when the courtier Ibn al-Muqaffaʿ (d. circa 139/756) complained to the Abbasid caliph al-Manṣūr (r. 136–58/754–75) that cities of the empire, including Kufa and Hira, had exceedingly different and contradictory legal rules. Even within the same city, he opined, what was permitted in a part of Kufa was forbidden in another part. In his pursuit of legal security, where laws are consistent across all Abbasid territory, Ibn al-Muqaffaʿ called for all legal opinions and their evidence to be collected so that the caliph would choose one "correct" opinion for each case, creating a permanent code. Once this code was made, judges would be required to follow it.[18] This attempt at codification was completely rejected by jurists,[19] allowing interpretive freedom, with its concomitant legal indeterminacy, to continue to be the dominant paradigm in Islamic law for another three centuries.

The failure of al-Manṣūr's courtier to endow the caliph with the power of legal interpretation was followed by another attempt by the Abbasids to assert their authority over scholars, when they embarked on the Qur'anic Inquisition (*miḥna*). The Inquisition, which was ostensibly initiated by the Abbasid Caliph al-Ma'mūn (r. 198–218/813–833) to support the Muʿtazilī theological position of the createdness of the Qur'an, started in 218/833 and lasted until 234/849.[20] The failure of the Inquisition led to a division of labor between jurists and rulers. Judicial authority came from the caliph, but the law came from scholars, creating a balance of power, a constitutional arrangement of sorts between the two sides.[21] The Abbasids' vision of the caliph's prerogative as the final arbiter on matters of law would not be attempted again until the Ottoman reforms of the nineteenth century, as we shall see in chapter 6.[22]

The triumph of jurists over the caliph in matters of law and orthodoxy only served to shift the task of codification from rulers to jurists, with the latter becoming increasingly aware of the social need for legal security, as the unpredictability of legal rules could shake the laity's confidence in the legal system of which they were the patrons. Living in late eleventh-century Baghdad under Seljuk rule, where a titular Abbasid caliph was kept to legitimize Seljuk control, al-Ghazālī presented the common position that a *mujtahid*'s legal opinion should match his new interpretation. This rule was not extended to the judge because, according to al-Ghazālī, if the judge's decisions were changed in keeping with changes in his interpretation, this would cause confusion in legal rulings and lead to a loss of confidence in the legal system among the laity.[23]

Placing such restrictions on the judges' ability to interpret the law marked the beginning of a process of transformation from a common law to a codification episteme. This transformation did not imply that Islamic law in the age of *taqlīd* had a clear-cut, fully determinate code. What is meant by the shift to a codification episteme is not a claim of total determinacy, but an epistemic shift whereby there was an increasing emphasis on legal determinacy. The road toward legal determinacy started with the rise of schools in the late ninth and early tenth centuries, and the stabilization of these schools by the eleventh century. It continued with the shift from a theoretical focus on the continuous creation of new doctrines through *ijtihād* to a focus on canonization through legal conformism.[24] This notion of canonicity was crystalized in the thirteenth century when scholars from fully developed schools, with clear methodological and substantive legal boundaries, started identifying "official" school positions on every point of law, whether based on preponderance (*tarjīḥ*) or pragmatic eclecticism, from the indeterminate, pluralistic corpuses of the four Sunnī schools.

Because of the fragmentation of juristic authority and the absence of one juristic voice, efforts to make the law more determinate would occur within the school unit. The gradual, incremental shift to the codification episteme was spectacularly epitomized by the rise of legal compendia (*mukhtaṣars*) in the thirteenth century. The activities of thirteenth-century jurists who wrote compendia of legal rules reduced determinacy within each school.[25] Owing to the constitutional balance achieved under the Abbasids between scholars and rulers, none of these compendia was selected by a sultan and declared the law of the land. The political and juristic authorities, however, required judges to follow the dominant view within their schools. These limits placed on judges and muftis can be found in juristic discourse whereby thirteenth-century judges—and to a lesser degree muftis—were assumed to follow school precedent through *taqlīd*,[26] and in court practice, where both muftis and judges had to follow their schools. This is why, as we shall see in chapter 4, judges would refer subjects of the law to other schools for less stringent juristic views, rather than issue rulings based on other school doctrines.[27]

Such bureaucratization of the function of the judge *ideal-typically* relegated him from a maker of the law to a bureaucrat, whose sole function was to "apply" the law. Judges played a minor role in changing or interpreting legal doctrine and their decisions did not add any authority to these legal compendia, which were produced by author-jurists, acting like legislators outside the courtroom. The authors of the legal compendia used legal reasoning less and less over time, producing univalent legal texts with an increasing level of determinacy.

These intra-school compendia were echoed in the fourteenth century in the comparative genre of legal writing, known as "juristic disagreement" (*ikhtilāf*), designed to promote pragmatic eclecticism within the codification episteme, as we shall see in chapter 2. The culmination of this process took place in the Mamluk period, specifically in Egypt and the Levant. Reducing indeterminacy was meant to enable legal authorities to dispense justice with minimum interpretive interference on the part of judges, thus regularizing law across vast territories and ensuring legal security. To be sure, this was an ideal that was not always attained. Islamic law was increasingly becoming more determinate, and traces of ambiguity of legal rules that remained were incrementally reduced by jurists over the course of the Mamluk and Ottoman periods. Many unresolved doctrinal questions were addressed by successive generations of jurists, further reducing indeterminacy.

The Institutionalization of Pragmatic Eclecticism

The practice of forum selection among the laity took place before the formation of schools, when it was achieved by choosing different jurists mostly in ritual matters. Not long after the death of the Prophet, some early Muslims relied on geographical differences in legal doctrines to facilitate their transactions. It is plausible and in fact expected that some people would seek less stringent legal rules. This practice seems to have been discussed by early jurists. Sulaymān al-Taymī (d. 143/760), who was among the generation following the Companions known as the Followers (*tābiʿīn*), was quoted by Ibn ʿAbd al-Barr (d. 464/1071) as saying, "All evil converges on him who takes the less stringent opinions of every scholar."[28] Al-Awzāʿī (d. 157/773), the leader of a school in Syria that did not long survive his death, was also reported to have stated that whoever follows the scholars' anomalous opinions is not a Muslim. He went so far as to avoid the more lenient legal doctrines of different regions as a precaution against such eclecticism.[29]

Before the formation of Sunnī schools and the canonization of legal methodology, forum selection could only operate efficiently outside the court in the realm of fatwas, which mostly deal with moral as opposed to strictly legal matters, despite the overlap between the two.[30] In the courtroom, forum selection requires a level of legal determinacy, whereby a legal subject can choose a forum based on a clear legal result that is known to the parties to legal notarization and litigation beforehand. Ideal-typically, this was not the case under the regime of *ijtihād*, which limited the scope and efficiency of forum selection. It was the rise of legal determinacy and the shift from a common law model (epitomized by *ijtihād*) to a codification episteme (epitomized by *taqlīd*) in Islamic law that provided the institutional setting, not for the rise of forum shopping but for increasing its efficiency in the court system. Attempts at institutionalizing forum shopping in the Egyptian-Levantine legal system started in the early twelfth century, after the stabilization of schools and the rising hegemony of *taqlīd*, as I show in the following pages.

As we saw above, the Abbasids failed to prevail over jurists in the struggle over the determination of who had the power to be the arbiter of legal and theological orthodoxy. With the Abbasids' loss of Egypt and the Levant to the emerging Tulunids (r. 868–905), the latter were equally aware of the importance of law and legal centralization in asserting their power vis-à-vis the Abbasids. A crackdown on the local legal administration was an important target of the Abbasid authorities during the Qur'anic Inquisition. There was an attempt to homogenize the legal system and enforce Ḥanafism as the legal doctrine of the Abbasid center. The Shāfiʿī and Mālikī local centers of power were targeted, with jurists belonging to these two schools being prohibited from teaching in the central mosque. There was systematic humiliation of the local elite, who were mostly Mālikīs, some of whom were publicly whipped. The attack on the Shāfiʿī and Mālikī legal administration and a concomitant process of Ḥanafization were reversed with the fall of Egypt to the emerging independent Tulunids (r. 868–905). The Tulunids tried to stake their claims to political and legal independence from the Abbasids by reversing these Ḥanafization efforts. Ibn Ṭūlūn was even willing to pay a tribute to the Abbasid caliph in exchange for having the power to appoint judges in his realm of influence. He appointed a Shāfiʿī judge in Damascus, who later became the chief judge of all Tulunid territories. The Tulunids rescinded the ban imposed on jurists to teach Shāfiʿī doctrine in the central mosque and appointed a Shāfiʿī chief judge, reversing decades of persecution under the Abbasid Inquisition. In doing so, the Tulunids privileged a Sunnī legal school that was neither associated with the Abbasid metropole nor the local Egyptian Mālikī elite, two centers of power viewed as a threat to the new Tulunid order.[31]

The Tulunids' attempts at independence from Baghdad were short-lived, as the Abbasids were able to reconquer Egypt in 292/905, installing the Ikhshidids (r. 935–69) as governors by the Abbasid caliph.[32] But in 969 CE Egypt was about to experience the rise of an empire that transformed it into an emerging power and ended its direct political submission to the Abbasids forever. The Ismāʿīlī Fatimids marched from North Africa, which they had ruled since 909, to Egypt and established Cairo's namesake "al-Qāhira," from which they ruled until 1171 CE. The Fatimids were able to maintain their control over large territories that extended from North Africa to the northeastern Mediterranean, including the Hijaz, for more than two hundred years. Following in the footsteps of previous Egyptian rulers, the Fatimids took advantage of the breakdown of Abbasid authority, the deteriorating economy in Baghdad, and the rise of warring petty states in the Fertile Crescent—factors that made the Persian Gulf trade route less profitable—to lure trade through Egyptian ports. By the end of the tenth century, much of the trade between the Indian Ocean and the Mediterranean was diverted from the Persian Gulf to Egypt. By combining agrarian wealth with commercial expansion, Cairo became a flourishing regional powerhouse, competing with Baghdad for influence and making great accomplishments in art, culture, and learning.[33]

The motivation behind the Abbasid desire to codify Islamic law must have existed for the Fatimids as well, but it was not possible for them to upset the delicate balance of power between rulers and scholars. Instead of attempting to codify as the Abbasid courtier had tried, the Fatimids opted for legal pluralism at the expense of the "school loyalty" (*tamadhhub*) approach, which was attempted by the Abbasids in Egypt during the Inquisition when Shāfiʿī and Mālikī jurists were not allowed to teach in the central mosque.[34] The Fatimids sought to create an equal status for four different schools. In 525/1130–31, the Fatimid vizier Ibn al-Afḍal appointed four chief judges (Mālikī, Shāfiʿī, Ismāʿīlī, and Imāmī). Nothing is surprising about the choice of Mālikī and Shāfiʿī chief judges in Cairo since the majority of Egyptians were affiliated to these two schools, which was in some ways owing to the development of most of the doctrines of these schools in Egypt.[35] The choice of chief judges from the other two schools was not motivated by the needs of the population over which the Fatimids ruled, but rather by the desire of the rulers to promote Shīʿism in Egypt. Despite the clear political motivation behind the appointment of Shīʿī chief judges, a pragmatic motivation cannot be ruled out in the case of the other chief judges. Given the virtual absence (save for some extant papyri) of court records from this period, it is hard to assess the institutional significance of these appointments or determine the extent to which pragmatic eclecticism was promoted by the Fatimids.[36] The Fatimids' decision to appoint four chief judges from different schools would not have been possible had the schools not been fully formed entities with clear boundaries, doctrinal canons, and hermeneutic methodologies to deal with questions that fell outside the canon. These transformations had already taken place in Sunnī Islamic law by the time the Fatimids invaded Egypt.[37]

In 1169 CE, Egypt fell to the Zengid general Shirkuh, who died the same year, leaving control of the country to his nephew Saladin, marking the beginning of the Ayyubid dynasty, which controlled Egypt until 1250. Under the Ayyubids, Saladin sought to institute protectionist policies, excluding Western merchants from trade through the Red Sea. This policy contributed to increasing the wealth of local merchants such as the fabled Karimi merchants, who had virtually no rivals in the Red Sea trade.[38] The Ayyubids followed in the institutional footsteps of the Fatimids. In 641/1243–44, the Ayyubids established professorships for each of the four schools of law, perhaps as a prelude to institutionalizing pragmatic eclecticism, but these attempts were short-lived.[39] The Ayyubid dynasty was supplanted by the Mamluks (r. 1250–1517), who at the height of their power reigned over much of the Levant, Egypt, and the Hijaz. The shifting regional and commercial patterns that started with the diminishing fortunes of Baghdad, a reality that the Fatimids and Ayyubids were able to use to their advantage, continued under the Mamluks. Nothing is more telling of these shifting fortunes than the rise of the Karimi merchants in Egypt. From the twelfth century onward, Egyptian Karimi merchants and Franks dominated trade between East and West, and the taxes levied on them by the Mamluk authorities constituted an essential source of income for the functioning of the Mamluk state. The exponential growth in Egypt's trade and power led to an expansion of the Mamluk bureaucracy, where the government in Cairo created new official positions and departments to regulate and tax a thriving mercantile economy.[40] By the thirteenth century, Cairo had become an important urban center that was, in the words of André Raymond, "a bustling city where the individual lives in anonymity."[41]

The expansion of the Mamluk bureaucracy as well as the commercial need for a reliable legal system—capable of providing merchants with a flexible contract law that could facilitate the management of the wealth that they have accumulated—created the institutional need, nay necessity, for institutionalizing forum selection in the regime of *taqlīd*. This process started with Sultan Baybars' requiring the Shāfiʿī chief judge to choose deputies (*nuwwāb*) from among the other three schools, presumably to permit transactions and contracts not deemed legitimate under Shāfiʿī law. The fact that this decision both comes on the heel of similar Fatimid and Ayyubid decisions shows that this institutional need was not coincidental and that political authorities were fully aware of its importance. The culmination of this evolutionary process would take place in 663/1265 when Sultan Baybars (r. 658–76/1260–77 CE) appointed three chief judges in Cairo, in addition to the Shāfiʿī chief judge, thus providing equal representation for the four Sunnī schools at the highest levels of judicial administration. This decision would be replicated in Damascus a year later. Baybars' decision was viewed rightly by Yossef Rapoport as a strategy to provide litigants with the flexibility of choosing from the doctrines of the four schools.[42]

The decisions made by the Fatimids, Ayyubids, and Mamluks in the twelfth and thirteenth centuries were meant to institutionalize an existing practice of pragmatic eclecticism that started mostly outside the courtroom. This institutional transformation reflects the culmination of a long and incremental process of evolution that corresponded to the stabilization of *taqlīd*. Perhaps nothing shows more clearly the commercial importance of the necessity of facilitating pragmatic eclecticism than the fourteenth-century royal decree appointing a Ḥanbalī judge quoted below. Ironically, the Ḥanbalī school, which had very limited following in Mamluk territory, proved essential in facilitating certain commercial transactions, owing mostly to the school's laissez-faire approach to contracts. As the shift from the common law to the codification episteme was taking hold, the regime of *taqlīd* placed limitations on the judges' ability to provide the flexibility needed for the functioning of the Mamluk state, which was bound as much as its subjects, at least in theory, by Islamic law. By the fourteenth century, pragmatic eclecticism would become the norm in Mamluk courts, as is clear in the following royal decree appointing ʿAlī b. Munajjā ʿAlāʾ al-Dīn al-Tanūkhī (d. 750/1349) as the chief Ḥanbalī judge in Mamluk Damascus:

> The people [of Damascus] are often in need of a judge from this *madhhab* [the Ḥanbalī school] in most contracts of sale and lease, in sharecropping contracts (*muzāraʿa* and *musāqāh*), in settlements over damages caused by force majeure (*jawāʾiḥ samāwiyya*) according to the principle of "No one should be harmed or cause harm to others" (*lā ḍarara wa lā ḍirār*), in marrying off a male slave to a free honorable woman with the permission of his master, in stipulating in a [marriage] contract that a bride should be permitted to stay in her hometown, in dissolving the marriage of a husband who deserted his wife without maintenance and without granting her a divorce, and in the sale of dilapidated endowments that are of no use to their beneficiaries who cannot repair them themselves.[43]

Ottoman Ḥanafization versus Mamluk Pragmatic Eclecticism

When the Ottomans arrived in Egypt in 1517, they found an institutionally pluralistic legal system, epitomized by the above decree, with legal subjects able to forum shop in courts, especially in matters of personal status law, and, more important, in contract law. The Mamluks used Ḥanbalī legal doctrines to allow the drawing of certain contracts that were not permissible under the other three schools.

The royal Mamluk decree appointing ʿAlī b. Munajjā ʿAlāʾ al-Dīn al-Tanūkhī (d. 750/1349) as the chief Ḥanbalī judge in Mamluk Damascus explains some of the transactions in which the Ḥanbalī school offered the most convenient rules. These areas of law revolved around *money and women* as the Mamluk list of transactions permitted only by Ḥanbalīs indicates the motivation behind the appointment of a Ḥanbalī judge. As we will see in chapter 4 dealing with seventeenth- and eighteenth-century courts, pragmatic eclecticism was exercised mostly for questions related to both money and women. The decree contains the following examples of transactions permitted only by the Ḥanbalīs:

- Contracts of sale and lease
- Sharecropping contracts
- Settlements over damages caused by force majeure
- Marrying off a male slave to a free woman with the permission of his master
- Stipulating in a marriage contract that a husband cannot force his bride to leave her hometown
- Dissolving the marriage in the case of the husband's desertion of his wife without providing her with maintenance
- The sale of dilapidated endowments that are of no use to their beneficiaries

But before we can comprehend the continuity of Mamluk pragmatic eclecticism throughout the Ottoman period, we need to examine the internal political situation in Egypt on the heels of the Ottoman conquest, to which we now turn. Before leaving Egypt, Selim I (r. 1512–20) appointed a renegade Mamluk leader, Khāyir Bey, as the first governor of Egypt.[44] Khāyir Bey offered general amnesty to all Mamluks,[45] and the Mamluks returned to the old political and administrative positions they had occupied before the Ottoman conquest.[46] Rather than supplanting the Mamluk elite, the Ottoman conquests created a new administrative hybrid. The administration of Egypt was neither a continuation of the Mamluk system nor an imposition of an Ottoman system.[47] Because of Ottoman immigration to Egypt for administrative and military posts, as well as economic and religious activities, an Ottoman elite was slowly created alongside and overlapping with the Mamluk elite, leading to assimilation between the two groups, especially among the sons of Mamluks known as *awlād al-nās*.[48]

Although the new rulers allowed the Mamluks to maintain most of their control of the administration of Egypt in exchange for paying tribute to Istanbul,[49] it was the legal system where they tried to assert their authority and integrate Egypt into the Ottoman Empire. The Ottomans embarked on a process of legal homogenization and centralization, largely through the erosion of the authority of the schools and the adoption of a single official state legal school. They pursued a policy of purges of local judges, notaries, and witnesses.[50] As soon as Egypt was conquered, Selim I appointed a judge in the Ṣāliḥiyya Madrasa who stopped the judicial authorities (*nuwwāb*) and witnesses (*shuhūd*) from notarizing contracts, causing great disruption in the judiciary (*iḍṭarabat aḥwāl al-aḥkām al-shar'iyya*). The renowned historian Ibn Iyās adds that the judge installed by Selim was indeed more ignorant than a donkey (*ajhal min ḥimār*) and knew nothing about Islamic law. According to Ibn Iyās, the judge was also corrupt.[51] At least for the early decades of the sixteenth century, the Ottomans attempted to replace the predominantly Shāfi'ī and Mālikī judiciary with Ottoman Ḥanafīs. These purges drew the ire of the scholarly elite. Ibn Iyās, an eyewitness of the Ottoman conquest of Egypt, had much criticism for the Ottomans, whom he viewed as unjust and outright barbaric.[52]

The Ottoman attempts at Ḥanafization riled not only local jurists but also the laity, who faced occasional disruptions in their ability to navigate the legal system. In his *Quḍāt Miṣr*, Aḥmad b. Aḥmad al-Damīrī (d. 1030–35/1621–25) described the Ottoman judge Muḥammad Shāh b. Ḥazm, who arrived in Egypt less than fifty years after the Ottoman conquest, as rigid and unfamiliar with Egyptians, who were accustomed to lenience (*ṭubi'ū 'alā al-līn*).[53] This rigidity must have referred to Ottoman rejection of Mamluk legal pluralism. Such lenience, which was mainly linked to money and women as we shall see in the courts of seventeenth- and eighteenth-century Egypt, is the reason why Ottoman Ḥanafization failed at completely supplanting Mamluk legal pluralism. Despite the judicial purges directed at non-Ḥanafīs and the elevation of Ḥanafism to the top of the legal hierarchy, the Ottoman school loyalty (*tamadhhub*) approach, epitomized by the Ḥanafization drive, never prevailed. The hybridization that took place in military, economic, and political administration was replicated in the realm of law. What emerged from this struggle between local Mamluk legal pluralism and the Ottomans' desire to Ḥanafize and centralize is that Ḥanafism retained an official status guaranteeing that the majority of court cases were brought to Ḥanafī judges, as we shall see in chapter 4, and that Ottoman Ḥanafīs sat atop the legal hierarchy, but forum shopping continued to thrive in Ottoman courts.[54]

Why did the Ottomans eventually abandon Ḥanafization? The answer to this question lies in money, women, and their relationship to the political, social, and economic history of Egypt. Because of the division of labor between government and scholars, born of the constitutional arrangement created in the classical period, the Ottomans were not able or willing to crush scholarly opposition to their rule. Neither were they able or willing to pay the price of completely uprooting the powerful Mamluk households and forms of government. The Mamluks retained control over the administration of Egypt and continued to be the feudal lords even as it became part of the Ottoman Empire. By the seventeenth century, the chiefs of the major Mamluk households were the most powerful group in Cairo through their control of rural tax-farms.[55] In addition to the Mamluk and scholarly elites, the merchant elite, who certainly overlapped with other elite groups, continued to thrive, with Cairo remaining an important center of interregional and international trade, especially the trade in coffee, drugs, dyestuffs, and Indian textiles after the Ottoman conquest.[56] Although pragmatic eclecticism was not reserved only for the rich and powerful as we shall see in our discussion of Ottoman courts in chapter 4, the merchant class stood to benefit from it more than the laity. The elite classes were more likely to notarize commercial transactions, especially the alienation of endowment properties, which were essential to the functioning of the economy and benefited the ruling elite, the scholarly elite,[57] and the merchant class throughout the Mamluk and Ottoman periods. Owing to the centrality of freedom of contract ethos of the Ḥanbalī school to commercial transactions, especially those involving endowment properties—which made up about one-fifth of all arable lands in Egypt by the end of the eighteenth century[58]—the elite's economic activities depended on certain transactions that were habitually concluded according to Ḥanbalī law under the Mamluks.

The needs of these old elite groups—the Mamluks, scholars, merchants, and the emerging Ottoman elite—dominated Egyptian socioeconomic life.[59] These old and new elite groups overlapped and became at some junctures indistinguishable from one another. A continuation of the initial Ottoman policy of Ḥanafization would have caused social and economic disruption, which would have been felt most acutely by merchants and elite urban women, who had greater divorce rights under pragmatic eclecticism. Elite women in the Ottoman period administered their own property and played an active role in the marketplace, with 30–40 percent of deeds registered in the last half of the eighteenth century made out by women. Elite Mamluk women both in the Mamluk and Ottoman periods controlled their own wealth and in some cases managed family wealth as well. According to Afaf Lutfi Sayyid-Marsot, elite Mamluk women were often trained to manage investments.[60] Part of the reason for the increasing influence of women in economic activities in Ottoman Egypt is the high rate of attrition among Mamluks, leaving wives who had more than one husband and accumulated wealth through inheritance.[61] In the Ottoman period, women founded large numbers of new endowments (*awqāf*), in which most of their wealth was protected.

Let us return to the fourteenth-century Mamluk appointment decree to discuss the two areas of accommodation to women. The first was enabling women to stipulate in their marriage contracts certain conditions that would prevent husbands from forcing their wives to leave their hometowns and the second granted women a judicial divorce in case the husband deserted his wife without providing her with maintenance. These two cases assume a certain level of mobility that would have been more common among merchants. Indeed, the very fact that women were able to determine the place of their residence and to get a divorce when an absent husband could not provide maintenance indicates a certain class.

In her discussion of eighteenth-century Egyptian women, Sayyid-Marsot said, "It is difficult for me to believe that a wealthy woman had no power in her society, no matter how closed that society may have been."[62] Such accommodations and assumptions about mobility indicate that these particular pragmatic eclectic benefits primarily served elite women, who controlled their own wealth and had expectations that were not necessarily held by women of the lower echelons of society. According to Sayyid-Marsot, some marriage contracts from the Ottoman period stipulated that the wife has the right to wear whatever she pleased and to visit her mother whenever she pleased. Other contracts gave women the right to divorce should the husband take a second wife.[63] These types of stipulations were not permitted under Ḥanafism, the official Ottoman school, which is why the ability of the judiciary to have Ḥanbalī judges at the bench was essential to facilitating these types of transactions.

The needs of the Mamluk-Ottoman, the merchant, and the scholarly elite (with these groups often intersecting and overlapping), as well as those of urban elite women, were served through pragmatic eclecticism. The challenge posed to the economic interests of the elite classes of Mamluk society under Ottoman rule must have been at least partly responsible for the local opposition to Ottoman Ḥanafization. This is not to say that there was no doctrinal reason for the scholars' opposition to Ḥanafization. Ḥanafization was considered a form of official *tamadhhub* (strict school loyalty) that, as we shall see in chapter 2, jurists such as al-Shaʿrānī deemed fanatical and disrespectful to the other schools. This critique must have stiffened opposition to Ottoman Ḥanafization.[64] But perhaps the most decisive factor that guaranteed the failure of Ḥanafization is the threat it posed to the elite classes, of whom the Ottoman elite later became part.[65]

The early disruption to Mamluk legal pluralism failed in the face of opposition from jurists and perhaps a growing awareness among the Ottoman authorities of the significance of pragmatic eclecticism to commerce and accommodations of the needs of urban elite classes including urban women. It is not surprising then that the utilization of the Ḥanbalī school's laissez-faire approach to contracts by the Mamluks in the fourteenth century was echoed much later in the amendment of the Ottoman Mecelle, promulgated in 1877 as the Civil Code of the Ottoman State. The amendments were designed to promote freedom of commercial transactions by borrowing Ḥanbalī concepts of contractual freedom in a predominantly Ḥanafī code. Despite the official status of Ḥanafism in the Ottoman Empire, nineteenth-century Ottoman commercial reformers found the most suitable contractual legal doctrines to be in the Ḥanbalī school. Thus, in the fourteenth-century Mamluk sultanate, as in Cairo under Ottoman rule and well into the nineteenth-century Ottoman Empire, Ḥanbalism represented a numerical minority, but both the Mamluks and the Ottomans found in Ḥanbalism important concepts that were essential to the smooth functioning of the economy. This explains the striking continuity in the practice of pragmatic eclecticism after the shift in Islamic law to the codification episteme under the regime of *taqlīd*.

The *longue durée* institutional, sociopolitical setting of Islamic law in Egypt during the periods of *taqlīd* and *ijtihād* saw a shift from the common law to the codification episteme. This was followed by a shift from *tamadhhub* centralization, that is, centralizing Islamic law by imposing one school and persecuting others, to pragmatic eclectic centralization in which schools were utilized to achieve a division of labor in a system of more determinate legal rules. It is not surprising then that there was so much opposition among jurists to strict school loyalty (*tamadhhub*) and an increasing acceptance of school boundary-crossing. Another very important prerequisite for the rise of pragmatic eclecticism is the theological debate about the ontological multiplicity of truth to which we turn.

The Ontological Multiplicity of Truth

Now that I have discussed the codification episteme, I shall briefly address the debate over the ontological multiplicity (*ta'addud al-ḥaqq*) versus unity of truth in Islamic law, since it is often invoked in the debate over pragmatic eclecticism, as we shall see in the next chapter.

The Multiplicity vs. Unity of Truth Debate

As we saw above, Sultan al-Ẓāhir Baybars (d. 676/1277) decided to provide representation for all Sunnī schools in the form of a chief judge appointed to protect the rulings issued by the judges of their respective schools. Prior to his decision, there was only one chief judge, who hailed from the Shāfiʿī school.[66] Safeguarding differences among schools led to the formation of a legal system in which no judge could punish a subject for contradicting the ruling of his school, so long as his ruling had the backing of another school. This quadruple system protected against the type of incidents that Baybars had likely faced at the beginning of his reign in which the Shāfiʿī chief judge overturned the decisions made by judges whose rulings contradicted the views of his school.[67] By making this decision, Baybars was taking a position on a debate that had been preoccupying jurists before his time.

The practice of pragmatic eclecticism within this pluralist system required that members of each school believe in the probability of the correctness of other opinions, even if they preferred their own school's views and saw them as closer to the truth (*aqrab ilā al-ṣawāb*). For jurists to accept Baybars' pragmatic legal system, endorsing a certain degree of relativism and probabilism was essential.[68] Such a theory of pragmatic eclecticism would not have been possible under the scripturalist approach to law promoted by early Muʿtazilīs such as Bishr al-Marīsī, al-Aṣamm, and Ibn ʿUlayya, who emphasized certainty in matters of law. According to this strand of thought as articulated in debates between Ibn ʿUlayya and al-Shāfiʿī, certainty can be achieved by relying on consensus to the exclusion of single-transmitted Prophetic reports and by restricting analogical reasoning to cases of essential sameness.[69] The dominance of al-Shāfiʿī's thesis, which valorized single-transmitted reports and embraced uncertainty in matters of law, was nicely epitomized by the famous principle "Ours is the right way but it can conceivably be wrong and our opponents' way is wrong but it is conceivable that it is right." By the thirteenth century, the ethos of relativism advanced by al-Shāfiʿī would develop into a theory with different variations, growing in opposition to scripturalist legal absolutists.

This relativism with regard to juristic opinions that are not based on apodictic evidence was achieved in two ways, either through the belief that there are multiple correct *mujtahids* (a minority view among legal theorists in the Mamluk period), or through the notion that the identity of the correct *mujtahid* is ultimately unknowable, while subscribing to the doctrine that there is only one correct opinion. Believing in the knowability of truth makes the pursuit of less stringent juristic opinions less of an option, since the jurist is always expected to search for that objectively knowable truth and to reject the views of any school that contradicts his findings. Conversely, believing that it is impossible to objectively identify the correct *mujtahid* is effectively a prerequisite for the pragmatic utilization of legal diversity. This is why it is important to understand the debate over multiplicity versus unity of truth in legal matters before we embark on a discussion of juristic attitudes toward pragmatic eclecticism. There are several issues at stake in this debate, namely: (1) Is every *mujtahid* in legal matters correct? (2) If there is only one correct *mujtahid*, are the others blameworthy (*āthim*) for being wrong? (3) Is the one correct *mujtahid* always knowable?

There was general agreement among jurists that there may be only one correct *mujtahid* on issues for which there is apodictic evidence. Their disagreement was more specifically over whether every *mujtahid* may be considered correct on issues for which there is no apodictic evidence (*lā qāṭiʿa fīhā*). One group argued that every *mujtahid* may be regarded as correct and that God's ruling in this case corresponds to each *mujtahid*'s opinion (*ẓann*). The proponents of this view were called the *muṣawwiba* because they considered every *mujtahid* to be correct (*muṣīb*). Others contended that there may only be one correct *mujtahid*. The proponents of this view were often called the *mukhaṭṭi'a* because they considered some *mujtahids* to be mistaken in their rulings.[70]

The *muṣawwiba* essentially believed that on issues in which there is no scriptural evidence or consensus (*ijmāʿ*), there is no divine ruling at all. In such cases, the jurist must strive in his *ijtihād* to reach what he believes to be God's ruling. Some, whom the Shāfiʿī al-Juwaynī (d. 478/1085) called the extremists (*ghulāh*), even argued that when a person is presented with more than one opinion, he or she may choose what he or she prefers without having to weigh the different views against one another. According to al-Juwaynī, Abū Isḥāq al-Isfrāyīnī (d. 418/1027) described this opinion as heresy (*zandaqa*).[71] This was the view of some supporters of *tatabbuʿ al-rukhaṣ*, as we shall see.

Al-Juwaynī presented the argument of Abū Bakr al-Bāqillānī (d. 403/1013), who contended that there is no need for *tarjīḥ* since every *mujtahid* is correct (*kullu mujtahidin muṣīb*), and no single *mujtahid* is closer to the intention of the lawgiver than the other. Al-Juwaynī countered that there can only be one truth, though it remains unknowable (*al-ḥaqqu wāḥidun lā bi-ʿaynih*). In his view, if the jurist does not exercise *tarjīḥ* when faced with contradictory pieces of evidence, this will lead to the suspension of God's rulings (*taʿṭīl ḥukm min aḥkām Allāh*).[72] Al-Ghazālī (d. 505/1111) discussed the debate in his *al-Mustaṣfā* but came down on the side of the *muṣawwiba*. According to him, there is no one specific truth in jurisprudential questions for which there is no apodictic evidence (*al-fiqhiyyāt al-ẓaniyya*).[73]

According to the Mālikī jurist Abū ʿAmr ʿUthmān b. ʿUmar b. al-Ḥājib (d. 646/1248), the proponents of multiple truths cite the hadith "My Companions are like stars, whomever you follow will guide you aright" (*aṣḥābī ka'l-nujūmi bi-ayyihim iqtadaytum ihtadaytum*) to support their position. Their argument is that had the Companions been wrong, they would not have constituted guidance (*hudā*). Ibn al-Ḥājib countered that they all represent guidance simply because they did what they were required to do as *mujtahids* and *muqallids* and not because their opinions were all correct.[74]

Within the camp that supported a single correct opinion, there were disagreements regarding whether the correct *mujtahid* is objectively knowable and whether it is possible that some issues have no conclusive evidence (*lā qāṭiʿa fīhā*). Some accepted the possibility that there may be an absence of apodictic evidence on some issues. In such cases, the correct *mujtahid* is judged to be unknowable (*ghayra muʿayyan*), and the other *mujtahids* are not to be blamed on account of their opinions. This position, which was promoted by Abū Isḥāq al-Isfrāyīnī (d. 418/1027), al-Juwaynī, and Ibn al-Ḥājib, among others, would emerge as the dominant view among Sunnī jurists by the end of the classical period.[75]

Others, such as the Muʿtazilī theologians Abū Bakr al-Aṣamm (d. 201/816) and Bishr b. Ghiyāth al-Marīsī (d. 218/833), purportedly held the position that there is always apodictic (*qaṭʿī*) evidence to be discovered. The *mujtahid* who fails to find the correct answer was therefore, according to this view, considered blameworthy.[76] Again, al-Juwaynī described this group as extremists (*ghulāh*),[77] while al-Ghazālī noted that this view was popular among the opponents of analogy (*nufāt al-qiyās*). Al-Ghazālī explained that some of the Muʿtazilīs of Baghdad who held this position went so far as to require even the layperson to seek evidence and examine it for oneself (*al-naẓar wa ṭalab al-dalīl*).[78]

As Ibn al-Ḥājib and his commentator Shams al-Dīn al-Iṣfahānī (d. 749/1349) explained, those who argue for only one correct *mujtahid* contended that when two *mujtahids* disagree on a ruling, their *ijtihād* is either based on evidence (*dalīl*) or not. If it is not based on any evidence, then both have made an error. If one bases his ruling on evidence, while the other does not, the person lacking evidence is in error. If both follow different pieces of evidence but one argument is more preponderant (*rājiḥan*), then this is the correct opinion (*taʿayyana*), and the other is an error. Finally, if no such preponderance is possible, both pieces of evidence should be ignored (*tasāqaṭā*).[79]

Thus, according to this position, if truth cannot be discovered, ruling on the matter should be abandoned. This view does not accept contradictory opinions, which cannot be equated with the truth lodged in the mind of God, the Lawgiver. Ibn al-Ḥājib countered that pieces of evidence are given preponderance by people according to their different proofs (*amārāt*), and therefore it is not possible to objectively determine which one is the correct opinion.[80]

Another question raised in the course of this debate is whether it is possible for two probable proofs (*amārāt ẓanniyya*) to be epistemically equal. According to Ibn al-Ḥājib, this is possible, but he claimed that this view was rejected by earlier authorities like Aḥmad b. Ḥanbal (d. 241/855) and the Ḥanafī jurist Abū al-Ḥasan ʿUbayd Allāh al-Karkhī (d. 340/952). To argue that probable proofs cannot be equal implies that performing *tarjīḥ* among them is always possible, a position that supports the doctrine of the knowability of truth in all legal questions and is, therefore, less epistemically accommodative of pragmatic eclecticism.[81]

The view that it is not possible for two opinions to be epistemically equal was the minority position. The proponents of this position argued that if the two proofs are considered epistemically equal, people may either choose to follow both contradictory proofs, which is a logical impossibility, or alternatively they may follow one of the two, which in this case would necessarily involve an arbitrary designation (*taḥakkum*). Thus different people may choose different proofs (*mukhayyaran*), which means that what is permitted for someone will be forbidden for another. Finally, people may abstain from following either proof, which amounts to mendacity (*kadhib*) since there is an implication that certain things are neither forbidden nor permitted.[82]

In practical terms, the position that the truth on probable matters is unknowable—for instance because both proofs are on the same epistemic level—resembles the ontological multiplicity of truth doctrine in that different *ijtihād*ic views on matters in which there is no apodictic evidence are equally valid. The main difference is that the former doctrine makes the important distinction between truth as lodged in the mind of God and truth as understood by humans. Since we do not know which *mujtahid* is correct, legal pluralism must be accepted.

Legal Pluralism and the Scope of Unknowability

The dominant position within Sunnī jurisprudence came to be that when dealing with epistemically probable evidence, the truth of a legal question is present in the mind of God but remains effectively unknowable. Often it is hard to determine whether a given jurist, who supports the unity of truth doctrine, considers this truth to be knowable on a particular legal issue, partly because the knowability of truth was not often discussed in substantive law. Even within the dominant view that supports the unknowability of truth when there is no apodictic evidence, there was a wide variance on how this was interpreted on the substantive legal level. For some jurists, all issues of disagreement (*khilāf*) belong to the probable category in which truth is unknowable, essentially equating the existing reality of legal pluralism with unknowability. Others narrowed the scope of unknowability to a minimum by expanding the issues for which apodictic evidence is deemed to be available.

Some jurists went further by claiming that it is easy to attain this truth through a scripturalist approach that may be applied with limited training, showing little regard for the complex scholastic disputations of the jurists.[83] According to Ibn Taymiyya (d. 728/1328), many jurists such as Ibn Ḥanbal and most of the *salaf* accepted the possibility of an absence of apodictic evidence for a ruling. He cautioned, however, that the existence of disagreement among jurists over a ruling does *not* necessarily indicate that the evidence in this case is only probable.[84] He added that there is a difference between issues that are subject to *ijtihād* and juristic disagreement (*khilāf*), contending that there are issues of juristic disagreement on which there is apodictic evidence (*qaṭʿiyya*). *Ijtihād*, which can only be exercised in non-apodictic legal questions, may not be exercised on these issues since there is one clear answer. He thus rejected the position that equates epistemic uncertainty with juristic disagreement, which, as he explained, was held by many among his contemporaries (*kamā iʿtaqada dhālika ṭawāʾifun min al-nās*),[85] drawing, instead, a clear distinction between the sociological reality of the existence of issues of juristic disagreement and the normative acceptance of this diversity as equally valid.

Ibn Taymiyya held that there is a single truth for all rulings in the Sharīʿa, while allowing for the possibility of the existence of probable evidence and for its concomitant unknowability. He exonerated *mujtahids* from blame when they erred, and accepted the unknowability of truth in some cases. Nevertheless, he narrowed the instances of legitimate juristic differences to a bare minimum through his strictly scripturalist approach that privileged the opinions of the Companions over those of later jurists. For instance, he cited Ibn ʿAbd al-Barr's explanation of the causes of juristic disagreement (*ikhtilāf*) as follows: (1) two reliable (*ṣaḥīḥ*) contradictory Prophetic traditions; (2) one reliable Prophetic tradition contradicting a weak one (*ḍaʿīf*); (3) a tradition (*qawl*) of a Companion contradicting a Prophetic tradition; (4) an absence of scriptural sources (*naṣṣ*), and the existence of only contradictory views expressed by the Companions; or (5) a new opinion contradicting one or two views held by the Companions. Ibn ʿAbd al-Barr confirmed that whoever holds an opinion contradicting the tradition of a Companion (*qawl*), a weak Prophetic tradition, or any of the opinions of the Companions on which there is a consensus (*ijmāʿ*) is decidedly in error.[86] Owing to the eponyms' divergent positions on the elevation of the Companions' reports to the status of apodictic evidence, Ibn Taymiyya's position flies in the face of many of the legal doctrines of the four schools.

According to Ibn Taymiyya, who agreed with Ibn ʿAbd al-Barr's explication of how to deal with the textual sources, there are limited situations in which truth is unknowable, namely, when there are two contradictory textual sources, or where the two sources have been lost and the

Companions did not agree. In this case, a *mujtahid* who chooses one text over another by exercising preponderance (*tarjīḥ*) should not be judged to be wrong.[87]

Ibn Taymiyya's student Ibn Qayyim al-Jawziyya (d. 751/1350) attacked the dichotomy of attitudes toward theological issues (*masāʾil al-uṣūl*), a reference to *uṣūl al-dīn*, and legal issues (*masāʾil al-furūʿ*), in which scholars typically rejected differences over the former while accepting them in the latter. According to these scholars, Ibn al-Qayyim wrote, disagreement on theological issues renders a person an infidel. Seeing this distinction as artificial, he averred that there is right and wrong on both types of issues.[88] In his argument against the proponents of *taqlīd*, he stated that following different jurists instead of striving for the correct opinion implies that God's law consists of contradictions. Utterly rejecting this position, he declared that there can only be one direction for prayer (*qibla*), and that the rest are wrong. It is incumbent upon people, therefore, to seek the one correct truth (*ṭalab al-ḥaqq*).[89]

Ibn Qayyim's view is contrasted with the other end of the spectrum, at which some jurists considered all opinions within the four schools to belong to the category of unknowability, rejecting the presence of apodictic evidence in cases of juristic disagreement. According to them, truth lies somewhere within the judgments of the four schools. Needless to say, this view that equated juristic disagreement with the unknowability of truth or valid areas of *ijtihād* was more conducive to accepting pragmatic eclecticism, as we shall see below.

The tendency toward narrowing unknowability, which is arguably linked to the development and collection of the hadith literature, also emphasized the notion, based on a Prophetic tradition, that the Ummah will split into seventy-three groups that are doomed to hellfire, except for the one following the Prophet and his Companions.[90] This position was hostile to juristic differences. Thus, for instance, according to the Ḥanbalī al-Barbahārī (d. 329/940–41), one of the early opponents of juristic differences, marriage is only permissible if there is a legal guardian, witnesses, and a dower (*mahr*). He thus rejected the opinion that marriage is permitted without a male guardian (Ḥanafīs) and the opinion of those who did not require witnesses for the validity of marriage contracts (Mālikīs).[91]

Also, following Ibn Ḥanbal's rejection of *tatabbuʿ al-rukhaṣ*, he warned against choosing the Medinan opinion permitting music.[92] Similarly, Ibn Taymiyya supported the view that a person who drinks date wine (*nabīdh*) should be subjected to the prescribed punishment because even though it is an issue of juristic disagreement, it is not an issue of valid *ijtihād*. Truth here is knowable, despite Abū Ḥanīfa's position. Ibn Taymiyya added to this example a long list of matters of juristic disagreement for which he only saw one demonstrably correct *mujtahid*.[93]

The narrowing of unknowability in the work of Ibn Taymiyya and Ibn Qayyim contrasts sharply with the wider scope of unknowability held by al-Ghazālī and Ibn al-Ḥājib. Al-Ghazālī, for instance, accepted the controversial differences among schools that were rejected by Ibn Taymiyya, Ibn Qayyim, and al-Barbahārī. According to al-Ghazālī, drinking date wine, permitting women who are of age to conclude their marriages in the absence of a male guardian, and executing Muslims for the murder of non-Muslims are all valid areas of juristic disagreement, where there are multiple truths.[94]

Ibn al-Ḥājib took a similar position when his interlocutors, who rejected the unknowability of the correct *mujtahid*, cited the problematic example of a *mujtahid* who married a woman to a man in the absence of a legal guardian (*walī*), which is permitted in the Ḥanafī school. Then a second *mujtahid*, who considered the first marriage invalid, married her to another man but, this time, with the consent of a guardian. Ultimately, the question is: are both men legally married to the same woman? By citing this unusual example, proponents of the knowability of the correct *mujtahid* attempted to refute the notion that since we cannot know which *mujtahid* is correct, both marriages are valid from the human perspective, as opposed to truth in the mind of God. According to Ibn al-Ḥājib, given that there is one correct *mujtahid*, each must follow his own belief until a subsequent judicial decision is issued, which becomes binding on both.[95]

These examples show that even when scholars agreed in principle on the theological debate over the ontological multiplicity versus unity of truth, their attitudes toward legal diversity varied considerably. These varying positions were often informed by their respective approaches to what constitutes apodictic evidence, as well as their attitudes toward the origins of differences among the four schools and the legal value of different reports attributed to the Prophet and his Companions.

The Meaning of "Every Mujtahid is Correct"

In light of the above discussion, it becomes clear that the dictum "Every *mujtahid* is correct" (*kullu mujtahidin muṣīb*) did not necessarily imply subscribing to the multiplicity of truth doctrine. For instance, Ibn al-Ḥājib's commentator Shams al-Dīn al-Iṣfahānī (d. 749/1349)—who agreed with Ibn al-Ḥājib's position that there is only one correct *mujtahid*—added, nevertheless, that every *mujtahid* is correct because all have succeeded in their goal of seeking their respective subjective truths (*fa-yakūnu al-kullu muṣīban li-taḥaqquqi maṭlūbih*), even if they do not attain truth in the mind of God. This is not to be regarded as a contradiction with his initial position that there is only one correct *mujtahid*.[96] After all, the legal implications of the unknowability of truth position are similar to those of the multiplicity of truth doctrine.

Al-Juwaynī, who believed that there is only one truth in the mind of God, stated that every *mujtahid* is correct insomuch as each fulfilled what is required of him, which is to follow where his *ijtihād* led him.[97] Despite Ibn Taymiyya's different perception of legal authority, which ultimately narrows his view of the scope of unknowability, he made a distinction between truth lodged in the mind of God (*al-ḥaqqu al-ladhī ʿinda Allāh*, or *bāṭin*), and truth as perceived by the human mind (*ẓāhir*). This distinction, according to Ibn Taymiyya, is more accurate than the designation of absolute right and wrong, which many Ḥanbalīs and other jurists followed.[98] Thus "*Kullu mujtahidin muṣīb*" was used by both sides of the debate either in support of the ontological multiplicity of truth or in drawing a distinction between divine truth and human approximations of it.[99]

Conclusion

The shift from *ijtihād* to *taqlīd*, which started with the formation of schools, was a cumulative process that transformed Islamic law from a model of judicial discretion, similar to the common law, to a codification episteme. The Abbasid courtier Ibn al-Muqaffaʿ attempted to codify Islamic law, but owing to the failure of his proposition, as well as the failure of the Qur'anic Inquisition, it was incumbent upon jurists to manage the stability of the legal system without the intervention of a sovereign. Aware of the need for the stability of legal rules, jurists devised institutional mechanisms and topoi to limit individual interpretation and take law making out of the courtroom. By the thirteenth century, Islamic law was semicodified in the form of *mukhtaṣars*. To be sure, the maturation of *taqlīd* did not lead to a "code" in the modern sense of the word, but rather shifted the emphasis from judicial discretion to higher levels of legal determinacy and stability.

Pragmatic eclecticism represented the final stage in the institutionalization of *taqlīd* and the transformation of Islamic law from a common law system to a codification ethos. Both the Fatimids and the Ayyubids attempted to institute pragmatic eclecticism, but it was the Mamluks who succeeded in establishing a legal pluralistic system that served the interests of the elite members of Mamluk society, especially women. The Mamluk decision to opt for pragmatic eclecticism, despite juristic disagreement over the permissibility of this practice, was motivated mostly by the interests of elite groups, including merchants and women. When the Ottomans arrived in Egypt, they were on a mission to Ḥanafize the judicature, but decades after the Ottoman conquests, partly owing to local opposition, the Ottomans abandoned their Ḥanafizing drive. Pragmatic eclecticism remained the main area of flexibility under the *taqlīd* hegemony, benefiting the Ottoman-Mamluk elite.

Prior to and simultaneously with these judicial developments, the debate over the multiplicity versus unity of truth led to the acceptance of legal pluralism in large areas of the law. By the end of the classical period, the dominant view in Sunnism accommodated legal pluralism, paving the way for the acceptance of pragmatic eclecticism. The views on the issue of multiplicity versus unity of truth were as follows:

1. There are multiple truths.
2. There is only one truth lodged in the mind of God:
    a. This truth is unknowable, and thus, from the human perspective every *mujtahid* is correct.
        i. Unknowability is equated with actual juristic disagreements (*khilāf*).

ii. The scope of unknowability is restricted through a wider definition of apodictic evidence.

b. Truth is always knowable, with the implication that *mujtahids* must always attempt to discover it. Those who fail to discover it are not only in error, but they are also blameworthy.

As we shall see in the next chapters, these views were frequently invoked in the debate over pragmatic eclecticism. Believing in the multiplicity of truth or that truth is one but unknowable in matters of actual juristic disagreement were often the theoretical preconditions for accepting pragmatic eclecticism.

PART TWO

Juristic Discourse Prior to the Nineteenth Century

2

Tatabbu' al-Rukhaṣ in Juristic Discourse Prior to the Nineteenth Century

IN THIS CHAPTER, I analyze the evolution of the attitudinal transformations toward *tatabbu' al-rukhaṣ* starting as far back as the eponyms of the four Sunnī schools and ending at the early nineteenth century,[1] that is, before the attempts to modernize the Egyptian legal system. I start with the dominant view in the formative and classical periods, followed by the paradigmatic shift that started around the thirteenth century and continued to compete with the early doctrine. Although a few modern historians have made references to instances of eclecticism prior to the nineteenth century using the term *takhayyur*, there has not been a discussion of the history of attitudes toward *tatabbu' al-rukhaṣ*, the pre-nineteenth-century equivalent of *takhayyur*.[2]

Rukhṣa and *Tatabbu' al-Rukhaṣ*

Rukhṣa, literally "permission" or "dispensation," is the relaxation or suspension of a legal rule under certain circumstances. One example is the suspension of the obligation to fast during Ramadan while being ill or on a journey. This *rukhṣa* is available to all the four Sunnī schools, but the choice turns into obligation if one fears death in the event of abstaining from taking advantage of the *rukhṣa*.[3] This type of *rukhṣa* is not the result of legal pluralism as it is available within each school. Washing over one's shoes instead of washing the feet during ritual ablution is another example. A person performing the ritual ablution can choose whether to wipe the exterior of his shoes or take them off and wash his feet.[4]

A second type of *rukhṣa* is one that is usually based on differences of opinion among schools, known as *tatabbu' rukhaṣ al-madhāhib* (literally "pursuing the dispensations of the schools"), or more simply as *tatabbuʿ al-rukhaṣ* or *ittibāʿ al-rukhaṣ*.[5] These terms were used in the Mamluk and Ottoman periods to refer to the conscious decision to pursue the juristic opinion perceived to be most expedient from any of the four Sunnī schools. In this sense, any act of *talfīq* (combining two doctrines in the same transaction) can be seen as a form of *tatabbuʿ al-rukhaṣ*. The term *tatabbuʿ al-rukhaṣ* was also used less commonly to describe the act of choosing the most expedient of multiple opinions within the same school. Those who opposed this legal strategy oftentimes associated it with the Qur'anic term *ittibāʿ al-hawā* (following whims).[6] Some jurists even used *tatabbuʿ al-rukhaṣ* interchangeably with *ittibāʿ al-hawā*. This negative association might explain the tendency among some modern reformers to opt for the use of the term *takhayyur*, as explained below.

A diachronic discussion of attitudes toward pragmatic eclecticism and references to practice, whether done across school boundaries or within the same school, will demonstrate that change in Islamic law was in fact a response to social realities. There was no abrupt break with the approach of the formative and classical periods, but rather a new strand of thought began to compete with the earlier approach, gaining momentum over time, particularly in the Ottoman period. Both opponents and supporters of pragmatic eclecticism abounded in all four schools of Sunnī law. There is some irony in the fact that not only supporters, but also opponents of pragmatic eclecticism found it convenient to enlist the help of like-minded jurists from among the other schools. Indeed, some jurists justified their frequent engagement with the authorities of other schools on this issue by arguing that this is a topic that requires such eclecticism.[7] Let us now turn to the earliest approaches to pragmatic eclecticism.

Opposition to Pragmatic Eclecticism

Before the rise of schools, *tatabbuʿ al-rukhaṣ* referred to the selection of the less stringent juristic opinions of *mujtahids*, which often varied along geographical lines. Opposition to this legal strategy started quite early in Islamic juristic discourse. Sulaymān al-Taymī (d. 143/760), who was among the generation following the Companions known as the Successors (*tābiʿīn*), was quoted by Ibn ʿAbd al-Barr as saying that "All evil converges on him who takes the less stringent opinions of every scholar."[8] Al-Awzāʿī (d. 157/773), the leader of a school in Syria that did not long survive his death, was also reported to have stated that whoever follows the scholars' anomalous opinions is not a Muslim. He went so far as to avoid the more lenient opinions of different regions as a precaution against *tatabbuʿ al-rukhaṣ*.[9]

Two Prophetic traditions were cited by supporters of pragmatic eclecticism in particular, namely (1) "Differences among the *umma* are a blessing" (*ikhtilāfu ummatī raḥma*), referred to hereinafter as the "*ikhtilāf* hadith"; and (2) "My Companions are like stars, whomever you follow will guide you aright" (*aṣḥābī ka'l-nujūmi bi-ayyihim iqtadaytum ihtadaytum*), referred to hereinafter as the "Companions hadith." Although these traditions were often invoked in the discourse of postclassical supporters of pragmatic eclecticism, they were not used by the eponyms in the same way.

A version of the first tradition is mentioned in *al-Fiqh al-Akbar*, which is problematically attributed to Abū Ḥanīfa (d. 150/767), although not yet in the form of a Prophetic tradition.[10] For Abū Ḥanīfa and his later commentator Abū Manṣūr Muḥammad al-Ḥanafī al-Samarqandī (d. 333/944), the context of the hadith had nothing to do with pragmatic eclecticism. It was primarily cited in defense of the Companions against Shīʿī attacks.[11] The Ḥanbalī jurist Abū Muḥammad al-Ḥasan b. ʿAlī al-Barbahārī (d. 329/940–41) mentioned the Companions hadith in a somewhat similar context, namely, in paying respect to the Companions as opposed to endorsing a notion of pragmatic eclecticism.[12]

It seems that the Companions hadith was considered irrelevant by Muḥammad b. Idrīs al-Shāfiʿī (d. 204/820) or perhaps it was unknown to him, as he did not mention it in his discussion of *ikhtilāf* in *al-Risāla*. He simply divided juristic disagreements into forbidden and permitted, citing the Qur'an to condemn disagreement when textual evidence points to one opinion. He held that when the Companions disagree, one should search out the view that corresponds to the textual sources, consensus, or analogy.[13] Al-Shāfiʿī, who rejected jurists' acceptance of legal opinions without verification through a link to the sources of law, did not permit jurists to exercise "blind following" of legal opinions, itself a prerequisite for the permission of pragmatic eclecticism for jurists.[14] Even from the viewpoint of the layperson, al-Shāfiʿī does not have a place in his theory for the laity's exercise of pragmatic eclecticism.[15]

Al-Shāfiʿī's view resembles an opinion attributed to the eponym of the Mālikī school, Mālik b. Anas (d. 179/795), that some of the Companions of the Prophet were right and others wrong and that, therefore, one must exercise *ijtihād* with regard to their juristic opinions. In Ibn al-Ṣalāḥ al-Shahrazūrī's (d. 643/1245) estimation, Mālik did not believe such differences to be a blessing (*tawsiʿa*).[16] But Malik's view of pragmatic eclecticism for the laity and jurists is hard to assess. The situation is less ambiguous in the case of the eponym of the Ḥanbalī school, Aḥmad b. Ḥanbal (d. 241/855), who is reported on the authority of his son Abdullāh to have said that if someone were to follow the people of Kūfa on date wine (*nabīdh*), the people of Medina on music (*samāʿ*), and the people of Mecca on *mutʿa* marriage, such a person is a sinner (*fāsiq*).[17] Similarly, asked about what a person should do when faced with conflicting opinions, he stated that the choice should be based on the view that best supports the Qur'an and Prophetic traditions, implying that only one opinion is supported by the sacred source texts.[18]

The early authorities of the schools were also opposed to the practice and perceived there to be a consensus against it. The Ẓāhirī jurist Ibn Ḥazm (d. 456/1064), for instance, disapproved of people following their "whims" (*al-hawā*) by taking the less stringent views (*rukhaṣ*) of jurists. He even argued that there was consensus over the ban on following such *rukhaṣ*. He voiced much criticism for Abū Ḥanīfa's followers, including Abū Ḥanīfa's disciple Muḥammad al-Shaybānī (d. 189/805), accusing them of picking and choosing the opinions of those Companions that fit their whims. According to him, such practices were far from piety and might even lead to fornication (*zinā*), a reference to invalid marriages caused by pragmatic eclecticism. The proponents of such views "only follow a devastating *taqlīd*, a rotten opinion, and misleading whims (*ittibāʿ al-hawā al-muḍill*)."[19]

Ibn Ḥazm was diametrically opposed to *taqlīd*, emphasizing the need for the lay fatwa-seeker (*mustaftī*) to inquire about the source of the fatwa. If the fatwa is not explicitly derived from the textual sources, the fatwa-seeker should not take it. According to him, pragmatic choices of varying legal opinions are strictly forbidden. This attitude is clear in his epistemic hierarchy for different types of evidence. If a fatwa-seeker is given two different fatwas, which one should he or she choose? Ibn Ḥazm, who operated within an *ijtihād*ic paradigm fully anchored in the textual sources, gave preference to the fatwa based on the hadith literature rather than on the Qur'an. According to him, such a hierarchy would resolve some contradictory fatwas.[20] In his *Marātib al-Ijmāʿ*, he claimed that there is consensus that following the less stringent interpretation (*ṭalab rukhaṣ kull ta'wīl*) is a forbidden act, even a sin.[21] His near contemporary, Ibn ʿAbd al-Barr (d. 463/1071), declared that he knew of no disagreement among jurists (*khilāf*) on this matter.[22]

Can the layperson follow the view of al-Shāfiʿī in some cases and Abū Ḥanīfa in others? Al-Juwaynī stated that if this were the case, there would have been no point in writing his book on preponderance (*tarjīḥ*). He explained that the layperson has to abide by one of the schools. In response to the argument that people often followed different Companions on different issues, he pointed out that the situation of people in the Companions' day was different because they did not have a fully developed legal system covering all possible transactions, unlike the school system. According to him, people had no choice but to follow different Companions on different issues out of necessity (*ḍarūra*), but this was no longer the case with the rise of legal schools.[23]

The Shāfiʿī jurist al-Ghazālī (d. 505/1111) used the term *takhyīr* to refer to a nonpragmatic choice that is made between equally valid proofs. He juxtaposed *takhyīr* with the practice of making a specific choice, that is, always choosing the more stringent or less stringent juristic opinion. He rejected this approach as arbitrary (*taḥakkum*).[24] He strongly opposed the selection of the more convenient juristic opinion, establishing a clear dichotomy between evidentiary choices (*tarjīḥ*) and choices based on desire (*tashahhī*). When faced with conflicting juristic opinions, the *muqallid* should treat them the same way in which a *mujtahid* deals with contradictory pieces of evidence. In such instances, the layperson must opt for the opinion expressed by the more knowledgeable or more pious jurist (*afḍal*).[25]

Al-Ghazālī was aware of the seeming contradiction between his view that the layperson must exercise *tarjīḥ* among the *mujtahids* and his position that every *mujtahid* is correct. He preempted any critique by arguing that it is possible that a *mujtahid* may be unaware of existing apodictic evidence. Such a mistake, he averred, is less likely to be made by the more knowledgeable jurist. If laypeople's choices were not controlled, he added, they would follow their whims (*muttabiʿīna li'l-hawā*) and become like beasts, unbridled by God's law. Forcing them to follow the more qualified jurist is better than giving them a choice (*takhyīrihim*). His mistrust of the potential motivations that can drive the choices of laypeople is clear in his conclusion that if two jurists appear to be equally correct, laypeople are given the choice but only out of necessity (*ḍarūra*). This is the same situation faced by the *mujtahid* who has to resort to *takhyīr* when two pieces of evidence enjoy the same level of strength. In al-Ghazālī's usage, the term *takhyīr* and its derivatives, which are used in a nontechnical sense, do not imply utility, although there is a concern that unrestricted choice (*takhyīr*) may lead to utilitarian manipulation.[26]

What about muftis facilitating pragmatic selections on behalf of the layperson? Ibn al-Ṣalāḥ al-Shahrazūrī clearly stated his opposition to muftis choosing less stringent (*tarkhīṣ*) or more stringent juristic opinions (*taghlīẓ*), regardless of the evidentiary grounds of these opinions. This choice is only allowed, according to him, to help the fatwa-seeker avoid perjury with respect to an oath. A mufti, he added, is not permitted to abandon his school's opinion on an issue in favor of a less stringent opinion, but choosing the safer opinion (*aḥwaṭ*) is allowed. He even claimed that there is consensus over the prohibition of pragmatic choices that are not based on the exercise of preponderance.[27]

Ibn al-Ṣalāḥ outlined five juristic approaches to the situation in which the layperson is faced with two conflicting fatwas: (1) he may follow the more stringent opinion (*aghlaẓ*); (2) he may follow the less stringent opinion (*akhaff*); (3) he may seek the opinion of the more knowledgeable and pious jurist; (4) he may ask another mufti; or (5) he may select one view arbitrarily (*yatakhayyar*). Ibn al-Ṣalāḥ clearly rejected the choice of the less stringent opinion, urging the fatwa-seeker, instead, to exercise *tarjīḥ*. If the fatwa-seeker fails to reach a conclusion, he must then ask a third mufti and follow that opinion. If this is not possible and the disagreement is over whether something is prohibited or permissible, he must consider it prohibited because it is the safer option (*aḥwaṭ*). If it is not a matter of prohibition and permissibility, then he may select what he pleases (*takhyīr*) out of necessity in such a rare instance (*ḍarūratun fī ṣūratin nādira*).[28]

There are also indications that pragmatic eclecticism caused outrage among jurists. This was the case with the Ḥanafī jurist Ibn al-Najjār (d. 660/1261), who took advantage of Shāfiʿī and Ḥanafī rules to facilitate his marriage and divorce. His behavior caused a stir among Ḥanafī and Shāfiʿī jurists.[29] This opposition is understandable in light of the polemical nature of the competition among Sunnī schools during that period. The struggle between the Shāfiʿīs and Ḥanafīs in Nishapur is a case in point. Although Richard W. Bulliet sees the struggle as having been political, rather than legal or theological, the least that can be gleaned from this episode is that legal-theological designations were employed to mobilize the masses against one another. Thus they were at least valid rallying points. Similar tensions, and even clashes, among the schools can be seen in twelfth-century Syria as well, a phenomenon that continued well into the Mamluk period.[30]

Opposition to *tatabbuʿ al-rukhaṣ* continued throughout the Mamluk period. Ibn Taymiyya (d. 728/1328) warned against following the errors of scholars (*zallāt*) and against following the less stringent juristic opinions (*rukhaṣ*).[31] He claimed that there is consensus over the prohibition of fatwas and judicial rulings that are based on whims rather than the exercise of *tarjīḥ*.[32] His student Ibn Qayyim al-Jawziyya (d. 751/1350) held that whenever the Companions of the Prophet disagreed, Ibn Ḥanbal chose (*takhayyara*) the view that was closest to the Qur'an and Sunna (note well that the root *kh-y-r* does not signify pragmatism in Ibn Qayyim's writing). If unable to establish one view as corresponding to the scriptures, he would transmit it as a *khilāf* issue without choosing one side over another.[33] Like his teacher, Ibn Qayyim al-Jawziyya engaged in a long discussion of the scholar's error (*zallat al-ʿālim*), which he used as evidence against the validity of *taqlīd*. He contended that since scholars are fallible, one should not accept all their juristic opinions. According to him, those who adhere to *taqlīd* follow jurists both when they are right and when they are in error, without due recourse to *tarjīḥ*.[34]

Opposition to *Taqlīd*

In this section, I discuss opposition to *taqlīd,* which by extension constituted a rejection of pragmatic eclecticism. In their promotion of *ijtihād,* opponents of *taqlīd* rejected the notion that there is a dearth or absence of *mujtahids.* They followed two approaches in their refutation of *taqlīd,* namely, drawing a distinction between the term "*taqlīd*" and "*ittibā*'" and emphasizing the simplicity of *ijtihād.* The concept of *ittibā*' (literally, to follow) means following the textual evidence, rather than accepting an opinion solely based on the authority of the jurist holding the opinion. According to these anti-*taqlīd* jurists, even the layperson should not accept a juristic opinion without verifying its scriptural evidence. This position effectively amounted to a rejection of much of the practice of *iftā*', which allowed the jurist to address legal questions with a yes or no answer.[35] The proponents of this distinction tended to be some of the strongest opponents of *tatabbu' al-rukhaṣ.* The discourse of the fatwa, according to this approach, must directly invoke the authority of God by invoking the textual sources, as opposed to appealing to the authority of individual jurists.

The conceptual distinction between *taqlīd* and *ittibā*' can be seen in Ibn 'Abd al-Barr's argument that if a *muqallid* can produce a proof (*ḥujja*), it is no longer considered *taqlīd,* even if such evidence is never examined by the jurist to derive laws. He attributed the linguistic distinction to the Mālikī jurist Abū 'Abd Allāh b. Khuwayyiz al-Mindād al-Baṣrī (d. 390/999–1000).[36] Ibn 'Abd al-Barr's approach was countered by the mainstream Sunnī position, represented by al-Khaṭīb al-Baghdādī and al-Ghazālī. They accepted *taqlīd* because if laypeople were required to exercise *ijtihād,* that would lead to the destruction of the earth (*kharāb al-dunyā*), since people will no longer farm the land or attend to their crafts.[37] At one point, al-Ghazālī even suggested that laypeople are not practicing *taqlīd* in the sense of "slavish imitation" since the layperson's obligation to follow the opinion of the mufti is confirmed by consensus; therefore, such an action is based on proof and cannot be called *taqlīd,*[38] but he did not provide an alternative term.

The second approach used by the opponents of *taqlīd* was to claim that exercising *ijtihād* is within the reach of everyone and, therefore, it does not require the full scholarly dedication that might lead craftsmen to abandon their trades.[39] We can see this, for instance, in Ibn Taymiyya's division of *tarjīḥ* into two types, one of which is based on specific proofs (*dalīl khāṣṣ*) and the other on general proofs (*dalīl 'ām*). The exercise of *tarjīḥ* for the *muqallid* involves a general proof, that is, choosing the mufti possessed of more knowledge and piety. Ibn Taymiyya, however, preferred to rely on specific proofs (*dalīl khāṣṣ*) that give preponderance to one juristic opinion over another through the assessment of evidence. He even argued that peoples' ability to give preponderance to one opinion over another through a direct assessment of the evidence itself may in fact be easier than identifying which mufti is more knowledgeable or pious.[40] This strand of thought that encouraged the pursuit of textual evidence (rather than pragmatic eclecticism), even among the laity, has continued well into the modern period, as we shall see below.

To summarize, we have seen thus far that almost all sides of the debate on the multiplicity versus the unity of truth prior to the thirteenth century agreed on the prohibition against *tatabbu' al-rukhaṣ*. Al-Juwaynī, who supported the unity of truth in the absence of apodictic evidence, was one of the opponents of *tatabbu' al-rukhaṣ*, along with his student al-Ghazālī who supported the multiplicity of truth doctrine. Opponents also included Ibn Taymiyya and his student Ibn Qayyim, who held that there is only one truth and narrowly defined the scope of unknowability of truth with regard to legal rules as we saw in chapter 1. They both rejected *taqlīd*, and, by extension, utilitarian choices inspired by mundane social rather than hermeneutic considerations, and sought to make a distinction between *taqlīd* and *ittibā'*, with the latter meaning following the evidence rather than the authority of jurists. Opponents of *taqlīd* outright rejected pragmatic eclecticism.

Pragmatic eclecticism across school boundaries was also rejected by proponents of the less popular strict school loyalty (*tamadhhub*) position, which opposed any change of school on a single transaction. This position continued to coexist with the mainstream Sunnī approach permitting *tarjīḥ* across school boundaries into the Ottoman period. The Ḥanafī jurist Ibrāhīm b. Bīrī (d. 1099/1687) held that the layperson or the jurist may change his school holistically but not in a single transaction. Thus a Ḥanafī is not allowed to follow a Shāfiʿī or a Mālikī mufti.[41] He then cited the Ḥanafī Shams al-Dīn al-Qahistānī (d. 953/1546) as stating that scholars who believed in the doctrine of the multiplicity of truth on legal matters, such as the Muʿtazilīs, permitted the laity to choose from whatever school they desired (*mā yahwāhu ay yamīlu ilayhi qalbuh*). According to Ibn Bīrī, those who upheld the unity of truth doctrine, including himself, considered those who took from every school its less stringent opinions (*rukhaṣ*) to be sinners.[42] The strict school-loyalty position was rejected by most jurists. The Shāfiʿī al-Samhūdī (d. 911/1505) even speculated that the sole motivation behind the strict school-loyalty position was the fear of laypeople exercising *tatabbuʿ al-rukhaṣ*.[43]

The above are just some examples of the early opposition to *tatabbuʿ al-rukhaṣ*. This strand of thought, which continues well into the modern period, is a deeply rooted position, which explains why the opponents of *tatabbuʿ al-rukhaṣ* claimed the existence of a consensus over the matter prior to the thirteenth century.[44] This consensus would itself be challenged over the course of the Ayyubid, Mamluk, and Ottoman periods, as we shall see in the remainder of this chapter.

On the Permissibility of *Tatabbuʿ al-Rukhaṣ*

Not all forms of *tatabbuʿ al-rukhaṣ* generated as much disagreement historically. Al-Samhūdī (d. 911/1505), for instance, drew a distinction between different types of *tatabbuʿ al-rukhaṣ* based on who makes the decision. The first type is the decision of a judge who may choose his rulings based on what is more beneficial to the legal subject, as opposed to following the inherent logic of the evidence or applying the preponderant opinion within his school. The second type deals with the decision made by a person in his or her capacity as a legal subject. The third type is the fatwa that is issued by a mufti in accordance with the opinion of a different school or on the basis of a weak opinion in his own school.[45] Most discussions of *tatabbuʿ al-rukhaṣ* in juristic discourse are related to the second and third types.

The agency behind the decision to exercise pragmatic eclecticism is directly related to whether the issue is brought before a mufti or a judge, which is, in turn, connected to whether the matter is ritual, moral, or strictly legal. The choice of a judge, as we shall see in chapter 4, is quite often made by the subject of the law but sometimes by the judges themselves. The situation is different with nonbinding legal opinions (fatwas) issued by muftis. Their nonbinding nature affords legal subjects greater agency in shopping around for more convenient juristic opinions. In what follows, I first discuss juristic attitudes toward *tatabbuʿ al-rukhaṣ* as practiced by legal subjects, especially when they have full agency in their choice of forum in the court context, or when they approach a mufti.

Subjects of the Law

Save for a few references to an earlier authority that supposedly supported *tatabbuʿ al-rukhaṣ*, namely the Shāfiʿī jurist Abū Isḥāq al-Marwazī (d. 340/951),[46] it is not until the thirteenth century that we find scholars making arguments in favor of this practice, which was already taking place among the laity. The Andalusian Ayyubid-era Sufi authority Muḥyī al-Dīn b. ʿArabī (d. 638/1240) was one of the earliest voices attempting to reconcile legal practice with juristic discourse. In his magnum opus *al-Futūḥāt al-Makkiyya*, which he started in 599/1201 and finished in 629/1231, he criticized contemporary jurists for preventing laypeople from following the *rukhaṣ* of the schools, and for obliging them to abide by a single school at all times. He explained that the jurists of his time regarded the pursuit of the *rukhaṣ* of other schools as a manipulation of the law and described their attitude as "the epitome of ignorance." To illustrate his point, he lamented the fact that a Mālikī mufti would prevent a Mālikī layperson from following the *rukhṣa* of the Shāfiʿī school.[47] He would rather grant legal subjects full agency in seeking the less stringent juristic opinions among different schools, as he treated *rukhaṣ* as a gift from God.[48]

Ibn ʿArabī's view seems to have been the exception in this period, as most of the jurists of his time were against this practice. The habit of laypeople availing themselves of the practice, however, does not seem to have been a novelty in the early thirteenth century as evidenced by the amount of attention given to the debate over this topic in the eleventh and twelfth centuries, as well as by references to people's behavior. The debate, in this case, was not merely theoretical speculation but rather reflected a commentary on legal practice. Al-Ghazālī's mistrust of laypeople, which we saw earlier, and his assertion that, left to their own devices, they would follow their whims and become like beasts unbridled by God's law, was most likely informed by actual practice before Ibn 'Arabī's time.[49] The reports of strong opposition and accusations of sinfulness against those who pursue less stringent juristic opinions are themselves an indication of early practice that predates Ibn 'Arabī. Even if the judiciary was not institutionally accommodative of such practices, people must have fatwa-shopped in the case of both rituals and potential legal disputes, regardless of whether or not they could do that in the courtroom.

Drawing upon the theological-legal debate of the multiplicity versus the unity of truth, another Ayyubid jurist, the Shāfiʿī 'Izz al-Dīn b. 'Abd al-Salām (d. 660/1262) argued that whether laypeople follow the *rukhaṣ* or the *'azā'im*, both decisions fall within the purview of truth. Referring to the unknowability of truth doctrine, he argued that those who hold that there may be only one correct *mujtahid* do not know which one he is.[50] In another work, Ibn 'Abd al-Salām supported a layperson's adoption of a different school in a single transaction, so long as the rule does not invalidate a judge's decision (*mimmā lā yunqaḍu fīhī al-ḥukm*), that is, so long as it does not violate a clear textual source, consensus, or obvious analogy.[51]

Ibn 'Abd al-Salām's Mamluk-era Mālikī student al-Qarāfī (d. 684/1285)—who lived in Cairo when Baybars appointed four chief judges—attributed to Abū Zakariyyā Yaḥyā b. Abī Malūl al-Zanātī (d. 525/1131) the view that switching schools is permitted, so long as it meets three conditions. First, the different views should not be combined in a way that violates consensus, as in the example of someone who concludes a marriage without a dower, a male guardian, or witnesses, thereby violating consensus because none of the schools would accept such a marriage in its entirety. His second condition is that the layperson must sincerely believe that the *mujtahid* whom he follows is knowledgeable and/or pious. Third, he must not expediently follow the less stringent opinions from the different schools (*tatabbu' rukhaṣ al-madhāhib*).[52]

Al-Qarāfī, who did not agree with al-Zanātī's stringent restrictions on school boundary-crossing, proceeded to cite an unnamed scholar of the view that switching schools is permissible, so long as the change does not lead to contravening consensus, *fiqh* rules (*qawā'id*), the textual sources, or a clear case of analogy. According to al-Qarāfī, following the *rukhaṣ* that bring about relief to the subject of the law (*mukallaf*) is permitted. After all, there was consensus among the Companions that people who obtained fatwas from Abū Bakr and 'Umar could seek fatwas from other Companions.[53] Given al-Qarafī's tendency to cite his authorities, it is curious that he avoided disclosing the source behind this position by using the formula "another/others said" (*qāla ghayruh*). This may suggest that this nascent view was not backed by any prominent jurists, or perhaps its backers were controversial. Might it be a reference to Ibn 'Arabī?

Be that as it may, the novelty of this strand of thought toward a greater acceptance of *tatabbu' al-rukhaṣ* is partly evinced by its Ottoman proponents' invocation of their thirteenth-century counterparts as the earliest voices for pragmatic eclecticism. The earliest supporter of pragmatic eclecticism, Ibn 'Arabī, is usually left out in later references. This is perhaps partly owing to his controversial mystical views, which might have dissuaded some later jurists from explicitly referencing his views or openly acknowledging his juristic contributions.[54] Later jurists, however, do not fail to acknowledge the contribution of Ibn 'Abd al-Salām, an important node of authority that supported *tatabbu' al-rukhaṣ*. The authority of Ibn 'Abd al-Salām was invoked by the Mālikī jurist Ibn 'Arafa (d. 803/1400) in his argument for *tatabbu' al-rukhaṣ*.[55] Ibn 'Arafa, as cited in the *Mi'yār* by al-Wansharīsī (d. 914/ 1508), confirmed that both the proponents of the doctrine that every *mujtahid* is correct and those holding that there may be only one correct *mujtahid*, albeit unspecified (*lam yu'ayyinūh*), justify accepting the choices of laypeople, whether they choose to follow more stringent or less stringent opinions.[56] Ibn 'Abd al-Salām's view was cited later in the Mamluk period by al-Samhūdī, who stated that the layperson is permitted to follow in each transaction whichever jurist he wished to follow and that even if he were to follow a jurist in a given transaction, there was no obligation to continue following him for future transactions.[57] In the Ottoman period, 'Abd al-Ra'ūf al-Munāwī (d. 1029/1620) would also cite Ibn 'Abd al-Salām as one of the main proponents of *tatabbu' al-rukhaṣ*.[58]

The Ḥanafī jurist Ibn al-Humām (d. 861/1457) was another important node of authority in the debate. He claimed that there is no *shar'ī* reason why people should not be permitted to pursue what is easier for them (*akhaff*), so long as they had not acted on a different opinion previously.[59] He added that the Prophet also favored what made things easier for people. His commentator Ibn Amīr al-Ḥājj (d. 879/1474) agreed with him, taking his argument further by attacking the consensus over the prohibition of *tatabbu' al-rukhaṣ*, which was claimed to exist by the Mālikī jurist Ibn 'Abd al-Barr (d. 463/1071). Ibn Amīr al-Ḥājj bolstered his argument further by citing the two main figures that pioneered this juristic position in the early Mamluk period, namely, Ibn 'Abd al-Salām and al-Qarāfī, but no mention was made of Ibn 'Arabī.

A point usually raised by opponents of *tatabbu' al-rukhaṣ* is that Aḥmad b. Ḥanbal had considered it a sin (*fisq*). Ibn Amīr al-Hājj countered that there are two versions to the report, one of which does not have Ibn Ḥanbal describing the practice as a sin. According to Ibn Amīr al-Hājj, a number of Ḥanbalīs argued that if someone followed stronger evidence or if that person was a layperson, he or she would not be considered a sinner. He added that Abū Ya'lā (d. 458/1066) interpreted Ibn Ḥanbal's statement as not referring to the context of *taqlīd*, implying that the reference was to following whims in the exercise of *ijtihād*.[60] The Shāfi'ī al-Zarkashī (d. 794/1392) would continue challenging Ibn Ḥanbal's opposition by arguing that some Ḥanbalīs held that Ibn Ḥanbal in fact supported *tatabbu' al-rukhaṣ*. Ibn Ḥanbal was even quoted as telling one of his disciples not to insist on his own opinion (*madhhab*) and to let people seek out less stringent views (*da'hum yatarakhkhaṣū bi-madhāhib al-nās*).[61]

The voices supporting the practice that one finds in the fifteenth century are multiplied manyfold over the sixteenth through the eighteenth centuries. Although opposition to *tatabbu' al-rukhaṣ* never ceased to exist throughout the Ayyubid, Mamluk, and Ottoman periods, there was a noticeable discursive shift, with an increasing number of jurists recognizing the existence of a vibrant debate. Even opponents of the practice no longer claimed a clear consensus on the subject. Thus, for instance, the Shāfi'ī jurist al-Samhūdī (d. 911/1505) who opposed the practice, nevertheless presented the other view, explicitly stating that there was no consensus on this issue and dismissing the consensus claimed by Ibn

Ḥazm. He suggested, instead, that Ibn Ḥazm might have been referring to complex *rukhaṣ* (*al-rukhaṣ al-mutarakkiba*), a reference to *talfīq*, or that he must have been referring to *tatabbuʿ al-rukhaṣ* in *ijtihād*, not in *taqlīd*. The implication here is that if *ijtihād* rather than *taqlīd* were to motivate the person's choices, this would not be *tatabbuʿ al-rukhaṣ*, since correspondence to another jurist's less stringent view is only a coincidence.[62]

The question of consensus was significant because, without consensus, the attribution of sin to those who practice pragmatic eclecticism can be rejected. To this effect, al-Samhūdī cited al-Zarkashī as stating that it would be unacceptable to label the person who follows less stringent juristic opinions a sinner (*fāsiq*) because every *mujtahid* is correct (*kullu mujtahidin muṣīb*). He contended that even if we were to believe that there is only one correct *mujtahid*, the existence of a sufficient doubt as to which one is correct must preclude any accusation of sin.[63] A rejection of the consensus claim and the accusation of sinning meant that a judicial ruling based on *tatabbuʿ al-rukhaṣ* may no longer be overruled. To most Mamluk and Ottoman jurists, a person exercising *tatabbuʿ al-rukhaṣ* could not, for this reason, be labeled a sinner.

The Ḥanafī jurist Amīr Bādshāh (d. 972/1564), in his commentary on Ibn al-Humām's *al-Taḥrīr*, also cast doubt on Ibn Ḥazm's claim that there was consensus, referring to the existence of two versions of Ibn Ḥanbal's statement on whether choosing less stringent opinions qualifies as a sin.[64] In a similar fashion, the Shāfiʿī jurist Shams al-Dīn Muḥammad b. Aḥmad b. Ḥamza al-Ramlī (d. 1004/1595) argued that *tatabbuʿ al-rukhaṣ* was not a sin (*fisq*) but merely an error (*ithm*) that did not invalidate the legal act itself. Unlike an error, a designation of sin has serious legal ramifications, for, according to most jurists, a sinner cannot testify in court, nor serve as a judge or mufti.[65] Similarly, although Shams al-Dīn al-Ramlī did not support *tatabbuʿ al-rukhaṣ*, he refused to accept its designation as a sin by the jurists of the formative and classical periods.[66]

Another important authority that permitted *tatabbuʿ al-rukhaṣ* for subjects of the law was the renowned Ḥanafī jurist Zayn al-Dīn b. Nujaym (d. 970/1563). He was asked if a person—having submitted his claim to a judge—can change that judge for pragmatic reasons:

> Question: If a person made a claim on someone before a judge supporting his claim with only one witness, as he did not have another, can he drop the claim and select another judge who would allow one witness and an oath?[67] Answer: He is permitted to do so, so long as he has not yet requested (*yas'al*) a ruling from the judge.[68]

In this case, if the person were to go forward with his or her claim under Ḥanafī law, it would not be possible to obtain the desired result because the Ḥanafī school requires at least two witnesses.[69] Ibn Nujaym, however, allowed the litigant to seek another judge in this instance, even if the claim had already been submitted. As we shall see in chapter 4, this fatwa represents actual practice in Ottoman Cairo and Bulaq in the seventeenth and eighteenth centuries.

While pursuing less stringent juristic opinions by crossing school boundaries has historically been controversial, doing so within the same school was sometimes looked upon differently. For instance, the Ḥanafī jurist ʿAlī al-Qārī (d. 1014/1605) discussed the selection of less stringent juristic opinions within the Ḥanafī school with regard to the use of written documents in transmission (*riwāya*), such as the transmission of hadith. He cited Abū Ḥanīfa's opinion that the narrator should memorize what he is to narrate from the time of hearing it until he delivers it. The proponents of this view were suspicious of written documents and only accepted memory as a form of transmission.[70] A more pragmatic approach was that of his disciple Muḥammad al-Shaybānī, who held that one can use writing for narration, even if the document was not in the possession of the narrator, which increases the likelihood of tampering. ʿAlī al-Qārī described al-Shaybānī's opinion as a *rukhṣa* and Abū Ḥanīfa's opinion as a *ʿazīma* (the more stringent option).[71] Al-Shaybānī's opinion was meant to make the process easier for people, which is why, according to al-Qārī, it was chosen in the latter's time to be the dominant opinion in the school (*wa-ʿalayhi al-ʿamal al-ān*).[72]

Jurists who permitted pragmatic eclecticism sometimes faced stiff opposition from school loyalists, who completely rejected forum-shopping. While debating the issue of juristic disagreements, the Shāfiʿī ʿAbd al-Raʾūf al-Munāwī (d. 1029/1620) noted the common position of an interlocutor who opposed juristic disagreement (*ikhtilāf*) by citing Qurʾan 3:103, which warns Muslims against falling into division. This argument against juristic disagreement, according to al-Munāwī, was only advanced by people who had a diseased heart (*fī qalbihi maraḍ*). He added that many scholars have risen in defense of juristic disagreement in substantive legal issues (*furūʿ*) against the zealots who favor some imams over others (*al-mutaʿaṣṣibīn li-baʿḍ al-aʾimma*). This tendency had apparently become a strong trend in his time (*ʿammat bihī al-balwā wa ʿaẓima bihī al-khaṭb*).[73]

Another important node of authority in the permission of pragmatic eclecticism is the Ḥanafī jurist Ḥasan b. ʿAmmār b. ʿAlī al-Shurunbulālī (d. 1069/1658). He wrote a treatise dedicated to *taqlīd* after he was asked for a fatwa on whether a Ḥanafī who bled after performing the ritual ablution could follow Mālik's opinion that such bleeding does not invalidate one's ablution. According to al-Shurunbulālī, it is permissible to choose Mālik's opinion, so long as there is no *talfīq*. This choice was valid, he added, regardless of whether or not there is a pressing need for it, and whether or not the person has previously followed the rule of a different school on the issue.[74] He gave an example of this in practice with the following story in which a Shāfiʿī jurist switched to the Ḥanbalī school to avoid having to repeat his ritual ablution:

> Al-Imām al-Ṭarṭūshī, may the mercy of God be upon him, said that one time the call for the Friday Prayer was made, and the judge Abū al-Ṭayyib al-Ṭabarī started reciting Allāhu Akbar when he was hit by a bird dropping. He said, "I am a Ḥanbalī," and started praying.[75]

The pragmatic eclectic camp continued to gain supporters throughout the Ottoman period. The Ḥanafī jurist Aḥmad b. Muḥammad al-Ḥamawī (d. 1098/1686) used the same arguments deployed by Amīr Bādshāh and Ibn Amīr al-Ḥājj in support of *tatabbuʿ al-rukhaṣ*. He quoted at length Amīr Bādshāh's rejection of Ibn Ḥazm's claim to consensus and the view that *tatabbuʿ al-rukhaṣ* is a sin. He also cited jurists who approved of the practice from different schools such as ʿIzz al-Dīn b. ʿAbd al-Salām, Ibn al-Humām, and al-Samhūdī.[76]

The Shāfiʿī jurist Muḥammad b. Sulaymān al-Madanī al-Kurdī (d. 1194/1780) indicated that not only would he allow an individual to follow the opinion of a school other than his own, but he would also permit people to follow a weak opinion within the same school. He even accepted nonauthoritative opinions in the four schools in order to facilitate people's transactions. He cited 'Umar al-Baṣrī and al-Subkī (most likely a reference to the Shāfi'ī Taqī al-Dīn al-Subkī [d. 756/1355]) as stating that legal subjects can follow the nondominant opinion of the school, but that this is not permitted for muftis and judges.[77]

In his discussion of *tatabbu' al-rukhaṣ*, the Mālikī jurist al-Dasūqī (d. 1230/1815) engaged mostly jurists from the seventeenth and eighteenth centuries. He explained away the opposition of Ibrāhīm al-Shabrakhītī (d. 1106/1694) to pragmatic eclecticism by suggesting that he was referring to pursuing the less stringent juristic opinions when they violate the textual sources and clear analogy (*mukhālif al-naṣṣ wa jalī al-qiyās*).[78] Despite al-Dasūqī's very permissive attitude toward *tatabbu' al-rukhaṣ* both within and without school boundaries, he did not allow the mufti or judge to issue fatwas or rulings respectively for legal subjects according to the weak opinions of their schools. Only when the mufti or judge searches for legal rules for himself is he allowed to rely on the weak opinion of his school, and only when there is a pressing need to do so (*khāṣat nafsihi idhā taḥaqqaqat al-ḍarūra*). As such, he may not issue such fatwas for others, as he can only be certain about exigent cases of necessity (*ḍarūra*) with regard to himself. He may, however, issue fatwas for his friends or acquaintances on the basis of necessity when he knows their particular circumstances.[79]

Al-Dasūqī then discussed whether it is better to follow the weak opinion of one's own school or the dominant view of another. According to him, when a Mālikī jurist searches for legal views for himself, using the preponderant opinion of another school takes priority over the anomalous (*shādhdh*) or the less preponderant (*marjūḥ*) opinion in the Mālikī school (*bal yuqaddamu 'alayhi qawlu al-ghayri in kāna rājiḥan*). He even created a hierarchy for Mālikīs whereby al-Shāfi'ī's views get priority over Abū Ḥanīfa's views, citing the Mamluk Mālikī jurist al-Qarāfī to support his point.[80]

Al-Dasūqī's Shāfi'ī student Ḥasan al-'Aṭṭār (d. 1250/1835) likewise expressed his support for *tatabbu' al-rukhaṣ* and argued that there was never consensus over the issue. After citing the views of Ibn al-Humām,

Amīr Bādshāh, al-Samhūdī, and al-Shurunbulālī, he explained away Ibn Ḥazm's position against pragmatic eclecticism by suggesting that what he objected to was *tatabbuʿ al-rukhaṣ* in *ijtihād*, not *taqlīd*, or that he was referring to *rukhaṣ* compounded in the same legal transaction, namely, *talfīq*.[81] Al-ʿAṭṭār, furthermore, disagreed with the position of Ibn al-Ḥājib and al-Āmidī to the effect that if someone acts on a particular case according to one school, he must follow that school in all similar future transactions. He cited al-Samhūdī's example of someone who, as a follower of the Ḥanafī school that grants the neighbor the right of preemption (*shufʿa*), seeks to acquire his neighbor's building. After the transaction, however, the same person adopts the Shāfiʿī school, thus depriving his neighbor of the same right to preemption when he resells the property. According to al-ʿAṭṭār, a person could follow the Ḥanafī school and then the Shāfiʿī school in a similar type of transaction, so long as the object of the transaction is not the same. Thus, in the above example, had the buyer subsequently followed the Shāfiʿī school with respect to another property, this would have been acceptable in his view.[82]

Author-Jurists and Muftis

There is a view held by some historians that *takhayyur*, that is, the selection of less stringent juristic views for pragmatic reasons (referred to in the primary sources as *tatabbuʿ al-rukhaṣ*) and *talfīq* were forbidden for both jurists and state authorities.[83] I problematize this claim by showing that there was an influential discourse that enabled jurists, as well as state authorities, represented by judges to exercise pragmatic eclecticism.

There is evidence that jurists were changing schools for practical considerations, with some reportedly switching schools to obtain certain salaried positions. Such decisions were clearly motivated by pragmatic and expedient considerations, not by a reassessment of the school's hermeneutic. Aware of this practice, al-Suyūṭī (d. 911/1505) quoted a jurist who applied for a job at al-Shaykhūniyya school as saying, "My school is the school of bread and food."[84] Similarly, the Shāfiʿī jurist Shams al-Dīn Muḥammad b. Mūsa al-Lakhmī, known as Ibn Sanad (d. 792/1390), was reported to have temporarily become Mālikī and then returned to the Shāfiʿīs in order to assume some of their official positions.[85] This change of school was not concerned with a particular legal view, but it was, rather, a holistic change meant to advance the jurist's career. In addition to the holistic change, jurists switched schools on single transactions to obtain a less stringent view, either for themselves as subjects of the law or for others when they functioned as muftis or judges.

Although there was a clear dichotomous distinction in the primary sources between *tarjīḥ*—based on assessment of evidence—and *tatabbuʿ al-rukhaṣ*, in which there is no evaluation of evidence but rather a focus on the legal result, these were both ideal types that experienced some degree of overlapping. Sometimes the motivation for the selection of one opinion over another was couched in the language of *tarjīḥ*, even though the jurist might have acknowledged that his choice was motivated by social needs. There were also situations in which social needs—couched in the discourse of *tarjīḥ*, the contingencies of the time, or people's practice (*ʿumūm al-balwā*)—prompted author-jurists to issue fatwas or to pen *furūʿ* manuals elevating some less prominent opinions to the level of *rājiḥ*.[86]

What was more common, however, is drawing a distinction between the *rājiḥ* (the preponderant position) and the *madhhab* opinion (the actual school position) in cases where the dominant opinion within the *madhhab* was a weaker one, selected out of necessity (*ḥāja*) over the *rājīḥ*, which is evidentially stronger. In this case, the *madhhab*-opinion would be used in opposition to *tarjīḥ*. For instance, in his discussion of which Ḥanbalī juristic opinions to include in his *Muntahā al-Irādāt*, the Ḥanbalī jurist Ibn al-Najjār (d. 972–1564) said he would only include opinions that had undergone *taṣḥīḥ* or that had been used in practice (*illā idhā kana ʿalyhi al-ʿamal*). He viewed *taṣḥīḥ* as a process that is distinct from practice despite the potential overlap,[87] with the former being subject to a hermeneutic, evidentiary assessment, and the latter sometimes involving an epistemically weaker opinion chosen for pragmatic reasons.

This tension between the hermeneutic exercise of preponderance (*tarjīḥ*) and pragmatic eclecticism is evident in Hallaq's discussion of two instances of doctrinal change. The first is the early Ḥanafī exclusion of all movable property from being the object of a judge's written communications.[88] An examination of al-Bazzāzī's (d. 827/1424) *al-Fatāwā al-Bazzāziyya* illustrates that the motivation behind the change was expressed in the language of need (*ḥāja*), as opposed to the discourse of preponderance.[89] This emphasis on need was used to justify pragmatic eclecticism within the school by allowing a non-preponderant opinion to be practiced in courts and in issuing legal opinions (fatwas).[90] The second example that Hallaq cites is the disagreement between Abū Ḥanīfa and Abū Yūsuf over whether documentary evidence sent from one judge to another but without indicating the sender's name should be accepted as valid. Abū Ḥanīfa held that such a communication is null and void, whereas Abū Yūsuf did not deem the ambiguity sufficient to invalidate the document. The chief justice al-Damghānī al-Kabīr (d. 477/1084) revived Abū Yūsuf's opinion against the position of Abū Ḥanīfa, which was heretofore the dominant opinion of the Ḥanafī school. This change was clearly not based on hermeneutic or evidential grounds, nor was it based on majoritarian *tarjīḥ*, that is, giving preponderance to one opinion over another owing to the wide support it enjoys among jurists.[91] Al-Damghānī al-Kabīr resorted to the weaker opinion of Abū Yūsuf, which was said to be "strange," as the basis of practice (*wa kānat gharība fi'l-ʿamal*) in lieu of Abū Ḥanīfa's view, which was considered the preponderant position. However, other judges followed suit in their courts, until this became a common practice (*sunnatun ma'lūfa*).[92] This reformulation of the dominant doctrine in the Ḥanafī school was exercised by author-jurists, who wrote authoritative works of substantive law. These are instances of jurists exercising vertical pragmatic eclecticism within their school to select legal opinions that are less stringent or more fitting to their social circumstances. Such pragmatic eclectic ways were also exercised by muftis.

Legal Advice or Mere Transmission. The standards for judges (*qāḍīs*) were generally far stricter than those for laypeople. The restriction on judges that prevented them from following a school other than their own was harder to relax because it was seen as potentially leading to greater unpredictability and instability in the legal system, which was the primary explanation for the rise of *taqlīd* and the shift to the codification episteme.

The doctrine that has come to dominate Islamic law after the rise of *taqlīd* was that the mufti should issue his legal opinion and the judge his rulings in accordance with the preponderant view (*rājiḥ*) of their schools.

In the Ottoman period, this view remained largely unchanged for judges, who could engage in pragmatic eclecticism indirectly by referring litigants to judges from other schools, as we shall see in chapter 4. As for muftis, however, one finds a strand of thought permitting *tatabbuʿ al-rukhaṣ* in the issuance of legal advice. Since the mufti's opinions are not binding on anyone except himself, lifting the restrictions placed on muftis to follow the dominant doctrines of their schools represented an embracement of greater flexibility that would ultimately benefit legal subjects without destabilizing the system. Thus some jurists allowed muftis to issue legal advice based on the weak opinions of their schools, but only if they made it clear to the fatwa-seeker that it is a weak opinion. Others assuaged opposition to muftis issuing legal opinions based on other schools by insisting that the mufti should answer the fatwa-seeker in the form of a transmission (*riwāya*), not as a fatwa. Such an ad hoc semantic maneuver was an attempt to circumvent the prohibition of issuing fatwas based on schools other than one's own. According to Aḥmad b. Ḥijāzī al-Fishnī (d. 978/1570), the mufti is not, in this situation, issuing a legal opinion, but rather relating the opinion of another jurist.[93] The tension between the two strands for and against pragmatic eclecticism was clear in the notion that muftis should not pursue less stringent opinions on behalf of the fatwa-seeker (*al-tarkhīṣ wa'l-tashīl*), on the one hand, and that legal opinions should take into consideration the situation of the fatwa-seeker, on the other.[94]

The distinction between transmission and fatwa can also be found in al-Kurdī's invocation of Ibn Ḥajar al-Haytamī's (973/1567) argument that legal opinions in later times (a reference to the regime of *taqlīd*) were based on transmission, not *ijtihād*. Therefore, according to al-Haytamī, it does not matter whether the transmission is from one's school or from another.[95] Similarly, an anonymous Shāfiʿī jurist, author of a treatise entitled "Risāla Jalīla fi'l-Taqlīd,"[96] would allow muftis to issue legal opinions according to any of the four schools, and to base them on weak opinions within the schools as well. He even permitted the mufti to issue legal opinions based on the views of the Companions. The fatwa-seeker, he argued, must be informed of such departures from school doctrine, which are mere transmissions (*riwāya*).[97] Proponents of the distinction between fatwa and *riwāya*, which was referenced frequently in the late Mamluk and Ottoman periods, assumed that all contemporary muftis in the state of *taqlīd* were not creating legal opinions (*iftāʾ*) per se, but simply narrating the views of earlier authorities (*ʿalā jihat al-ḥikāya*).[98]

In this sense, the mufti is almost indistinguishable from the layperson, who, according to Ibn Amīr al-Ḥājj, is not permitted to issue legal opinions but may narrate an opinion that he received from a mufti to another layperson.[99] In such cases, there was no claim of exercising preponderance (*tarjīḥ*) on the part of muftis because they were not qualified to do so. The motivation behind their "transmission" of a wide range of juristic opinions, including those of other schools, weak opinions, or opinions of the Companions, was the immediate resolution of a legal problem that the fatwa-seeker was facing. Needless to say, these practices were faced with stiff opposition from some quarters. One disapproving observer was Ibn Khaldūn (d. 808/1406), who complained that some muftis, trying to satisfy the whims of fatwa-seekers, issued legal opinions that exploited the different schools on an arbitrary basis and without any guidelines.[100]

We have seen thus far that there were two processes of pragmatic eclecticism: one vertical and one horizontal. The first type occurred within the same school by elevating a less preponderant opinion to the level of practice (*madhhab*-opinion), replacing the preponderant view (*rājiḥ*).[101] The second type took place by crossing school boundaries when the *madhhab*-opinion failed to provide the desired flexibility. These vertical and horizontal processes of pragmatic eclecticism were aimed at challenging legal inertia when enough pressure built up against existing laws and legal change became a necessity, in which case weaker opinions within the school were elevated above the preponderant school view (*rājiḥ*) in practice. Legal subjects and muftis also had access to a wide range of juristic opinions by crossing school boundaries to accommodate varying socioeconomic needs. Pragmatic eclecticism was reinforced by the stabilization of *taqlīd* and the gradual marginalization of preponderance (*tarjīḥ*) in favor of a focus on legal result through *tatabbuʿ al-rukhaṣ*. This process of the marginalization of preponderance is given credence, for instance, by Rudolph Peters's observation that jurists in the Ḥanafī school had gradually begun to feel that they were losing their ability to distinguish between correct and incorrect opinions. According to him, later Ḥanafī scholars claimed that they were no longer able to reason based on proofs or on content and were increasingly reliant on formal rules. By the twelfth century, according to him, jurists began to argue that there was a hierarchy of authority, which gave Abū Ḥanīfa's opinions the highest position, followed by those of his disciple Abū Yūsuf, then the opinions of his other disciple Muḥammad al-Shaybānī, and finally the opinions of Zufar or al-Ḥasan b. Ziyād.[102]

This process fit in well with the institutionalization of *taqlīd* and the general shift in the locus of authority from the hermeneutic exercise of absolute *ijtihād* or *tarjīḥ* to the juristic hierarchy within the school unit.[103] In this context, the school and its internal hierarchy increasingly became the center of legitimation as opposed to the direct authority of legal evidence. A psychological distance was created between the legists, whether judges or jurisconsults, on the one hand, and scriptural and analogical proofs, on the other. The link between the legist and God's law now had to go through the school hierarchy. Needless to say, the shift was one of emphasis, since such authority and hierarchies had existed prior to the twelfth century, but with the entrenchment of the *taqlīd* hegemony, breaking with such hierarchies through *ijtihād* or even *tarjīḥ* became less common. Even when the term "preponderant" (*rājiḥ*) was used in juristic discourse, it was frequently a description of the existing school position perceived to be weightier than other competing views on a given issue, rather than an actual process of weighing evidence.[104]

This shift in the utilization of preponderance (*tarjīḥ*) within the Ḥanafī school from an evidence-based reasoning to an emphasis on juristic authority meant that jurists were in some ways like laypeople. Just as laypeople were required by some jurists to choose the best mufti (*afḍal*)—based on an assessment of their knowledge and piety—a similar hierarchy for *muqallid* jurists was created. It was not based on the individual's legal opinions but on the character of the founders of the *madhhab*. The eponym naturally occupied the highest position in the hierarchy, followed by his best and most renowned disciples.[105]

Jurists' Practice of Tatabbuʿ al-Rukhaṣ in Legal Responsa. That legal practice informed juristic discourse can be seen clearly in the legal responsa literature (fatwas). The Ḥanafī jurist al-Bazzāzī (d. 827/1424), who was widely quoted in later Ḥanafī works, attempted to resolve a case involving a woman who, despite not reaching the menopausal age of fifty-five, had not had her period for six months after her divorce.[106] The solution, according to him, was to follow the Mālikī school, which would allow her to wait for three more months of *ʿidda* and remarry afterward. Such a marriage, according to al-Bazzāzī, though not accepted by the Ḥanafī school, was valid and could not be overruled since it was backed by the Mālikī school. He urged his readers, who were mostly Ḥanafī jurists, to memorize this case because of its common occurrence.[107]

In North Africa and Spain, which lacked the legal pluralism characteristic of Egypt and Syria, the discussion of juristic choices focused on differences within the Mālikī school. For instance, al-Wansharīsī (d. 914/ 1508) cited a question sent to Ibn ʿArafa (d. 803/1400) about the practice of muftis in Granada who treated the contradictory juristic opinions attributed to Mālik as valid areas of juristic disagreement (*khilāf*). Thus they issued fatwas based on those different opinions, even though specialists of legal methodology (*ahl al-uṣūl*) held that when the mufti cannot determine their chronological order (so as to choose the latest opinion), he must suspend judgment (*fa-lā yaʿmalu bi-muqtaḍā wāḥidin minhumā*). The suspension of judgment was rejected by Ibn ʿArafa because it would lead to the loss of much of Mālik's jurisprudence. Thus, on grounds of necessity (*ḍarūra*), a decision would have to be made.[108]

The fatwa genre contains many references to licenses granted to muftis to exercise pragmatic eclecticism. The Egyptian Shāfiʿī jurist al-Samhūdī (d. 911/1505) presented the following question that the Mālikī mufti and judge of Tunis Abū Muḥammad ʿAbd al-Ḥamīd b. Abū al-Barakāt al-Ṣadafī passed on to ʿIzz al-Dīn b. ʿAbd al-Salām (d. 660/1262) for a fatwa:

> If you permit it [*tatabbuʿ al-rukhaṣ*],[109] what is your argument? If not, what would be your reasoning for forbidding it? Bear in mind that every *mujtahid* is correct. One does not have to follow the more qualified jurist, according to al-Bāqillānī [(d. 403/1013)]. In addition, specialists of legal methodology (*ahl al-uṣūl*) have said that the Companions of the Prophet did not restrict their legal opinions (*fatwas*) to Abū Bakr and ʿUmar.

> Instead, some Companions, who were inferior to them in knowledge (*'ilm*), issued *fatwas* in their presence, which is stronger evidence than what Abū Ḥāmid [al-Ghazālī] said.[110]

This question, which was cited by al-Samhūdī to show the scope of disagreement among jurists over this issue, was about whether Mālikī muftis could choose from the stock of Mālikī school opinions to facilitate people's transactions (*al-tawassu' 'alā al-nās*), without any recourse to preponderance.[111]

This eclecticism can also be found in the Ḥanafī fatwas. In order to enable people to return to their marriages after a "for-compensation" (*khul'*) divorce,[112] muftis from the Ḥanafī school dug up some peripheral opinion that *khul'* did not constitute a *ṭalāq* (repudiation). This means that the *khul'* divorce would not count against the husband's maximum number of three utterances of *ṭalāq* at which point his wife would have to marry someone else and get divorced before she could remarry him. According to Muḥammad al-Fiqhī (d. 1147/1734), other muftis would provide a legal opinion to the same effect but derived from the Ḥanbalī school.[113] Al-Fiqhī generally welcomed such pragmatism, contending that muftis should provide people with less stringent legal opinions, especially to those who are weak. He added that this should be particularly the case with endowments (*awqāf*), which belong to God. According to him, in cases of disagreements among jurists, the mufti should always choose the opinion that is most beneficial to the endowment. To support his position, he cited al-Bazzāzī's view that a mufti should always choose the opinion that he thinks would bring about the greatest good (*maṣlaḥa*).[114]

Al-Fiqhī, however, was aware that such pragmatism could be abused. For instance, he cursed (*'alyhi la'natu Allāh*) those muftis who issued legal opinions based on anomalous juristic views (*mahjūr*). On another occasion, he called them "immoral" (*fājirīn*).[115] This fear of juristic abuse explains his opposition to allowing muftis to be paid in exchange for issuing legal opinions because this, according to him, would lead them to follow their whims (*ittibā' al-hawā*). He condemned the practice in his time of receiving compensation to issue legal opinions, which led muftis to expediently provide people with less stringent opinions merely for the sake of profit.[116]

This fear of manipulating the legal system through bribery was perhaps one of the reasons that kept the opposition against *tatabbuʿ al-rukhaṣ* from completely disappearing. Al-Fiqhī's opposition to the practice of muftis in his time is an example of this tension between juristic discourse and practice. Prescriptive jurists treated such practices as anomalies that needed to be put aright, whereas descriptive jurists used practice as a justification for a doctrinal adjustment, thus laying the ground for the rise of a strand that challenged the opposition to *tatabbuʿ al-rukhaṣ*, as well as the claim of consensus on the topic.

Judges (Qāḍīs)

Jurists did not grant judges the same flexibility they did muftis. While most jurists in the age of *taqlīd* did not permit judges to issue rulings based on a school other than their own (exceptions to this rule exist in the early decades of Ottoman rule), they allowed them to refer cases to judges of different schools to give legal subjects more favorable results. In this sense, judges provided both the sanction for eclecticism and the knowledge of which judge would provide a less stringent juristic view, as we shall see in chapter 4, which deals with court practice.

In his *Ādāb al-Qāḍī*, the Ḥanafī jurist al-Ṭarsūsī (d. 758/1357) argued that a Ḥanafī judge may choose to delegate judgment to a Shāfiʿī judge in cases requiring the validity of a supplementary oath (*al-yamīn al-muḍāfa*).[117] In the late Mamluk period, the Shāfiʿī jurist al-Asyūṭī (d. 880/1475) wrote *Jawāhir al-ʿUqūd wa-Muʿīn al-Quḍāh wa'l-Muwaqqiʿīn wa'l-Shuhūd* (The pearls of contracts: manual for judges, scribes, and witnesses) containing formulas for contracts in all fields of law. He discussed some of the points of disagreement among the four schools.[118] He advised the reader that after drawing up a contract, he or she should refer it to the judge of whichever school would allow it. He thus prescribed the choice of judges based on the most conducive legal outcome as opposed to one's school affiliation.[119] Ibn Ḥajar al-Haytamī (d. 973/1567), on the other hand, argued that the practice of delegating another school's judge to rule according to his school on a particular issue had long been tolerated by practical consensus (*ijmāʿ fiʿlī*) and had been practiced for hundreds of years, which in itself is an indication that it was permissible.[120]

In 1178/1764, the Ottoman jurist Muḥammad b. ʿAbd Allāh ʿAlī Zādah authored a short practical guide for judges and court scribes instructing them on contract formulae. One of the lines repeated in many of the formulae is an expression of the judge's awareness of the differences among the four Sunnī schools on this subject (*ʿāliman bi'l-khilāf al-jārī bayna al-a'imma al-ashrāf*).[121] Since the judge, by the eighteenth century, was not required to exercise *ijtihād*, for which this knowledge of juristic disagreement would be necessary, it is likely that such knowledge was meant to help legal subjects choose the less stringent school opinions. Indeed, according to the text of one endowment (*waqf*) deed in this collection, correspondence with the opinion held by any of the imams seems to have been sufficient for the officiation of a contract (*ʿalā ra'y man yarāhu min ʿulamā'inā raḥimahum Allāh*).[122]

In a sense, the increasingly permissive attitudes toward *tatabbuʿ al-rukhaṣ* among jurists when practiced by muftis and judges paralleled the attitudes toward it when exercised by subjects of the law. The mufti's right to veer from the dominant opinion of his school was unrestricted by some jurists, while others restricted it to the particular circumstances of the fatwa-seeker. Thus, when the late Ottoman Shāfiʿī jurist al-Sayyid ʿUmar al-Baṣrī was once asked about how a mufti should deal with issues on which Shams al-Dīn al-Ramlī and Ibn Ḥajar al-Haytamī disagreed,[123] he answered that the mufti should rule according to what he found preponderant if he is capable of exercising juristic preponderance (*min ahl al-tarjīḥ*), but that it would be better for the mufti to simply rule according to the particular circumstances of the fatwa-seeker.[124] Thus, instead of weighing legal opinions evidentially, it was considered better for muftis to weigh them in accordance with social and personal needs.

This instance in which the particular state of the fatwa-seeker is assessed by the mufti brings us to another question concerning the limits placed on the permissibility of *tatabbuʿ al-rukhaṣ*. The above views supporting this simple form of pragmatic eclecticism, which marked an important evolution in the practice of *taqlīd*, did not necessarily restrict its permissibility to cases of necessity. Other views tied its permissibility to the context and the particular condition of the fatwa-seeker. I briefly discuss this theme as an independent attitude toward *tatabbuʿ al-rukhaṣ*, where its implementation was circumscribed by the concepts of necessity (*ḍarūra*) and need (*ḥāja*). I first discuss the limitation of necessity and need, followed by al-Shaʿrānī's theory, which represents an important evolution in the theory of *tatabbuʿ al-rukhaṣ*. Finally, I discuss the post-Shaʿrānī invocation of necessity and need to justify *tatabbuʿ al-rukhaṣ*.

The Limitation of *Ḍarūra*

In addition to outright acceptance or rejection of *tatabbuʿ al-rukhaṣ*, some jurists emphasized the concept of necessity (*ḍarūra*) to legitimize the practice of pursuing less stringent juristic opinions. These jurists may be called "*ḍarūra*-pragmatists." Needless to say, this distinction between the two approaches was not always clear-cut. Some jurists permitted the practice of *tatabbuʿ al-rukhaṣ* with no preconditions on some occasions, while appearing to restrict its employment to cases of *ḍarūra* or social needs on other occasions.[125]

In his fatwas, the Shāfiʿī jurist Taqī al-Dīn al-Subkī (d. 756/1355) identified six key motivations behind atomistic school boundary-crossing as follows: (1) when the person believes that the other school's opinion is more correct (*rājiḥ*) than that of his own, in which case it is permitted to follow the other opinion; (2) when the person believes that his imam is more correct or when he does not have an opinion either way, but switches school as a precaution (*iḥtiyāṭan*), which is also permitted; (3) when the motivation behind switching schools is to seek a *rukhṣa* because of some need (*hāja*) or out of necessity (*ḍarūra*), in which case he is also allowed to choose another school's opinion; (4) when there is no need (*hāja*) or necessity (*ḍarūra*), which is not permitted, as it constitutes following one's whims (*hawāh*); (5) when one frequently follows the less stringent opinions, making *ittibāʿ al-rukhaṣ* his religion, which is forbidden; and (6) when school boundary-crossing leads to a complex reality (*ḥaqīqa murakkaba*), a reference to *talfīq*, which is also forbidden by consensus.[126]

Similarly, the Shāfiʿī jurist al-Zarkashī (d. 794/1392) argued that when people have doubts or despair, they should pursue the less stringent juristic opinions, lest these feelings should increase. He contended that such eclecticism (*ittibāʿ al-rukhaṣ*) is preferable (*maḥbūb*) because the Prophet said, "God likes [people] to follow His *rukhaṣ*." According to him, following the less stringent juristic opinions should, however, be supervised by the mufti, who must examine the state of the fatwa-seeker to ensure that his circumstances merit a less stringent rule (*rukhṣa*). He cited al-Subkī's view, albeit without identifying him, that when the selection of the less stringent opinions becomes habitual, an indication that it has exceeded the restriction of personal need or necessity, the selection of the less stringent opinions is not permitted.[127]

The utilization of *ḍarūra* in al-Subkī does not correspond to al-Ghazālī's famous delineation of necessities (*ḍarūriyyāt*), since al-Subkī described it as a *ḍarūra* that is "taxing" (*ḍarūratun arhaqathu*).[128] The traditional concept of necessity (*ḍarūra*) that was devised by al-Juwaynī and al-Ghazālī, by contrast, was framed within the major objectives of the Sharīʿa to preserve religion, life, intellect, procreation, and property, rather than as a means to avoid a mere inconvenience. While al-Ghazālī attempted to identify *ḍarūra* more objectively by giving it some measurable criteria,[129] later jurists drew upon the word in an ad hoc, nontechnical sense in order to justify a desired outcome that has nothing to do with al-Ghazālī's necessities.

Because this ad hoc use of necessity (*ḍarūra*) and need (*ḥāja*) is hard to gauge, one way of verifying their existence was through considering the frequency of the practice of pragmatic eclecticism. In other words, a necessity or a need should not occur to the same person very frequently, and therefore if someone utilizes pragmatic eclecticism frequently, she is indeed manipulating the permission, rather than genuinely responding to a difficult situation. Frequency becomes a litmus test for the genuineness of one's circumstances. Thus al-Subkī forbade exercising *tatabbuʿ al-rukhaṣ* so frequently that it itself becomes an article of one's faith, although he supported its infrequent use when there is a genuine need.[130] Owing to the loose handling of the terms "need" (*ḥāja*) and "necessity" (*ḍarūra*), some jurists were reluctant to permit the practice of *tatabbuʿ al-rukhaṣ* without some form of restriction, imprecise as it may be, with some attempting to base its use on the strength or weakness of one's faith, as we saw in the case of the person who is stricken by doubts about his or her faith.[131] An attempt at more precise criteria was made, however, in Sufi circles with their greater attention to people's different spiritual conditions and states of mind. This brings us to al-Shaʿrānī's theory, a very important evolution of the theory of pragmatic eclecticism, which was invoked throughout the Ottoman and modern periods by supporters of pragmatic eclecticism. Owing to the centrality of al-Shaʿrānī in the theory of pragmatic eclecticism, I will discuss his contribution in detail in what follows.

Al-Shaʿrānī's Theory of Pragmatic Eclecticism

The Shāfiʿī mystic and jurist al-Shaʿrānī (d. 973/1565) represents an important and early stage of evolution in the discussion of *tatabbuʿ al-rukhaṣ*. His novel theory of legal pluralism elaborated on the work of the prominent mystic Ibn ʿArabī (d. 638/1240). In *al-Mīzān* (the scales), al-Shaʿrānī introduced a theory of juristic disagreement, in which he argued that all legal rules in the four schools have a dualistic nature of leniency and strictness. He argued that the less stringent juristic opinions are for those who are weaker in faith or body, explaining that the Prophet always addressed people according to their abilities. Different rules are also intended to address the needs of Muslims at different times and therefore legal pluralism is a blessing. According to him, since the Sharīʿa has one source, when a person who is weak in faith and spirit draws water from that source, his water is as good as the water drawn by a saint.[132]

According to al-Shaʿrānī, laypeople (*ʿawāmm*) are in a constant state of weakness, unlike scholars (*ʿulamāʾ*) and mystics (Sufis), whom he referred to as the people of piety (*ahl al-waraʿ*) and of high religious status (*al-akābir*).[133] As such, they can always follow the less stringent juristic opinions. Weakness and strength were mostly defined in terms of religious knowledge, whether esoteric or exoteric, although there were also other weaknesses, those of body and faith. A lack of religious knowledge always allowed the layperson to be in the weak category, whereas physical weakness sometimes exempted the *ʿulamāʾ* and Sufis from following the more stringent juristic opinions. Since there were no formal criteria for determining what constitutes weakness of body or faith, the choice was left to the discretion of legal subjects and *muftis*.

Just as with the concept of *ḍarūra*, al-Shaʿrānī's concept of "ability" was used to justify availing oneself of a position held by a jurist that would otherwise be forbidden. In this sense, his approach was an evolution of the concept of necessity (*ḍarūra*) as applied by al-Subkī and al-Zarkashī.

According to al-Sha'rānī, however, one cannot choose freely between strictness (*'azīma*) and leniency (*rukhṣa*), but rather according to one's own ability. He cited the example of washing one's head during the ritual ablution. The Prophet is reported to have washed his entire head on at least one occasion and only some of his head on others. According to al-Sha'rānī, this is not a case of abrogation (*naskh*) because, otherwise, such a position would be tantamount to discrediting some of the schools that held a different view. Here we see his descriptive approach, where existing school doctrines are all part of a legal system that has different manifestations of the same source. Rather, he interpreted the conflicting views on washing the head as an example of dispensation (*rukhṣa*), in which one is required to wash his entire head in the summer, for instance, but only partially in the winter. As such, every strict view has an opposing one that is more lenient in another school, or even within the same school.[134]

According to al-Sha'rānī, the Shāfi'ī view that touching one's genitals invalidates the ritual ablution is based on a Prophetic tradition to that effect, and so is the opposing Ḥanafī opinion that it does not invalidate the ablution. These seemingly contradictory traditions, he contended, were designed for two different types of people. The more strict tradition is meant for the superior believers (*akābir al-mu'minīn*), whereas the more lenient one is aimed at the general laity.[135] Similarly, the Prophetic traditions "Drink, but do not get drunk"[136] and "What is inebriating in large quantities is forbidden in small quantities" are both part of the Sharī'a. They lie along the two ends of the strictness/leniency spectrum, and both are applicable, but for different people.[137]

Al-Sha'rānī even established the normativity of practice in the age of *taqlīd* by citing earlier juristic practice in favor of his position. He contended that earlier jurists issued fatwas according to all of the four schools, such as the Shāfi'ī jurist Badr al-Dīn b. Jamā'a (d. 733/1333) and the Mālikī Shihāb al-Dīn al-Burlusī, known as Zarrūq al-Fāsī (d. 899/1493). He also quoted the observation of his teacher al-Suyūṭī (d. 911/1505) that many jurists issued fatwas according to the doctrines of the four schools for those among the laity since they were not obligated to abide by a single school. In the eyes of al-Sha'rānī, these jurists were merely providing fatwas based on people's needs.[138]

According to al-Shaʿrānī, this diversity of legal opinions did not result from arbitrary human interpretations of the textual sources. They were indeed ordained by God to fit the different natures of His subjects.[139] God's foreknowledge dictated the existence of this diversity, as what may be good for one person may not be appropriate for another, and what may be good for a person at one time may not necessarily be so under different circumstances. God, he continued, in His infinite wisdom, has willed that what may be considered beneficial or harmful under the law is not intrinsically so in an absolute or categorical manner. Sometimes a thing may be beneficial to someone but harmful to another and vice versa. Thus a person who is not weak in body or faith may be losing out by choosing the less stringent rulings.[140] Al-Shaʿrānī based his theory of legal pluralism on the multiplicity of truth doctrine (*taʿaddud al-ḥaqq*), thus disagreeing with the vast majority of his contemporaries. According to him, his predecessors had been mistaken for having held that there is only one truth in legal matters.[141] By al-Shaʿrānī's time, the multiplicity of truth position had fallen so far out of favor that proponents of this doctrine were often condemned as espousing "Muʿtazilī ideas."[142]

Al-Shaʿrānī provided evidence for his theory from the practice of the earlier generations of Muslims, citing, for instance, ʿUmar b. al-Khaṭṭāb's statement that God gives rules according to people's conditions and times. He added that early jurists such as Mujāhid and Mālik refused to issue fatwas in hypothetical situations because of their conviction that fatwas should always be issued by the scholars of their time when the events in question occur to customize the fatwa to the state of the fatwa-seeker. These early jurists, al-Shaʿrānī reasoned, believed that the particular needs of the individual should always be borne in mind while issuing a fatwa.[143]

In addition to his textual proofs, al-Shaʿrānī described a mystical experience through which he was convinced that every *mujtahid* is correct. While he was performing his pilgrimage in Mecca, he explained, a voice from the sky told him, "We have given you scales (*mīzān*) that you may use to determine the opinions of *mujtahids* and their followers till the Day of Judgment. But none of those in your age would appreciate them."[144] According to him, this gnostic knowledge of the "scales" was a blessing from God who allowed the eye of his heart to see the fountain of Sharīʿa, out of which came the different opinions of jurists. This personal experience confirmed for al-Shaʿrānī that every *mujtahid* is correct and that no school of law may be deemed better than another.[145]

The Background of al-Shaʿrānī's Theory

Al-Shaʿrānī's *Kashf al-Ghumma* explains the background of his theory. According to him, laypeople complained that their practice was sometimes rejected by jurists from other schools. Jurists rejected their tendency to mix the rules of the different schools, which created a deep sense of guilt and a fear that their ritual and legal transactions were not based on the divine law.[146] They did not know which of the jurists' opinions represented the truth and needed a book containing all the proofs supporting the opinions of the four schools on different legal and ritual issues, as well as the clear traditions of the Prophet and the rightly guided caliphs.[147] The preaching of some jurists who rejected their practice of mixing schools must have caused these feelings of guilt among the laity, leading some to believe that they were required to search out the textual sources directly rather than rely on juristic writings. In light of these concerns, al-Shaʿrānī responded that it is sufficient for laypeople to simply follow the jurists' opinions.[148]

This view that even laypeople are required to seek the scriptural sources in their requests for fatwas can be found throughout the Islamic tradition in purist circles that emphasized the importance of a direct connection between rulings and the authority of the textual sources, rather than through the mediation of jurists. Some even considered laypeople's requests for textual evidence to be a form of *ijtihād* for the layperson.[149] This view was similar to those expressed by the so-called "extremists" (*ghulāh*) as we saw in the discussion of the multiplicity versus the unity of truth.

There was awareness among jurists before al-Shaʿrānī's time of laypeople's practice of asking for scriptural evidence, which must have been at least partly influenced by the purist approach. The Ḥanafī jurist Ibn al-Humām, for instance, argued that if the fatwa-seeker asks for the proof (*dalīl*) of a fatwa, the mufti has to provide it unless it is too ambiguous. His commentator Ibn Amīr al-Ḥājj (d. 879/1474) explained that the motivation for giving the layperson legal proofs is to make him content with the fatwa (*li-tudhʿina nafsuhu liʾl-qabūl*).[150] Al-Shaʿrānī's concern about the practice of laypeople echoed Ibn ʿArabī's references in *al-Futūḥāt al-Makkiyya*, in which he condemned the rejection of pragmatic eclecticism, a practice regarded by many as a manipulation of religion.[151] Al-Shaʿrānī was aware of the similarity between his project and that of Ibn ʿArabī and clearly referenced *al-Futūḥāt al-Makkiyya* in his discussion,[152] developing Ibn ʿArabī's thought into a theory of whose novelty al-Shaʿrānī was well aware. He even excused the opponents of his book, stating, "I do not know anyone who had written something like it before."[153]

Al-Shaʿrānī's theory was an attempt to counter the purist tendency,[154] which required laypeople to seek scriptural evidence for their legal opinions, the school loyalty (*tamadhhub*) position represented by the Ottoman attempts at Ḥanafization, and the *ḍarūra*-pragmatists' restriction of pragmatic eclecticism to the conditions of *ḍarūra* and *ḥāja*, often limited by the frequency of utilization. Unlike *ḍarūra*-pragmatists, al-Shaʿrānī's theory expands *ḍarūra* and *ḥāja* beyond the individual and into whole classes of people. Any layperson by virtue of being a layperson is in a constant state of weakness. No further illustration of necessity or need is required, no frequency litmus test. Al-Shaʿrānī's theory was primarily an attempt to buttress Mamluk legal pluralism in the face of early Ottoman attempts at Ḥanafization, in which the Ottomans tried to purge the non-Ḥanafī Egyptian judicature to replace it with a uniform Ḥanafī regime.[155]

Post-Shaʿrānī Permission of Pragmatic Eclecticism on Grounds of Necessity

Using necessity (*ḍarūra*) to justify pursuing the less stringent juristic opinions in the different schools became very common in the Ottoman period, with this position being attributed usually to al-Zarkashī. For instance, the Shāfiʿī jurist Zayn al-Dīn b. ʿAbd al-ʿAzīz al-Malībārī (d. 987/1579) contended that *tatabbuʿ al-rukhaṣ* is forbidden unless the person is stricken by doubts to the point that he may abandon the Sharīʿa altogether.[156] Similarly, the Shāfiʿī ʿUmar Muḥammad al-Fāraskūrī (d. 1018/1609) invoked the concept of *ḍarūra* in its ad hoc sense by contending, in verse, that while changing schools may be permissible when there is a pressing need, the practice of *tatabbuʿ al-rukhaṣ* is otherwise forbidden.

In his discourse, a distinction is made between the pragmatic selection of juristic views for *ḍarūra* and *ḥāja* and when such selection becomes so frequent that it becomes clear that it is not based on genuine need, with the latter being labeled as *tatabbuʿ al-rukhaṣ*.[157]

> *You may follow this [school] in a transaction and that in another if need be*
> *(idhā iḥtajta ilayhī);*
> *So long as you do not pursue the rukhaṣ, the ruling is not against the text;*
> *And there is no combination of two schools, wherein no one accepts the*
> *combination [talfīq].*[158]

Again, in al-Fāraskūrī's work, the need in which the less stringent opinion (*rukhṣa*) was anchored and by which it was justified was not defined in the technical sense governing the term in the discourse of the "purposes of the law" (*maqāṣid al-Sharīʿa*).[159] Instead, the legal subject was placed in charge of making the decision as to whether she or he had a need that warranted the use of another juristic opinion. Furthermore, the Ḥanafī jurist Muḥammad al-Fiqhī rejected the view that a layperson must weigh contradictory legal opinions and choose the view with which his heart is most comfortable (*yamīlu ilayhi qalbuh*). According to him, the layperson's perception of what is more correct is irrelevant. Rather, when faced with contradictory opinions, the layperson must follow the methods of the eponyms, namely to pursue the less stringent opinions (*wa mā huwa al-arfaq*) and heed the changing conditions of legal subjects. He cited examples of the opinions of later jurists being chosen over those of Abū Ḥanīfa simply because of a change in people's needs.[160]

Similarly, the Shāfiʿī jurist Muḥammad b. Sulaymān al-Madanī al-Kurdī (d. 1194/1780) justified his position on *tatabbuʿ al-rukhaṣ* not on textual evidence but by reference to social needs. He cited Ibn Ḥajar al-Haytamī's *al-Fatāwā al-Kubrā*, according to which al-Subkī relied on a weak opinion to permit the sale of an absent commodity based on people's exigent needs (*li-iḥtiyāji ghālib al-nāsi ilayhi*). According to al-Haytamī, this is no serious matter (*al-amru fī dhālika khafīfun*) since the standards required of the laity are not the same as those demanded of jurists (*lā yukallafu ʿawāmm al-nās bimā yukallafu bihī al-faqīh al-ḥādhiq al-niḥrīr*).[161] This notion that laypeople are morally weaker than jurists is an extension of the views of al-Zarkashī and al-Shaʿrānī.[162]

Another example of the invocation of necessity to legitimize pragmatic eclecticism is mentioned by the Ḥanafī jurist Ibn ʿĀbidīn (d. 1252/1836) in his *Sharḥ al-Manẓūma*, where he stated that some of the opinions of Abū Ḥanīfa were abandoned either because of the corruption of the people of his time (*bi-sabab fasād ahl al-zamān*) or because of necessity (*ʿumūm al-ḍarūra*). This is why, for example, later jurists after the tenth century (*al-muta'akhkhirīn*) issued legal opinions permitting payment for teaching the Qur'an, which contradicts the view of Abū Ḥanīfa. His description of these doctrinal changes was not framed in the language of preponderance (*tarjīḥ*) but rather in the parlance of necessity (*ḍarūra*).[163] This mobilization of necessity and need is similar to the invocation of the same tools in the discourse of the proponents of *tatabbuʿ al-rukhaṣ* both in legal opinions (fatwas) and in the courts. Ibn ʿĀbidīn would also base the choice of legal opinions from among the different positions of the Ḥanafī school on the situation of the person involved. According to him, the plurality of juristic opinions within each school may be utilized to select whatever is easier for people (*mā huwa al-arfaq bi'l-nās*).[164] He did not use the term *tatabbuʿ al-rukhaṣ* to refer to these processes of doctrinal change based on social need partly because the term *tatabbuʿ al-rukhaṣ* was more commonly used in connection with school boundary-crossing. Horizontal pragmatic eclecticism across school boundaries was more controversial than choosing more appropriate juristic opinions from within the same school. We now move on to the question of how legal subjects and practitioners gained the knowledge necessary to navigate legal pluralism.

The Rise of the Ottoman *Ikhtilāf* Manuals Genre

Another indication that the acceptance of *tatabbuʿ al-rukhaṣ* was increasingly gaining traction was the noticeable rise of a specific type of *ikhtilāf* literature, which consisted of short treatises written as professional manuals for legal practitioners. These manuals were often concerned with a single area of the law in the four schools. Only substantive legal rules were provided, eschewing the legal reasoning and proofs underpinning them. This type of *ikhtilāf* literature is a far cry from the earlier disputation-based (*jadal*) literature.[165]

This literature can be traced back to the Mamluk period, most notably to the work of the Shāfiʿī jurist ʿAbd al-Raḥmān al-Dimashqī, who in 780/1378 wrote *Raḥmat al-Umma fī Ikhtilāf al-A'imma* in an attempt to provide an easy manual that could be memorized by legal practitioners wishing to learn the four schools' rules. It was a brief work that left out the proofs for the different opinions and their arguments (*mujarradatun ʿan al-dalīli wa'l-taʿlīl*).[166] In addition to its clear educational purpose, this practical guide served as a manual for practitioners with limited legal training, whose objective was to help laypeople and religious figures navigate legal pluralism without becoming entangled in the minutiae of legal reasoning.[167]

Some of the earlier *ikhtilāf* literature elaborated on the reasoning behind juristic opinions and mobilized proofs in support of each opinion. One of the main objectives of the earlier *ikhtilāf* genre was marked by the exercise of *tarjīḥ* on the most appropriate legal opinions. An example of this is the *Ḥilyat al-ʿUlamā' fī Maʿrifat Madhāhib al-Fuqahā'* of the Shāfiʿī scholar Abū Bakr al-Qaffāl al-Shāshī (d. 507/1114), not to be confused with Muḥammad al-Qaffāl al-Kabīr al-Shāshī (d. 365/975).[168] Some earlier *ikhtilāf* works contained many chains of transmission for the authorities supporting different opinions. The opinions of different authorities within the schools or of the Companions of the Prophet were frequently mentioned alongside the dominant opinions within each school.[169] Other *ikhtilāf* works were primarily concerned with how different conceptions of *uṣūl* principles could lead to *ikhtilāf* in substantive law, such as Ibn Rushd's *Bidāyat al-Mujtahid wa-Nihāyat al-Muqtaṣid*.[170] There were also instances of juristic disagreement manuals being restricted to only the opinions of the eponyms.[171]

This style of *ikhtilāf* legal manuals increased in importance in the Ottoman period. The focus and function of this new genre was resolutely taken aboard by Ottoman jurists. The Shāfiʿī jurist ʿUmar Muḥammad al-Fāraskūrī (d. 1018/1609), who wrote an *ikhtilāf* manual in rhymed prose, stated that many jurists had written on *ikhtilāf*, but that they typically elaborated more than necessary (*fa-ṭawwalū wa bi'l-marāmi ajḥafū*). He decided for this reason to set aside legal proofs and explanations (*tārikan al-ishāba wa'l-taṭwīla, ḥādhifan al-dalīla wa'l-ta'līl*).[172] Similarly, in his work *Mabāhij al-Umma fī Manāhij al-A'imma al-Arbaʿa*, Nūr al-Dīn al-Shāfiʿī (d. 1044/1634) reminded his audience that the differences among the four schools are a blessing from God (*wa-ikhtilāfuhum niʿmatun minhu musdātun wa-raḥma*).[173]

In some Ottoman *ikhtilāf* texts, the purpose of the genre is expressed quite explicitly. For example, in his book on marriage contracts in the four schools, the Shāfiʿī jurist Abū al-ʿAbbās Aḥmad b. ʿUmar al-Dayrabī (d. 1151/1738) stated that his father and others had asked him to write a book on marriage in the four schools because such a book would help people exercise *taqlīd*, even if it was not based on their own school. Invoking the *ikhtilāf* hadith mentioned above, he argued that such eclecticism is acceptable because differences among the four eponyms are a blessing from God (*raḥma*). This book, he added, would not contain unnecessary information (*khālin ʿan al-ḥashw wa'l-taṭwīl*).[174]

In a similar fashion, the Shāfiʿī jurist ʿAbd al-Muʿṭī al-Samalāwī wrote a treatise in 1198/1783 on marriage in the four schools. He was motivated by the questions of townspeople (*ahl al-mudun*) and jurists from the countryside (*fuqahā' al-aryāf*) concerning the different rules for marriage contracts in the four schools. He explained that peasants would typically ask jurists for the different opinions of the different schools because they sought to enter into marriage contracts that best conformed to their needs, since they were not bound by any particular school.[175]

In his commentary *Sharḥ ʿalā al-Jawhar al-ʿAzīz*, the Mālikī ʿAbd Allāh b. Ḥijāzī al-Sharqāwī (d. 1227/1812) offered a set of options from the four schools with regard to conditions without which the marriage of an orphan girl is considered null and void. Because of the strictness of the Mālikī school, he encouraged people to choose the less stringent positions of the other three schools on this issue.[176] The author of the original work (*matn*) upon which this commentary was based, Muḥammad b. Sālim al-Muʿayṣirāwī, also alerted his readers in another passage to further differences among the schools, urging them to follow whomever they wished (*qallid li-man tahwā wa-tābiʿ*).[177]

This new evidence of the vernacularization of legal knowledge supports Nelly Hanna's observation that the legal doctrines of the four schools seem to have been understood by laypeople and that it was common knowledge in the Ottoman period.[178] This knowledge must have been propagated through this *ikhtilāf* literature. The clear references to questions by peasants and other commoners about the differences among the schools show that there was demand for such knowledge and that jurists tried to fill that need with this simplified *ikhtilāf* genre. Al-Samalāwī's reference to jurists from the countryside (*fuqahā' al-aryāf*) can plausibly be read as referring to minor religious figures who never left their villages for higher education at al-Azhar or some other renowned institution. Al-Samalāwī's reference to lay townspeople (*ahl al-mudun*), who also sought this knowledge in order to navigate the legal system,[179] should be taken to refer to the middle classes, or the literati among nonscholars, who benefited from the "textualization of society" in the Mamluk period, leading to a vibrant reading culture from the Mamluk period onward among traders and craftsmen.[180]

This *ikhtilāf* genre became very succinct, and it was even presented by some jurists in verse, an indication that it was intended for memorization by legal professionals. A similar phenomenon can be found in European legal history. Nicolas Dourbault versified *La Coutume de Normandie* in 1280, and the renowned Italian jurist Giuseppe Aurelio Gennaro (d. 1761) versified *Le Digeste* in Latin. Edme-Hilaire Garnier-Deschênes versified *La Coutume de Paris* in 1768.[181] Joseph-Henri Flacon-Rochelle versified the French Code Napoléon in 1805, the objective being to "engrave the articles of the code more easily in the memory."[182]

A manual of this sort helped legal practitioners—whether muftis, judges, or minor religious scholars—provide legal advice to legal subjects by drawing upon the four schools to serve different social needs without having extensive legal training. It was the proliferation of these manuals in the Ottoman period that enabled legal subjects, through the mediation of their local religious authorities, to gain a functional knowledge of the law that served them in their various transactions.

Conclusion

Why did it take jurists this long to permit pragmatic eclecticism? In the age of absolute *ijtihād*, pragmatic eclecticism was taking place on a much smaller scale. Geographical differences were utilized by both the laity and jurists to facilitate their transactions, but this use must have been limited in the courtroom since, in theory, a *mujtahid* judge could come up with a novel view. Needless to say, judges were most likely constrained in actual practice by the legal options laid down by the jurists of their locality, a "living tradition," in Schachtian terms. With the rise of stable school doctrines and the dominance of the *taqlīd* hegemony, the legal landscape changed dramatically. Pragmatic eclecticism was utilized on a larger scale owing to the increasing predictability of the legal system and the slow shift toward a codification episteme. This was the moment in the praxeological history of pragmatic eclecticism that jurists felt it necessary to offer a justification for that practice. The institutional transformations that started with the Fatimids and were continued by the Ayyubids, culminating in Baybars's decision to appoint four chief judges, contributed to increasing social pressure on jurists to offer a justification for pragmatic eclecticism.

Some jurists from the thirteenth century onward broke away from the formative period's opposition to pragmatic eclecticism. Their debate put an end to the putative consensus of previous generations of jurists, bringing the practice into the realm of valid juristic disagreement. People exercising *tatabbu' al-rukhaṣ* could no longer be dubbed as sinners, thus depriving them of legal probity (*'adāla*), which would have barred them from practicing as judges or muftis, or testifying in court. The lack of consensus also meant that judicial rulings based on these strategies would not be overruled, since the very practice was, by the Mamluk period, considered a legitimate issue of juristic disagreement.[183]

The discussion of whether it is better to follow the anomalous rules of one's own school or the preponderant ones of another would have been pointless had school boundary-crossing been unanimously forbidden. This does not mean that the anti-*tatabbu' al-rukhaṣ* camp was ever completely silent. Jurists continued to oppose pragmatic eclecticism up to the modern period, and, as such, there was no abrupt break with the formative period. Rather, a new strand of thought started to compete with the juristic position of the formative and classical periods, gaining more traction over time. This new strand of thought frequently referenced social practice as a justification for the acceptance of pragmatic eclecticism.

The pragmatic utilization of legal pluralism was not restricted to subjects of the law. A parallel discussion permitted jurisconsults to exercise *tatabbuʿ al-rukhaṣ* on behalf of legal subjects by providing them with less stringent juristic opinions. Some jurists contended that muftis should issue legal opinions based on the situation of the fatwa-seeker, so long as their declarations were not issued as legal opinions but rather as transmissions (*riwāya*). The role of muftis was complemented by the role played by author-jurists who compiled legal manuals. Muftis participated in this system by providing legal advice to subjects of the law, while author-jurists wrote professional manuals to help legal subjects seek the school that could provide the best outcome for their court transactions. In this sense, muftis acted somewhat like lawyers, and—along with author-jurists and minor legal practitioners—bridged the knowledge gap, enabling people to navigate the system to their own advantage.

While *taqlīd* provided the legal system with predictability, pragmatic eclecticism afforded it its much-needed flexibility. The evolution of *taqlīd* and pragmatic eclecticism represents a tight balancing act between the two legal ideals of stability and flexibility. This balancing will become clearer in our discussion of the practice of pragmatic eclecticism in the courts. Furthermore, the methods used by Mamluk and Ottoman jurists to accommodate legal change would be used in the modern codification of Sharīʿa, as we shall see in chapter 6.

3

Talfīq in Juristic Discourse Prior to the Nineteenth Century

IN THIS CHAPTER, I analyze attitudes toward *talfīq* in juristic discourse from the first mentions of the term in the Mamluk period until the late Ottoman period. I discuss the emergence of the term for the first time in discussions of *tatabbuʿ al-rukhaṣ* in the Mamluk period, early opposition to it, and the rise of a pro-*talfīq* camp. I analyze their arguments, which referenced not only the practice of the earlier school authorities, but also the practice of the laity making both of them equally normative. I finally discuss the nature of legal relativism in this pragmatically eclectic, pluralistic system as perceived by jurists.

> A person who marries his daughter off with no guardian (*walī*) according to the Ḥanafī school, no witnesses according to the Mālikī school, and no dower according to the Shāfiʿī school turns marriage into fornication.[1]

The term *talfīq* comes from the verb *laffaqa*, which is to sew two pieces of cloth together.[2] In its technical legal sense, the term is used to refer to putting together elements of two or more doctrines to create a new one. The marriage example mentioned above is one type of *talfīq*, which Hallaq and Aharon Layish name *synchronic*, in which there is a combination of two or more juristic opinions in the same legal transaction. A second type of *talfīq*, which they term *diachronic*, refers to when an individual follows the doctrine of a *mujtahid* in a transaction and then switches to another *mujtahid* before the legal effect of the first case has been exhausted. An example of diachronic *talfīq* is when an individual exercises the right of preemption (*shufʿa*) to a neighbor's piece of land, following the Ḥanafī school, which guarantees adjoining neighbors this preferential right. Later, however, she chooses to adopt the Shāfiʿī school for a future sale, thus depriving her neighbor of the same right to preemption that she herself had once claimed.[3]

The Rise of *Talfīq* in Juristic Discourse

The common wisdom is that *talfīq* came to be considered a lawful practice only in the nineteenth century, when legislators used it for the development of legal codes to accommodate modernity.[4] Hallaq and Layish argue that the practice of *talfīq* was outright forbidden prior to the nineteenth century.[5] This view led Layish to describe the practice as a form of "legal opportunism" (as if such eclecticism and transplantation were peculiarities of Islamic law of the modern period) aimed at enabling legislators in Muslim majority societies to create legal codes compatible with the dictates of European modernity. He thus concludes that the modern codification of Sharīʿa was a development that occurred outside the classical tradition.[6] This view was challenged by Lutz Wiederhold, who points out that the issue of *talfīq* was in fact debated prior to the nineteenth century.[7] Similarly, studying two legal opinions from the seventeenth and eighteenth centuries, Birgit Krawietz shows two sides to the debate over the prohibition of *talfīq*.[8] Yet despite the reliance on *talfīq* in modern codification efforts, there has not been any extensive study of it to my knowledge.[9]

It is not until the Mamluk period that we see any references to *talfīq*. Jurists operating in the formative and classical periods saw no need to discuss it because they had already forbidden *tatabbuʿ al-rukhaṣ*, a more general term that was later semantically dissected to give birth to *talfīq*. In the jurists' attempt to explain away the references in which early legal authorities clearly prohibited pragmatic eclecticism, they had to create a distinction between eclecticism in the same transaction or in two separate transactions. By semantically splitting *tatabbuʿ al-rukhaṣ* into these two types, they were able to deflect the early authorities' prohibition from all types of eclecticism to only one complex type that was not as widely practiced, to wit, *talfīq*, which acted somewhat like a foil for *tatabbuʿ al-rukhaṣ*. Jurists were thus able to claim that the opposition of earlier jurists referred only to *talfīq*, not to *tatabbu' al-rukhaṣ*. They sacrificed the infrequent situations in which such eclecticism is compounded in the same transaction in order not to directly challenge the authorities of the schools and to maintain justificatory continuity. This ad hoc solution, which, in this case, was a form of "legal scaffolding," is typical of the regime of *taqlīd*, where distinctions were made to effect legal change without reinterpreting the sources of law.[10]

This solution was no longer satisfactory for Ottoman jurists who generated more arguments to permit both types of pragmatic eclecticism. The motivation behind this rationalization was to systematize and reconcile legal practice with juristic attitudes. One may legitimately wonder why it took this long for jurists to deal with such a gap between the actual practice of *talfīq*, once it was semantically divorced from *tatabbu' al-rukhaṣ* in the thirteenth century, and the shift in juristic attitudes toward *talfīq*. Such a time lag should not be surprising since it is common for legal systems—or any philosophical system for that matter—to maintain inconsistencies for long periods of time. In his study of the Ḥanafī school, Behnam Sadeghi shows that there were some clear inconsistencies that were either not dealt with by jurists at all or that took them centuries to rationalize.[11]

Based on the evidence presented below, I argue that the virtually unanimous opposition to *talfīq* characteristic of the Mamluk period was challenged in the sixteenth through eighteenth centuries, despite the persistence of strong opposition to the practice throughout the latter period. The growing acceptance of *talfīq* is reflected in juristic discussions in which even some opponents of this legal strategy refused to overrule *talfīq*-based judicial decisions. As I point out in chapter 5, nineteenth-century reformers invoked the juristic arguments advanced by proponents of *talfīq* from the sixteenth through eighteenth centuries to support its use in the modern codification of Islamic law.

The earliest discussions of *talfīq* are uniformly opposed to the practice. Though the dating is not exact, the term *talfīq* begins to be discussed in juristic discourse sometime in the early Mamluk period, not long before the Mālikī jurist al-Qarāfī pointed to a consensus on its prohibition.[12] This claim of a consensus indicates that there was a prior discussion, but it could not have been much earlier than al-Qarāfī owing to the absence of the term in earlier detailed discussions of *tatabbuʿ al-rukhaṣ*. The first Ḥanafī to discuss *talfīq* is said to have been Najm al-Dīn b. Ibrāhīm b. ʿAlī al-Ṭarsūsī (d. 758/1357).[13] In the earliest Mamluk-era writings on the topic, *talfīq* was mentioned only pejoratively as a misguided practice in the courts.[14]

As we saw in chapter 2, the late Ayyubid and early Mamluk period witnessed the birth of a pro-*tatabbuʿ al-rukhaṣ* camp supported by an increasing number of jurists, often referencing court practice and the contingencies of social needs. Conversely, *talfīq* was usually singled out by the proponents of this new trend as the only forbidden type of pragmatic eclecticism because it combines rulings in a manner that is unacceptable in any of the schools and/or as it creates new situations, thus violating consensus. Most jurists, regardless of their position on *tatabbuʿ al-rukhaṣ*, seem to have distanced themselves from the practice of *talfīq*, and this discourse continued throughout the Ottoman period.

The strand of thought opposing *talfīq* in Ottoman juristic discourse continued well into the eighteenth century. As we saw in the previous chapter, some jurists explained away earlier references forbidding *tatabbuʿ al-rukhaṣ* by claiming that they were directed at *talfīq*. The Shāfiʿī jurist Ibn ʿAlān al-Makkī (d. 1057/1647), for instance, completely rejected both synchronic and diachronic forms of *talfīq*,[15] even though he accepted *tatabbuʿ al-rukhaṣ*.[16] The Shāfiʿī jurist Abū al-ʿAbbās Aḥmad b. ʿUmar al-Dayrabī (d. 1151/1738) wrote a book that was designed to allow laypeople to pick and choose from among the less stringent juristic opinions, yet he did not accept *talfīq*.[17] Muḥammad b. Sulaymān al-Madanī al-Shāfiʿī al-Kurdī (d. 1194/1780) was another Shāfiʿī jurist who permitted *tatabbuʿ al-rukhaṣ* but completely rejected *talfīq* as unlawful.[18] This uniform approach was to change in the Ottoman period when a heated debate erupted over the issue.[19]

The discussion of *talfīq* often assumed that the two legal opinions in question came from two different schools. Some jurists, however, expressed their opposition to *talfīq*, even when practiced within the same school. For example, Ibn Bīrī (d. 1099/1687) cited as an example of *talfīq* the case of a person who wishes to endow to himself a number of trees. Such an endowment involves two legal issues: First, can an individual make an endowment to himself? Second, can he make an endowment of a moveable item? There are different opinions on both of these issues in the Ḥanafī school. In order to make this transaction permissible, different aspects of the rules of two authorities within the Ḥanafī school were combined. Abū Yūsuf allowed the endowment of moveable items, but did not allow the endowment of items to oneself; whereas Abū Ḥanīfa allowed endowment to oneself, but did not allow the endowment of moveable items. According to Ibn Bīrī, such an endowment should be forbidden because the actual transaction would not be permitted by either authority, albeit for different reasons.[20]

The Rise of a Pro-*Talfīq* Camp: An Acerbic Debate

Opposition to *talfīq* remained strong throughout the Ottoman period, but the consensus claimed earlier by Mamluk jurists came to be gradually challenged. Al-Qarāfī's support of simple pragmatic eclecticism, so long as it does not lead to *talfīq*, was cited and challenged by later jurists. Amīr Bādshāh (d. 972/1564), for instance, invoked the example of a person who follows the Shāfiʿī opinion that rubbing is not required in the process of ritual ablution and the Mālikī opinion that touching a woman without desire does not invalidate the ritual ablution. He disagreed with al-Qarāfī that such a prayer is invalid, arguing that the opponents of *talfīq* failed to come up with any proof to forbid such a practice.[21]

Some dissenting voices ignited a heated debate in the seventeenth and eighteenth centuries, transforming the practice of *talfīq* into a matter of disagreement (*ikhtilāf*) in the process. The Ḥanbalī jurist Marʿī b. Yūsuf b. Abī Bakr al-Karmī (d. 1033/1623), the mufti of the Ḥanbalīs in Egypt, issued a fatwa permitting the practice of *talfīq*. The controversy erupting from his fatwa remained the subject of a response several decades later, when another Ḥanbalī jurist, Abū al-ʿAwn Muḥammad b. Aḥmad al-Saffārīnī (d. 1188/1774), wrote a treatise specifically to refute the argument for permission.[22]

According to the Ḥanafī jurist Ibn Mullah Farrūkh al-Makkī (d. 1061/1650), some of his renowned contemporaries prohibited *talfīq*, citing the example of someone who follows one school in one part of his prayer and another in another part. He explained that he had not been able to find any evidence for this prohibition (*lam ajid li-imtināʿi dhālika burhānan*).[23] By the time the Ḥanafī jurist Ibrāhīm b. Bīrī (d. 1099/1687) wrote his treatise, he was able to say with confidence in its opening that *talfīq* was an issue over which there was juristic disagreement. According to him, there had been many questions about the validity of *talfīq* in *taqlīd*, with some people permitting it and others forbidding it. Even though he came out strongly against the practice, he noted that those who argued against it often did so without providing evidence, while those supporting it only cited substantive law (*furū'*) in the form of legal opinions (fatwas). He set out, in his treatise, to provide more conclusive evidence against it,[24] while being fully aware of the connection between the practice of *iftā'* and the discourse permitting *talfīq*, which he considered insufficient as a basis for normativity.

The debate was so acerbic that some jurists resorted to ad hominem attacks to denounce their opponents. For instance, Ibn Mullah Farrūkh al-Makkī described anyone who refused to follow al-Shāfi'ī in combining two prayers when traveling (*al-jam'*) and who subsequently missed the prayer because he did not wish to exercise *talfīq* as "an ignorant and fanatical imbecile" (*al-jāhil al-muta'aṣṣib al-ghabī*).[25] Another example in which insulting words were exchanged was cited by Ibrāhīm b. Bīrī (d. 1099/1687) in his treatise prohibiting *talfīq*, in which he discussed how his views had drawn the ire of an unnamed proponent of *talfīq*. This scholar insulted Ibn Bīrī over the issue in public in a manner that, as he put it, "reduces his good deeds and increases his bad deeds" (*takallama 'alayya fī majlisihi bimā yuqallilu ḥasanātihi wa yukthiru sayyi'ātih*).[26]

It was generally unusual for jurists to denigrate their peers or use insulting language in their writings, especially on matters of juristic disagreement. The following comments by al-Nābulsī (d. 1143/1730) found in his later response to al-Makkī's stand on *talfīq* suggest that the debate was a defining issue for some jurists:

> See how this person [al-Makkī], who is deficient in understanding (*al-qāṣir al-fahm*), thought that *talfīq* was permitted based on the view [of Ibn al-Humām] that the layperson can choose in each transaction the opinion of a *mujtahid* that is easier for him. What is really meant by the transaction is the entire transaction, not part of it.[27]

The high passions in this acrimonious debate were the result of the high stakes involved. The prohibition of *talfīq* practically rendered the legal practices of the laity invalid, since there was a perception that it is hard to avoid *talfīq* in prayers, wherein laypeople were thought to be frequently mixing school doctrines in carrying out their ritual ablutions and in performing their prayers. As we shall see, jurists were very concerned about the validity of people's practice, especially with regard to ritual worship. We now turn to the different strategies adopted by both sides of the debate to support their positions.

The Arguments of the Pro-*Talfīq* Camp

Attribution to Earlier Authorities

Jurists permitting the practice of *talfīq* defended it in several ways. They argued that opposition to the practice was only a recent development and could thus be dismissed as a departure from the formative period. A work written in 1051/1641 by Ibn Mullah Farrūkh al-Makkī (d. 1061/1650) cited Ibn Nujaym al-Miṣrī (d. 970/1563) as stating that negative views toward *talfīq* were only expressed by later scholars (*muta'akhkhirīn*), and that earlier authorities did not forbid *talfīq*.[28] Al-Makkī is right that there were no references made by earlier authorities to forbidding *talfīq*, but this is the case simply because the term had not emerged in juristic discourse until the thirteenth century when the semantic shift took place.

In their efforts to find support for their sanctioning of the practice, scholars sometimes related stories attributed to the eponyms of the four schools, portraying them as accepting the practice of *talfīq*. For instance, Ibn Mullah Farrūkh al-Makkī wrote of how al-Shāfiʿī once had a haircut and subsequently performed his prayers with much hair scattered on his clothes, which, according to his own old doctrine, invalidated his ritual ablution. When asked about this, he answered that he was confronted with a problem (*ibtulīnā*), so he turned to the school of the people of Iraq, meaning the Ḥanafīs.[29] This was taken to be an example of *talfīq* because al-Shāfiʿī fused his performance of ritual ablution, which was based on his old doctrine, with a relaxation of his opinion regarding the ritual purity of hair.

Supporters of *talfīq* also related an anecdote in which Abū Yūsuf (d. 181/798), after having performed his ritual ablution, was informed that there was a dead rat in the water. He responded, "I will take the view of the people of Medina that if the volume of water is two jugs (*qullatayn*) or more,[30] it does not carry dirt (*khubth*)."[31] Others, while accepting the story, argued that Abū Yūsuf was exercising *ijtihād*, and, therefore, his action did not constitute an example of *talfīq*. In other words, his independent legal reasoning merely happened to agree with that of the jurists of Medina and therefore there was no fear that utility was the motivation behind the decision. The way jurists argued that he was exercising *ijtihād* to support one position or *taqlīd* to support another can be classified as ad hoc reasoning, since the choice of either option is not based on legal methodological engagement. The claim that he was exercising *ijtihād* or *taqlīd* was not backed up by clear evidence.

Thus the Ḥanafī jurist ʿAbd al-Ghanī al-Nābulsī maintained that Abū Yūsuf relied on the same evidence as the Shāfiʿīs and was not simply imitating or borrowing their opinion (*taqlīd*). The wording of the story does not, however, support al-Nābulsī's interpretation of Abū Yūsuf's action as *ijtihād*, since Abū Yūsuf (if the story is to be believed) stated explicitly that he took the "opinion" of the people of Medina (*idhan na'khudhu bi-qawli ikhwāninā min ahli al-Madīna*). To counter this, al-Nābulsī argued that Abū Yūsuf's use of the term "opinion" (*qawl*) was metaphorical, suggesting that he did not take their opinion but, rather, "their evidence" (*akhadha bi-dalīlihim wa sammāhu qawlahum majāzan*).[32] This claim of personal *ijtihād* was also invoked by Ibn Mullah Farrūkh al-Makkī, who was aware of a version of the story that had Abū Yūsuf following his new *ijtihād* for six months after the incident and returning to his old *ijtihād* subsequently.[33] Other opponents of *talfīq* cited another version mentioned in *al-Quniyya* of the Ḥanafī jurist al-Zāhidī (d. 658/1259), in which Abū Yūsuf was said to have repeated his prayer because he considered his first prayer to be invalid. The proponents of *talfīq* did not accept this version.[34]

Another manner in which the proponents of *talfīq* tried to strengthen their position was through seeking out examples of its practice in earlier Ottoman juristic discourse. Al-Makkī, for instance, cited Zayn al-Dīn b. Nujaym al-Miṣrī (d. 970/1563) as having allowed combining the contradictory opinions of Ḥanafī authorities by establishing an endowment (*waqf*) of moveable properties to oneself.[35] He saw this as evidence that earlier authorities supported *talfīq*.[36]

By the late eighteenth century, we find the Egyptian Mālikī jurist al-Dasūqī (d. 1230/1814) pointing to two opinions among the Mālikīs regarding the practice of *talfīq*. The first was that of the Egyptians, who prohibited it, and the second was that of the North Africans (*maghāriba*), who allowed it. He sided with the North African opinion, which he indicated was the preponderant view (*wa-rujjiḥat*). It is not clear whether he meant that his personal assessment was that the North African view is more accurate or that it is the dominant Mālikī position.[37]

Practice as a Justification for the Permissibility of Talfīq

Social practice or custom has always played an important role in Islamic law. Custom was used to fill in areas of the law that were not scripturally determined. One example would be the role of custom in contracts, whereby what is considered customary in a particular social context functions as an implicit condition in the contract, unless there is a stipulation to the contrary.[38] But can social practice itself be normative, thus leading to a doctrinal change in an existing legal doctrine? The juristic discourse on *talfīq* offers some insight into this question. Jurists in general were well aware that *talfīq* was taking place in practice. Evidence of the practice includes debates regarding whether a ruling based on *talfīq* must necessarily be overruled. An example of this is the question of whether a judge should overrule the ruling of another judge in a case where a sinful (*fāsiq*) witness testifies against an absent person. This case constitutes an example of *talfīq* because the Shāfiʿīs do not accept the testimony of a sinner, but allow ruling in absentia, whereas the Ḥanafīs do not allow ruling against someone in absentia but allow the testimony of a sinner.[39]

In juristic discourse, there were two distinct approaches to the reality of *talfīq* in social practice. One approach was to treat it as an anomaly that needed to be put aright. Al-Shurunbulālī, for instance, cited the Shāfiʿī jurist Shihāb al-Dīn Aḥmad b. ʿImād al-Iqfihsī (d. 808/1405–6) on the authority of the Ḥanafī Qāsim b. Qaṭlūbaghā al-Miṣrī (d. 879/1474), as stating that if a judge's decision contains *talfīq*—which is the practice of "ignorant judges" (*kathīrun min jahalati al-quḍāti yafʿalūna al-ḥukma al-mulaffaq*)—it should be overruled.[40] The second approach treated the practice of *talfīq* as evidence of its validity and tried to adapt juristic discourse to this practice. I discuss the second approach in what follows.

Practice was, as it happens, often invoked in the discussion of *talfīq*. Ibn Mullah Farrūkh al-Makkī interpreted Ibn al-Humām's comments in *al-Taḥrīr* to the effect that he did not see why it should be forbidden (*lā yadrī mā yamnaʿu minhu*) as referring to *talfīq*. Al-Makkī then cited al-Qarāfī's opposition, whose view he felt under no obligation to follow, despite his recognition of al-Qarāfī's renown as an expert of legal methodology (*min fuḍalāʾi al-uṣūliyyīn min al-Mālikiyya*). The reason for his rejection of al-Qarāfī's view was that he had found some Ḥanafī references not only to its permission, but also to its occurrence (*qad wajadtu ʿan baʿḍi aʾimmatinā mā yadullu ʿalā jawāzihi, bal wuqūʿihi*).[41] Ibn Mullah Farrūkh al-Makkī's wording indicates that social practice was itself normative as a gauge of permissibility.

Ibn Mullah Farrūkh al-Makkī also tried to justify *talfīq* with reference to the *al-Fatāwā al-Bazzāziyya* of Muḥammad b. Muḥammad b. Shihāb b. Yūsuf al-Kurdarī al-Bazzāzī. Al-Bazzāzī referred to cases in which women were able to testify by following the Ḥanafī permission for women to testify on these cases. But their testimony, which was invalid under the Shāfiʿī school, was conducted against an absent person.[42] This is an instance of *talfīq* because the Ḥanafī acceptance of women's testimony in these specific cases was combined with the Shāfiʿī acceptance of a ruling in absentia in the same transaction. But the problem lies in the inverse: women's testimony in these cases would not be accepted by the Shāfiʿīs and the fact that it concerned absent parties would not be permitted by the Ḥanafīs.

Al-Makkī also cited an example in which *talfīq* was utilized to validate people's prayers. According to him, when a person erroneously replaces the verb "to worship" (*naʿbudu*) with the verb "to eat" (*naʾkulu*) in the recitation of the opening chapter of the Qurʾan, the *Fātiḥa*, this creates two problems. The first is missing a word of the *Fātiḥa*, which would invalidate the prayer according to the Shāfiʿīs since they consider the *Fātiḥa* to be an essential component of the prayer. The second is the issue of making errors in recitation, which is not acceptable to the Ḥanafīs but is pardoned by the Shāfiʿīs. To solve this problem, some of the scholars of Khawārizm, al-Makkī explained, validated the prayer by combining the Shāfiʿī opinion allowing for a few mistakes in the recitation with the Ḥanafī view that the *Fātiḥa* is not an essential part of the prayer.[43] Needless to say, from the jurists' perspective, introducing this flexibility saved many people from violating the ritual aspect of Islamic law.

As we saw above, support for *talfīq* often generated considerable outrage, as was the case with al-Karmī's treatise on the permission of *talfīq*, which raised the ire of some Ḥanbalīs. In his treatise, al-Karmī explicitly stated that it would be unrealistic to try to change people's practice and, on this basis, *talfīq* ought to be legitimized, "wherever this takes place, especially as performed by the laity, who are unable to do otherwise" (*bal haythu waqaʿa dhālika ittifāqan khuṣūṣan min al-ʿawāmm al-ladhīna lā yasaʿuhum ghayra dhālika*). He thus demonstrated that practice can be normative.[44] We saw above that insulting words were sometimes exchanged among jurists over this contentious issue. We may recall that Ibn Mullah Farrūkh al-Makkī decried some members of his school as zealots for refusing to follow al-Shāfiʿī in combining their prayers during travel (*al-jamʿ*). For this reason, he considered *talfīq* to be a practical need, without which one stands the risk of missing prayer.[45]

The important place that practice occupied in juristic discourse belies Coulson's claim that the Mālikī legal work *al-ʿAmal al-Fāsī* is the single instance of a "realist" form of Islamic jurisprudence that follows the practice of the courts rather than preceding it.[46] The descriptive strand of juristic discourse, which I have outlined in the debate over *talfīq* and which was concerned with the law not as it ought to be but as it actually is in practice, continued to compete with the prescriptive approach throughout the Ottoman period and well into the modern period. But beyond the clear acceptance or rejection of *talfīq*, there was a middle position to which we now turn.

Diachronic versus Synchronic *Talfīq*

We have seen thus far that approaches to *talfīq* varied from wholesale acceptance to complete rejection. Another approach used by proponents of the practice of *talfīq* was to distinguish between combining juristic opinions in the same transaction (synchronic) and in two separate, albeit related, transactions (diachronic). For example, according to some jurists, following one imam in ritual ablution and a different imam in prayer does not invalidate the prayer because the ablution and the prayer can be seen as two separate acts, even though the legal effect of the first act had not yet been exhausted by the time of the second act.[47]

Another example offered was that of a woman who is divorced for a third time and is therefore unable to remarry her now ex-husband unless she first consummates a marriage with a different man. If she contracts her own marriage, without a male legal guardian, which is permitted under Ḥanafī law, would this marriage be acceptable to her new Shāfiʿī husband? Opponents of *talfīq* argued that it would be permissible for the Shāfiʿī husband to accept her Ḥanafī marriage as valid and marry her, so long as he follows the Ḥanafī school in everything related to this marriage.[48] Since her marriage to the new husband (*muḥallil*) is separate from her remarriage to her former husband and the subject of both transactions is the same (or the legal effect of the first act has not been exhausted), it constitutes a case of diachronic *talfīq*.

Jurists were generally more open to diachronic than to synchronic *talfīq*. Al-Khaṭīb al-Timurtāshī (d. 1004/1595) only permitted diachronic *talfīq*, citing the example of a Ḥanafī judge who settles a dispute between parties to a pledge (*rahn*) contract that was drawn up under a Mālikī judge. The schools differ on whether accretions to the collateral are considered part of the collateral or belong to the pledger. The Ḥanafī judge would consider the fruit of a tree pledged as collateral to be part of the collateral (*thamaratu al-rahni takūnu tabaʿan li'l-aṣl*). The Mālikī opinion, by contrast, would consider the fruit to belong to the pledger. Al-Timurtāshī indicated that the Ḥanafī judge may adjudicate a dispute over this contract according to his school because although it deals with the same collateral, the original contracting transaction is separate from any later dispute arising over the accretion of the collateral.[49] Presumably the pledger would prefer the Ḥanafī judge since this would give her possession of the fruit, whereas the pledgee would be more inclined toward the Mālikī judge. In such situations, where there is a conflict of interest, jurists developed a system of procedure to determine whose choice gets priority, as we shall see in chapter 4.

That this distinction between synchronic and diachronic *talfīq* was growing in importance can be seen through the arguments of its detractors. Although the Shāfiʿī jurist al-Fishnī (d. 978/1570) was opposed to both synchronic and diachronic *talfīq*, he admitted that the Mālikīs allowed diachronic *talfīq*. In order to argue that this was just as unacceptable as the synchronic type, he offered the example of a Shāfiʿī who follows the Ḥanafī school during a land sale in order to take advantage of the right of preemption (*shufʿa*) to which adjacent neighbors are entitled in Ḥanafī law. According to him, if the Shāfiʿī asserts preferred status, on Ḥanafī grounds, in order to buy a piece of land being sold by his neighbor, he should not then be allowed to switch back to the Shāfiʿī school in order to sell the same piece of land to someone else and deny his neighbor the same right of preemption.[50]

Talfīq and *Ijtihād*

In most of the debates that we have examined, *talfīq* is assumed to be exercised within *taqlīd*, where the choice is motivated not by a hermeneutic exercise but rather by an assessment of the utility of the resulting rule. The distinction between exercising *talfīq* in one's personal *ijtihād* or merely in a state of *taqlīd* was used by both sides of the debate to support their arguments, as we saw above. The anti-*talfīq* camp of jurists, who claimed that a consensus existed on its prohibition in earlier generations, explained away cases in the earlier sources where the rules of more than one school appeared to be combined as instances of *ijtihād*. For example, according to the Shāfiʿī school, the ritual ablution requires wiping only part of the head, and touching the genitals invalidates the ablution. By contrast, according to the Ḥanafī school, while touching the genitals does not invalidate the ablution, the whole head must be wiped. A *mujtahid* may theoretically come to the conclusion through his own legal reasoning (*ijtihād*) that he must wipe over part of his head and that touching the genitals does not invalidate the ablution. According to the opponents of *talfīq*, historical examples of the practice do not constitute evidence of early *taqlīd*ic *talfīq*. They are interpreted as instances of personal *ijtihād* in which the *mujtahid*'s view happened to coincide with the Ḥanafī position in one area and with the Shāfiʿī position in another. According to Ibn Bīrī, his contemporaries invoked, as evidence for the validity of *talfīq*, the judicial practice in which a judge rules against an absent person on the basis of a sinner's testimony. In his attempt to explain away this evidence of the practice of *talfīq*, he responded that such judicial decisions were not based on *talfīq*, but were, rather, exercises of *ijtihād* on the part of the judge.[51]

Some proponents of *talfīq* even turned the opponents' *ijtihād* argument on its head by contending that if *ijtihād*ic *talfīq* is permitted, then the practice of *taqlīd*ic *talfīq* should raise no concerns.[52] A story is cited in support of this position according to which ʿUmar b. al-Khaṭṭāb once changed his ruling in the same case. According to al-Makkī, if ʿUmar was justified in changing his *ijtihād*, those following established opinions (*muqallids*) should also be allowed to change their *taqlīd*, and if, furthermore, *talfīq* is permitted when reached through *ijtihād*, it should also be allowed in instances of *taqlīd*.[53]

Leadership in Prayer (*al-Iqtidā'*) and *Talfīq*

Validating people's prayers was an important motivation behind the growing acceptance of *talfīq*, as we saw above. One important orthopraxic theme in which *talfīq* was invoked relates to communal prayer. Communal prayers require a leader, an imam, and at least one other worshipper. The worshipper must make a mental act of resolution (*niyya*) to follow the leader's prayer and then the worshipper will follow the leader's motions. According to the Ḥanafīs, the validity of the worshipper's prayer depends on that of the leader, but this is not the case for the Shāfiʿīs.[54] Is the prayer of a *ma'mūm* (the worshipper being led) valid, when the imam comes from a different school with different rules? A jurist's position on this issue was often an indication of whether he was for or against the practice of *talfīq*.

The controversy here was principally concerned with whether the prayer of the imam had to conform to the requirements of the *ma'mūm*'s school, or whether it is sufficient for the imam's prayer to meet the requirements of his own school, even if it is different from that of the *ma'mūm*. Since the validity of the prayer of the *ma'mūm* in Ḥanafism hinges upon his or her own prayer as well as that of the imam, if the imam is not praying in the manner of the *ma'mūm*'s school, then to follow that imam constitutes a form of *talfīq*. A Ḥanafī *ma'mūm* who is led by a Shāfiʿī imam would be combining the Ḥanafī and Shāfiʿī schools in his or her own prayer. Ḥanafī opponents of *talfīq* argued that the *ma'mūm*'s prayer is only valid if the imam's prayer follows the school of the *ma'mūm*, whereas proponents of *talfīq* insisted that the prayer is valid, so long as it meets the requirements of the school of the imam.

Al-Shurunbulālī claimed that earlier authorities considered the prayer of the *ma'mūm* to be invalid if his imam's prayer was invalid from the *ma'mūm*'s point of view. Although al-Shurunbulālī was one of the supporters of *tatabbuʿ al-rukhaṣ*, he was staunchly opposed to *talfīq*. He cited the views held by earlier authorities against following an imam from a different school in support of his position. For a Ḥanafī to be led in prayer by a non-Ḥanafī, the non-Ḥanafī imam must not do anything to render his prayer invalid under the Ḥanafī school, even if his prayer may still be valid under his own. For example, if a Shāfiʿī imam bleeds, he has to renew his ritual ablution in order for the prayer of a Ḥanafī following him to be valid, since bleeding invalidates the ablution in the Ḥanafī school. Al-Shurunbulālī added that, had it been the case that *talfīq* were permitted, earlier authorities would not have set this condition for those led by imams from other schools.[55] Similarly, other opponents of *talfīq* such as the Ḥanafī jurists al-Sindī and ʿAbd al-Ghanī al-Nābulsī saw validity as dependent upon meeting the requirements of the school of the *ma'mūm*. According to them, fulfilling the requirements of the imam's school is not sufficient.[56]

Unlike al-Shurunbulālī, al-Mullah ʿAlī al-Qārī (d. 1014/1605) did not engage the issue of *talfīq* at all in his discussion of leadership in prayer. According to the majority of jurists, he stated, so long as the imam is known to avoid areas of *khilāf* (*idhā kāna yaḥtāṭu fī baʿḍi mawḍiʿ al-khilāf*), it is permitted to follow him even if he belongs to a different school. He added his own explanation to this juristic opinion by arguing that what it indicates is not a categorical prohibition, but rather, the appropriate legal value here is undesirable (*karāha*) rather than prohibited. If the imam were a Shāfiʿī who happens to renew his ablution after bleeding, which is not required under his school, it is permitted to follow him. But even if he does not avoid areas of disagreement, it is not strictly prohibited to follow him. He cautioned, however, that finding an imam who performs his prayers and ablutions in accordance with the requirements of all the four schools is rare.[57]

The positions of al-Shurunbulālī and al-Mullah ʿAlī al-Qārī contrast sharply with that of Ibn Mullah Farrūkh al-Makkī (d. 1061 /1650), who argued that what matters for the validity of prayer is the position of the imam, not the *ma'mūm*. Like al-Shurunbulālī, he dealt with leadership in prayer as part of his wider discussion of *talfīq*.[58] He accused those who refuse to be led in prayer by an imam from another school of exhibiting "fanaticism" (*maḥḍ taʿaṣṣub*). Thus a Muslim who finds himself in the presence of an imam from a different school has no choice but to follow him, even if his prayer is considered invalid according to the *ma'mūm*'s school.[59]

Invalid Instances of Juristic Disagreement

How relativist was the discourse permitting pragmatic eclecticism? We saw in chapter 1 that the majority of jurists agreed that there is only one truth in the mind of God and that in the absence of apodictic evidence this truth is unknowable. Some jurists widened those instances of unknowability by equating them with the historical reality of juristic disagreement, while others such as Ibn Taymiyya and his student Ibn Qayyim significantly narrowed the scope of unknowability, rejecting many of the opinions of some of the eponyms and the tendency among many jurists to equate knowability with consensus and unknowability with juristic disagreement. According to this view, the eponyms were not immune from flagrant errors, and, therefore, there may be areas constituting invalid instances of juristic disagreement. We have also seen the proponents of the ontological multiplicity of truth doctrine widen their definition of the absence of such evidence so as to include all areas of juristic disagreement among the four Sunnī schools. According to al-Shaʿrānī, for instance, there were no violations of apodictic source texts in the views of the eponyms of the four schools, and, therefore, his conception of legal pluralism incorporated all the opinions of the four Sunnī schools. The reality of legal pluralism was fully embraced.

Similarly, Ibn al-Ḥājib (d. 646/1249) considered all instances of juristic disagreement as unknowable and tolerated some of the most controversial opinions within the schools, such as Abū Ḥanīfa's famous permission of drinking date wine (*nabīdh*) so long as it does not lead to inebriation. Ibn al-Ḥājib and his commentator the Shāfiʿī jurist Shams al-Dīn al-Iṣfahānī (d. 749/1349) agreed that a person who drinks date wine (*nabīdh*) and plays chess is not a sinner (*fāsiq*), even while they continued to affirm the unity of truth doctrine and the existence of a single correct *mujtahid*. In this example, drinking date wine is only permitted by Abū Ḥanīfa, whereas chess is prohibited by the Ḥanafīs and Ḥanbalīs but permitted by some Shāfiʿīs. Thus the *muqallid* who plays chess and drinks date wine follows the Ḥanafī school on one view but abandons it on the other to take advantage of the less stringent Shāfiʿī position on chess. Implied in this approach is the assumption that the rules of the eponyms are all equally valid and that even the opinion that date wine is permissible does not contradict the textual sources. Ibn al-Ḥājib also accepted as valid such issues of juristic disagreement as the opinion that women of legal age and sound mind can contract their own marriages without a guardian, as well as the contradictory opinion that considers a male legal guardian to be necessary to the validity of a marriage contract.[60]

Between the two extremes of equating unknowability with all issues of juristic disagreement and of narrowing the scope of unknowability in *fiqh* significantly, there were several particularly controversial issues espoused by the Ḥanafī school that were not accepted by jurists from the other schools. As we saw above, jurists such as Taqī al-Dīn al-Subkī (d. 756/1355) and al-Zarkashī—who permitted pragmatic eclecticism in cases of necessity or need (*ḍarūra* or *ḥāja*)—only took issue with a small number of cases. They considered them to be invalid instances of juristic disagreement, arguing that they contradict clear textual evidence, obvious analogy, or consensus (*ijmāʿ*). This view had practical ramifications since there was a general agreement among jurists that any judge's decision that contradicted these sources must be overruled.[61]

Exacting the death sentence on a Muslim who kills a non-Muslim (*dhimmī*), for instance, was not accepted by some non-Ḥanafīs because it was seen to contradict a clear scriptural source,[62] meaning that any judicial decision to this effect must be overruled according to their schools.[63] Unlike the Ḥanafīs, the majority of Shāfiʿīs, Mālikīs, and Ḥanbalīs consider the tradition "A Muslim should not be killed for an unbeliever" (*Lā yuqtalu muslimun bi-kāfir*) as conclusive evidence supporting their view.[64] Thus, according to Taqī al-Dīn al-Subkī, a Shāfiʿī witness to a murder committed by a Muslim against a non-Muslim should not testify to that effect before a Ḥanafī judge, as such a testimony would lead to a Muslim being killed for an unbeliever, which is prohibited under Shāfiʿī law. Thus, if the blood money is rejected by the victim's family and the Ḥanafī judge issues a death sentence, this should not be approved by a Shāfiʿī judge if he has the power to overrule the decision.[65]

Similarly, it is permissible in the Ḥanafī school for a free person to be executed in punishment for the murder of a slave, whereas the Shāfiʿīs only permit the payment of blood money when this difference in status exists. As a result, some Shāfiʿī jurists argued that a Shāfiʿī executioner who kills a free person for the murder of a slave, even if it were at the orders of a Ḥanafī judge, is liable for retaliation or blood money (*wujūb al-qiṣāṣ wa'l-ḍamān ʿalā al-jallād*).[66] Similarly, the Ḥanbalī Ibn Mufliḥ (d. 763/1362) held that a judge's decision to kill a Muslim for murdering a non-Muslim must be overruled on the grounds that it contradicts clear scriptural sources.[67]

Other examples can be found in the work of the Central Asian Shāfiʿī jurist al-Ardabīlī (d. 799/1396), whose work *al-Anwār li-Aʿmāl al-Abrār* was widely known in Egypt. Al-Ardabīlī outlined a number of rulings that he thought must be overruled when referred to a Shāfiʿī judge for enforcement. These include a judge's decision to allow a woman whose husband had been missing for four years to remarry after the expiration of a waiting period (*ʿidda*) at the end of the four-year period. According to him, although this view is accepted by the Mālikīs and the Ḥanbalīs, it should, nonetheless, be overruled by Shāfiʿī judges. Other examples that must be overruled by the Shāfiʿīs, according to al-Ardabīlī, include temporary (*mutʿa*) marriage contracts, and the decision to exclude equal retribution (*qiṣāṣ*) in murder cases committed with a heavy object (*muthqal*), which is held by the Ḥanafīs. At the same time, there are decisions in other schools that Shāfiʿī judges may not overrule, such as marriage contracts with no guardians or witnesses and contracts witnessed by sinners.[68]

The Shāfiʿī jurist Ibn Ḥajar al-Haytamī (d. 973/1567) listed a number of legal rules that contradict the clear textual sources, such as a sale in which the buyer is not allowed to return the purchased item during the selling session (*nafī khiyār al-majlis*) and the practice of forgoing the death penalty (*qiṣāṣ*) in the case of murder by a heavy object (*muthqal*), noted previously. He indicated that there is a debate over whether or not such court decisions may be overruled, adding that the majority of jurists support doing so.[69]

The Ḥanafī jurist al-Bazzāzī also pointed out instances of differences among the schools in which the ruling of a judge is not respected. For example, in the Shāfiʿī school, a sexually impotent husband who had divorced his wife cannot return her to the marriage (*rājaʿahā*) against her will. According to al-Kurdārī, however, any such decision by a Shāfiʿī judge must be overruled, and the husband should be allowed to force her back into the marriage. Al-Bazzāzī argued that the Shāfiʿī opinion contradicts a clear scriptural text, as the Qur'an declares in 2:228: "And their husbands have more right to take them back" (*wa buʿūlatuhunna aḥaqqu bi-raddihinna*).[70]

This line distinguishing between acceptable and unacceptable differences of opinion among the schools continued to be drawn throughout the Ottoman period. Thus the Shāfiʿī jurist ʿUmar Muḥammad al-Fāraskūrī (d. 1018/1609) argued, for instance, that changing schools is allowed when there is a pressing need, so long as the ruling that one follows does not contradict any clear scriptural evidence.[71]

In the face of these irreconcilable doctrinal differences, to what degree, in practice, were members of a given school able to overturn other schools' legal rulings deemed to contradict the source texts or an obvious case of analogy? Needless to say, the ability of a school to protect its rulings and to overrule the decisions of other judges depended, to a large extent, on the political power of the school. There is some evidence to suggest that, in Ottoman Egypt, the Ḥanafī legal establishment tried to preempt the rulings of non-Ḥanafī judges in certain key areas of disagreement. The issue of ruling in absentia furnishes a case in point. Ḥanafī Ottoman jurists tried to enforce their school position by not allowing non-Ḥanafī judges to hear such cases.[72] Whether this attempt was successful or not in actual practice is an issue that ought to be the subject of a future study. It is likely that the line drawn between acceptable and unacceptable differences remained little more than a theoretical consideration for the non-Ḥanafī schools in Ottoman territories since they lacked the political backing of the Ottomans.

Conclusion

Hallaq and Layish's view that both diachronic and synchronic types of *talfīq* were forbidden before the nineteenth century is in need of revision.[73] There was an attitudinal shift that took place in the early thirteenth century with regard to pragmatic eclecticism. Part of the ad hoc reasoning devised by Ayyubid and Mamluk jurists was to create a semantic shift, singling out a new concept as the forbidden type and permitting most forms of pragmatic eclecticism. *Talfīq* appeared as a foil for *tatabbu' al-rukhaṣ* around the thirteenth century. Throughout the Mamluk period, *talfīq* was almost unanimously rejected by jurists. It was not until the sixteenth century that voices permitting *talfīq* emerged, leading to a very acerbic debate in which jurists exchanged insulting language over this issue. Some jurists restricted their support to diachronic *talfīq* or forbade both types, while others saw no reason for forbidding it. But many jurists on both sides were well aware that *talfīq* was taking place in practice. The pro-*talfīq* camp frequently referred to the practice of the laity especially in rituals to justify its permission.

More important, by the end of the Ottoman period, jurists had become aware that the issue was subject to debate. Like *tatabbu' al-rukhaṣ*, *talfīq* became part of the repertoire of the juristic disagreement (*ikhtilāf*) literature, marking an important development in attitudes toward it. Rulings based on *tatabbu' al-rukhaṣ* and *talfīq* could no longer be automatically overruled. This was precisely the view of the majority of jurists examined in this study. The new status and recognition granted to the practice of *tatabbu' al-rukhaṣ* and *talfīq* came to be accepted even by some of those who opposed these legal strategies.[74] This development suggests that Islamic law continued to be dynamic throughout the Ottoman period, as jurists exhibited an ability to revise the doctrine of the formative and classical periods. This revision was clearly motivated by the practice of the laity, but the primary catalyst for the rise of pragmatic eclecticism, as we saw in chapter 1, was to facilitate the financial and class-based needs of elite groups, especially women and merchants.

As we shall see in chapter 5, modern jurists have used these Ottoman arguments to present the case that the pragmatic utilization of Sunnī legal pluralism is still open to debate. One factor that enabled later attitudes to compete with the doctrine of the formative period was the tendency for jurists to update their authorities. While someone like al-Ghazālī (d. 505/1111) remained a significant figure, the views of the likes of Ibn Ḥajar al-Haytamī (d. 973/1567) became arguably more important in the Ottoman period.[75]

To better appreciate the juristic discourse on pragmatic eclecticism, I next present a study of a thousand and one cases from three courts in Cairo and Bulaq. I illustrate the utilization of pragmatic eclecticism by both subaltern and elite groups to take advantage of the immense diversity of opinions among the four Sunnī schools—born of multifarious geopolitical and socioeconomic settings from Transoxania to North Africa—to respond to new challenges and accommodate evolving socioeconomic realities.

PART THREE

Court Practice Prior to the Nineteenth Century

4

Pragmatic Eclecticism in Court Practice

A Thousand and One Cases

IN THIS CHAPTER, I present examples of both types of pragmatic eclecticism from the records of three Egyptian courts in the seventeenth and eighteenth centuries, not long before the modernization efforts of Mehmed Ali in the nineteenth century. I first briefly discuss the practice of courts prior to the Ottoman period, followed by a study of the utilization of *tatabbuʿ al-rukhaṣ* in early modern Ottoman Egyptian courts. Since the motivation behind the choice of forum is not always mentioned in the court records, I will partly rely on case patterns in determining whether or not the choice of legal forum was motivated by utility. In addition to case patterns, explicit references to motivation as well as specific individuals' litigation history will reveal that *tatabbuʿ al-rukhaṣ* was in fact an important element of flexibility in the Ottoman Egyptian legal system. Using the same sample and after examining *tatabbuʿ al-rukhaṣ*, I will explore cases of *talfīq*, which was often achieved through combining more than one judge in the same transaction. In the process, I will discuss the social status of the people involved in these legal transactions to ascertain whether pragmatic eclecticism primarily catered to the needs of elite classes or to wider segments of Egyptian society.

Recall that in chapter 2 we discussed the context of al-Shaʿrānī's theory of legal pluralism as a response to early Ottoman attempts at Ḥanafization in the sixteenth century. Al-Shaʿrānī not only rejected legal purism in which juristic views were chosen based on hermeneutic exercises of preponderance, but also the school loyalty (*tamadhhub*) position underlying Ottoman Ḥanafization. His theory epitomizes the resistance against Ottoman legal homogenization and represents a valorization of local, Mamluk legal pluralism. By the seventeenth century, as the court records examined here show, the Ottoman Ḥanafization drive would peter out. However, in actual court practice, while the sweeping majority of cases in the sample were adjudicated by Ḥanafī judges, the other three schools were utilized pragmatically, thus maintaining, nay valorizing, Mamluk legal pluralism.[1]

Tatabbuʿ al-Rukhaṣ

As discussed in chapters 2 and 3, the number of jurists who defended the practice of *tatabbuʿ al-rukhaṣ* and *talfīq* increased exponentially during the Ottoman period. While *tatabbuʿ al-rukhaṣ* had been steadily gaining support among jurists as early as the Ayyubid period, the practice of *talfīq* did not manage to achieve widespread acceptance until the Ottoman period. Jurists were increasingly advocating these practices partly because they were being used in the courts so extensively as to effectively become a social necessity. In addition, forbidding school boundary-crossing (whether in the form of *tatabbuʿ al-rukhaṣ* or *talfīq*) would have invalidated the ritual prayers of many among the Egyptian laity, where school rules on prayers and ritual ablution were perceived by jurists to have been mixed.[2]

In a collection of fatwas authored by the Shāfiʿī jurist Tāj al-Dīn al-Fazārī (d. 690/1291), he stated that in 1264, while Baybars was laying siege to the Palestinian coastal town of Arsuf, some legal questions were sent to the jurists of Damascus. One of these questions was about whether a person affiliated with the Shāfiʿī school could seek out the less stringent rules (*yatatabbaʿ al-rukhaṣ*) of the other schools.[3] Al-Suyūṭī also told a similar account according to which Baybars himself had asked the Shāfiʿī chief judge Tāj al-Dīn b. Bint al-Aʿazz about a similar issue, which the latter refused to deal with. When Baybars then asked him to appoint a Ḥanafī judge to adjudicate on the matter, he refused once again.[4] The chief judge's refusal to cooperate with Baybars was cited by some scholars such as Sherman A. Jackson as the main motivation behind the sultan's decision to appoint four chief judges.[5]

Yossef Rapoport found the explanations surrounding the relationship between Baybars and the Shāfiʿī chief judge to be insufficient. According to him, the expansion of the system to other towns in the Mamluk Empire and previous attempts to implement the policy going as far back as the Fatimids point to deeper institutional concerns. He concluded that the four chief judgeships were meant to introduce flexibility into an increasingly rigid system of *taqlīd*.[6] Baybars's decision in 1265 should, therefore, be seen as the first successful attempt at the institutionalization of pragmatic eclecticism to facilitate legal transactions. Before we look at the court records, it is important to discuss first the question of who chooses the forum of adjudication in court.

Selecting the Forum of Adjudication

As we saw above, the question of who had the agency to exercise pragmatic eclecticism depended on whether subjects of the law were dealing with a judge or a mufti, which itself depended somewhat on whether the issue was related to ritual matters or to cases of litigation and notarization. Legal subjects generally had more power in choosing a mufti, although such freedom was sometimes subject to geographical limitations, such as when there was an absence of muftis representing particular schools in some localities. Sometimes the practice of the laity was faced with stiff opposition from jurists as we saw above in the accounts of both Ibn ʿArabī and al-Shaʿrānī. In the court context, however, the laity's agency was somewhat more limited because there were other players with a stake in court transactions. Rulers sometimes imposed certain school doctrines that they perceived to advance state interests.[7] The Mālikī school was used strategically by the state in the Mamluk period to crack down on heresy.[8]

Some legal theorists give the impression that judges were primarily responsible for selecting the appropriate forum of adjudication. In multiple legal works, judges were allowed to refer cases to other schools in order to facilitate a legal transaction not permitted in their school, as we saw in chapter 2. Taqī al-Dīn al-Subkī (d. 756/1355), for instance, would allow a Shāfiʿī judge to refer a case involving written documents to a Mālikī judge because the Shāfiʿī school does not accept written documents as evidence.

He also accepted the referral of a case involving the establishment of an endowment to oneself (*waqf ʿalā al-nafs*), which is considered invalid in the Ḥanafī school, to a Ḥanbalī judge who would permit this transaction under his school.[9] Similarly, the Ḥanafī jurist Muḥammad b. Shihāb b. Yūsuf al-Kurdārī (d. 827/1423) permitted a judge to refer cases that cannot be adjudicated according to the Ḥanafī school to other schools.[10] This discourse, as we shall see in the remainder of this chapter, is confirmed by court practice.[11]

There is also evidence that some jurists operated on the assumption that subjects of the law had a role in selecting the school used to adjudicate their cases, either as a result of their own affiliation with a particular school or owing to pragmatic considerations related to the outcome of adjudication. Al-Qarāfī (d. 682/1283), writing in the early Mamluk period, discussed the monopoly of the Shāfiʿī chief judge of his day. He complained bitterly about muftis who would respond according to their own views, even when the petitioner had made clear that his school affiliation was different from theirs. In his view, the school affiliation of the person bringing the case should decide the forum of adjudication. Thus, he averred, a member of the Mālikī school is not bound by what al-Shāfiʿī says, nor vice versa.[12] In most cases, the state did not have a stake in the legal outcome and the process was one of cooperation between the judge and the legal subject, unless there was a conflict of interest among the litigants.[13] That legal subjects had the power to choose the forum of adjudication is clear in discussions of which litigant has the priority of forum in the case of a conflict of interest among litigants. Al-Asyūṭī (d. 880/1475) included this question in *Jawāhir al-ʿUqūd wa-Muʿīn al-Quḍāh wa'l-Muwaqqiʿīn wa'l-Shuhūd* (The pearls of contracts: Manual for judges, scribes, and witnesses). He used hypothetical cases to guide legal practitioners. In the following case of a custody dispute, he discussed the differences among the schools as follows:

> [Hind] came to the court of [ʿAmr], presided over by the Shāfiʿī, Ḥanafī, or Ḥanbalī judge. She brought her divorced husband [Zayd], claiming that he had contracted a valid marriage with her according to the Sharīʿa. They consummated the marriage, bearing a child named [ʿUthmān] in

> his house, whose age is such and such. He then concluded a final divorce dated such and such. She received her said child after the divorce according to the legal (*shar'ī*) right to custody. She was then married to a different man named [Khālid], which waived her right to custody of her said child. His father took him away from her after she married the said person. But she was then divorced irrevocably from the said husband. During the present claim, she has no husband and therefore is entitled to custody of her said child after taking him from his father's custody. But he has refused to give him back to her . . . The judge rules that she should obtain custody of her said child.[14]

According to al-Asyūṭī, the woman could only have obtained a favorable decision granting her custody of the child by referring to the Shāfi'ī, Ḥanafī, or Ḥanbalī schools. Al-Asyūṭī provides another version in which the husband preempted her by bringing the same case before a Mālikī judge. In this instance, al-Asyūṭī reasoned that the ruling would be in favor of the husband.[15] The underlying assumption in al-Asyūṭī's discourse is that either parent is free to choose the judge who would be most likely to grant him or her custody. But faced with this conflict of interest over the forum of adjudication, he would give priority in selecting the judge to the litigant who files the claim first.[16]

Al-Asyūṭī again described the conflict of interest among litigants with a hypothetical example of a maternal sister, a paternal sister, and a maternal aunt. The three of them are in dispute over the custody of their nephew or niece, whose mother had passed away. Each school would grant custody to a different relative:

> The judge asked the three aforementioned women. The paternal sister said, "I have priority to take custody under the Shāfi'ī and Ḥanbalī schools." The aunt said, "I have priority under the Mālikī school." The maternal sister said, "I have priority under the school of Abū Ḥanīfa."[17]

Legal subjects were assumed by jurists to have the freedom to choose their forum of adjudication. This assumption is palpable in an ongoing debate in the literature on which of the litigating parties has the prerogative to choose forum where the outcome entails a material difference for each. Within the Ḥanafī school, Abū Ḥanīfa's two disciples disagreed about how the selection of forum can be resolved when there is a conflict of interest. Abū Yūsuf left the choice up to the plaintiff (*al-ṭālib*), whereas Muḥammad al-Shaybānī gave it to the defendant (*al-maṭlūb*), which became the dominant opinion within the Ḥanafī school.[18] This view was further solidified through a sultanic decree, stipulating that judges were no longer allowed to hear cases if the defendant had not agreed to the choice of forum.[19] This view was not shared by the Egyptian Mālikī jurist al-Dasūqī (d. 1230/1815), who reasoned that it should be up to the plaintiff and not the defendant to select the judge before whom the case is heard. If both are plaintiffs, then the person who gets to the judge first has priority. If they arrive at the same time, the judge is required to draw lots.[20]

Regardless of how precedence was granted, what is clear is that forum selection was mostly the prerogative of legal subjects, not imposed by the state (as is the case in modern legal practice). In cases of notarization in which there was no conflict of interest, subjects of the law selected their judges freely, sometimes with the help of the legal establishment, which would direct them toward the school best suited for their transaction.

The above case, in which each party would have different claims under the different schools, explains the evolution of the professional *ikhtilāf* manuals (discussed in chapter 2) as a tool for navigating through school differences. The simple practical language, free of legal disputation and focused on the dominant opinion in each school, appears to be intended for quick reference in cases where a clearly advantageous legal outcome could be gained by bringing the case before the judge of a specific school. The simplified, practical approach to school differences seen in the *ikhtilāf* manuals provided basic knowledge of the differences among schools,[21] suggesting that individuals may have approached legal experts for advice as to which judge would give them the outcome they were seeking.

As we will see in the cases below, the Ottoman *ikhtilāf* manuals would prove particularly useful in the notarization of contracts, as most Sunnī schools placed arduous restrictions on many types of contracts. Muftis, who as we saw practiced *tatabbu' al-rukhaṣ*, assisted legal subjects in navigating legal pluralism both within their own schools and across school boundaries.[22] Let us now turn to the court records to verify the claims made by jurists about court practice.

The Sample

In this section, I provide a praxeological account that I hope will complement the picture that has thus far emerged out of juristic discourse on the nature of pragmatic eclecticism in legal practice. I examine a thousand and one cases from four court registers to demonstrate that the theoretical debates raging during the seventeenth and eighteenth centuries and the references to practice provide an accurate reflection of actual court transactions. In order to answer the question of whether *tatabbuʿ al-rukhaṣ* was used in the courtroom, I explore the motivation behind the consistent use of certain schools for specific types of cases. The figure below shows that Ḥanafism was the dominant school in terms of the pure number of cases brought before Ḥanafī judges. When non-Ḥanafī schools were utilized, there was almost always a clear pragmatic motivation that is sometimes explicitly stated in the court records. The sheer number of instances in which pragmatic decisions were made suggests that pragmatic eclecticism was practiced in the courts on a large scale.

If we add to this picture what we know of the demographics of school affiliation in Egypt, it becomes clear that there was a disproportionate use of some schools, which can only be explained by pragmatic considerations. Although it is difficult to determine the exact proportion of followers for each of the different schools, what is indisputable is that Mālikism and Shāfiʿism had historically maintained a large presence in Egypt, which was an important center for the development of these two schools. The majority of Muslims in Egypt have traditionally adhered to either the Shāfiʿī school (especially in Lower Egypt) or the Mālikī school (especially in Upper Egypt).[23] This is also clear from the Fatimid experiment with the appointment of four chief judges prior to the Mamluk period.[24]

Out of the four Sunnī schools, Ḥanbalism had the least following in Egypt, while Ḥanafism did not gain ground until the Ottoman conquest in 1517. The majority of the Ottoman elite adhered to Ḥanafism, which was the official school of the empire. The more ambitious members of the

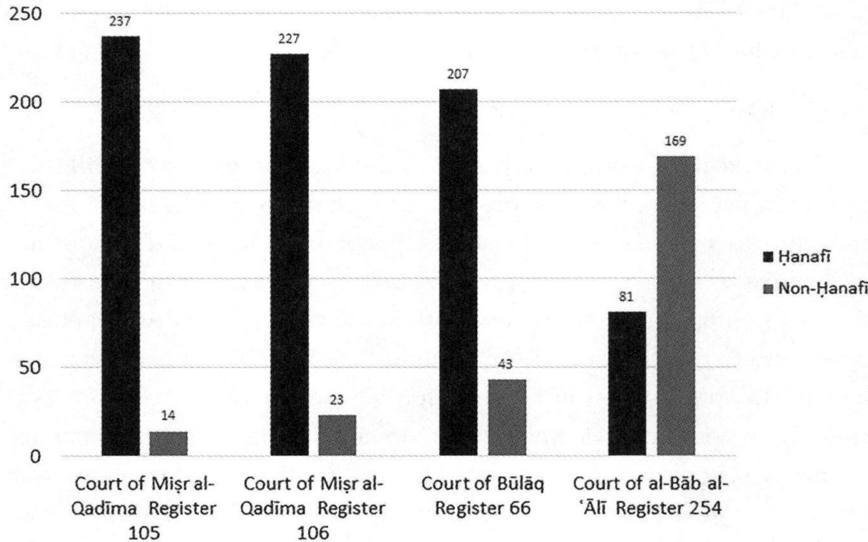

2. School distribution of 1,001 cases from premodern Egyptian courts. Courtesy of Margaret Gilligan, 2014.

Egyptian scholarly establishment were motivated to change their affiliation by the prospects of official positions and financial gain. There is, however, no evidence to suggest that Ḥanafism managed to unseat Shāfiʿism and Mālikism as the dominant schools in Egypt in the Ottoman period.[25]

My procedure in the following discussion is as follows. I discuss the rationale for the selection of the courts. I then examine some patterns behind the cases observed in the sample, such as the establishment and sale of endowments, agreements to long rental contracts on endowments (*waqf*), loans with interest, establishment of ownership based on physical control, conditional sales, and marriage, as well as dower and maintenance disputes. In addition to determining whether *tatabbuʿ al-rukhaṣ* was used in the Ottoman period, such an examination of the types and proportions of cases that were adjudicated by Ḥanafī versus non-Ḥanafī judges will shed light on the level of predictability that was established within the pluralistic legal system and on the complementary relationship that emerged among the four schools. After discussing *tatabbuʿ al-rukhaṣ*, I shall turn to the examination of cases in which *talfīq* was used. Unlike *tatabbu' al-rukhaṣ*, the examination of *talfīq* will not require exploring the frequency of the case types and patterns, since it is practiced within the same transaction and thus stands out on its own without the need to tease it out through the patterns observed in the courtroom.

The sample of court records was obtained from the National Archives of Egypt (Dār al-Wathā'iq al-Qawmiyya) in 2009 and 2010. The time span for these cases stretches from 1091/1680 to 1172/1758.[26] These courts, chosen to provide a diverse sample, include a variety of types of transactions, with parties to the transactions coming from a broad range of socioeconomic backgrounds. The court of Miṣr al-Qadīma, for instance, represents a diverse Cairo neighborhood court, with a larger concentration of Christians as well as artisans and other working classes. The types of cases brought before this court included a large percentage of personal status law transactions involving marriages, divorces, cases of remarriage following a divorce, and custody disputes, representing 29 percent of the total sample.[27] This representation is contrasted with only 11 percent of the sample from Bulaq and 2 percent of the sample from al-Bāb al-'Ālī.

The court of Bulaq was located in the commercial Nile port city of Bulaq, just outside Ottoman Cairo and in the contemporary period a neighborhood of Cairo. Certain types of commercial transactions were more prevalent in this court owing to the role of this city as a commercial center, especially in the grain trade.[28] The third court surveyed, that of al-Bāb al-'Ālī, attracted members of the Mamluk-Ottoman military elite, partly because there was a minimum monetary amount set for the transactions brought to this court.[29] According to official decrees, any transaction with a value higher than five hundred silver pieces had to be brought to al-Bāb al-'Ālī.[30] Furthermore, al-Bāb al-'Ālī enjoyed special jurisdiction over cases of sale or long rental contracts on endowments (*awqāf*), as stated in the following decree:

> None of the scribes of the two Qisma courts and other courts in Miṣr al-Maḥrūsa, Bulaq and Miṣr al-Qadīma should handle cases designated for the al-Bāb al-'Ālī Court such as the sale of endowments (*istibdālāt*),[31] long rental contracts of endowments, and the addition of conditions to endowment deeds, sale of agricultural land and sale of salaries, rental

> contracts on agricultural land and other forbidden things that have become customary. These issues should only be handled by the scribes of al-Bāb [al-ʿĀlī].[32]

As early as the seventeenth century, stern official decrees threatened judges of neighborhood courts with dismissal if they heard these types of cases outside of al-Bāb al-ʿĀlī.[33] The restriction of cases involving sales and long rental contracts on *waqf* properties to the main court was owing to the belief that such cases were particularly susceptible to corruption.[34] The perception was that al-Bāb al-ʿĀlī was better controlled and more easily overseen by the legal establishment, as it was presided over by the chief judge himself, making it less likely for any corruption to occur.[35] One of the main functions of this court was to ensure that endowments were not sold or rented for long periods of time (exceeding three years) without verifying that the conditions required under the school in question were met. This requirement is why we frequently see references in the court records to the "legal justification" (*al-musawwigh al-sharʿī*) for a sale or long rental contract on endowment properties.[36]

Because of the special jurisdiction of al-Bāb al-ʿĀlī, the number of cases related to endowments amounts to 176, which represents 70 percent of the total sample from this court. Of these, 168 deal with the sale or long rent of endowments. It should be noted that the Ḥanafī school forbids or restricts some transactions related to endowments that the Mālikīs and Ḥanbalīs allow. The Ḥanbalī school thus monopolized the notarization of long rental contracts on *waqf* properties since these contracts were not permitted by the Ḥanafīs of that period. Another frequent transaction that also became a specialty of the Ḥanbalīs of the period under examination was the alienation of endowments known as *istibdāl*, literally meaning "exchange."[37] While Ḥanafī judges handled 93 percent of the cases brought to Miṣr al-Qadīma and 82 percent of the cases brought to Bulaq, judges of al-Bāb al-ʿĀlī had a majority of cases brought to non-Ḥanafī judges. Most of these cases were handled by Ḥanbalī and Mālikī judges, whose schools set fewer restrictions on the sale of endowments. Out of 250 cases, a total of 117 cases were brought before Ḥanbalī judges (47 percent) and 48 before Mālikī judges (19 percent), while only 81 cases were presided over by Ḥanafī judges (32 percent), and four cases represented instances of *talfīq* (2 percent).[38]

Case Patterns

Based on the following case patterns, I contend that Ḥanafism enjoyed a default status, meaning that most cases were brought before Ḥanafī judges unless there was a pragmatic reason to refer them to other schools. The importance of the default status of Ḥanafism was that it provided much-needed predictability to the legal system despite the quadruple pluralism of the Sunnī schools, as well as a certain level of flexibility with the provision of less stringent opinions from the other schools. This was not what was envisioned by the initial Ottoman policy of Ḥanafization implemented soon after the conquest of Egypt. Yet while this policy failed to completely do away with Mamluk legal pluralism, it did succeed in giving Ḥanafism an official status, making it the default *madhhab* on issues in which no pragmatic considerations necessitated a non-Ḥanafī school.[39]

Although it is clear that the motivation behind the selection of a non-Ḥanafī judge was most often pragmatic, it cannot be ruled out that legal subjects undergoing litigation were in some cases affiliated with the school that offered the least stringent opinion. This type of coincidence, which might occur in the sample, is unlikely to distort the findings, especially if we locate case types in which there was a disproportionate use of one school above the others. This becomes more evident when the favored school for a given case type is compared to its actual proportion of followers in Egypt, such as Ḥanbalism, for example, which had far fewer followers than the other schools. In what follows, I discuss some of the case patterns observed in the sample to show the motivation behind the choice of different forums of adjudication in the courts.

Exchange and Sale of Endowments (istibdāl)

The Islamic institution of endowments (*waqf*) controlled many properties since it was a chief means of protecting assets from taxation and confiscation. Establishing an endowment was also sometimes used as a means of distributing inheritance shares beyond the prescriptions of

Islamic law. All four schools of Islamic law forbade the outright sale of an endowment once a commitment was made to "freeze" it in the form of a *waqf*, which implies that it cannot be "unfrozen" for a *waqf* was meant to be held in perpetuity. Certain legal strategies were nonetheless used to dispose of these properties. There were some types of transactions related to endowments that were restricted under the Ḥanafī school, especially by later jurists who were attempting to crack down on the perceived corruption in the endowment system.

The most permissive with regard to *istibdāl* was the Ḥanbalī school, but within the Ḥanafī tradition there was much disagreement over endowments. Some Ḥanafī jurists such as the famous al-Ṭarsūsī (d. 758/1357) completely forbade *istibdāl*. Others forbade it unless the endower expressly stipulated that the overseer was allowed to exercise *istibdāl* in the endowment deed.[40] Even some of those who permitted it in the Ḥanafī school laid stringent conditions on the kinds of properties purchased in exchange for the endowment property. The prominent Ḥanafī jurist Ibn Nujaym, for instance, placed the stringent condition that the exchange must occur within the same transaction and that no money should change hands.[41] This decision was meant to avoid the practice of selling endowments without replacing them with other productive properties, which was common practice in his time. These Ḥanafī restrictions advocated by Ibn Nujaym, whose works played an important role in the standardization of Ḥanafī law in the Ottoman period, explain the selection of the Ḥanbalī school for this kind of transaction in the records that we have examined, given its fewer restrictions on cases of *istibdāl* for money (*bi'l-darāhim wa'l-danānīr*).[42]

The greater flexibility of Ḥanbalism toward *istibdāl*, coupled with a desire for consistency on the part of the judicial establishment, resulted in a complete monopoly over this type of case, despite the dearth of Ḥanbalīs in Egypt. Out of the 1001 cases that I have examined, there were only eighty-five cases of *istibdāl*, all of which were brought to Ḥanbalī judges. It was also clear that money changed hands in these transactions, with no evidence of new properties replacing the sold endowments.[43] The terms for buying and selling were even sometimes used interchangeably with the term *istibdāl*, as in one case in which a certain Ḥājj Aḥmad in 1172/1758 "bought and exchanged" (*ishtarā wa istabdala*) a clothes factory from its "seller and exchanger" (*bāyiʿihi wa mubaddilih*).[44] The formula "bought and exchanged" here referred to a single financial transaction consisting of a sale, with no replacement of the sold endowment. The two terms were lexical couplets that were presented as synonyms in this type of transaction.

One of the common themes that emerge in discussions of endowments, whether in the Mamluk or the Ottoman periods, is that widespread corruption led to a loss of endowments, which was perceived to be a sign of the weakness of the state. *Istibdāl* was often cited as a sign of this institutional, economic, and political decline.[45] I contend that these negative characterizations of *istibdāl* and the endowment institution in general are sometimes unwarranted, especially with regard to family endowments (*al-waqf al-ahlī*), which were designed for relatives rather than charities. Given that the motivation behind locking up properties in the case of a family endowment was to protect them against confiscation, the use of *istibdāl* to sell such properties should not be portrayed as a sign of "corruption" since the original intentions behind founding such properties was achieved. In this case, the founder's intention was not to give away her property to charity but rather to pass it on to her family to dispose of as they wished after her passing.[46]

In most of the endowment cases that I have seen in the court records, the founder typically established the endowment for herself and her descendants. This was often followed by a clause at the end that assigned the revenue of the endowment to a mosque on the condition that all the endower's descendants die out. The following record offers one such typical example:

> The founder establishes the endowment for his children, then for the children of his children, then for their offspring . . . till they are all deceased. If all are deceased, then the revenue of this endowment shall be spent on the needs of the mosques of the great teacher, al-Imām al-Shāfiʿī and ʿAmr b. al-ʿĀṣ.[47]

The utilization of the Ḥanbalī school, with its fewer restrictions on the sale of an endowment, enabled the beneficiaries to treat endowments as private properties, matching the intention of the endower. Through *istibdāl*, derelict and frozen endowment properties were brought back into the private economy, which was made possible by crossing school boundaries. Thus, with the vast majority of endowment cases being of the noncharitable type, laying the blame for the economic and commercial ails of Middle Eastern societies on the endowment system needs to be revised.[48]

Given this observation, there needs to be a rethinking of the role that the endowment system played in the stagnation of the means of production, since the majority of endowment properties functioned for all intents and purposes as private properties. While establishing endowments was a way to protect private properties, *istibdāl* was a creative way to liquidate these assets. The ability of the Ottoman legal system to facilitate such sales illustrates a functional flexibility in the legal system that was able to free up the means of production since the objects of these endowments were often factories, real estate, and agricultural lands. Because of the vast number of properties frozen within the endowment system, enabling their sale by eclectically selecting less stringent juristic views was an economic necessity. According to Afaf Lufti al-Sayyid Marsot, one-fifth of all arable land in Egypt at the end of the eighteenth century was locked in endowments.[49]

Sale of Endowments (isqāṭ)

Another procedure used to effectively sell an endowment is *isqāṭ*, which literally means "dropping" an endowment and usually refers to the sale of the usufruct (*manfa'a*) of a property. The Ḥanafī school did not permit the sale of an abstract right in exchange for a sum of money,[50] while the Mālikī school permitted such a sale and so it was used in almost all such cases. The main difference between *istibdāl* and *isqāṭ* is that the intention of the *istibdāl* transaction, technically speaking, is to replace the property in question with another that is productive owing to its state of dereliction. In *isqāṭ*, the right to use the property is exchanged for money without transferring the ownership of its corpus (*'ayn*). In the case of *istibdāl*, the judge had to verify that there is a justification for the exchange, to wit, that the property in question is no longer productive and needs to be replaced, but such justification was not required for *isqāṭ*. Hence, many cases of *istibdāl* contain a statement indicating that the property is in ruins.

In the records of Miṣr al-Qadīma, there are fifteen cases of *isqāṭ*, all of which were brought to Mālikī judges. Likewise, all twenty-four cases of *isqāṭ* in Bulaq were brought to Mālikī judges,[51] while all thirty-four cases of *isqāṭ* in al-Bāb al-ʿĀlī were also brought to Mālikī judges.[52] The unusual consistency of such cases clearly suggests that loyalty to one's school affiliation is a less likely explanation than pragmatic eclecticism.

Establishing an Endowment on the Usufruct of a Property

Out of a total of twenty-three cases concerning the establishment of endowments in the three courts I have examined, fifteen were brought before Ḥanafī judges, three before Ḥanbalī judges, two before Mālikī judges, and three involved multiple judges. The fifteen cases brought to Ḥanafī judges did not involve a transaction that was prohibited in the Ḥanafī school such as the establishment of an endowment on the usufruct (*manfaʿa*) of a place. The three cases brought before Ḥanbalī judges established endowments on the usufruct (*manfaʿa*) of properties, rather than the corpus (*ʿayn*), that is, the transfer of ownership of the actual property. In other words, if someone establishes an endowment on a house (*ʿayn*), the actual building will no longer be owned by her, but it will belong to the endowment beneficiaries. However, if she only establishes an endowment deed on the usufruct of the house, the building will still be owned by the founder, but its rent will belong to the endowment beneficiaries. Since establishing an endowment that does not include the physical property was generally forbidden in the Ḥanafī school,[53] these transactions were typically brought before Ḥanbalī judges. The reason for the choice of a Ḥanbalī judge was often provided in the text of the cases, as in the following example:

> The venerable Amīr Muḥammad, the Jurbajī of the Mustaḥfiẓān Corps . . . established an endowment on the usufruct of the entire place located in the protected Cairo . . . According to him [the Ḥanbalī judge], it is valid to establish an endowment on the usufruct of a place, even if the designated beneficiary is oneself. This is the view of the erudite scholar Shaykh ʿAlāʾ al-Dīn [al-Mardāwī al-Ḥanbalī] . . . issued on the twentieth of Dhū al-Qiʿda al-Ḥarām, in the year 1140.[54]

In one of the two cases brought before Mālikī judges, it is clear that the selection of the Mālikī school was also based on pragmatic grounds because the endowment was established on the rent of a place, rather than on its ownership, a transaction that was prohibited by the Ḥanafīs of the period but allowed by the Mālikīs.[55] However, there seems to be no pragmatic reason for the selection of the Mālikī judge in the second case.[56] It is possible that in this case, the legal subjects demanded the Mālikī school because they shared that school affiliation, but there is no way to verify this surmise. The remaining three cases involve multiple schools, and will be discussed below in the section on *talfīq*.

Rental Contracts on Endowment Properties

Long-term leases (exceeding three years) on endowment properties,[57] prohibited by the majority of Ḥanafīs in Egypt, were frequently brought before Ḥanbalī judges. Out of the 1001 cases examined in this study, one finds sixty-four cases of leases, thirty-six of which are long-term leases on an endowment and twenty-one are short-term.[58] All thirty-six of the long-term leases on endowment properties were brought before Ḥanbalī judges. In the following example, a case was originally brought to a Ḥanafī judge, who referred it to his Ḥanbalī deputy because it was not a transaction that could be conducted under Ḥanafī law:

> After the revered permission, our master, the greatest of the Shaykhs of Islam and the king of the great scholars . . . sent a letter to his deputy in the venerated judgeship in the aforementioned court, our master and leader the great Shaykh and Imām . . . the Ḥanbalī *shar'ī* judge to deal with what is mentioned below.[59]

While it is clear why the Ḥanbalī school was appealed to for long-term leases on endowment properties, it is not as clear why some short-term leases were also brought before Ḥanbalī judges. Out of twenty-one short-term leases, seventeen were handled by Ḥanafī judges and four by Ḥanbalī judges. Since the Ḥanafī school permits short-term leases, why were these four cases not brought before Ḥanafī judges as well? A closer examination of Ḥanbalī doctrine reveals that this choice must have been motivated by the renters' interests. The Ḥanbalīs provide certain benefits to renters, including a prohibition against increasing the rental value, as well as honoring the rental contract in the case of the death of one of the parties to the contract,[60] the dominant view in Ḥanafī law being that the death of the lessor nullifies the rental contract.[61] In addition, the favorable legal view motivating the selection of the Ḥanbalī judge is highlighted in all of these cases. The following case is one such example:

> According to him [the Ḥanbalī judge], it is forbidden to accept increase in rent and the rental contract is not terminated at the death of the two parties to the contract, the death of one of them, or the transfer of the oversight of the endowment.[62]

This issue of rental contracts was also studied by Abdul Karim Rafeq, who examined the first extant court register from sixteenth-century Damascus. Out of fifty short rental contracts, Ḥanafī judges authorized forty-six contracts, whereas only three contracts were authorized by Ḥanbalī judges and one by a Shāfiʿī judge. According to Rafeq, when the Ottoman administration was strong in the sixteenth century, Ḥanafī judges were in a position to enforce Ḥanafī law, which stipulates that agricultural endowment properties may only be leased for a maximum of three years and commercial properties for a maximum of one year.[63]

Rafeq argues that the ability of Ḥanafī judges to control 92 percent of the cases, which had to be short-term leases according to Ḥanafī doctrine, was a sign of the Ottoman Empire's strength at that point. He then compares his findings to the situation that obtained in the eighteenth century, when the number of long-term leases increased, with the majority being authorized by Shāfiʿī and Ḥanbalī judges. In one sample from 1189/1775–76, Rafeq finds thirty-seven long-term leases of more than three years, four of which were authorized by Ḥanafī judges in violation of the school's own rules. He explains this discrepancy between the results from the early and late Ottoman periods in terms of a shift in the power of the central government and the ability of officially appointed Ḥanafī judges to enforce Ḥanafī doctrine.[64] The situation in Egypt seems to have been quite different from that in Damascus, with Egyptian courts having a higher level of consistency in the utilization of the schools along pragmatic lines. A larger Syrian study of legal pluralism would be needed to better assess the roles played by the different schools in the legal process.

Loans with Interest

There were five cases of loans in the sample. Two of them were simple loans that were brought to Ḥanafī judges,[65] while the remaining three were brought before Shāfiʿī judges.[66] These three cases contained provisions for a votive offering (*nadhr*), which clearly indicated a stipulation of interest on the loans. Loans with interest are forbidden in all four schools of Islamic jurisprudence. However, legal strategies that allowed individuals to effectively loan money with the promise of paying interest did exist in the courts. In one example, after a loan contract was drawn, the person receiving the loan promised to pay a certain monthly donation to the lender, so long as he had not yet repaid the loan. This donation was to be terminated upon repayment of the loan.[67] This is a clear case of legal stratagems (*ḥiyal*), in which legal tricks were used to circumvent the Islamic ban on interest. There is no explicit mention of the reasons for selecting a Shāfiʿī judge in the cases in question. Some Ḥanafī and Shāfiʿī jurists permit the use of *ḥiyal*, whereas the Mālikīs and Ḥanbalīs are generally staunchly opposed to them,[68] but this still does not explain why these cases were not adjudicated under the official Ḥanafī school. Perhaps the answer to this question lies in one essential difference between Ḥanafism and Shāfiʿīsm. Under Shāfiʿī law, one cannot retract a promise of a gift made, whereas the Ḥanafīs permit such retractions.[69] The technical legal transaction in question here is in the form of a donation, and thus the votive offering (*nadhr*) follows the rules concerning gifts. This finding fits in well with Haim Gerber's study of Bursa and Istanbul in the seventeenth and eighteenth centuries in which he showed that contracts with interest were quite common. The contracts simply avoided the formal terminology of interest (*ribā*), using instead terms like *murābaḥa* (sale of a property at cost-plus profit).[70]

Establishing Ownership Based on Physical Control

The Shāfiʿī school assigns significant rights to the individual in physical possession of a property, described as *dhū al-yadd* (the one who controls the property), giving him or her uncontested control over it in the absence of any further proofs of ownership. Out of the 1001 cases examined in this study, there are six cases in which ownership is established on the basis of physical possession. Five of the cases were brought before Shāfiʿī judges because the Shāfiʿīs grant the most rights in the case of an uncontested possession of a property,[71] while only one case was brought before a Mālikī judge.[72] In one of the Shāfiʿī cases, a prominent merchant named ʿUmar had previously purchased a *waqf* property consisting of a piece of land with a decrepit building on it. In order to establish his ownership, he brought two witnesses to testify that he renovated the building with his own money and had physically controlled it (*waḍaʿa yadahu*) since then, having "dealt with the land in the same way owners would deal with their property, without any partner, challenger or disputer."[73] Based upon this, the record continues:

> He [the judge] ruled according to the school of the great Imām Abū ʿAbd Allāh M. al-Shāfiʿī b. Idrīs, may God be pleased with him, according to which, he must respect [the rights deriving from] his building, his right to dispose of it, and the priority to him (*taqdīm*) [in ownership] as the one who controls it (*dhū al-yadd*).[74]

Conditional Sale

Out of 1001 cases examined, there were 251 cases of sale of non-*waqf* items. All but five of these cases were regular, unconditional sales. The five conditional sale transactions were all brought before Mālikī judges, whereas all the unconditional sales were brought before Ḥanafī judges.[75] In the conditional sales, a Mālikī judge was needed to validate the contracts, as this type of transaction is not allowed under the Ḥanafī school.[76] The condition stipulated in these sales was that the buyer would reverse the sale and return the sold item to the seller if she or he redeemed it for the original sale price within a specified period of time, as in the following example:

> The aforementioned al-Zaynī Muṣṭafā bought . . . from his seller the aforementioned woman, Raḥma, . . . the entire building located in Miṣr al-Qadīma in the quarter of Ḥammām Ḥumdār . . . Then the pride of

his peers, the aforementioned al-Zaynī Muṣṭafā testified on himself that if the seller, Ḥājja Raḥma, returns to him the entire aforementioned amount, which is 18,800 silver *niṣf* or an equivalent amount of money from this date until the month of Rajab of this year, the sale will be considered null and void.[77]

Marriage

Out of the sample examined, there were eighty-three cases of marriage notarization, only two of which were brought before non-Ḥanafī judges and the rest before Ḥanafī judges. These two exceptions were handled by Mālikī judges, but there is no indication that this was arranged for pragmatic reasons. One of the two cases involved a marriage between minors.[78] The other concerned a marriage in which the dower was to be paid over ten years.[79] Both these types of cases would have been permitted by the Ḥanafī school.[80] There are even many similar cases of marriage of minors officiated by Ḥanafī judges in this sample.[81] The motivation behind the choice of the Mālikī school in these two examples remains obscure.[82] It is possible that it was a question of school affiliation and nothing more. But even if this were true, these cases represent the exception rather than the rule in the practices of Egyptian courts in the seventeenth and eighteenth centuries. Pragmatic considerations can explain the overwhelming majority of non-Ḥanafī adjudication.

Dowers and Spousal Maintenance

In case 203, presented to the court of Miṣr al-Qadīma, a woman by the name of Fāṭima claimed that her husband, Shaykh Yūsuf, a spice vendor in the quarter of Ḥumdār in Miṣr al-Qadīma, had not yet paid her dower or clothing allowance (*kiswa*).[83] The husband was then asked to pay thirty piasters in dower and thirty piasters in allowance, but he refused. The wife asked the Shāfiʿī judge to jail him, which he did. The choice of the Shāfiʿī school here must have been motivated by the school's strict rules against husbands. For instance, it allows the dissolution of a marriage after only three days of nonpayment, in contrast to the Ḥanafī school, whose grounds for divorce are far less accommodating of the wife. In fact, a Ḥanafī judge would not grant her a divorce on the grounds of nonpayment at all.[84]

In addition to the distribution of cases reflecting pragmatic patterns, further compelling evidence can be found in cases in which the same individual goes to the Ḥanafī judge for one transaction and then to a non-Ḥanafī judge for another. This pattern can be found, for instance, in documents 139 and 143. According to document 139, a man by the name of Shalabī b. Salāma al-Qahwajī sold half a building to his wife, Kūhiyya, a transaction that was brought before a Ḥanafī judge. In document 143, he sold Kūhiyya his rights to the long-term lease of an endowment property on which the building was constructed (*ḥikr*). This second case was brought before a Mālikī judge because it is related to the sale of the usufruct of an endowment property (*isqāṭ manfaʿa*).[85] In another case, a certain Yūsuf al-Jurbajī brought four transactions before the court, three before Ḥanafī judges, and one before a Ḥanbalī judge.[86] The motivation behind his choice of a Ḥanbalī judge for this one case was that the contract exceeded three years.[87]

Ḥanafism's Semi-Default Status

To summarize, Ḥanafism seems to have attained what may be termed a "semi-default status," in which most legal transactions were brought to Ḥanafī judges unless there was a pragmatic reason to resort to another school's doctrine. While there were exceptions to this general trend, the figures in the present sample strongly support this conclusion. This situation was the outcome of the official status of Ḥanafism and the control of Ottoman Ḥanafī judges over the judicial system in Egypt. This outcome is reflected in official Ottoman writings, in which Ḥanafism is always mentioned first, followed by the Mālikī, Shāfiʿī, and Ḥanbalī schools, in this order.[88] This official status did not reflect a complete break with Mamluk legal pluralism, but, rather, it meant the creation of a clear hierarchy. For the majority of cases, in which there were no significant differences among the schools, a Ḥanafī judge usually presided. The judges of other schools would be called upon solely when there was a particular desired outcome that was only allowed in that school.

Although the Ḥanbalī school had the least number of followers in Egypt,[89] its judges handled 117 cases out of 250 in the sample taken from the court of al-Bāb al-ʿĀlī. This number of cases was more than any other, including the Ḥanafī school, whose judges handled only eighty-one cases in this court. A further forty-six cases went before Mālikī judges, while not a single case from this sample was brought before a Shāfiʿī judge, despite the historical importance of this school in Egypt. This finding further supports the argument that the distribution of cases was not based on the status of the school or the affiliation of the legal subject, but on pragmatic considerations.

Out of the total of 1001 for all three courts, 752 (75 percent) of the cases were brought before Ḥanafī judges. The default status of the Ḥanafī school becomes clearest when we exclude the court of al-Bāb al-ʿĀlī (with its special jurisdiction, which made it more friendly toward Ḥanbalism and Mālikism): out of a total of 751 cases in three registers from the courts of Miṣr al-Qadīma and Bulaq, 672 cases were brought before Ḥanafī judges (89 percent) and 79 to non-Ḥanafī judges (11 percent).

Having given up on their earlier Ḥanafization endeavor, the Ottomans gave a semi-default status to the Ḥanafī school to ensure that Ḥanafī jurists were paid more than their non-Ḥanafī counterparts, since judges received a percentage of the value of legal transactions. In this manner, a financial as well as a power hierarchy was created in the Egyptian judiciary. At the top of this hierarchy sat the chief judge, an important authority in the Ottoman bureaucracy, whose income was guaranteed to be the highest within the Egyptian legal system, given that most high-value cases had to be brought before the court over which he presided, namely al-Bāb al-ʿĀlī.

In most of the non-Ḥanafī cases, there is a clear legal outcome for which the other schools were selected. Evidence for this conclusion can be found in the conventions of the court records themselves. In some cases in which a non-Ḥanafī judge is chosen, we sometimes see a phrase preceding the non-Ḥanafī ruling emphasizing its legality in the school of the presiding judge. This is particularly common in cases of *talfīq*, discussed in the next section. We even sometimes come across jurists who submit cases before a judge from a school different from their own, clearly for pragmatic reasons. The esteemed Ḥanafī jurist Badr al-Dīn Ḥasan al-Maqdisī, who was a professor at al-Azhar and also a mufti, leased an endowment property for seventy-one years, which would not be permitted under his school. His school affiliation and his work as a jurisconsult did not dissuade him from using a Ḥanbalī judge to facilitate his transaction.[90]

It is through such cases that we are able to obtain an insight into the Egyptian Ottoman legal system, which, as we saw, facilitated the alienation of endowment properties, thus bringing dilapidated factories and real estate back into the economic cycle. This result was all achieved through the utilization of Sunnī legal pluralism within the context of *taqlīd*. This approach is a far cry from that of the Ottoman judicial authorities in the immediate aftermath of the conquest of Egypt, when the Ottomans were rigorously engaged in a process of institutional Ḥanafization. Using the same sample, I now turn to the court practice of *talfīq*.

Talfīq in Court Practice

As we saw in chapters 2 and 3, juristic attitudes toward *tatabbuʿ al-rukhaṣ* started changing as early as the thirteenth century, leading to a semantic split whereby *talfīq* was singled out as the only type of *tatabbuʿ al-rukhaṣ* that was forbidden. The institutional practice of *tatabbuʿ al-rukhaṣ*, which goes at least as far back as Sultan Baybars, continued to operate within the Ottoman legal system, but with a clear positioning of Ḥanafism at the top of the legal hierarchy. In the Ottoman period, we witness a heated discussion over the validity of *talfīq* in the juristic discourse of the sixteenth through eighteenth centuries, with clear references to its practice. The strong opposition among jurists toward this legal strategy has led some historians to believe that the application of *talfīq* in the modern period was an innovative practice with no precedent in Islamic law prior to the nineteenth century (see chapter 3). Contrary to this widely held view, the following sample of cases from the National Archives of Egypt (Dār al-Wathāʾiq) in Cairo illustrates the way in which *talfīq* was practiced in the seventeenth and eighteenth centuries.

The norm in Islamic judicial proceedings is that there is only one judge presiding over each case. When more than one judge adjudicates the same case, I contend, it is usually done for the sake of *talfīq*, in which different judges are called upon to validate different aspects of the same case. Often the motivation behind having more than one judge is explicitly stated in the court records. There were no cases in this sample in which the juristic opinions of different schools were combined in a legal transaction by a single judge.

There is another form of *talfīq* discussed in juristic discourse in which two judgments from different schools are rendered over a period of time on the same object of a transaction, such as the same building or the same piece of land. This type of *talfīq*, known as diachronic *talfīq* as explained in chapter 3, was commonly used in the management of endowment properties. One example of diachronic *talfīq* deals with an individual who initially rented an endowment property in 1035/1626 under the authority of a Ḥanbalī judge, and then in 1039/1630 the same piece of property was subject to a sale of *isqāṭ* under a Mālikī judge.[91] This type of *talfīq* was very common in the court records.[92] Often we find a transaction concluded by one judge with a reference to a previous transaction under a different judge dealing with the same property. Conversely, transactions performed under more than one judge in the same document were much less common, and to them I now turn.

Two or More Judges on the Bench

There is evidence in the court records that Ḥanafī judges would refer a case to judges from the other schools when the Ḥanafī school did not allow for the notarization of a particular transaction. This referral took the form of a permission granted to a non-Ḥanafī judge to take over the case. This permission came at the beginning of a number of cases notarized by non-Ḥanafī judges, with a line that reads, "After the honorable permission (*ba'da al-idhn*) of our master to the Ḥanbalī judge . . ."[93] In other examples, this authorization was at the end of the document, with a line that typically reads as follows: "He ruled according to this, a *shar'ī* ruling, validated and executed [*muttaṣilan wa munaffadhan*] by our master the Ḥanafī *shar'ī* judge."[94]

The word *ittiṣāl*, the active participle of one of the terms figuring in the previous example of authorization, was often used at the beginning of some cases to mean "authorized by," as in the phrase "before the Mālikī and the *ittiṣāl* [authorization] of the Ḥanafī."[95] This was one way in which the presence and permission of the Ḥanafī judge was felt. In other cases, we see another form of Ḥanafī engagement in the transactions conducted by other judges, expressed in the records through apposition. In this case, the name of the Ḥanafī judge would come after the presiding judge, without either of them serving a *talfīq* function, as explained later in the section on the presence of multiple judges in the absence of *talfīq*.

Out of the 1001 cases examined in this study, only twenty-one cases were brought before more than one judge.[96] Seven of these cases came from Miṣr al-Qadīma (Register 105), ten from Bulaq (Register 66), and four from al-Bāb al-ʿĀlī (Register 254). There were no cases with multiple judges in Register 106 of Miṣr al-Qadīma. In some of the twenty-one cases, we see a clear utilization of *talfīq*, where two judges were chosen to validate different parts of a contract, as was the case in document 199 in Miṣr al-Qadīma, dated 1092/1681.[97] According to this document, a woman by the name of Riḍā brought her case for marriage annulment before a Shāfiʿī judge, followed by a marriage in the same contract adjudicated by a Ḥanafī judge. The selection of two different judges in the same document was motivated by a triple divorce that had taken place prior to this transaction, which would have normally necessitated her marrying another man (*muḥallil*) prior to remarrying her first husband.[98] In order to avoid this unwanted intermediate marriage, Riḍā utilized a legal procedure that is only permitted in the Shāfiʿī school. She annulled the marriage by claiming that the two witnesses to the original marriage contract did not possess the necessary qualities for probity (*ʿadāla*). According to the Shāfiʿīs, evidence that the witnesses to a marriage contract lack probity renders it null and void (*bāṭil*).[99]

The Shāfiʿī view was, therefore, advantageous because if the original marriage was considered void based on this technicality, then the same couple may be remarried without a *muḥallil*. Furthermore, although the original marriage was considered invalid, the parties were not subject to punishment for fornication owing to the presence of an exculpating "doubt" (*shubha*) since they truly, albeit erroneously, believed themselves to be married. For the same reason, the paternity of any children Riḍā bore from the marriage could still be attributed to the husband. The case record carefully documents not only the component of the case that has been approved by the Shāfiʿī judge, but makes the effort of citing the specific legal authority from within the school that permits it, namely, "Shaykh al-Islām al-Ramlī [Shams al-Dīn] in his *Sharḥ al-Minhāj* in the section on marriage."[100] Because of the ingenuity of this case as well as the seeming banality with which it was treated, it is fair to argue that such pragmatic eclecticism was the norm in this court. The case reads as follows:

> Before the Shāfiʿī *sharʿī* judge, the woman Riḍā, daughter of Shaykh Suwaydān al-Ḥarīrī al-Rifāʿī, claimed that her husband, the respected Muḥammad son of al-Ḥājj Muḥammad son of the late Khalīl . . . that before this date, he had married her with two witnesses who did not have legal probity . . . No *sharʿī* judge, who views the above-mentioned contract as valid, ruled that it is. The aforementioned husband consummated the marriage. He then divorced her from his matrimonial authority thrice before this date . . . Then she left [the court] and returned with the respected Shiḥādha, son of the late Ghannām al-Aḥmadī, and Manṣūr b. ʿĀmir al-Qahwajī in the above-mentioned quarter and asked them to bear witness [to her claim] . . . Each one of them testified in front of our master the *sharʿī* judge . . . The aforementioned claimant asked our master the *sharʿī* judge, referred to above, to do what is required by the honorable Sharīʿa in this regard. He responded by ruling that she deserves the *mithl* dower from her husband,[101] the defendant mentioned above, and annulled the marriage contract . . . and that the sexual intercourse that resulted from this [marriage] is based on *shubha* (doubt) and is sufficient grounds for proving paternity . . . following the rules of his illustrious school, which include the validity of renewing the marriage contract with her without the need for a *muḥallil,* as stated by Shaykh al-Islām al-Ramlī [Shams al-Dīn] in his *Sharḥ al-Minhāj* in the section on marriage . . . And in front of the Ḥanafī judge, the aforementioned honorable Muḥammad paid his fiancée, the aforementioned woman Riḍā a dower . . . The aforementioned wife accepted that from him to herself in the *sharʿī* fashion and the marriage became effective . . . on the fourteenth of Shaʿbān al-Muḥarram, one of the months of the year 1092.[102]

Had the case stopped with the annulment of the marriage, this would have been an example of simple *tatabbu' al-rukhaṣ*.[103] But Riḍā did not have a guardian to contract her marriage. Had a guardian been present, who would have accepted the dower on her behalf, the case could have proceeded with the same judge.[104] But while marriage without a guardian is not allowed under the Shāfi'ī school, the Ḥanafīs permit it. The Shāfi'ī judge who had helped her avoid marrying a *muḥallil* could not have officiated over her remarriage in the absence of a legal guardian (*walī*). Thus the contract as a whole required the use of *talfīq*, though it was spread over two legal transactions. In the second transaction, which completed the contract, the Ḥanafī judge presided over the new marriage in which Riḍā represented herself, as evidenced by the statement "the aforementioned wife accepted that from him to herself."[105] Although both transactions were inscribed on the same document, this is an instance of diachronic rather than synchronic *talfīq*.[106]

The Social Status of the Legal Subjects. The above example of *talfīq* was an innovative way to solve a serious problem for Riḍā and her husband. The question, however, arises as to whether this type of solution was available only to those among elite classes, who had the resources to manipulate the system and who as we saw in chapter 1 were the catalyst behind the institutionalization of pragmatic eclecticism in the Mamluk period and its continuation under the Ottomans. The text of the case suggests that the participants were regular people. This is made clear mainly by the absence of honorary titles. Riḍā is merely a woman or "*ḥurma*." Her father is "Shaykh Muḥammad," and her husband is "the respected Muḥammad." Her husband's father is "al-Ḥājj Muḥammad, son of the late Khalīl." The first witness is referred to as Qahwajī, namely, a waiter in a coffee shop, while the other is the "respected Shiḥādha" and his father "the late Aḥmadī." They clearly did not belong to the military elite, the high *'ulamā'*, the *ashrāf*, or the merchant class. By drawing up the document in this manner, Riḍā and her husband in fact went against an Ottoman sultanic order issued in the sixteenth century that forbade a woman to contract her own marriage without a legal guardian. This decree was supported by the fatwa collection of none other than the famous Shaykh al-Islām Ebu's-su'ud, which went against the view of Abū Ḥanīfa.[107] To get a sense of the subaltern social status of Riḍā and her family, compare the references made to them with the following:

> Before our master, the deputy Ḥanafī judge, in the presence of our master, the Shaykh, the imam, the gallant scholar, the descendant of scholars, the leader of great scholars, the best of teachers and researchers, Shihāb al-Dīn Aḥmad, son of our late master Shaykh Sālim al-Mālikī, one of the people of knowledge and teaching at al-Azhar Mosque.[108]

The utilization of pragmatic eclecticism was thus not restricted to the powerful military elite, the *'ulamā'*, or the merchant classes. It was equally practiced by the subalterns, issuing from different socioeconomic strata. While these subaltern masses may not have been the primary target behind the institutionalization of pragmatic eclecticism, they were certainly happy beneficiaries of this practice. They were able to take advantage of the diversity of legal opinions to facilitate their transactions in Ottoman courts. As we saw above, Yūsuf al-Jurbaji, who was an *amīr* in the 'Azbān military corps, selected different judges according to his legal needs.[109] Similarly, Riḍā, a simple woman, used the system to resolve her family problem.

Divorce for Compensation (khul'). In addition to the above case of annulment and subsequent remarriage, we can also see a clear pragmatic motivation behind the choice of multiple judges in some cases of divorce. Of the 1001 cases surveyed, nine were simple repudiations (*ṭalāq*), and thirty-three were divorces offered in exchange for a compensation to be paid to the husband, known as *khul'*. All nine cases of repudiation were brought before Ḥanafī judges, although one case had a Shāfi'ī judge alongside the presiding Ḥanafī counterpart.[110]

In twenty-nine out of the thirty-three cases of *khul'*, the presiding judges were Ḥanafīs. In these cases, the wife waived her right to the portion of the dower that would have remained hers had the husband initiated the repudiation with no compensation, but she retained her rights to any previously unpaid maintenance. In the remaining four cases of *khul'*, we found that *talfīq* was used to deny women some of their financial rights. Mālikī and Ḥanafī rules were combined in such cases to achieve this outcome, as can be seen in the following case:

> Each one of them [the two judges] ruled according to what is acceptable to him [his school], which for our master the Ḥanafī *shar'ī* judge means losing any past *kiswa* [clothing allowance] and *nafaqa* [maintenance] owed to the mentioned divorcée and to our master the aforementioned Mālikī *shar'ī* judge means losing the *mut'a*[111] and *'idda*[112] money owed to the aforementioned divorcée, even if it were established.[113]

According to the Shāfi'īs, Mālikīs, and Ḥanbalīs, previous maintenance is not immediately waived because of a *khul'*.[114] On the other hand, according to the Ḥanafīs, while a *khul'* does not entail waiving any future financial rights, such as any maintenance during the *'idda* period, this is not the case with earlier debts.[115] Thus the wife in the above case lost her right to any unpaid *kiswa* (clothing allowance) and *nafaqa* (maintenance) from past years of marriage according to the Ḥanafī school. By employing *talfīq*, she was similarly denied her rights to any *mut'a* and *'idda* money on the authority of the Mālikī judge. In this case, the Ḥanafī school would not have waived her right to the *'idda* and *mut'a* money, since such payments had not been established at the time of the contract.[116]

The description of *talfīq* is explicit in these cases, containing the repetition of whole phrases and formulaic language, which suggests that the use of *talfīq* to obtain this particular result in cases of *khul'* was common.[117] The reason behind the use of *talfīq* in the above four cases could have been the result of an agreement made between the respective spouses since, according to the consensus of the four schools, the husband's consent is essential to the validity of a *khul'* divorce. This might explain a woman's willingness to agree to some less than ideal conditions. Despite their agreement to forgo their financial rights, the decision can still be considered pragmatic in the sense that these women, in the face of a recalcitrant husband refusing to agree to a *khul'*, likely preferred losing greater financial rights to staying in an unhappy marriage.

It is possible that the husband had not paid past maintenance and wished to have that explicitly stated along with the Mālikī exclusions as a precaution to avoid future litigation. Regardless of the motivation or how this case came to be negotiated behind closed doors, the utilization of *talfīq* is explicit in the document. This consistency is somewhat similar to the employment of Sunnī legal pluralism in the legal reforms of the nineteenth and twentieth centuries as we shall see in chapter 6.

The Establishment of Endowments. Three cases, which deal with the establishment of a *waqf*, represent instances of *talfīq*.[118] One case begins by recording a peculiar debate between the founder of the endowment and the guardian (*mutawallī*) appointed by the court, ostensibly in response to the desire of the former to repeal the endowment. The founder brought his case to a Ḥanafī judge since Abū Ḥanīfa's view is that endowments are not binding. The guardian challenged the founder, saying that, in the view of Abū Yūsuf and al-Shaybānī, an endowment is binding as soon as it is issued. The Ḥanafī judge, for his part, decided that an endowment established by an individual for herself or himself is binding upon the authority of the most prominent disciples of the Ḥanafī school,[119] and that the *waqf* cannot be repealed.[120] Thus the document confirms the validity of the endowment and rejects the founder's request, but the reestablishment of the endowment required the presence of a Ḥanbalī judge, since it contained an endowment of the usufruct of a property, which is not permitted by the Ḥanafīs.[121]

In a similar example from the same court, we see not only the Ḥanafī and Ḥanbalī judges presiding over the case but the Mālikī judge as well. The Ḥanbalī is present to validate the endowment of the usufruct of the place (*khulū*), whereas the Mālikī is needed to validate the endowment of a rent, both of which consist of an endowment of the usufruct of a place, which is not permitted by the Ḥanafīs. The document states that according to the Ḥanafī judge, the endowment is valid, and "the endowment of the usufruct of a place and its rent are validated by the Mālikī and Ḥanbalī judges."[122]

The third case comes from the court of al-Bāb al-ʿĀlī, in which we find Mālikī and Ḥanbalī judges being selected to validate different aspects of the case. The reasons for bringing these transactions before the two judges are explicitly stated in the document: "according to the Ḥanbalī judge, establishing an endowment to oneself on the usufruct of a place or its ownership is permitted, and according to the Mālikī judge, it is allowed to change and amend the endowment deed."[123]

Two or More Judges with No Evidence of Talfīq

As we saw above, we are able to explain the selection of multiple judges in most cases along pragmatic lines, but sometimes that choice may not be clearly ascertained. In most such cases, a non-Ḥanafī judge is needed to validate a transaction that is not permitted by the Ḥanafīs, with the Ḥanafī judge continuing to preside over the case alongside the non-Ḥanafī, as can be seen in the statement "before the Mālikī and Ḥanafī judges" (*ladā al-Mālikī wa'l-Ḥanafī*). This mention is different from cases in which the Ḥanafī judge simply authorizes a non-Ḥanafī judge to take over a case.

Four cases involve the sale of a usufruct of a *waqf* that were brought to Mālikī and Ḥanafī judges sitting in tandem, when they could easily have been brought before the Mālikī alone.[124] The presence of a Ḥanafī judge in these instances does not seem to serve any functional purpose, except perhaps to signal that permission had been granted to the other judge to hear the case. Similarly, there are two cases involving manumission that were brought before Mālikī and Ḥanafī judges in Bulaq that could have also been brought to either judge alone.[125] Also from Bulaq, there is a case in which a conditional sale was brought before Ḥanafī and Mālikī judges, though the Mālikī judge could have presided over the transaction alone since the Mālikīs permit this sale.[126]

In al-Bāb al-ʿĀlī, we find two cases in which two judges presided, but no evidence of *talfīq* can be found. In one example, the Mālikī judge was needed to alter the terms of an endowment in a procedure in which Mālikī judges were typically utilized, but the Ḥanafī judge, whose presence was not required, was also seen presiding over the case.[127] In another case involving the establishment of an endowment, Mālikī and Ḥanbalī judges presided. It is not clear from the case why both were needed since the transaction could have been performed by either judge.[128]

While all cases of *talfīq* required the presence of more than one judge since no single judge was allowed to rule in accordance with more than one school, the presence of other judges did not always signify an example of *talfīq*. Since in most of these cases, the seemingly redundant judge happens to be Ḥanafī, it is conceivable that this was yet another manner in which the Ḥanafī establishment authorized transactions performed by non-Ḥanafī judges. We saw earlier, three other ways in which such an authorization was granted. Thus the use of multiple judges with the formula of placing two judges on the bench (evoked in expressions such as "*ladā al-Ḥanafī wa'l-Mālikī*") cannot always be interpreted as instances of *talfīq*.

Collaboration between Ottoman Legal Authorities and Azharī Scholars

Pragmatic eclecticism seems to have been accepted not only by the legal establishment but also by the high *'ulamā'*. The court records are full of prestigious religious scholars attending court cases and sitting with the judge. Sometimes they acted as witnesses, but they frequently seem to have served no particular legal function; nor did they appear to provide any legal advice to the judge. Many professors at al-Azhar also attended these cases, such as the prominent Shaykh Badr al-Dīn al-Maqdisī al-Ḥanafī[129] and Shaykh Salīm al-Mālikī.[130] Their presence was sometimes clearly honorary.[131]

There are also examples of such prominent scholars being themselves parties to these types of contracts. For instance, the Shāfi'ī 'Aṭiyya al-Ajhūrī established an endowment under the Mālikī school, with his Shāfi'ī affiliation not constituting a hurdle in that transaction.[132] Jurists' wide acceptance of these practices and their attendance at the court in some formal or informal capacity reemphasizes what we argued in chapters 2 and 3 concerning the shift in attitudes in juristic discourse toward a wider acceptance of pragmatic eclecticism.

As we have seen thus far, the legal system constituted an interaction between three main players: local jurists, Ottoman judges, and non-jurists, whether belonging to elite or subaltern groups. Not only did the interaction of a woman like Riḍā with the law get cited by jurists to justify acceptance of pragmatic eclecticism as we saw in chapters 2 and 3, but also local jurists created a unique legal system that surpassed the Ḥanafī Ottoman center in its pluralistic pragmatism. This development must be read against the backdrop of resistance to Ottoman rule in the early years of the conquest in which jurists such as al-Sha'rānī (discussed in chapter

2) privileged local Mamluk legal pluralism over Ottoman Ḥanafization. It should also be read against the persistent Mamluk efforts to regain independence from the Ottomans. These efforts were successful under the Mamluk ʿAlī Bey al-Kabīr, who ruled over a de facto independent state.[133]

Conclusion

Pragmatic eclecticism was widely practiced in Egyptian Ottoman courts of the seventeenth and eighteenth centuries, with Ḥanafism gaining a semi-default status with regard to court transactions. As such, cases brought before non-Ḥanafī judges can usually be explained in terms of pragmatic eclecticism whether in the form of *tatabbuʿ al-rukhaṣ* or *talfīq*. Legal subjects, regardless of their social status, were able to take advantage of these legal strategies. The widespread utilization of pragmatic eclecticism coupled with the fact that it was not exclusively monopolized by elite groups indicates that it was part of the legal mainstream. We have seen examples of subalterns using both *tatabbuʿ al-rukhaṣ* and *talfīq* to serve their diverse legal needs. One notable example is the case of Riḍā and her husband, who were able to avoid a permanent dissolution of their marriage through the employment of *talfīq*.

The flexibility of the legal system brought about by the Ottoman embracement of legal pluralism—despite their initial experimentation with Ḥanafization—served some important social and economic functions. Just as Riḍā and her husband were able to solve an undesirable family problem, owners of real estate could also circumvent some of the restrictive rules on the sale of endowment properties. They were able to sell the endowment properties that they had established primarily to protect from the encroachment of the military elite, to prevent their breakup through inheritance, or to avoid paying taxes on them. This allowed these endowments to function much like privately owned properties. The prevalence of these cases belies the notion that the endowment system led to the stagnation of the means of production.[134] Legal pluralism was used to reinforce private ownership and to bring these otherwise frozen properties back into the market.

The legal pluralism that existed within the Egyptian legal system was utilized for multiple purposes. We saw the legal establishment allowing a woman to give herself in marriage, thus contradicting not only the legal opinions of famous Ottoman muftis such as Ebu's-su'ud but also sultanic decrees. When it came to *khul'* divorce, we also saw examples in which women were denied some financial rights also through the exploitation of existing legal pluralism. It appears that this was perhaps the only legal means by which these women were able to obtain a divorce from their recalcitrant husbands.

As we have seen in chapters 2 and 3, the pressure created by the practice of the courts on juristic discourse challenged legal inertia and eventually led to a shift in the juristic views in the early years of the thirteenth century, which contradicted the juristic opposition to pragmatic eclecticism characteristic of the formative and classical periods. Ottoman jurists, who participated in the debate over pragmatic eclecticism, attended many court cases in which these practices were taking place, and some of them were themselves parties to some of these transactions. It was therefore not surprising to see the Shāfi'ī jurist 'Aṭiyya al-Ajhūrī establish an endowment under the Mālikī school.[135]

Just as nineteenth-century legal pluralism allowed for the creation of a predictable legal code, the legal pluralism of the seventeenth and eighteenth centuries was already being implemented in a consistent fashion. In the seventeenth and eighteenth centuries, one could predict, for instance, that the *istibdāl* sale of an endowment would be brought before Ḥanbalī judges and that *isqāṭ* sales would most likely be brought before Mālikī judges. Furthermore, all conditional sales would be brought before Mālikī judges, whereas all nonconditional sales would be brought before Ḥanafī judges. In this sense, Sunnī legal pluralism functioned as a de facto unwritten legal code. The process was efficient and often predictable. Unless there was litigation, it was clear to all the parties of the legal process where a particular case would go. In the case of litigation, certain mechanisms for establishing priority for the choice of forum were put in place.

Needless to say, this predictability belies Max Weber's notion of *Kadijustiz*. For Weber, a truly just legal system should be stable, predictable, grounded in general rules, and impersonal. According to him, Islamic law, or *Kadijustiz*, was characterized by arbitrariness and irrationality. Its judgments were ad hoc and not derived from general principles. The judge ruled in every case on the basis of personal, particularistic grounds. There was, he added, a clear disconnect between this arbitrary practice and the universal legal code of Islam, which he categorized as a rational law. It was a one-judge system, in which the decisions of the judge could not be appealed. Unlike the practice of courts, Islamic substantive law itself was rational and consistent, but rigid, which explains why judges had to depart from it.[136] I hope that the stunning balance between the two legal ideals of stability and flexibility of Egyptian courts shown in the previous chapters has put such claims to rest, and offered a new critique of Weber's assumption of the gap between theory and practice in Islamic law.

In chapter 5, I demonstrate that there was no shift in juristic attitudes toward pragmatic eclecticism in the nineteenth and twentieth centuries, as the same Ottoman authorities and arguments were invoked. I also address the confusion among some historians over the distinction between *tatabbuʿ al-rukhaṣ* and *talfīq* and how this confusion might have been responsible for the virtual absence of any substantive discussion of *tatabbuʿ al-rukhaṣ* in Islamic legal historiography.

PART FOUR

The Sweep of Modernity

5

Juristic Discourse on Pragmatic Eclecticism in Modern Egypt

WE HAVE THUS FAR SEEN that juristic opposition to *tatabbu' al-rukhaṣ* characteristic of the formative period was challenged in the thirteenth century, with *talfīq* emerging as a foil for *tatabbu' al-rukhaṣ*. After the failure of the Ottoman policy of Ḥanafization in Egypt, both legal strategies were utilized in early modern Cairo and Bulaq. There was a dynamic dialogic interaction between juristic discourse and court practice, between the laity and legal authorities prior to the nineteenth century.

In this chapter, I discuss what happens after the eighteenth century, with the rise of the "legal reform" discourse associated with modernization. I discuss attitudes toward pragmatic eclecticism in the nineteenth and twentieth centuries to show that there was a sense of continuity in juristic discourse. I also examine different approaches to legal reform in the nineteenth and twentieth centuries to explore areas of continuity and discontinuity with the Ottoman period. The discussion of juristic discourse in this chapter will set the stage for the developments that were introduced to the legal system in the nineteenth and twentieth centuries, the topic of chapter 6.

Confusion over the Meaning of *Talfīq*

Before we start our discussion of juristic attitudes toward pragmatic eclecticism in the modern period, it may be helpful to resolve some of the confusion generated over the term "*talfīq*" in the secondary literature. The most accurate characterization of *talfīq* as a legal concept was outlined by Layish and Hallaq, whose description captures the way it was understood by pre-nineteenth-century jurists. They outlined the two types of *talfīq—diachronic and synchronic*—discussed above, albeit without discussing the parent term "*tatabbuʿ al-rukhaṣ*."[1] Other modern scholars have extended the meaning of *talfīq* to include any selection from other schools, which Muslim jurists identified as *tatabbuʿ al-rukhaṣ*. Coulson remarks on the confusion over the meaning of the term, but then ascribes the following two meanings to *talfīq*, the first of which is any departure from the doctrine of one's legal school in order to draw rulings from other Sunnī schools, whereas the second refers to *talfīq* proper. His first definition, which does not mention the term *tatabbuʿ al-rukhaṣ* at all, blurs the line between *talfīq* and *tatabbuʿ al-rukhaṣ*, allowing the former to encompass any form of school boundary-crossing.[2] Some of Coulson's examples of *talfīq* in modern Egyptian law are indeed instances of *tatabbuʿ al-rukhaṣ*[3] rather than *talfīq*.[4]

In a similar fashion, we find the absence of a distinction between *talfīq* and *tatabbuʿ al-rukhaṣ* in Albert Hourani's work, in which he refers to *talfīq* as the practice of permitting the judge to choose an interpretation of the law that best fits the circumstances, regardless of whether or not this interpretation comes from his own school. He states that ʿAbduh's *talfīq* involved a systematic comparison of all four schools of law.[5]

The same confusion obtains in Malcolm Kerr's discussion of *talfīq*. Although he accurately describes the two types of pragmatic eclecticism, he characterizes both of them as types of *talfīq*. One type is when "an individual might follow one school in marriage procedure, another in determining inheritance, and still another in establishing a *waqf* or in performing prayers," while the other is performed in a single process, as in the case of a marriage in which the Ḥanafī rules of consent and the Shāfiʿī rules on the dowry are observed in the same contract.[6] Pre-nineteenth-century jurists encountering such eclectically-selected laws in legal manuals would have seen them as representing simple eclecticism (*tatabbuʿ al-rukhaṣ*) rather than *talfīq*. The term *talfīq* had in fact not yet emerged in its technical sense when the following story was reported by al-Bayhaqī (d. 458/1066) in his *al-Sunan al-Kubrā*, in which a certain Ismāʿīl al-Qāḍī is quoted as having stated,

> I entered into the company of al-Muʿtaḍid who showed me a book in which the more lenient of the anomalous opinions of the scholars [*al-rukhaṣ min zalal al-ʿulamāʾ*] were collected. I said, "The author of this book is a heretic [*zindīq*]." Al-Muʿtaḍid said, "Are these traditions not authentic?" I said, "They are, but whoever permitted the drinking of inebriants, did not permit *mutʿa* marriage, and whoever permitted *mutʿa* marriage, did not permit the drinking of inebriants. Every scholar makes an error [*zalla*]. Those who collect the errors of scholars and follow them lose their faith." Then al-Muʿtaḍid ordered the book burned.[7]

The book referred to here, consisting apparently of the anomalous opinions of different scholars, was considered an example of *tatabbuʿ al-rukhaṣ* by pre-nineteenth-century jurists because although there were different, divergent opinions contained in the same book, each opinion belonged to only one scholar. This begs the question: did the two technical terms evolve in the writings of modern reformists such as ʿAbduh and Riḍā, leading to this new conflation of the two terms under the rubric of *talfīq*?

Did the Meaning of *Talfīq* Evolve in Modern Juristic Discourse?

Surprisingly, there is virtually no evidence in the juristic literature that I have examined from the nineteenth and twentieth centuries to suggest that Muslim jurists used the terms interchangeably. I was able to locate one potential exception in which the Syrian jurist Muḥammad Saʿīd al-Bānī (d. 1351/1933) made an ambiguous statement in his book *ʿUmdat al-Taḥqīq fi'l-Taqlīd wa'l-Talfīq*. He encouraged muftis to give fatwas to the laity that suit their abilities, "even if this led, in some cases, to combining schools (*tadākhul al-madhāhib*), which some call *talfīq*."[8] This reference could be read to refer to what was commonly referred to in the premodern period as *tatabbuʿ al-rukhaṣ*. The difference seems clear in the writings of other modern jurists such as Rashīd Riḍā. When sent the following fatwa, it was clear from Riḍā's response that he understood it to be an example of *talfīq*:

> I performed my ritual ablution, but before I prayed I had bleeding in my mouth that was more than my saliva. Thus my ritual ablution was

> invalidated because I follow the school of the great [al-aʿẓam] Imam [Abū Ḥanīfa]. I wanted to pray according to the school of al-Shāfiʿī because that does not invalidate the ablution in his school. Can I do that?[9]

In the above example, the Ḥanafī fatwa-seeker would be mixing Ḥanafī rules of ablution with Shāfiʿī rules in the same transaction, which constitutes a classic example of *talfīq*. Riḍā used the term *talfīq* in his response to the question.[10] When he was asked whether it is permitted for the layperson to follow each school in its *rukhaṣ* even if the motivation is a weak excuse, he described it as an example of *ittibāʿ al-rukhaṣ*.[11] In the above examples, one cannot sense any evolution in the meaning of these terms in Riḍā's discourse. Elsewhere, Riḍā even invoked a typical example of *talfīq* cited in pre-nineteenth-century sources, namely the endowment of moveable items to oneself. The Ḥanafī school allows the endowment of moveable items to oneself, which is a *talfīq* of Abū Yūsuf's opinion permitting the establishment of an endowment (*waqf*) to oneself, though not of moveable items, and Muḥammad al-Shaybānī's opinion allowing the endowment of moveable items but not to oneself.[12] Riḍā called for the establishment of a committee of jurists to compile a book of jurisprudence of legal transactions (*muʿāmalāt*), in which juristic views from the four Sunnī schools would be selected to achieve the public weal (*maṣlaḥa*). Being aware of the negative views among jurists toward *talfīq*, he was sure to reassure the reader that such a book would not necessarily involve *talfīq* (*wa-lā yalzamu min hādhā al-talfīq*).[13]

The meaning of *talfīq* does not seem to have undergone a semantic shift in more recent juristic discourse. For instance, writing in 1964, Mohammad Ahmad Farag El Sanhoori and Abdul-Rahman al-Qalhūd described *talfīq* as "eclecticism in the same transaction."[14] The contemporary scholar Muḥammad Ibrāhīm al-Ḥifnāwī understood *talfīq* as the construction of a new juristic view that no *mujtahid* holds (*al-ityānu bi-kayfiyyatin lā yaqūlu bihā mujtahidun*), evoking the manner in which pre-nineteenth-century jurists described the term.[15] He cited the playful verses of Abū Nawwās as an example of *talfīq*.

> The Iraqi had permitted date wine and its consumption
> Forbidding only constant partaking and inebriation

The one from Hijaz said the two drinks are but one
Because of their disagreement, we are permitted to drink wine[16]

In these verses, Abū Nawwās played on the differences between the Ḥanafī and the Shāfi'ī schools on *nabīdh* (date wine). Abū Ḥanīfa argued that it is not forbidden unless inebriation takes place, whereas al-Shāfi'ī insisted that *khamr* (grape wine) and *nabīdh* are the same, making both of them permissible for Abū Nawwās through what is effectively a *talfīq* of both opinions. Abū Nawwās combined the Ḥanafī opinion that date wine is permitted with the Shāfi'ī opinion that the rule for date wine is effectively the same as for grape wine, concluding that the consumption of both is thus permissible.

By drawing a distinction between *talfīq* and *tatabbu' al-rukhaṣ*, we are able to better trace the evolution of the pragmatic utilization of legal pluralism. After all, there are many jurists, especially in the late Ottoman period, who accepted *tatabbu' al-rukhaṣ* but remained unflinchingly opposed to *talfīq*. Disentangling these two terms is, thus, crucial for a more accurate understanding of the areas of continuity and discontinuity between the modern and premodern periods.

Modern Juristic Attitudes: Continuity or Discontinuity?

In this section, I focus on juristic attitudes toward pragmatic eclecticism from the early nineteenth century to the 1930s of the twentieth century, when three important figures in the debate over pragmatic eclecticism died, namely Muḥammad Sa'īd al-Bānī (d. 1351/1933) and Muḥammad Rashīd Riḍā (d. 1354/1935), and Muḥammad Bakhīt al-Muṭī'ī (d. 1354/1935). During this period, jurists were as divided about the status of *tatabbu' al-rukhaṣ* and *talfīq* as their Ottoman counterparts. Ottoman authorities continued to be invoked by jurists in the nineteenth and twentieth centuries. For instance, in his *Radd al-Muḥtār*, Ibn 'Ābidīn (d. 1252/1836) engaged the debate on pragmatic eclecticism to enable the wife of a missing husband (*zawjat al-mafqūd*) to remarry after four years of the latter's absence.[17] He cited the opinion of Shams al-Dīn al-Qahistānī (d. 953/1546) that in cases of *ḍarūra*, the judge is allowed to follow the Mālikī school. He also cited Sirāj al-Dīn 'Umar b. Ibrāhīm b. Nujaym al-Ḥanafī (d. 1005/1596) as stating that there was no need for a Ḥanafī judge to follow the opinion of a Mālikī since the issue could be brought before a Mālikī judge instead.[18]

The North African jurist ʿAbd al-Qādir al-Shafshawīnī, who died in Cairo in 1313/1895, was cited by Muḥammad Saʿīd al-Bānī as stating that changing schools for the pursuit of more lenient opinions (*rukhaṣ*) may be permitted in some transactions for people who do not have the strength to bear more stringent rulings, so long as this does not involve the use of *talfīq*. People who have the strength to do so (*ahl al-quwwa*), however, are not allowed to switch schools pragmatically. This reference to people's varying degrees of strength is reminiscent of the discourse of the *ḍarūra*-pragmatists discussed above, such as al-Subkī, al-Zarkashī, and al-Shaʿrānī. Although "strength" is not explained by the author, it usually refers to physical and spiritual fortitude, as we saw in chapter 2.[19] Thus a person is expected to follow her mufti in all transactions, but if that person has a weakness of heart or body, she may switch schools in pursuit of a less stringent juristic opinion, lest she should be dissuaded from following the law altogether. This strand of thought, which supported *tatabbuʿ al-rukhaṣ* but not *talfīq*, was quite common among Ottoman jurists.

Even jurists opposed to pragmatic eclecticism in the modern period were aware of the contested nature of this issue and presented it as subject to debate. For instance, despite his opposition to pragmatic eclecticism in both its complex and simple forms, the Shāfiʿī Abū Bakr b. al-Sayyid Muḥammad Shaṭā al-Dimyāṭī (d. 1310/1892) discussed the whole spectrum of views on the subject. He reiterated Shams al-Dīn al-Ramlī's (d. 1004/1595) opinion that those who practice *tatabbuʿ al-rukhaṣ* are committing an error (*ithm*), rather than a sin (*fisq*). Not only did al-Dimyāṭī acknowledge the view permitting *tatabbuʿ al-rukhaṣ* for people experiencing doubts, but also the view allowing it for people who merely follow their whims (*tashahhī*), so long as their choices do not lead to *talfīq*.[20]

The nineteenth-century Ḥanafī jurist Muḥammad al-ʿAbbasī al-Mahdī (d. 1315/1897), who held the position of Mufti of Egypt for no less than forty-nine years, was once asked for a fatwa regarding a layperson who had divorced his wife using the *ḥarām* formula.[21] This divorce formula is considered revocable under Shāfiʿī law if the husband had intended it to be revocable, whereas the Ḥanafīs consider it irrevocable regardless of the husband's intention. Thus, in such cases, the person in question had to resort to a Shāfiʿī mufti, who duly issued the desired fatwa, allowing the couple to resume their marriage. But the situation gets more complicated:

> Then he had an argument with her and divorced her using the triple-divorce formula. He had already sought a fatwa in the first instance of the *ḥarām* formula from someone who believes in the validity of their remarriage. Thus, is he not allowed to change his *taqlīd* [once again] in pursuit of fatwas because this has become his school in this transaction? Does this mean the *ṭalāq* is effective and his wife can no longer remain married to him until she has taken another husband?[22]

The husband was now faced with finding a mufti from yet another school that would help him avoid the irrevocability of his triple divorce. While al-Mahdī took no issue with the first act of switching to the Shāfiʿī school to avoid falling into an irrevocable divorce, he disallowed in this case a second change of school for purposes of expedience.[23] As he explained, "He is not permitted to change after this incident because this would constitute *talfīq*, which is not allowed, notwithstanding the permission of Ibn al-Humām and others."[24]

Al-Mahdī, on a different occasion, argued that the legal opinions issued by non-Ḥanafī muftis had no legal effect in Egypt because only Ḥanafī law was considered applicable.[25] While he allowed the exercise of *tatabbuʿ al-rukhaṣ* in principle, he also accepted the extra-Sharīʿa limitations imposed by the ruler favoring the Ḥanafī school, which was part of the Egyptian state policy of Ḥanafization stipulating that muftis were not allowed to issue non-Ḥanafī legal opinions (more on this in chapter 6). Despite his position on school boundary-crossing in pursuit of less stringent juristic views, al-Mahdī also rejected the legal opinions issued by Ḥanafīs if not based on authoritative Ḥanafī doctrine. According to him, such legal opinions were invalid and muftis who issued them should be subjected to discretionary punishments.[26]

One way the proponents of *tatabbuʿ al-rukhaṣ* in the modern period explained away the opposition of the early scholars was by focusing on the motivation behind its utilization. The Shāfiʿī jurist Aḥmad al-Ḥusaynī (d. 1332/1914) presented both sides of the debate and singled out as forbidden a legal selection motivated by frivolity (*talahhī*), such as in the case of a Ḥanafī who follows al-Shāfi'ī in granting permission to play chess or a Shāfi'ī who follows Abū Ḥanīfa in allowing the drinking of *muthallath*.[27] The reason for forbidding the selection of such opinions is that frivolity itself is forbidden. Accordingly, whether *tatabbu' al-rukhaṣ* may be considered permissible also depends on the issue in question. According to al-Ḥusaynī, Ibn Ḥanbal's general opposition to *tatabbu' al-rukhaṣ* only referred to this type.[28] He contended that the person who exercises *tatabbu' al-rukhaṣ* is not sinful. In the manner of the Ottoman jurists, he explained away Ibn Ḥazm's anti–*tatabbu' al-rukhaṣ* views by suggesting that Ibn Ḥazm was referring to pragmatic selections within the context of *ijtihād*, not *taqlīd*.[29] In addition to al-Ḥusaynī, the late nineteenth- and early twentieth-century jurist Muḥammad Munīb al-Hāshimī (d. 1334/1915) engaged the same pre-nineteenth-century authorities in his argument for the validity of both forms of pragmatic eclecticism, showing that there was a lack of consensus on the subject.[30]

In a fatwa issued in 1919 by Muḥammad Bakhīt al-Muṭī'ī (d. 1354/1935), Egypt's grand mufti from 1914 to 1920, *talfīq* was presented as subject to disagreement (*ikhtilāf*) among the jurists of all schools. He focused in his defense of *talfīq* on whether it is permissible to break the "multiple-opinion scholarly consensus" of a given period by arriving at a third opinion never before devised by the four schools, that is, the new *talfīqic* view. In such an instance, al-Muṭī'ī saw no harm in coming up with a third view, that is, a *talfīq* opinion blending the positions of two schools. For example, when a Mālikī performs his ritual ablution according to the Mālikī school, but washes only part of his head according to the Shāfi'ī school, this mixing of the two schools represents a third opinion, which al-Muṭī'ī permitted, so long as the resulting third view does not breach well-established regular consensus.[31] As we saw above, two Egyptian muftis had contradictory views on *talfīq*, which is evidence that the issue was never fully resolved in the modern period.

In 1923 the Syrian jurist Muḥammad Sa'īd al-Bānī (d. 1351/1933) published a book entitled *'Umdat al-Taḥqīq fi'l-Taqlīd wa'l-Talfīq*, in which he discussed various views on the two pragmatic strategies, drawing on al-Sha'rānī's *al-Mīzān*, discussed in chapter 2. He cited al-Sha'rānī's examples of contradictory Prophetic traditions, and his argument that they do not constitute contradictions because the Prophet treated people according to their abilities. In addition to citing al-Shaʿrānī's *al-Mīzān*, he also cited, to a lesser extent, Ibn ʿArabī's view. Al-Bānī's modern project was to search for a relativist approach to legal pluralism in which legal opinions are issued according to any of the four Sunnī schools in the manner that best caters to the needs of the fatwa-seeker in the modern context. After all, the argument goes, the laity are not bound by a single school because they do not understand the texts and rules of the different schools. According to him, the four schools represent different Sharīʿas that are equally valid.[32]

Al-Bānī's discourse closely resembles al-Shaʿrānī's *al-Mīzān*, a book that has clearly influenced his thinking on the topic. Al-Shaʿrānī's influence on nineteenth-century scholars has already been pointed out by Leila Hudson, who has demonstrated through a study of probate inventories (*tarikāt*) that he was the single most important author in nineteenth-century Damascus. His works appeared in 50 percent of the inventories she examined, with *al-Mīzān* being the most popular text.[33] This work, in which al-Shaʿrānī articulated most succinctly his theory of legal pluralism, was extremely influential in the nineteenth and twentieth centuries.[34]

In his discussion of *talfīq*, al-Bānī stated that jurists were divided over its status, and recommended following the view of later authorities (*al-muta'akhkhirīn*), who permitted it. Although he respected the earliest authorities (*al-salaf*), he admitted being put off by the views of Ibn Taymiyya and his student Ibn al-Qayyim, and being partial to the position of the *muta'akhkhirīn* on this matter. He invoked the same Ottoman arguments in support of *talfīq* such as the anecdote about al-Shāfiʿī's praying with hair on his clothes and Abū Yūsuf's being informed after praying that a rat had been found in the water with which he performed his ritual ablution.[35] Echoing some of the arguments of Ottoman jurists, he justified his argument for *talfīq* on the basis of social practice. According to him, a rejection of *talfīq* would be tantamount to judging the rituals and *muʿāmalāt* (legal transactions) of the laity as invalid since *talfīq* is already the norm in common practice. He explained that women use *talfīq* more than men, especially in their ritual ablutions in public bathrooms, where, for instance, they use combs made out of bone, and they reuse water that has already fallen into the basin to perform their ritual ablution, both being points of disagreement among the four schools.[36] As we saw in chapter 3, other jurists such as the Ḥanbalī Marʿī al-Karmī (d. 1033/1623) likewise invoked practice to justify the permission of *talfīq*.

Al-Bānī then quoted the Damascene jurist Jamāl al-Dīn al-Qāsimī (d. 1332/1914) as having said that the term *talfīq* was not used in the early period, and that it did not appear until the fifth century AH.[37] According to al-Qāsimī, there is nothing wrong with mixing different rulings in the same transaction or ritual. Thus he permitted the performance of major ritual ablution (*ightisāl*) with an amount of water measuring less than two jars, even with a drop of wine in it (in accordance with the Mālikī school), and without rubbing (in accordance with the Ḥanafī school). He also permitted washing only some of the hair during ritual ablution (in accordance with the Shāfiʿī school), even if the person were to have minor bleeding, and even if her or his prayer was performed according to the Ḥanafī school. Al-Qāsimī concluded, "Many jurists of all schools have permitted *talfīq*."[38]

Addressing modern legislation, al-Bānī supported the attempts coming out of Egypt in the early 1920s that were aimed at unifying the schools into one legal system (*tawḥīd al-madhāhib*), in which the most suitable opinions were to be selected from the four schools in matters of personal status.[39] He contended that this Egyptian experiment was aimed at the well-being (*maṣlaḥa*) of the family and society in general. He also suggested that if people of his time are faced with stricter rules, there is a danger that they would have no choice but to give up their Sharīʿa obligations altogether.[40] While this fear of abandoning the Sharīʿa is axiomatic of the Islamic encounter with modernity in the discourse of modernists, it was also a concern of pre-nineteenth-century jurists as we have seen.

Al-Bānī was even supportive of the *taqlīd* of juristic views falling outside the four schools when such a choice advanced the public weal. He believed that the political authority had no choice but to call on scholars to discover the laws that best suited the times, rejecting the opinions they abandon, lest there be chaos. He argued against those who refuse to go beyond the four schools in adapting the law to the spirit of the age (*rawḥ al-zamān*), and against those whom he called school fanatics (*muta'aṣṣib li-madhhab*), who only wished to abide by their own schools. According to him, choosing Islamic juristic opinions even from outside of the four schools would be better than resorting to man-made laws.[41]

The opposition to these ideas to which al-Bānī was referring would emerge some years later when the Egyptian government passed the Family Law of 1929. Three Azharī scholars coauthored a treatise that same year outlining their objections to the new law. They were opposed to the use of *talfīq* but not to *tatabbu' al-rukhaṣ*.[42] Among their chief complaints was that the new law relied on some weak opinions, as well as views issuing from outside the four schools. They cited as one example Article 25, which stipulates that a mother could retain custody of her children beyond the seven years prescribed by the Ḥanafī school. According to them, legislators supported their choices by invoking some peripheral views within Ḥanafism.[43]

Another provision to which the Azharī scholars objected was Article 6, according to which a repudiation (*ṭalāq*) counts as one even if the husband states a higher number. The legislators cited some of the Companions of the Prophet as holding this view, including 'Alī b. Abī Ṭālib, Ibn Mas'ūd, and 'Abd al-Raḥmān b. 'Awf. The Azharī scholars did not object to the utilization of *tatabbu' al-rukhaṣ* as such but rather to the legislators' avoidance of the four schools altogether by resorting directly to the opinions of the Companions.[44]

Nathan Brown has discussed the puzzling political silence toward the legal reforms of the nineteenth and twentieth centuries, and Noah Feldman wonders, "Why was the scholarly opposition to codification not more absolute?" In the case of the Ottoman Mecelle, Noah Feldman offers some reasons for this silence such as the fact that codifiers themselves were Muslim jurists and therefore they assumed that these changes would incorporate their expertise rather than supplant it.[45] Opposition to the modern codification of Islamic law was limited to a few critiques that did not reveal a strong sense of crisis on the part of scholars. This silence can partly be explained in terms of the presence of similar debates throughout the Ottoman period and the jurists' own perception of continuities with pre-nineteenth-century jurisprudence.[46]

Al-Bānī's position against the Azhar objectionists resembles the view of Muḥammad Rashīd Riḍā (d. 1354/1935), one of the leaders of the modernist movement.[47] Riḍā held a position similar to the *ḍarūra*-pragmatists, who permitted *tatabbu' al-rukhaṣ* only when there is a pressing need (*ḥāja*) to do so.[48] He pointed out that *tatabbu' al-rukhaṣ* is subject to disagreement among jurists, adding that many forbade it, even though it remained essential for *taqlīd*. He also evoked the differences of opinion over *talfīq* in his fatwas, siding with its supporters whose evidence he found more convincing.[49] He went so far as to suggest that *talfīq* is part and parcel of the Ḥanafī school, in which opinions sometimes consist of more than one jurist's opinion, and, therefore, it is essential for the practice of *taqlīd*.[50]

More recently, some of the opponents of *talfīq*, such as the contemporary Ḥanbalī jurist 'Abd al-'Azīz b. Ibrāhīm al-Dukhayyil, presented the issue as subject to disagreement among earlier jurists.[51] Al-Dukhayyil followed one of the dominant trends in the Ottoman period by forbidding *talfīq*, while allowing *tatabbu' al-rukhaṣ* when there is a need (*ḥaraj*). In the case of a need, people are permitted to search in the legal opinions of jurists for a more lenient resolution (*makhraj*) to their legal predicaments. He invoked the same premodern arguments and recounted commonly used anecdotes in their defense such as Abū Yūsuf's previously mentioned story of ritual ablution with water that has been rendered impure by a rat. He explained away Abū Yūsuf's *talfīq* by suggesting that he merely exercised a novel *ijtihād*, and that therefore this did not constitute an example of *talfīq*.[52] This argument is identical to the ones encountered in the juristic discourse of the Ottoman period.[53] Nineteenth- and twentieth-century scholars did not present the issue as a break with the juristic past, but as continuous with the Ottoman period. This discursive continuity was, however, contradicted with a rupture in juristic practice in the nineteenth century under the rule of Mehmed Ali, followed by a return to legal pluralism in the partial codification of personal status law, as I show in the next chapter.

The Rise of *Takhayyur*

Takhayyur and *takhyīr* come from the root *kh-y-r* (forms V and II respectively in Arabic morphology), which means "to select." The use of *tatabbu' al-rukhaṣ* is more often associated with crossing school boundaries, whereas *takhayyur* and *tarjīḥ* were mostly exercised within the same school. Prior to the nineteenth century, *takhayyur* and *takhyīr* were used interchangeably and in a nontechnical manner in instances where there was a conflict of evidence for the *mujtahid* or a conflict of fatwas for the person exercising *taqlīd* (*muqallid*). When unable to give preponderance (*tarjīḥ*) to one legal opinion over another through an assessment of evidence, the jurist could either suspend judgment (*tawaqquf*), or simply select one of the competing pieces of evidence or legal opinions. In the context of *taqlīd* as exercised by the laity and *muqallid* jurists, al-Ghazālī (d. 505/1111) explained that the motivation behind *takhayyur* may be based on wishes (*tamannī*) and whims (*tashahhī*) or on following the better jurist (*al-afḍal*), defined as the more knowledgeable or more pious. In this example, the choice of the better jurist is similar to exercising *tarjīḥ* for the layperson who cannot examine the evidence directly, but at least he or she can inquire about the more knowledgeable or more pious jurist.[54] The root *kh-y-r* was also used to refer to a situation in which a jurist, faced with two different pieces of evidence, had to exercise *tarjīḥ* to determine which was preponderant. Should the latter prove impossible, the jurist was allowed to choose (*takhayyur*), the assumption being that such a choice would not be influenced by any pragmatic considerations. For instance, the Shāfiʿī jurist al-Juwaynī used *takhyīr* to refer to an arbitrary choice that is based on neither evaluation of evidence nor utility.[55] Ibn al-Ṣalāḥ (d. 643/1245) too discussed the situation of being faced with more than one juristic opinion on the same issue. He used *takhayyur* in contradistinction to *tawaqquf*, namely, failing to give preponderance to one opinion over another. Again, unlike *tatabbuʿ al-rukhaṣ*, *takhayyur* does not explicitly refer to pragmatism as the motivation behind a given choice, but it is also sometimes used in contradistinction to *tarjīḥ*.[56]

The Mālikī jurist al-Qarāfī (d. 684/1283) employed the *kh-y-r* root in a similar fashion. He argued that when there are two pieces of evidence supporting two different directions for the *qibla*, one has to choose (*yatakhayyar*) one of them.[57] In this example, the choice is arbitrary since there is no pragmatic motivation behind choosing either direction. In fact, according to al-Qarāfī, the choice must be arbitrary in order to avoid unjustifiably privileging one piece of evidence over another. In the absence of any definitive evidence, he reasoned, both options ought to be treated as equal, which is implicit in the term *takhayyur.*[58] Taqī al-Dīn al-Subkī (d. 756/1355) likewise discussed the presence of two contradictory pieces of evidence, recommending *takhayyur* over *tawaqquf.*[59] The same applies to laypeople in the context of fatwa. Tāj al-Dīn al-Subkī (d. 771/1370) cited Ibn al-Ṣalāḥ as stating that when there are two muftis, one may select (*takhayyara*) one of them. This selection is specifically distinguished from *tatabbu' al-rukhaṣ,* which, according to him, was prohibited by most scholars.[60]

The influential Ḥanafī jurist Ibn 'Ābidīn (d. 1252/1836) used *takhayyur* in a similar nontechnical fashion. According to him, choices of substantive laws should ultimately be based on an assessment of evidence; therefore, judges and muftis are not allowed to choose (*yukhayyar*) unless they are qualified *mujtahids.* If they are *muqallids,* they should follow the opinion of a more knowledgeable jurist.[61] In this sense, *takhayyur* was used in the same way as *tarjīḥ*. The different ways in which the root *kh-y-r* was used indicates that it was used in its lay meaning and had not attained a technical meaning similar to *tatabbu' al-rukhaṣ*.

It was only around the first half of the twentieth century that the term *takhayyur* came to be used in a technical sense similar to *tatabbu' al-rukhaṣ* by some jurists. The term's usage in the twentieth century came to occupy the same semantic space that was historically reserved for *tatabbu' al-rukhaṣ*. This evolution was most likely motivated by a desire to steer clear of the negative connotations associated with *tatabbu' al-rukhaṣ*. The earliest possible usage of the new signifier that I could find appeared in a 1935 eulogy written by the rector of al-Azhar, Muṣṭafā al-Marāghī (d. 1435/1945) on the occasion of the passing of Muḥammad Rashīd Riḍā, in which he described Riḍā as following the way of the *salaf,* defining them as men of knowledge who selected rules that were beneficial to people and suitable for their age (*takhayyur al-aḥkām al-munāsiba lil-zamān wa'l-nāfi'a lil-umam*).[62] The semantic evolution of *takhayyur* and its replacement of *tatabbu' al-rukhaṣ* by some jurists explain the absence of the latter term from discussions of reform by modern legal historians.[63] However, the term *tatabbu' al-rukhaṣ* never disappeared from modern juristic discourse, but its use was virtually restricted to its opponents, who dug up the negative term and the juristic discussions of it to discredit pragmatic eclecticism, as we shall see later in this chapter.

To sum up, I have thus far established the continuity of the discourse of pragmatic eclecticism in the period between the nineteenth century and the 1930s and demonstrated a lack of consensus on the topic in much the same way pragmatic eclecticism was contested prior to the nineteenth century. I have also argued that the term *takhayyur* experienced a conceptual semantic shift around the early twentieth century. In what follows, I explain the mobilization of the debate over pragmatic eclecticism by different actors *mostly* from around the middle of the twentieth century until the contemporary period. I discuss the tensions among purists, pragmatists, and *ḍarūra*-pragmatists, which continued to frame debates about the place of Islamic law in Egypt in the twentieth- and twenty-first centuries. I contend that the new hegemonic, universalist discourses of human rights and their entrenchment in international treaty obligations, initiated by the proclamation of the UN Declaration of Human Rights in 1948, reinforced the need for novel approaches to legal reform that go beyond pragmatic eclecticism. International human rights discourses were solidified throughout the second half of the twentieth century through several treaties, including the International Covenant on Civil and Political Rights (adopted in 1966), the International Covenant on Economic, Social and Cultural Rights (adopted in 1966), the Convention on the Elimination of All Forms of Discrimination against Women (adopted in 1979), and the Convention on the Rights of the Child (adopted in 1989). The sweeping majority of Muslim nation-states emerging from colonial rule ratified these conventions, which were seen by purists as incompatible with Islamic law. Other jurists and lay Muslim intellectuals utilized both pragmatic eclecticism and novel hermeneutic strategies to accommodate human rights discourses, which they saw as representing the "essence" of Sharīʿa, and the rest, to them, was history.

Situating Pragmatic Eclecticism within Modern Approaches to Legal Reform

Let us return briefly to Rashīd Riḍā, one of the prominent figures of the modern Salafī movement. He wrote the best articulation of the tensions between the different approaches to legal reform in his time. More than a century ago, he identified five groups with different approaches to law making: (1) the supporters of *taqlīd* of the schools, whom we may call *traditional*; (2) secularists and "heretics" who do not accept Islam as a source of law but instead call for modern civilization (*ḥaḍāra ʿaṣriyya*), civil modes of organization (*al-nuẓum al-madaniyya*), and man-made legislation; (3) reformers, who believe that Islam and modernity can coexist through following the Qur'an, the authentic Sunna, and the guidance of the *salaf*, and refuse to be bound by any particular school; (4) oscillators, who reject *taqlīd* and call for *ijtihād*, claiming to promote reform when they instead corrupt the law because of their insufficient knowledge of the Arabic lexicon and the rules of legal methodology. Even stricter than the traditional *ʿulamāʾ*, they pass statements of permission or excommunication on everyone. They accept all Prophetic traditions including weak ones and excommunicate anyone who challenges their authenticity; and last of all (5) those who go beyond a desire to facilitate legal transactions for people, imposing heterodox meanings on the texts in a manner that is unjustifiable linguistically and akin to the heretical *bāṭinīs* (those who believe that the scriptures have inner esoteric meanings that can be discovered only by a select few) or worse. Of those belonging to this final camp, some go as far as to reject the Prophetic tradition literature, while others reject the traditions that are not amenable to their objectives. Riḍā argued that those who go too far in the accommodation of modernity by impugning the authenticity of the Prophetic tradition literature, in fact, drive people away from modernity and its arts and sciences.[64]

Riḍā's categories should be seen as ideal types, with some jurists approaching the middle of the spectrum rather than either extreme. Moreover, not only are the lines of demarcation vague, but one must also take into account the fact that some jurists switch their orientation during the course of their lives. The career of Rashīd Riḍā himself arguably offers a good example of such a change of orientation. The first camp, for instance, which we have called *traditional*, reflects a commitment to *taqlīd*, with the "traditional" reliance on pragmatic eclecticism, which dominated juristic discourse and court practice prior to the nineteenth century. This camp also exhibits a general aversion to *ijtihād* and to legal change that is not grounded in the authority of the jurists of the schools.

The second camp of reformers does not concern us here since it refers to secular critics of the legitimacy of a legal code inspired by Islamic law. They completely rejected the utilization of Islamic law in state legislation, and for this reason—without underestimating their role in legal modernization—they fall beyond the scope of this study. The third camp is composed of reformers such as Riḍā himself, although the term *reformers* is too general and vague to be of much use since every group describes its project as "reform." The clear reference to the accommodation of modernity and Islam as the central objective of this group justifies using the term *modernists* to refer to them instead. Riḍā described them as striving to unify the *ummah* by following a "middle path" (*manhaj wasaṭ*) that steers clear of the extremes of the other camps.[65] To describe the fourth camp, we will use the terms *purist, scripturalist,* or *textualist* interchangeably, given that their main objective in the present day is to purify Islam of accretions of human interpretation and the externalities of modern discourses.[66]

The final camp can, by the same token, be described as *liberalists,* a term that has been used by Hallaq to describe modernists who are distinguished by an endeavor to develop new hermeneutic paradigms.[67] My choice of the term *liberalist* is informed by an objective that unifies many of these reformers, namely, finding an *overlapping consensus* between their comprehensive religious doctrine and liberal democratic principles.[68] Most of the liberalists—though by no means all—are marked by their desire for a complete accommodation of Euro-American notions of liberalism, as opposed to aspiring to devise a new "Islamic modernity." A closer accommodation of modern discourses requires new hermeneutics, which liberalists endeavor to devise.[69]

The term *salafī* is often used to describe the third (modernists) and fourth (purists) camps, despite the radically different positioning of these two groups vis-à-vis modernity. Both the members of the radical al-Jamāʿa al-Islāmiyya and the modernist Muḥammad al-Ghazālī (and his followers) are self-described *salafīs*.[70] The term's positive connotation explains its appropriation by intellectuals with contradictory methodologies. Another reason for the shared heritage and terminology of various orientations of legal reform is the historical development of both Salafī approaches from the same learned circles.[71] However, it is important to emphasize that the notion that the first three generations of Islam (*salaf*) were superior to later generations and should be emulated is not in itself new. It has existed in Islamic history since at least as early as traditionalists such as Ibn Ḥanbal.[72] But it was not until the last century that this trend had gained much prominence.[73]

The failure of modernists to achieve their goal of legislating laws that were both Islamic and modern, covering all aspects of the law, has helped give momentum in the contemporary period to a more assertive form of modernism (the liberalist camp), which according to Riḍā imposed foreign meanings onto the textual sources and sometimes went as far as to reject the Prophetic tradition literature. Thus liberalists share many of the objectives of the modernists, but they frequently differ in terms of the degree to which they wish to accommodate modern discourses and, as a consequence, on the methodology used to bring about legal reform. Essentially, one of the main differences between these two groups is that while modernists believe in multiple modernities,[74] in which modern discourses can be dressed in an Islamic garb, liberalists attempt to fit Islam into modernity. It is a difference of the degree of accommodation they are willing to concede to modernity. Therefore, the greater the need for accommodation, the more necessary it is for liberalists to come up with creative hermeneutic strategies. They reject many of the perceived incompatibilities between Islam and a uniform, Euro-American–centric vision of what it means to be modern. Again, this is an ideal type and therefore I do not argue that every modernist who employs nontraditional methodology is necessarily an advocate of Euro-American modernity, as opposed to a specifically Islamic modernity. Like Riḍā, I argue that there are enough differences in terms of approach and methodology between modernists and liberalists to warrant a separate category for each.[75]

These four categories (excluding Riḍā's "secularists" camp) represent a rough continuum that extends from a rejection of the greater part of modern discourses such as human rights to their open embrace by seeking to readily accommodate its prevailing discourses and values. Although

Riḍā tended to view liberalists as heretical, their objective has much in common with the modernists: how to go about crafting an Islamic yet simultaneously modern society. Needless to say, some figures are harder to locate within this continuum than others. Even in the life of one intellectual, there are often inconsistencies and changes of trajectory that do not fit into consistent categories. This diversity of approaches—and at times incoherence—only serves to complicate the task of disentangling the intellectual projects of modern Islamic legal reform.

As we have seen, attitudes toward pragmatic eclecticism in the nineteenth and early twentieth centuries were similar to those held in the Ottoman period, with both sides of the debate engaging Ottoman authorities. The issue was never conclusively resolved in favor of one view over another, and the topic continued to be an issue of juristic disagreement. Those same debates have remained central to legal discourse in the twentieth- and twenty-first centuries. Riḍā's typology of modern approaches to legal reform remains highly relevant to the discussion of the future of post-Mubarak and post-Morsi Egypt. In what follows, I discuss these different approaches in twentieth- and twenty-first century Egypt, providing a brief general outline of the different strategies of legal reform in the modern period, with a specific focus on jurists' positions on pragmatic eclecticism.

Purism

As we saw in chapters 2 and 3, the premodern period was characterized by a struggle between purists, who were averse to nontextual human interpretation, and those who attached greater value to social factors such as the facilitation of people's legal and ritual practices. According to purists, pragmatic eclecticism represented a form of this human interference in the purity of God's legal prescriptions, as it was based on the "whims" of jurists and the laity, as well as on their own assessment of what constituted social weal.[76]

This purist tendency can also be found in the theological-legal discussions of the ontological multiplicity of truth, discussed in chapter 1, with regard to how they defined the unknowability of truth and its scope in legal matters. Some jurists filled the legal lacuna by attaching greater authoritativeness to reports attributed to the Companions of the Prophet and the Successor generation or the *salaf.* As we saw, Companions' reports were considered authoritative by some jurists such as Ibn Taymiyya and Ibn Ḥazm.[77] Purism thus refers to tendencies that have historically been associated with the *ahl al-ḥadīth* or traditionalism.[78] Although these tendencies have deeply influenced the evolution of Islamic legal methodology and substantive law, mainstream juristic opinion in the premodern period generally continued to give priority to later juristic positions over the views of the Prophet's Companions.[79]

To say that the views of people like Ibn 'Abd al-Barr, Ibn Ḥazm, Ibn Taymiyya, Ibn Qayyim al-Jawziyya, Ibn 'Abd al-Wahhāb, and al-Shawkānī, among others, provide inspiration to modern purism is to state the obvious. However, we cannot discuss these figures as a coherent group with identical methodological and substantive legal orientations. Within the early modern period, the so-called revivalists followed different approaches, making it hard to speak of them as a coherent movement, as Ahmad Dallal rightly points out.[80] There are, however, methodological similarities in their views on pragmatic eclecticism, as well as in their emphasis on the exercise of *tarjīḥ* and *ijtihād.*

Whereas early modernists such as 'Abduh and Riḍā were positioning themselves against the *taqlīd* of the traditional *'ulamā',* purist thinkers were hostile both to the traditional *'ulamā'* and to the reactiveness of modernists. Modern purism was a reaction not only against human interpretation and pragmatic eclecticism, as was the case with premodern purists, but also against modern discourses and the modernists' attempts to accommodate them. The purist trend is thus prone to emphasize a pristine Sharī'a, unspoiled by human interpretation, which may only be discovered through a fresh interpretation of the source texts (*ijtihād*) or through an evaluation of the correct legal rules from among existing juristic views by assessing the available evidence (*tarjīḥ*). This approach has thus given rise to a general tendency, with varying degrees of intensity, to reject other school opinions that do not correspond to the purists' legal hermeneutic methodology, as well as to their view of what constitutes scripture. In the early controversy between traditionalists (*ahl al-ḥadīth*) and people of opinion (*ahl al-ra'y*), the method of jurists was rejected because it was seen to favor the insertion of human reason and personal interpretation over a more literalist approach to the derivation of legal rules. This debate arose before the formation of the schools and eventually led to the adoption of a middle ground in legal methodology, whereby the textual sources gained more prominence in the derivation of substantive law. The traditionalist brand of law making was partly accommodated in al-Shāfiʿī's *Risāla*, and much has been written about this to warrant further elaboration.[81]

The tension within legal methodology over the role of human interpretation in the derivation of substantive law remained an essential part of Islamic legal history, with figures such as al-Bukhārī, Ibn Ḥanbal, Ibn Taymiyya, and Ibn Qayyim al-Jawziyya representing the minimalist approach to human interpretation.[82] The strong association between this approach and the Ḥanbalī school became even more pronounced after the death of Ibn Ḥazm, the last major representative of the Ẓāhirī scripturalists.[83] It was through the Ḥanbalī emphasis on *ijtihād*, *tarjīḥ*, and *ittibāʿ* (verification, or following) that they were able to challenge the corpus of the schools by rejecting some of the rules they perceived to contradict the religious source texts. This is also similar to the argument that al-Shaʿrānī's interlocutors put forward, according to which, as we saw, they held that receiving juristic opinions without textual sources is insufficient for the attainment of God's law.

One of the main differences between what Raymond William Baker calls the "new Islamists" (the modernists according to our scheme) and purists is that the former explicitly recognize that the texts have ambiguous meanings that can lead to legitimate differences of opinion. They reject the certitude claimed by those he calls "extremists" (our purist category).[84] It is this certitude that we see in some of the early views regarding the ontological unity of truth doctrine and its knowability (discussed in chapter 1). Some of the major proponents of this view argue that there is only one faith without schools and only one way, that is, the way of Prophet Muhammad, such that whoever follows anything other than the Qur'an and the Sunna is a disbeliever.[85] This claim of certitude can be sensed in the efforts of the eighteenth-century Muḥammad b. ʿAbd al-Wahhāb, who rejected many premodern jurists as "devils." Only a few figures, such as Ibn Taymiyya, were spared from his attacks. Deference to the schools of law was, according to him, an act of heresy, as many jurists relied on reason in their legal interpretation.[86]

The distinction between purists and modernists is particularly palpable in the revisions proposed by the leaders of al-Jamā'a al-Islāmiyya, who were involved in acts of violence against the Egyptian government in the 1990s. In 2002 they revised their views regarding the permissibility of taking up arms against the state, ultimately denouncing violence from their jails in a series of four works recanting their bellicose stance. In their revisionist works (*murāja'āt*), the members of al-Jamā'a al-Islāmiyya called for a gradual implementation of God's law, employing such words as *wasaṭiyya* (the middle path) and *yusr* (ease) to describe their revised agenda. This newly formulated middle path is one that attempts a balance between a strictly textualist approach and the application of unfettered reason. The concept of *yusr*, according to them, should not be used to pursue the errors of scholars (*tallaquff hafawāt al-'ulamā'*), a premodern epithet referring to *tatabbu' al-rukhaṣ*. They argued that *yusr* was used as a guise by extreme secularists (*ghulāt al-'almāniyyīn*) to rid people of the Sharī'a.[87] Their discourse is reminiscent of the premodern opponents of *tatabbu' al-rukhaṣ*, who warned against pursuing the errors (*zallāt*) of scholars.[88] Ironically, terms such as *yusr* and *wasaṭiyya* are also the preferred discursive tools of modernists such as al-Qaraḍāwī to rebut religious extremism (*al-ghulūw fi'l-dīn*).[89]

One of the striking features of these revisionist writings is their return to a somewhat more traditional approach, in which the authors invoked traditional nodes of authority to support their new position on violence, excommunication (*takfīr*), jihad, and the enforcement of public morality (*iḥtisāb*). In their revisionism, they no longer embraced a direct examination of the textual sources. They rather argued that the *salaf* warned against taking knowledge directly from books without receiving the guidance of scholars who are needed to mediate this knowledge. They explicitly criticized members of the movement for their direct examination of the source texts without the mediation of jurists.[90] These revisions can be seen as a rejection of the binary division between the social weal and legal purity, as well as a move closer toward the premodern understanding of *taqlīd*. In these revisions, the term *'ulamā' al-salaf* (early scholars) was frequently used to refer to the early period extending beyond the generation of the four eponyms. These revisionists incorporated many jurists from all four schools as late as Ibn ʿĀbidīn,[91] and even criticized Islamic groups that prohibited acts over which there is disagreement among jurists.[92]

The tensions between purism and traditionalism found in the revisions are a far cry from the discourse of the father of postcolonial Salafism, Muḥammad Nāṣir al-Dīn al-Albānī (d. 1999), who can be placed squarely within the purist camp. He outlined his general approach to reform that consisted of two stages of implementation. The first is a process of purification (*taṣfiya*), an intellectual enterprise with important legal ramifications in which the vast corpus of Islamic literature is purged of weak Prophetic traditions and the remnants of Judeo-Christian–inspired sources (*isrāʾīliyyāt*), as well as of juristic opinions that contradict the hadith. One of the main objectives of this process is to create a homogenous society and to avoid current legal fragmentation. Naturally, the second stage is to educate Muslims according to the revised "pure" program.[93] Al-Albānī's project suggests a rejection of the four schools and of school loyalty.[94] The opponents of school affiliation (*madhhabiyya*) in the modern period held a position similar to that of premodern purists, namely, that schools should not be followed without weighing the different opinions against one another through the process of *tarjīḥ*.[95]

In much the same way the scope of unknowability of truth was narrowed down by pre-nineteenth-century purists, modern purists believe that there is only one correct rule on most issues and that it can be reached through an examination of the textual sources. The work of Muḥammad Sulṭān al-Maʿṣūmī al-Khajandī (d. 1381/1960) is a clear example of this tendency, for not only did he argue that following one of the four schools is neither obligatory nor even recommended (*mandūb*), he also added that anyone who follows one specific school in all transactions is fanatical (*mutaʿaṣṣib*).[96]

Al-Khajandī rejected the fragmentation that schools bring to the Muslim community, arguing that school opinions consist of the interpretations of later generations (*al-qurūn al-mutaʾakhkhira*) of Muslims and are, therefore, not binding. His literalist approach is clear in the claim that the early imams (*aʾimmat al-salaf*) abided by the outward meaning (*ẓāhir*) of the source texts. He rejected the heavy mediation of jurists between the texts and legal rules, citing the exhortations of the eponyms Abū Ḥanīfa, Mālik, al-Shāfiʿī, and Ibn Ḥanbal to avoid using their juristic opinions for fatwa, unless one is fully aware of their sources.[97] Al-Albānī, in line with other purists both modern and premodern, was hostile to pragmatic eclecticism, which he tried to replace with an evidential "comparative jurisprudence" (*al-fiqh al-muqāran*) that was designed to discover legal truth from the mayhem of juristic disagreement. He described it as exercising evidential preponderance (*al-tarjīḥ bi'l-dalīl*).[98]

This comparative jurisprudence is very similar to the modernists' comparative approach to Islamic law, according to which all the legal opinions of the schools are to be compared and one opinion is to be selected on the grounds of its suitability for the conditions of modern times. The obvious difference is that the modernists' approach utilized pragmatic eclecticism to accommodate modern conditions, whereas the purists' reasoning was based on the exercise of preponderance (*tarjīḥ*). For the purists, using modern conditions as a point of reference constitutes an act of secularization. Thus they saw the partial codification of Islamic family law, which utilized pragmatic eclecticism, as a modern innovation. Al-Albānī attacked his opponents in the modernist camp, such as al-Qaraḍāwī, Muḥammad al-Ghazālī, and Muḥammad Abū Zahra, as "aberrant rationalists" (*al-ʿaqlāniyyīn al-shudhdhadh*) who select from every school according to their whims. Al-Albānī even made references to the early opposition to *tatabbuʿ al-rukhaṣ* by some of its avowed enemies in the formative period, such as al-Taymī and Ibn ʿAbd al-Barr, so as to support his position.[99]

Al-Albānī enumerated rules in the four schools that contradict the Prophetic tradition literature, arguing that all legal opinions must be strictly subjected to the textual canon in order to determine whether they withstand the test of divine authority. He attacked the *taqlīd* of the four schools as a contradiction to the Prophetic tradition, criticizing for instance personal status laws that enshrine the Ḥanafī opinion permitting adult women to marry themselves without the authority of a male legal guardian. According to him, Abū Ḥanīfa was in error since his opinion contradicted clear Prophetic traditions on the matter.[100] According to al-Albānī, only the "*salafīs*," the sole Muslim group to be spared hellfire (*al-firqa al-nājiya*), can guide their Muslim brethren along the right path.[101]

Al-Albānī also cited the example of drinking alcohol, noting that some books of jurisprudence continue to hold that there are different types of alcohol (*khamr*) and that only the type extracted from grapes is prohibited, while the other types made out of barley, corn, and dates may be consumed in moderation. As he pointed out, people defend this view not on its merits, but simply because their imam (Abū Ḥanīfa) held it, even though there are clear Prophetic traditions that contradict his position. To his dismay, this Ḥanafī position was cited by an unnamed Syrian jurist, who argued that it would be unnecessarily strict to prohibit small amounts of alcohol since there is a juristic opinion that permits it. The Syrian jurist clearly used the same pragmatic eclectic logic that we have encountered in previous chapters, which seeks to legitimize more lenient legal views from the vast corpus of the inherited juristic literature. Al-Albānī accused followers of this type of *taqlīd* of laziness and cowardice since they refused to admit that the fallible eponym was in error. According to al-Albānī, even the renowned Syrian jurist Muḥammad al-Ḥamīd al-Ḥamawī (d. 1969) was hesitant to reject the Ḥanafī view simply because of its pedigree in the school.[102] Another example that al-Albānī cited is the Ḥanafī opinion that a Muslim may be put to death for murdering a non-Muslim, which is not accepted by the other schools. He invoked the Prophetic tradition that states, "A Muslim should not be killed for an unbeliever."[103] As can be seen from these examples, Islamic law was strictly equated with the apparent (*ẓāhir*) meaning of the textual sources as al-Albānī interpreted them, and thus many interpretive disagreements based on history and social context were not accounted for in his definition of the law.

It is important to caution once more that although these purists might share similar approaches and attitudes to pragmatic eclecticism, *tarjīḥ*, and *ijtihād*, this does not necessarily mean that we can speak of them as a coherent group with a predictable set of methodological and substantive legal doctrines. On the topic of the permissibility of music, for instance, al-Albānī wrote a book refuting Ibn Ḥazm's view that listening to music is not forbidden.[104] Ibn Ḥazm, whose legal methodology is somewhat similar to the scripturalism and literalism of the purists, challenged the authenticity of the Prophetic traditions that forbid listening to music.[105] Al-Albānī, on the other hand, accepted these traditions despite the many challenges to their authenticity leveled by Ibn Ḥazm and others, and instead rejected the ones permitting music.[106] Whether al-Albānī's choice is based on a preconceived idea of a desired legal outcome or simply a preference for the views of his more valued authorities, such as Ibn Ḥanbal and Ibn Taymiyya, is difficult to determine.

Another opponent of pragmatic eclecticism who adopts a purist orientation to law is the contemporary Saudi scholar Sulaymān b. Ṣāliḥ al-Kharāshī, who criticizes the overly lenient orientation (*madhhab al-taysīr*) of Muḥammad al-Ghazālī and al-Qaraḍāwī through which, as he argues, they permitted many a forbidden act, giving priority to their intellects and whims (*'uqūlahum wa ahwā'ahum*). His main objective in one article was to criticize the Tunisian intellectual Rāshid al-Ghannūshī, who follows an eclectic approach to juristic diversity. Al-Ghannūshī, according to al-Kharāshī, forsook the principles of Islam for the sake of his political agenda. People with a sound knowledge of the truth inherent in the Qur'an and Sunna, al-Kharāshī adds, recognize al-Ghannūshī's approach as a deviation, while those lacking in knowledge may view it as virtuous.[107] Al-Kharāshī blames secularist pressures for the concessions made by the Muslim Brotherhood and their followers such as al-Ghannūshī. According to al-Kharāshī, there are well-established Islamic rulings (*aḥkām al-Islām al-thābita*) that the likes of al-Ghannūshī, who call themselves "progressive Islamists," have abandoned because they are no more than secularists masquerading as Islamists.[108]

Needless to say, legal codification was not popular among purists. They frequently made negative references to the personal status laws of Egypt and other Arab countries, where the laws were drawn from the four schools based on pragmatic considerations rather than on their preponderance.[109] According to the opponents of codification, jurists resorted to *tatabbu' al-rukhaṣ* in order to entrench European traditions in Islamic societies. The renowned Egyptian jurist Muḥammad al-Ghazālī was accused of adopting European values through the gate of eclecticism.[110] This debate over codification continues to be relevant in the contemporary period. In Saudi Arabia, for instance, where the government is pushing for codification, much opposition has come from purist circles.[111]

I hope to have shown the manner in which the premodern purist tendency, which rejected pragmatic eclecticism, has been carried forward by modern purists whose aversion to pragmatic eclecticism—mirroring that of their intellectual predecessors—was coupled with a rejection of the externalities of modern life and a particularly strong opposition to the positions of modernists. The purist discourse cannot be read in isolation from the modernists' discourse, to which we now turn.

Modernists

Relations among the four Sunnī schools in the formative period witnessed a slow evolution and oscillation from enmity and boundary-drawing to later fluidity and boundary-crossing. From the very beginning of modernist Salafism, there were two different approaches, which are well summarized by an unnamed friend of the Syrian modernist ʿAbd al-Ḥamīd al-Zahrāwī (d. 1334/1915) in an article published in *al-Manār*. The first approach was to consider all the juristic opinions held by the eponyms of the schools as a vital part of religion that must necessarily be accepted. On this basis, people were allowed to select from books of jurisprudence those opinions that best suited the conditions of the age. These juristic views ideally would be unified and collected in one book in order to create a general law that could be used by all Muslims. This approach, which was later described rather inaccurately as a practice of *talfīq*, is embodied to some extent in al-Shaʿrānī's *al-Mīzān*, as we have already seen. The second approach was not to treat the eponyms' views as part of the faith but as mere opinions reached through *ijtihād*. As such, if this were the case, then people today would be allowed to exercise *ijtihād* in much the same manner that their predecessors did.[112]

Rashīd Riḍā combined both approaches within his reform project, arguing that Islam could be revived and its guidance renewed by following the Qur'an, the authentic Sunna, and the guidance of the *salaf*, as well as by exploiting the knowledge of the imams of the four schools without being strictly bound to any of their teachings.[113] During the early stage of the reformist movement, there was already some tension between *ijtihād* in the sense of a complete renewal of jurisprudence without any commitment to the legal methodology and hermeneutics of the inherited premodern scholarship, and *taqlīd*, in which the jurist accepts the accretions of centuries of jurisprudence. Riḍā's approach to *ijtihād* was conservative. He stated that wherever the early Muslims (*al-ṣadr al-awwal*) established consensus (*ijmā*ʿ), these opinions cannot be rejected for a novel *ijtihād*. He added that Prophetic traditions that were used by the first generation of Muslims should be accepted even if rejected by a small number of scholars. The only traditions that Riḍā would allow jurists to impugn were solitary reports that were not used by the *salaf*.[114]

Both *ijtihād* and pragmatic eclecticism within the context of *taqlīd* have been the bread and butter of the modernist project since the nineteenth century. We still find the same approaches operating today in the discourse of contemporary modernists such as the influential Yūsuf al-Qaraḍāwī. In contrast with the approach of the purists' "comparative jurisprudence," al-Qaraḍāwī calls for the utilization of two types of *ijtihād*; the first type is *ijtihād intiqā'ī* (selective *ijtihād*), in which the most appropriate opinions in the four Sunnī schools are selected, while the other type is what he refers to as *ijtihād inshā'ī* (innovative *ijtihād*), namely, deriving new rules from the textual sources to meet new needs.[115] It is perhaps because of the negative connotations of the term *tatabbu*ʿ *al-rukhaṣ* that he uses the more positive "selective *ijtihād*." But as we saw above, this change into a more positive signifier did not placate his opponents who saw his pragmatic eclectic methods, regardless of what he calls them, as "aberrant," accusing him of selecting juristic views from schools according to his whims.[116]

Al-Qaraḍāwī contends that it is important for the jurisprudence of Muslim minorities living in non-Muslim countries (*fiqh al-aqalliyyāt*), and for modern jurisprudence generally, that the mufti not restrict himself to one *madhhab*. A modern mufti, therefore, should draw upon the four surviving schools and on the opinions of jurists whose school affiliation is unknown, as well as upon the views of the Companions. According to him, this diversity of stringent and lenient juristic views proffers the opportunity to compare them and exercise preponderance (*al-muwāzana wa'l-tarjīḥ*).[117] It should be noted here that al-Qaraḍāwī uses the term "preponderance" (*tarjīḥ*) to refer to pragmatic eclecticism. As we have seen, as an ideal type, *tarjīḥ* means giving preponderance to one opinion over another by weighing the different pieces of evidence. Social needs were rarely explicitly considered among the criteria on which preponderance was based, even though these needs must have motivated new interpretations. Direct references to social needs were usually invoked under the rubric of *tatabbu' al-rukhaṣ*. What al-Qaraḍāwī referred to here is a preference for a juristic view that is more suited to the time, as opposed to an assessment of evidence to the exclusion of the social context of modernity. But instead of using the rubric of *tatabbu' al-rukhaṣ* with its negative connotations to describe this type of pragmatic eclecticism, he preferred to use the more positive terms "preponderance" and "selective *ijtihād*" instead. Ironically, as we saw in the introduction and chapter 2, *tarjīḥ* was the term used in the premodern period to designate the categorical opposite of *tatabbu' al-rukhaṣ*.

The pragmatic eclectic approach of al-Qaraḍāwī has been operationalized by the Tunisian intellectual Rāshid al-Ghannūshī in an attempt to theorize a conception of an Islamic democracy and create an overlapping consensus with liberal democracy.[118] Al-Ghannūshī considers human rights as among the purposes of the law (*maqāṣid al-Sharī'a*), placing human rights under the needs (*ḥājiyyāt*) and improvements (*taḥsīnāt*) categories of the purposes of the law (*maqāṣid*), as opposed to the necessities (*ḍarūriyyāt*), which may at times take precedence over well-established legal doctrine.[119] In his discussion of the Universal Declaration of Human Rights (UDHR), he goes through the different articles of the Declaration and tries to show that they are largely in line with Islamic law. He achieves this objective through the mix of *ijtihād* and pragmatic eclecticism that has been used by the majority of modernists since the nineteenth century. He also discusses the juristic opinions on who has the right of *dhimma*, which he translates into the modern parlance of "citizenship" in a Muslim state. Al-Ghannūshī engages the juristic debate and eventually approves the Mālikī opinion that allows any religious group the right of *dhimma* in a Muslim state, rejecting the view that restricts it to Christians and Jews.[120]

On the issue of apostasy from Islam (*ridda*), which al-Ghannūshī describes as a crime (*jarīma*), he does not challenge the historicity of the death penalty given to apostates. He expounds, rather, on the different motivations behind the death penalty being assigned by premodern jurists, delineating two main approaches. One view treats it as a doctrinal "crime" that the head of state (imam) has no right to forgive, while the other treats it as the prerogative of the head of state and within his right of discretionary punishment (*ta'zīr*) to keep public order. He supports the second view, arguing that an actual crime only obtains when it is accompanied by acts of violence against the state and public order. This crime should be punished according to the seriousness of the threat it represents to society. The punishment is therefore not for the change of belief, but rather for armed struggle against the Muslim state.[121]

Al-Ghannūshī's eclecticism knows no sectarian or temporal boundaries. He cites both premodern and contemporary jurists, as well as Shī'ī and Khārijite scholars. For instance, he disagrees with Abū al-A'lā al-Mawdūdī that non-Muslims and women should not be part of the legislature of a Muslim state. He cites different juristic opinions on the topic, including those in support of non-Muslims and women serving as judges. He even invokes the view of some of the sects among the Khārijites that the head of state may be a woman.[122] He clearly sides with these views, even though they do not represent mainstream jurisprudence; but when it comes to non-Muslims assuming the presidency, his search for an overlapping consensus grinds to a halt.

Despite his determined search for an overlapping consensus between liberal democracy and Islamic law, al-Ghannūshī does not call for a universal Euro-American–centric democracy, but he instead prefers an Islamic democracy that has its own specificities. Speaking of the Bin 'Alī regime in Tunisia, he contends that the Islamic movement's true battle is against totalitarianism and Occidentalization (*taghrīb*). According to him, the only way Muslims could win this battle is by persuading people of the dangers of intellectual colonization. As part of this struggle, it is important, according to him, for Muslims to take pride in their cultural and religious heritage.[123] Thus his perceptions of an Islamic democracy and Islamic human rights are not always in line with Western perceptions. This attitude is clear in his position on the compatibility between his conceptualization of Islamic democracy and the UDHR on the issue of the equality of citizens, regardless of religious affiliation. According to him, while equality is the general rule in the Islamic democratic polity, there may be very limited situations in which citizens are not treated equally on account of culture or public order.[124] This last statement applies especially to excluding non-Muslims from the presidency, as he argues that the head of the Muslim state cannot be a non-Muslim.[125]

Al-Ghannūshī's discourse resembles the Cairo Declaration of Human Rights in Islam (CDHRI), which departs from the UDHR on this issue, as well as on the question of marriage between a Muslim woman and a non-Muslim man. In 1990 Muslim member states of the Organization of the Islamic Conference (OIC) declared their support for the CDHRI, which, although it opposes in Article I all discrimination "on grounds of race, color, language, sex, religious belief, political affiliation, social status," states clearly in Article V that "men and women have the right to marriage, and no restrictions stemming from race, color, or nationality shall prevent them from enjoying this right." As can be seen in Article V, the mention of religion is dropped, since the dominant interpretation of Islamic law explicitly forbids Muslim women from marrying non-Muslims and Muslim men from marrying women who do not adhere to Islam, Christianity, or Judaism. Articles I and V of the same document are thus at odds with one another.[126]

As we have seen thus far, the most important common denominator that links the two extremes of modern legal reform, modernists and purists, is that they share no commitment to traditional authority and *taqlīd*. For instance, Riḍā drew a distinction between the approaches of the *salaf*, the partisans of the Sunna, who favored a stricter reliance on the textual sources over the use of analogy and *taqlīd*, and those affiliated with a particular school, especially as the followers of each imam became increasingly hardened in their *taqlīd*. According to him, this school rigidity is a major contributing factor to the ailments afflicting Muslim society.[127] However, neither camp rejected the edifice of substantive Sunnī Islamic law wholesale. They were instead selective in the way they handled the massive layers of legal interpretation. Both camps relied mainly on premodern juristic discourses and authorities in constructing their rejection or embrace of modernity. Some jurists, who share many of the goals of modernists, have felt that the latter's methods were too beholden to the premodern tradition. They have therefore tried to devise new hermeneutics and/or reformulate the sources of scripture so as to bring more radical change to Islamic law.

The Liberalists

Riḍā's fifth camp, which for our purposes we have identified as the liberalists, refers broadly to a category of thinkers who, in Riḍā's words, would manipulate the meaning of the textual sources in a manner that is linguistically unjustifiable. According to him, others within this group reject the Prophetic tradition literature in order to accommodate modernity, but this strategy usually backfires as it drives people away from modernity altogether.[128] One of the strategies of the liberalists is hermeneutic, and the other relates to the definition of the textual sources themselves. This trend has been a strand of the wider modernist project since its inception. For instance, even Riḍā's friend Muḥammad Tawfīq Ṣidqī wrote in *al-Manār* that the hadith literature should not be used as a source of law, a position that Riḍā rejected outright. In the early twentieth century, al-Zahrāwī (d. 1334/1915) and the same Ṣidqī discussed the issue of hadith fabrications, arguing that the Prophetic tradition literature must be tested against the Qur'anic text.[129]

This tendency to do away with the hadith literature can still be seen, for instance, in the modern Qur'anist approach to Islamic law, which has persisted into the contemporary period. The challenge leveled by Jamāl al-Bannā (d. 2013) to the Prophetic tradition literature is another notable example of this approach. His work entitled *Naḥwa Fiqh Jadīd* (Toward a new jurisprudence), wherein he challenged the entire school system and the Prophetic tradition literature, generated much controversy, with al-Azhar calling for its ban.[130] Similar attacks were launched against representatives of new hermeneutic approaches such as the famous case of Naṣr Ḥamīd Abū Zayd.[131]

Critics of the hadith literature frequently focus on the text of the hadith (*matn*), rather than on the chain of narration (*isnād*), as a tool for weeding out much of this body of writing. This approach goes back to the formative period of Islamic law, although it was rejected as allowing human interpretation to legislate.[132] The *matn*-critical approach was rejected by a number of scripturally inclined scholars, who saw it as placing humans in the position of the Law-giver by allowing them to determine what may be palatable from the corpus of Prophetic traditions. For instance, in the premodern period, Ibn Qayyim al-Jawziyya piled criticism on scholars who subjected Prophetic traditions to a content test against the Qur'anic text.[133]

In the modern period, the liberalists took the *matn*-critical approach further to challenge most of the hadith literature. Jamāl al-Bannā, for instance, stirred controversy when he proposed a content test that he admitted would lead to the rejection of thousands of Prophetic traditions, most of which deal with the occult, contain negative statements about women, attribute miracles to the Prophet, assign a special status to certain tribes or caliphs, or violate freedom of belief. One example he cited of the substantive legal effect of subordinating the Prophetic traditions to the Qur'an is that the capital punishment for apostasy would be repealed, as the Prophetic traditions used to derive this law contradict the multiple Qur'anic references to freedom of belief. According to him, the Prophetic traditions that contain negative attitudes toward women must also be rejected since the Qur'an and the general life of the Prophet indicate that he respected women.[134]

In addition to redefining what falls within the category of scripture, the other strategy that Riḍā identified as being espoused by this camp is primarily hermeneutic.[135] Modern hermeneutic approaches to the Qur'an that abandon the hermeneutics of the premodern period frequently do so with the aim of "unreading patriarchy" in the Qur'anic text, such as has been attempted by contemporary scholars such as Asma Barlas, or of reframing the law in terms of general and more universal Islamic principles, potentially shattering the entire edifice of premodern legal hermeneutics, and of the *madhhab* as an institution, as was the case in Fazlur Rahman's approach.[136]

The stated objective behind adopting unconventional hermeneutic approaches and the redefinition of the sacred source texts is sometimes framed in terms of the need for an overlapping consensus between Islam and Western modernity. This approach has gained little support among stakeholders in the political Islamic project. For instance, Riḍā's aversion to this approach, which he saw as a threat to the middle road of *wasaṭiyya*, was mirrored by al-Ghannūshī's characterization of such attempts as Occidentalization (*taghrīb*).[137] One of the biggest challenges facing representatives of this camp is that they have not yet managed to gain the mass support needed to enable it to compete with both modernists and purists. In the final tally, pragmatic eclecticism within *taqlīd*—and to a lesser extent *ijtihād*—have been much more dominant in modernist discourse because their exponents have succeeded in making the argument that their approaches have the backing of the authoritative premodern legal tradition.

Conclusion

The secondary literature shows that some legal historians conflated *tatabbuʿ al-rukhaṣ* with *talfīq*, identifying both as instances of *talfīq*. This conflation may partly explain why the utilization of pragmatic eclecticism in the modern codification of Islamic law was largely perceived to be an alien development that was new to the history of Islamic law, given the stronger opposition to *talfīq* in premodern juristic discourse. At some point in the early twentieth century, there was a shift in the manner in which the term *takhayyur* was employed by some jurists, as it increasingly came to take up the semantic space normally occupied by *tatabbuʿ al-rukhaṣ*. This change can be attributed to the negative connotations of the latter term, which, despite such connotations, never disappeared from juristic discourse. It has continued to be utilized, but often by the opponents of pragmatic eclecticism. Modern jurists were as divided as were their Ottoman counterparts about the validity of both types of pragmatic eclecticism.

The *taqlīdic* approach to the challenges of modernity has proved less controversial and more acceptable to Muslims than the approaches of liberalists such as Jamāl al-Bannā, Amina Wadud, Fazlur Rahman, and Muḥammad Shaḥrūr, among others. The work of Rāshid al-Ghannūshī, in which he eclectically selects the juristic opinions that fit his own modern Islamic *weltanschauung* demonstrates the attractiveness of pragmatic eclecticism in the contemporary period.

The struggle between modernists and purists in the modern period replicates much of what we have seen prior to the nineteenth century, albeit with different emphases. While modernists tried to embrace modernity, purists viewed the modernist approach as a threat. Again, the law was a major arena in need of reform for purists. Like the modernists, purists conceived of a homogenous law, much like the legal systems of European countries, in which pluralism was initially regarded as a sign of antiquatedness. Within the purist camp, differences among jurists were seen as a sign of fragmentation, not of flexibility.

The debate over the permissibility of pragmatic eclecticism continued throughout the nineteenth and twentieth centuries. The issue remained subject to debate as it had been in the Ottoman period, and the tension between the two camps in juristic discourse continued well into the contemporary period. Modern reformers such as Riḍā, al-Ḥusaynī, al-Ḥifnāwī, al-Bānī, and others drew upon Ottoman juristic debates to justify their positions that mostly supported such eclecticism. In the nineteenth and twentieth centuries, approaches to legal reform drew on premodern legal strategies to accommodate the novel challenges of modernity, which brought its own discourses and epistemology.

Reformers such as Riḍā and al-Bānī supported the utilization of pragmatic eclecticism to accommodate the changing needs of society. They treated the entire spectrum of views within the four schools as a source from which legislators could freely choose. This attitude would later be adopted in the codification of personal status laws in Egypt, which faced surprisingly little opposition. Even the renowned Azharī Shaykhs, who opposed the personal status laws of 1929, did not reject the legislators' simple pragmatic eclecticism (*tatabbuʿ al-rukhaṣ*). Instead, they criticized complex pragmatic eclecticism (*talfīq*), as well as any attempt at drawing from outside of the four schools altogether. In the next chapter, which deals with the actual codification of personal status laws in Egypt in the nineteenth and twentieth centuries, I explore how legal reform was concretized in state laws, privileging the modernists' eclectic pragmatic vision that we have discussed in this chapter. In this sense, the modern state's privileging of the pragmatic eclectic camp resembles the Mamluk and Ottoman authorities' choice of pragmatic eclecticism to introduce flexibility into the regime of *taqlīd*.

6

Codification and the Arab Spring

Can the Sharīʿa Be Restored?

I HAVE DISCUSSED in the previous chapters the place of pragmatic eclecticism in juristic discourse in both the premodern and the modern periods. This chapter is primarily concerned with the operationalization of pragmatic eclecticism through the partial codification of Islamic law in Egypt in the modern period. I will also discuss the future of Sharīʿa in the context of the attempts to implement further codification of Islamic law in post–Arab Spring Egypt.

It is important here to caution that although I argue for continuity as far as the tools utilized by modern jurists to accommodate modernity, I do not claim that there was always continuity in terms of actual substantive law. As we will see, Oussama Arabi demonstrates that there was a radical transformation in Egypt's *khulʿ* law of 2000. Amira Sonbol has also shown ruptures in gender relations owing to the impact of nineteenth-century European gender values. Her discussion of transformation of the legal concept of the wife's obedience (*ṭāʿa*) to her husband into the modern institution of "house of obedience" (*bayt al-ṭāʿa*) in 1920 represented a clear rupture with premodernity. The incarceration of the wife in the "house of obedience" does not have premodern Islamic pedigree.[1]

In my earlier discussion of legal reforms in the modern period, I noted that there was very little opposition to these reforms within both traditional and modernist circles. Needless to say, the lines between these two orientations to law became blurred because of the efforts of Muḥammad ʿAbduh, Rashīd Riḍā, and Muṣṭafā al-Marāghī, among others. Even the limited traditional opposition to codification that we saw in chapter 5 was not directed at the pragmatic selection of less stringent juristic views per se, but rather at the practice of selecting opinions from outside the four schools, or of depending on the opinions of the Companions over those of later jurists. I also argued in chapter 5 that there was no substantial discursive shift on pragmatic eclecticism in the modern period. By making this argument of continuity, I seek to show that some of the strategies and tools of legal modernization were more local than they are perceived to be. But before delving into legal codification in the twentieth century, a brief word about legal modernity and a discussion of some important legal transformations that took place in the nineteenth century are in order.

Legal Transformations in Nineteenth-Century Egypt

Legal modernity is characterized by three main objectives: the unification of laws across ethnic, religious, and class segments of society; limiting laws to the borders of the nation-state; and achieving "justice," a notion that was epistemically and historically conditioned by colonialism and the discourses of modernity. In this study, I approach the process of legal modernization with these inherent assumptions about what constitutes legal modernity in the context of the modern nation-state.[2] In order to achieve these stated objectives, the new nation-state had to create a written, fixed code. Central to European notions of justice was the creation of an appeal system and a hierarchy within the courts, consisting of defined jurisdictions. Thus legal modernization involved two main processes: (1) the establishment of a legal hierarchy and (2) the codification of the law, whether Sharīʿa-based or of European provenance, within the borders of the nation-state.[3]

The common periodization scheme situates the beginning of Egyptian legal modernization in 1883, which is the date when national courts were established. Another view places the beginning of modernization in 1876 when the mixed courts were created.[4] These two views were challenged quite recently by scholars who argued for an earlier date.[5] Focusing on codification, the revisionists showed that such attempts started as early as 1829 with the creation of the first criminal code and continued up until the second half of the nineteenth century. Peters, for instance, argues that the period between 1829 and 1882 was more important to legal modernization in Egypt than the colonial period.[6] This view that much of the centralization and modernization of the legal system took place under Mehmed Ali was corroborated by Zeinab A. Abul-Magd's findings from the Qina province in Upper Egypt. She demonstrates that the Sharīʿa court was an important tool of the hegemonic policies of Mehmed Ali (d. 1849, and reigned 1805–49), for he made the court part of the state apparatus, with judges enforcing the new codes issued by the state.[7]

Whether the modernization of legal institutions started in the colonial 1880s or the Ottoman 1820s is important, for it shows that the legal sea change that took place in the nineteenth century was not a Western export in all its component parts. Some of these changes were directly related to the history of colonialism, but others have their roots in the local administrative, political, and social context of Ottoman Egypt. Some of these changes were introduced under Mehmed Ali, while others predated him. Mehmed Ali, for example, initiated policies in the nineteenth century that intensified state control and intervention into the lives of the population, and embarked on widespread modernization of the army and the judiciary.[8] As we saw in chapter 4, Ḥanafism had a default status in seventeenth- and eighteenth-century Egyptian courts, with most cases being brought to Ḥanafī judges unless there was a pragmatic reason to bring them to other judges. In the practice of nineteenth-century Egypt, this situation was changing rapidly under Mehmed Ali, who embarked on a process of Ḥanafization,[9] through which there developed increasingly rigid adherence to the Ḥanafī school. This narrowing was partly the result of Ottoman decrees requiring Egyptian judges to issue rulings in conformity with Ḥanafī law and partly the influence of modern perspectives on legal conformity and the European nineteenth-century anti-legal pluralism ethos. Throughout the nineteenth century, there was a strong tendency to exclude non-Ḥanafīs from judgeships.[10]

Prior to Mehmed Ali's Ḥanafization program, Mālikī and Shāfiʿī muftis attended cases in the court. In addition, any fatwa issued by a trustworthy mufti and based on one of the four schools was accepted. Mehmed Ali and his successors gradually transformed the legal system so that there was one Ḥanafī state mufti resident in the court, whose fatwa had to be observed. The culmination of this narrowing of the pluralistic Sunnī legal system occurred in 1839, when the Turkish governor of the Qina province in Upper Egypt sent a letter to the Mālikī mufti in Isna indicating that any fatwa would henceforth only be issued by the Ḥanafī mufti resident at the court and that there was no need to bring non-Ḥanafī fatwas to court since the official judge was Ḥanafī and ruled only according to the official school.[11]

This Ḥanafizing tendency—which in some ways resembles sixteenth-century Ottoman Ḥanafization efforts—can be seen clearly in a treatise written by the Mālikī jurist Ḥasan al-ʿIdwī al-Ḥamzāwī in 1855, in which he discussed the restriction of judgeships to one school. He confirmed that there was no contradiction to the rules of Sharīʿa in using only the Ḥanafī school given that Abū Ḥanīfa did not give priority to analogy over the textual sources. Ironically, he even invoked al-Shaʿrānī's relativist approach to legal pluralism enunciated in his *al-Mīzān* to support his acceptance of the strict school loyalty (*tamadhhub*) position of nineteenth-century Egyptian courts, despite al-Shaʿrānī's general aversion to this position.[12]

Mehmed Ali and his successors also engaged in efforts to centralize the government apparatus through extra-Sharīʿa legislation. In 1829–30, for instance, he issued his first criminal legislation, then the Agricultural Code (*Qānūn al-Filāḥa*) of 1830 and the Penal Code of 1945 (*Qānūn al-Muntakhabāt*).[13] After Mehmed Ali's reign, the reforms continued, culminating in the introduction of a European legal system in the modern sense of "a community's code of rules."[14] Not long after Mehmed Ali's reforms, the Ottoman Empire introduced its own reforms during the Tanzimat period (1826–78), in which new national courts were established and Western-style codes were adopted in commercial law (1850), penal law (1858), and commercial procedure (1861).[15]

In the post–Mehmed Ali period, the Egyptian legal system also experienced important developments in which Islamic law was restricted to the realm of personal status law. In 1876 the mixed courts were created, followed by the national courts in 1883. In the period between 1880 and

1897, modern Sharīʿa courts were established to deal with litigation in family matters. This system remained effective until Sharīʿa courts were abolished in 1956.[16] The Ottomans were able to codify the Sharīʿa in a civil code known as the Mecelle (1869–76), while, in Egypt, it remained uncodified until the twentieth century. There was an attempt in Egypt by Muḥammad Qadrī Pasha to introduce an Egyptian Islamic legal code similar to the Ottoman Mecelle in the nineteenth century, but it never attained official status.[17] Qadrī Pasha's code, which only contained the authoritative opinions of the Ḥanafī school, contrasts sharply with the Ottoman *ikhtilāf* genre that focused on differences among the schools to facilitate people's transactions (as we saw in chapter 2). His exclusive reliance on the Ḥanafī school fit in well with the dominant ethos of homogenization, which was characteristic of that period. This ethos continued throughout the nineteenth century, culminating in a Ministry of Justice decree issued on December 10, 1891, requiring all judges, muftis, and employees of the Public Prosecution to be Ḥanafīs.[18] It was not until the twentieth century that a partial codification of the Sharīʿa in Egypt was achieved, with a new role for Ḥanafism that was quite different from Mehmed Ali's Ḥanafization efforts and, in some ways, more similar to the courts of the seventeenth and eighteenth centuries.

Twentieth-Century Codification and De-Ḥanafization

Following the Ḥanafization project initiated by Mehmed Ali and continued by his descendants, a return to the pragmatic legal pluralism of the seventeenth and eighteenth centuries was achieved through the partial codification of Sharīʿa-inspired family law in the twentieth century. According to Article 280 of Law 31 of 1910, all family laws had to be based on the preponderant view (*rājiḥ*) of the school of Abū Ḥanīfa, except in cases in which there is an explicit stipulation to the contrary.[19] Such exceptions referred to the targeted amendments of Ḥanafī law that drew upon the other schools pragmatically to accommodate changing social mores and values with regard to the family and gender relations.[20] Since Ḥanafism was the official school, the selection of less stringent rules meant either the selection of a weak view within Ḥanafism other than the preponderant view or the choice of a view from a completely different school. These choices were made by Egyptian legislators with a view to solving specific social problems, as we shall see.

Using Pragmatic Eclecticism to Place Limits on Divorce

The modern perspective of the centrality of the nuclear family led modern legislators to find ways to limit the husband's power of divorce, which they saw as sometimes reaching the level of frivolity. This theme of Islamic legal reform had been enunciated earlier by al-Zahrāwī (d. 1334/1915), who criticized Islamic repudiation (*ṭalāq*) in which women find themselves separated from their husbands owing to a frivolous oath made by the husband. According to al-Zahrāwī, a beloved wife, who could be a mother with children, may thus become separated from her husband based on juristic views that consider frivolous utterances of *ṭalāq* as grounds for separation.[21]

These juristic views were not challenged in actual law until decades after al-Zahrāwī wrote his article. This challenge was done through *tatabbu' al-rukhaṣ*, from within and without the four schools. Article 1 of Law 25 of 1929 stipulates that *ṭalāq* uttered under the influence was invalid. This was not based on the official Ḥanafī school but rather on the opinion of Aḥmad b. Ḥanbal and some of the Companions. The same article states that repudiation issued under duress was also invalid. This article was based on the views of the Shāfi'īs, Mālikīs, and Ḥanbalīs, but not the Ḥanafīs. Conditional repudiation too (Article 2) was considered invalid following the views of Companions of the Prophet such as 'Alī b. Abī Ṭālib, Shurayḥ, and al-Ḥakam b. 'Utayba.[22] According to Article 3 of Law 25 of 1929, a double or triple repudiation may only count as one. This is not the preponderant opinion of the Ḥanafī school, nor of any other school for that matter. It is, rather, based on the opinions of a handful of Companions such as Ibn Mas'ūd and 'Abd al-Raḥmān b. 'Awf, and is a minority view in the Mālikī, Ḥanbalī, and Ḥanafī schools.[23]

In an explanatory memorandum delineating the motivation behind the enactment of Law 25 of 1929, the Ministry of Justice explained that Muslim women were constantly threatened with repudiation. Sometimes neither the husband nor the wife knew when repudiation would take effect, as in the example of a husband's use of the conditional repudiation formula. The ministry decided to narrow down the prerogative for repudiation as exercised by men, even if this meant following the opinions of jurists from outside the four schools, which the ministry argued is a perfectly valid exercise.[24] This is a clear example of pragmatic eclecticism, where what counts is the potential legal result rather than the weight of the evidence undergirding a given juristic view.

Women's Access to Divorce through Mālikī "Harm" (Ḍarar)

In addition to limiting the man's repudiation prerogative, modern legislators expanded women's "for-cause" divorce rights. Article 6 of Law 25 of 1929 grants women the right to divorce against the husband's will when they can prove cause, known in Islamic juristic discourse as "harm" (*ḍarar*). The Ḥanafī school is perhaps the least generous to women with regard to divorce rights. This gave rise to the occasional abandonment of Ḥanafī rules in favor of widening the grounds of divorce for women, a social need that the law recognized.[25]

The Mālikī school was the obvious choice for legislators as it offers the widest definition of harm, which ranges from verbal abuse and refusing to talk to the wife to homosexuality.[26] For instance, in a case brought to a Cairo court in 1930, a woman was able to obtain a judicial divorce on grounds of her husband's verbal abuse. Similarly, a divorce case was brought to the Alexandria Court of Karmūz over an incident in which the husband was caught in an uncompromising position with a man. The court granted the wife the divorce based on the Mālikī principle that if the husband prefers another woman over his wife, she may seek a divorce. The court argued that, by analogy, preferring a man over her also constitutes harm to the wife.[27]

Articles 12, 13, and 14 of Law 25 are also based on the Mālikī school, with the definition of harm including the husband's absence for a long period of time without providing maintenance. But even if maintenance is provided throughout, his abandonment of their spousal bed (*hajr fi'l-maḍja'*) could also constitute a sufficient cause for divorce. A memorandum issued by the legal establishment further explains that what matters is not whether the husband is to blame for his absence, but rather the establishment of the occurrence of harm.[28]

Expansion of the Principle of "Harm"

Between 1929 and 1979, no new laws promoting women's rights were advanced until Sadat enshrined in legislation some of the demands of Egyptian feminists. Law 44 of 1979 allowed women an automatic for-cause divorce in the event the husband takes a second wife. In order to speedily push his law through, Sadat issued an emergency legal decree, which was approved by parliament. It was known as Jihan's Law, in reference to the president's wife, Jihan Sadat, who was thought to be its main proponent. The following year, the law's constitutionality was challenged and the whole matter was referred to the Supreme Constitutional Court (SCC) for a ruling. It was not until 1985 that a ruling by the highest court established the unconstitutionality of the law on the grounds that the initial emergency decree promulgating it was issued in the absence of a real emergency.[29]

Two months later, the Mubarak regime introduced a similar law (Law 100 of 1985), which was identical to Law 44 of 1979 with one exception that was viewed as a compromise with the traditional religious establishment. Under the new legislation, a wife's right to divorce in the event that the husband takes a second wife was no longer automatic. She now had to prove in court that his second marriage constituted tangible harm to her.[30] Furthermore, Article 11b of the law requires the husband to declare his marital status in all marriage certificates. If he is married, the name of his wife and her domicile must be stated. The notary must then inform the wife of the new marriage by registered mail. The law also gives the first wife up to a year to sue for divorce on the grounds of harm.[31] Legislators attributed their granting wives the prerogative to seek a repudiation on grounds of harm if the husband takes another wife to both the Mālikī and the Ḥanbalī schools. Pragmatic eclecticism thus played an important role in relaxing some of the rigidities of the official Ḥanafī school.[32]

No-Cause Divorce for Compensation (Khul')

The latest attempt made by modern legislators to grant women greater divorce rights came in the form of Law 1 of 2000, which allows women a no-cause divorce with compensation, known as *khul'*.[33] The law was an attempt to narrow the scope of discretion left to judges in assessing what constitutes harm. In the case that a wife is unable to convince the court of the occurrence of harm, she may at least give up her dower or other financial rights in exchange for a "for-compensation" divorce. The new law does not even require the wife to explain the reasons for why she wishes to terminate the marriage.[34] The most striking and controversial part of the law is Article 20, which stipulates that if the husband does not consent, the court is required to issue a judicial divorce against his will once she restitutes to him the dower he had given her. The court's ruling in this case is *not* subject to appeal.[35] The late shaykh of al-Azhar Muḥammad Sayyid Ṭanṭāwī declared that the law was in full conformity with the Sharīʿa and that it was approved by a majority vote in al-Azhar's Islamic Research Academy.[36]

In 2001 the constitutionality of the law was challenged by a husband who was forced to divorce his wife against his will after the passage of the law. His argument was that in the Sharīʿa, *khulʿ* is contingent upon the consent of the husband. He added that any law that contradicts the Sharīʿa is unconstitutional since Article 2 of the constitution, according to the amendment of 1980, states that "the principles of Islamic Sharīʿa are the main source of legislation."[37] The Supreme Constitutional Court's response is a telling example of the interplay between *ijtihād* and *taqlīd* in modern legal reform. First the court established the validity of *khulʿ* in principle based on Qur'an 2:229. Then it proceeded to cite the Prophetic tradition in which Jamīlah Bint ʿAbd Allāh came to the Prophet and informed him that, though she did not reproach her husband Thābit b. Qays regarding his character or religion, she did not wish to be guilty of showing disrespect to him. The Prophet asked her what she had received from him, and she informed him that she received a garden. He asked if she would give him back his garden, to which she replied that she would. The Prophet then told Thābit, according to one version of the report, "Accept the garden and make one declaration of repudiation (*ṭalāq*)."

The SCC justices then explained that there are other reports in which the Prophet divorced her in Thābit's absence (implying that his consent was unnecessary). According to the court, there was disagreement among jurists over whether the Prophet's command to divorce her signified an obligation or a recommendation. The legislator who had to make a choice between these conflicting juristic views opted for the view of the Mālikīs (*akhadha bi-madhhab al-Mālikiyya*), allowing the judge, failing reconciliation, to divorce her against the husband's will. The court added that the selection of the Mālikī view was informed by the purposes of the law (*maqāṣid al-Sharīʿa*).[38] Having explained the reasoning behind the law, the court's verdict was that there is no contradiction between Article 2 of the Egyptian constitution that "the principles of Islamic Sharīʿa are the main source of legislation" and Article 20 of Law 1 of 2000.[39]

The SCC's reference to a supposed Mālikī permission of divorce against the husband's will is rather baffling. The majority of jurists from all four schools (including the Mālikīs) interpreted the command by the Prophet to be one of advice and guidance,[40] and therefore the authoritative view within Mālikism, and all the Sunnī schools for that matter, is that the husband's consent remains essential.[41] Oussama Arabi has already shown that the new law represents "a radical discontinuity" with Islamic legal doctrine.[42] Arabi's description is accurate when it is read as referring to a break with the dominant views within the four Sunnī schools. He argues that the discontinuity was the result of a direct appeal to the textual sources and that no such innovation would have been possible under the system of *takhayyur* or *talfīq*.[43] I, however, see in the discourse of the SCC a clear appeal to *taqlīd* and a shying away from *ijtihād*, as the court clearly indicated that the legislator had to choose between two existing juristic opinions that were competing with one another, rather than appeal directly to the texts for new interpretations. They simply "opted" for the Mālikī opinion.

This was the same way al-Azhar University professor Muḥammad Muhannā understood the legislators' legal reasoning. Shortly after the law was passed, in an article published in al-Azhar's *al-Muslim* magazine, he called the new legislation "the personal whims law" (*qānūn al-ahwāʾ al-shakhṣiyya*), playing on its alliteration with personal status law. According to him, the law was a clear example of Occidentalization. While he never challenged the validity of *khulʿ* in principle, he was opposed to imposing such an arrangement on the husband against his will. He averred that no school permits the judge to force the husband to divorce his wife, explaining, in the manner of premodern jurists, that—like any other contract—the *khul*'s validity hinges on the consent of both parties. He pointed out that the legislators conflated Mālikī judicial for-cause divorce on the grounds of harm with the no-cause *khul*ʿ, which, he maintained, had to be consensual in all schools.[44]

Muhannā added that resorting to an anomalous view in any of the thousands of books of jurisprudence is unacceptable. Using the same premodern trope mobilized against pragmatic eclecticism, he opined that allowing the judge to have this power of divorce can lead to cases of adultery,[45] the assumption being that the divorce may be invalid, and hence the woman's subsequent marriage would amount to adultery. It is not clear whether the legislators were disingenuously appealing to the authority of the Mālikī school or, as Muḥammad Muhannā held, wrongly conflating the Mālikī conception of harm (*ḍarar*), in which the judge can issue a divorce against the husband's will, with the Mālikī view on *khul*ʿ. Be that as it may, the legislators found it necessary to appeal to the authority of an established school, rather than reinterpret the hadith as a command by the Prophet in his capacity as a judge. This choice speaks volumes about the preferred approach of legal modernization, in which legislators choose to derive their authority from existing juristic views through *taqlīd* rather than *ijtihād*, despite the negative views of *taqlīd* in modern Islamic legal historiography.

The *khul*ʿ law made the news in March 2012 when a member of the Egyptian People's Assembly, Muḥammad al-ʿUmda, drafted a bill to abolish Article 20 of Law 1 of 2000. Although al-Azhar has no legislative powers under the Egyptian constitution in force in 2012, the People's Assembly, which was dominated by the Muslim Brotherhood (MB), decided not to proceed with the draft law until al-Azhar had been consulted. Members of the Islamic Research Academy, including Aḥmad ʿUmar Hāshim, ʿAbd Allāh al-Najjār, and ʿAbd al-Muʿṭī Bayyūmī, as well as al-Azhar University professors of jurisprudence Saʿd al-Dīn al-Hilālī and Ḥāmid Abū Ṭālib, argued that the law was fully in line with Sharīʿa. The scholars did not make reference to the Mālikī school or to any specific premodern jurist and simply cited the hadith without claiming a new *ijtihād*.[46]

Returning to legal practice prior to the nineteenth century, based on my own sample of Egyptian court records from the seventeenth and eighteenth centuries, I found no instances in which the husband was forced into a *khul'* arrangement by the judge. The language of the contracts implied that the husband's consent was essential. The wife or her representative would request (*sa'alat*) a divorce from the husband in exchange for forgoing some financial rights. Then the husband would agree to this arrangement and divorce her (*fa-ajāba su'ālahā li-dhālika wa-ṭallaqahā*).[47] According to Abdal-Rahman Abdal-Rehim, however, there were some instances of Ottoman judges enforcing a divorce against the husband's will, but such cases must have been rare.[48] In the Ottoman court records examined in the previous chapters, I did not find cases of harm using Mālikī law as was the case in modern legislation, perhaps because women had greater access to *khul'*, which was a very widespread practice in the Egyptian courts of the seventeenth and eighteenth centuries.

Age of Child Custody

Prior to Law 25 of 1929, the age of child custody reflected the dominant view within the Ḥanafī school, which is seven years for boys, and nine years for girls. Law 25 of 1929 gave the judge some power in considering the well-being of the child on a case-by-case basis, rather than what used to be an immediate transfer of custody from mother to father when the child reached the prescribed age in the Ḥanafī school. The law stipulates that once a girl reaches the age of nine and a boy the age of seven, the judge determines whether to extend the period to nine for the boy and eleven for the girl or transfer custody to the father. The legislators argued that the law was in line with the Ḥanafī school in which some jurists set the age at which girls and boys can be independent of their mothers at eleven and nine years respectively.[49] This was a case of vertical pragmatic eclecticism within the Ḥanafī school.

This law would later be amended by Law 100 of 1985, which raised the age of female custodianship to ten for boys and twelve for girls. After these ages have been reached, the judge may then allow the boy to remain in the custody of the mother until he reaches the age of fifteen and the girl until she is married if he believes this to be in their interest.[50] Finally, Law 4 of 2005 amended its predecessor, fixing the age at fifteen for both girls and boys, after which the judge may ask the child if she or he wishes to remain with the mother.[51] The legislators did not explain the reasoning behind the law, but had they explicitly resorted to pragmatic eclecticism, they would have had no difficulty in justifying their choices along those lines because of the striking divergences among jurists over defining the child's age of independence from the mother both within each of the Sunnī schools and across school boundaries. The Mālikī school gives custody to women until the boy reaches puberty and the girl consummates a marriage. Since many jurists estimate puberty at fifteen years of age if no clear physical signs of puberty exist prior to that age, it could have been argued by legislators, for instance, that this increase was based on the Mālikī school.[52] It is intriguing that legislators did not justify this law by reference to any of the Sunnī schools, as was customary in previous family law legislation. Law 4 of 2005 has recently been challenged by fathers, who argued that raising the age of custody to fifteen has denied them the right to participate in the upbringing of their children. Following the January 25, 2011, Egyptian Revolution, several sit-ins were organized by fathers in front of the office of Egypt's former grand mufti, ʿAlī Jumʿa, who agreed to examine the law's compatibility with Islamic law and to propose amendments if necessary. The fathers who organized the sit-in sought to return the age at which the father assumes custody to nine and seven, according to the Ḥanafī school, claiming that Law 4 of 2005 is contrary to the Sharīʿa.[53]

Unsurprisingly, the mufti's comments infuriated some women's rights activists for interfering in a legislative matter. They also saw the fathers organizing the sit-ins as opportunists, who feigned outrage at the violation of Islamic law to advance their interests. For instance, Iman Baybars, the chair of the Association for the Development and Enhancement of Women (ADEW), countered that the Sunnī schools disagree on the age of custody transfer and that the fathers' invocation of the Sharīʿa is only a pretext to change the law in their favor.[54]

Another critique articulated by the fathers is that the law gives priority of custody to a long list of female relatives as distant as the mother's aunt over the father in the event of the death of the mother. Ironically, the reason this is the case is because the law partially follows the Ḥanafī school, which is the same school that the fathers had invoked in their quest to reduce the age of custody. Conversely, the Shāfiʿī and Ḥanbalī schools have a much shorter list of female relatives receiving priority of custody over the father in the early years of the child's life.[55] This contestation between fathers and state legislation shows what is at stake in the codification of Sharīʿa.

Talfīq in the Courts

As we saw in the previous chapters, the very utilization of different school rules in the same law does not necessarily by itself constitute *talfīq*. It only occurs when a single legal transaction is based on two schools or two juristic views. Consider this example from a case brought to the Court of Asyūṭ in 1944: a wife gave up her rights to the delayed dower and the waiting period (*ʿidda*) maintenance in exchange for a *khulʿ* divorce, and the husband repudiated her accordingly. The question is: would this divorce still be valid in the absence of evidence of the sum of money given up by the wife? The court was to take the Shāfiʿī view that the divorce is valid even in the absence of such evidence. This same couple was married under Ḥanafī law and therefore their divorce under a different school constituted an example of diachronic *talfīq*.[56]

We also see examples of *talfīq* in Law 48 of 1946, which regulates endowments. Egyptian law permits temporary endowments based on the Mālikī school that are not permitted under Ḥanafī law. A temporary endowment raises another question: who owns the endowment after it expires? The law did not directly discuss the issue of ownership. Yet according to Article 17 of the law, when the endowment expires, the property returns to the endower if he or she is alive, but if she or he is deceased, it returns to the beneficiaries of the endowment. The first part of the article agrees with the Mālikī school, whereby the endower maintains ownership, whereas the second part is based on the Ḥanbalī school. Thus, when the endowment expires after the endower dies, the law terminates the endowment according to the Mālikī school and transfers ownership to its beneficiaries in accordance with the Ḥanbalī school, which represents an example of synchronic *talfīq*.[57]

Although *talfīq* was used in the courts on a limited scale, we still see examples of judges' aversion to it. There is a sense among some judges that once a law is based on one school, all future cases not covered in the law should be referred to the same school. This was the view of the judges of a case in the neighborhood of Sayyida Zaynab in Cairo in 1933, Case 3558, in which a woman argued that her husband's imprisonment constituted harm to her, invoking Article 6, Law 25 of 1929. The judges maintained that since this law was based on the Mālikī school, any incident related to it should be based on the same school. According to the court, Mālikism does not consider imprisonment in and of itself to constitute harm (*ḍarar*), and therefore no divorce may be granted on these grounds alone.[58]

This reluctance to resort to *talfīq* is also clear in Case 20 of 1960, in which a husband challenged the decision of the court to divorce him from his wife on the grounds of failure to provide maintenance. The lawyer argued that there was only one witness to his inability to provide such maintenance, which is not sufficient evidence under the school of Abū Ḥanīfa. The court decided that since the law was based on the Mālikī school, Mālikism takes precedence over the Ḥanafī school in terms of establishing the necessary procedures and conditions for witnesses.[59]

To sum up, it was traditional *taqlīd* that played the most important role in modern legislation, in contrast to *ijtihād*, which has taken up so much of the intellectual energy of modern historians. Most departures from the official Ḥanafī school were brought about through recourse to *tatabbu' al-rukhaṣ* or *talfīq*. Even in situations in which there was a reexamination of the source texts, such as when interpreting the Prophetic tradition about for-compensation divorce to indicate a command to the husband as opposed to a recommendation, modern legislators still endeavored to find a *taqlīd*ic justification for their position. This justification was achieved by attributing their view to the Mālikī school, rather than claiming fresh *ijtihād*.

The Selection of Legal Opinions in the Absence of Statutes

As we saw above, legislators employed pragmatic eclecticism in their efforts to remove some of the rigidities of Ḥanafism. For areas not covered by legislation, judges had to follow the preponderant view (*arjaḥ al-aqwāl*) of the school of Abū Ḥanīfa, as opposed to exercising pragmatic eclecticism or their own *ijtihād*. A judge's decision that strayed from the school of Abū Ḥanīfa was overruled.[60] But that does not mean that judges played a passive role in shaping legal doctrine. There were always instances in which no clearly dominant view within the Ḥanafī school could be found. In such cases, in particular, the judges' own beliefs informed their choices, setting precedents that were not always in line with the legislators' modernist agenda.

By way of example, the Ḥanafī school sometimes offers two competing opinions, with neither view assuming an exclusive preponderant status.[61] In this situation, the judge has to make a definitive selection. These juridical choices—in the absence of legislation—were an important manner in which judges influenced the legal process and either placed limits on the modernist legislation that we have examined thus far or supported it. For instance, there are two competing views in the Ḥanafī school regarding a woman's right to maintenance when she works outside of the marital home. One view denies them that right, while the other grants it to them. In the absence of an explicit stipulation in the law, al-Jundī, who was a judge in the 1930s–70s, gave preference to the second Ḥanafī view, which he considered "more suitable for the developments of our times." His focus on the legal result suggests that the decision was not based on an evidentiary evaluation of legal reasoning but rather on pragmatic considerations. Case 184 brought to the court of Asyūṭ in 1946 led to a ruling the following year that a woman who works outside of the marital home is still entitled to a maintenance allowance. In his explanation of the ruling, the judge challenged the Ḥanafī view that a woman is not entitled to maintenance if she works during the day outside of the marital home and spends the night with the husband. Here the judge's view contradicted those of some very important Ḥanafī jurists such as Zayn al-Dīn b. Nujaym al-Miṣrī (d. 970/1563), Sirāj al-Dīn b. Nujaym al-Ḥanafī (d. 1005/1596), and Ibn ʿĀbidīn (d. 1252/1836).[62]

In a court ruling in 1947, the judge at the court of Asyūṭ ruled that a man who had previously agreed to his wife's working cannot then withdraw his consent. In 1953, a court in Maghāgha went further (Case 753), ruling that a husband does not have the prerogative to stop his wife from working, so long as her work does not interfere with his rights over her.[63]

Another question not covered by modern legislation in Egypt is whether a woman is entitled to a wage for breastfeeding a child for the period before an agreement is drawn between her and the baby's guardian. This issue presented a challenge to judges because there are two contradictory views in the Ḥanafī school that enjoy almost the same level of strength. The first view, attributed to Zayn al-Dīn b. Nujaym al-Miṣrī, is that a woman is entitled to a wage for breastfeeding during the period before a contract is drawn up. The other view, supported by Ibn Ghānim al-Maqdisī (d. 1004/1596), is that she is not entitled to a wage for the period preceding such an agreement. In the end, the courts followed the opinion of Ibn Nujaym.[64]

But what about the wage for the custody of a child for the period preceding an agreement? The grand mufti of Egypt, al-Shaykh al-Mahdī (d. 1897), had issued a fatwa following the opinion of al-Maqdisī, denying the woman a wage for custody for the period prior to drawing up a contract. Some courts in the 1930s followed the fatwa of al-Mahdī, but others did not wish to have two standards for very similar types of cases, namely, the treatment of breastfeeding wages as opposed to custody wages prior to entering into a contract. In his discussion of this issue, al-Jundī added that women should be granted a wage in both situations for the sake of consistency. In 1936, case 410, brought before the court of Atsa, prompted judges to grant a woman such a wage, establishing the desired consistency by equating breastfeeding wages with custody wages.[65]

As we saw above, the state utilization of pragmatic eclecticism in codification introduced some flexibility to the legal system, while retaining the dominant status of Ḥanafism, a position that had its detractors. In 2002 an Egyptian man by the name of Magdī ʿAllām M. Saʿīd challenged the constitutionality of Article 3 of Law 1 of 2000, which states that wherever there are no legal provisions, judges must select the most preponderant view (*arjaḥ al-aqwāl*) of the school of Abū Ḥanīfa. He argued that this provision contradicts the Sharīʿa because it restricts law to the opinion of a single school, thus closing the door of *ijtihād*. He added that the practice of *ijtihād* is considered an obligatory duty (*wājib*) for Muslims of all times.[66] Although he lost his case, the question he raised presents new concerns with modern legislation: placing restrictions on legal flexibility through largely narrowing the definition of Sharīʿa as the dominant view of one school and the closure of the gate of *ijtihād*.

Can the Sharīʿa Be Restored?

Pragmatic eclecticism, which was heavily utilized in the modern codification of personal status laws, has often been described as a modern form of "juristic opportunism" and as a development that had no sound basis in the Sharīʿa.[67] According to Coulson, the growing utilization of *talfīq* and *takhayyur* in the modern period marked the end of traditional *taqlīd*.[68] Similarly, Hallaq judges the utilization of *takhayyur* in the codification of personal status laws as leading to an "arbitrary amalgamation of doctrines."[69] He argues that even where some traditional rules are to be found in modern nation-state laws such as the law of personal status, they have been uprooted from their indigenous context and therefore do not represent the Sharīʿa, which, as he argues, saw its demise by the middle of the twentieth century.[70]

Although Hallaq acknowledges that the popular Muslim imagination holds "these remnants to be an authentic and genuine expression of *fiqhī* family law," he rejects this belief because this sphere of law was severed from both the substance of classical *fiqh* and its methodology. The reason for his verdict is that new family laws did not maintain the Arabicate hermeneutics, nor "the human and institutional bearers of this complex epistemic tradition."[71]

In addition to these transformations, Hallaq explains that, in the modern period, the concept of necessity (*ḍarūra*) was transposed from the domain of substantive law to the realm of legal methodology, thus regulating the construction of substantive law generally.[72] The elevation of the concept of necessity to a higher status within juristic discourse is nothing new. As noted, "necessity" and "need" were often used by jurists in an ad hoc manner to justify pushing at the boundaries of legal inertia (see the introduction and chapter 2). In the course of the debates over *tatabbuʿ al-rukhaṣ* and *talfīq*, many jurists permitted these pragmatic strategies on account of need and necessity, with both terms being used in an unregulated sense, in a manner quite different from the way they were devised by al-Juwaynī and al-Ghazālī. Thus, as noted in chapter 2, al-Subkī permitted *tatabbuʿ al-rukhaṣ* when one encounters a "taxing necessity" (*ḍarūratun arhaqathu*), which is clearly not a life-threatening situation.[73]

We have also seen need and necessity, as well as the corruption of the age (*fasād ahl al-zamān*), being invoked as tools to justify the elevation of an epistemically non-preponderant view to the status of the dominant *madhhab*-opinion for pragmatic reasons, even though the evidence might not support the new *madhhab*-opinion. This is not to say that the concept of necessity did not evolve in the modern period. It certainly did, at least in terms of the sheer number of cases in which it has come to be invoked, but it is important to point out that the technical connection to the five necessities (*ḍarūriyyāt*) of al-Ghazālī had already been severed in some juristic discourses of the Mamluk period.

In order to rejuvenate the entire traditional system, Hallaq explains, Islamic law would have to be more than a dead "branch."[74] It must include "a theoretical, methodological, and perhaps, hermeneutic system," a new *uṣūl al-fiqh* that is suitable to the ever-changing conditions of modernity,[75] since the traditional theory of *uṣūl al-fiqh* is no longer well-suited to the exigencies of modern life.[76] Given the fact that the creation of a new legal methodology is not attempted by the "utilitarianists" (our modernist camp, see chapter 5) who rely on pragmatic eclecticism and the concept of necessity, Hallaq considers their approach inferior, compared with the more sophisticated "liberalists" such as Shaḥrūr and Fazlur Rahman.[77]

Hallaq valorizes legal methodology over substantive law, assuming that the marginalization of the former is a by-product of the modern period. He agrees with Nathan Brown that it was only in the modern period that there was a shift from focus on law-as-process to law-as-content, or as Nathan Brown puts it,

> I will suggest that important shifts in the meaning of the Islamic sharia have taken place in the Muslim world, and that these shifts are closely connected to the nature and viability of legal and educational institutions associated with the Islamic sharia in the past. As the Islamic sharia has become disconnected from these institutions, its meaning has changed in some fundamental ways. Most important, the sharia is approached less for its process than for its content. And because the shift

> in institutions and understanding has received much less attention from Muslims, widespread attempts to recreate older relationships (particularly involving the relationship between the Islamic sharia and the state) in fact involve a deepening rather than a counteracting of the transformation in the Islamic sharia.[78]

While it is true that there was a shift from process to content in Islamic law, I would argue that this shift came about much earlier than the modern period. Recall that there was a juristic disagreement (*ikhtilāf*) literature, particularly during the sixteenth through eighteenth centuries, in which only the substantive legal opinions of the different schools were given without any elaboration of the reasoning behind them. This genre, as we saw in chapter 2, was used precisely because there was a shift from process to substantive law, from legal methodology and the epistemological coherence of the *madhhab* to a focus on the content of the law. The premodern practice of pragmatic eclecticism, whether in the form of *tatabbu‘ al-rukhaṣ* or *talfīq*, confirms this observation. This shift of focus to content or legal result, rather than the process of reasoning, might partly explain the absence of strong opposition on the part of the *‘ulamā’* to the content-based "piecemeal" codification of Islamic law.

This shift from process to content saw juristic views being selected, not for their methodological consistency with legal methodology or based on the parameters of the single school's methodological, hermeneutic orientation, but according to their utility to society. The shift in emphasis from the methodological to the substantive is itself one of the most important developments that took place in Islamic legal discourse and practice in the premodern period. This development is not unique to Islamic law, as transplants akin to those resulting from school-boundary crossing and the focus on content are part of most legal systems. Having said that, it is important to caution here that the valorization and institutionalization of pragmatic eclecticism was not an inevitable part of the institutionalization of *taqlīd*. It is conceivable that a *taqlīd*-based system could have failed to produce the same shift toward the methodological "incoherence" inherent in the focus on the legal result (that is, the content rather than the methodological process) through *tatabbu‘ al-rukhaṣ*. Had legal theorists, for instance, adopted the position of school loyalty (*tamadhhub*), there would not necessarily have been such a shift to content since abiding by each school's dominant view would have preserved the perceived theoretical coherence of the school's methodology.[79] This counterfactual scenario would have certainly increased rigidity in the system of *taqlīd*, prompting jurists to find alternative avenues for legal flexibility to accommodate the evolving needs of Muslim societies.

Despite negative scholarly views of the modern codification of Islamic law, which is often described as inauthentic, the majority of Muslim reformers today focus on the content of Islamic law.[80] There is very little discourse on legal methodology, which, by contrast, tends to come mostly from the liberalist camp, one such attempt being Jamāl al-Bannā's "new jurisprudence" as we saw in chapter 5.[81] Despite the intellectual sophistication of some of the thinkers in this camp, theirs remains an elite discourse that has little support among Muslim activists. One must not overlook the view of those who see the restoration of substantive law—rather than the creation of a sophisticated new *uṣūl al-fiqh*—as a return to the Sharīʿa. The debate between Abū Yaʿrub al-Marzouqi and al-Būṭī is a case in point. Al-Būṭī's view, which represents the mainstream, should not be rejected as insufficient or unsophisticated offhand. As we saw in chapter 5, jurists using a mix of pragmatic eclecticism and *ijtihād* have offered solutions to many of the areas of perceived incompatibility between Islamic law and modern discourses of human rights. Al-Ghannūshī's book *al-Ḥuriyyāt al-ʿĀmma fi'l-Islām* suggests that eclecticism will continue to be the preferred approach of the proponents of political Islam for years to come.

Many traditional and modernist Islamic activists in Egypt support an expansion of the approach used in personal status laws to the rest of the Egyptian legal system. Even the call for the independence of al-Azhar and the restoration of its endowments are considered by Islamists as subsidiary to the restoration of Sharīʿa qua substantive law. After all, many Islamists contend that the Sharīʿa can be restored without such independence as happened in the codification of personal status laws in Egypt in the twentieth century. As we have seen, the debates taking place in Egypt today revolve around Sharīʿa as content. Recall, for instance, the bill to annul the *khul*ʿ law proposed by members of the Muslim Brotherhood–controlled and short-lived 2012 People's Assembly.

The challenge of modernity and its radical transformations is yet another historical evolution that the Sharīʿa has experienced in its long history. To say that Sharīʿa and its many institutions were never static in the premodern or modern periods is to state the obvious, but it follows that we should not privilege the understanding of one historical period over another, such as the privileging of *ijtihād* over *taqlīd*, jurists' law over statutory law, or, more generally, premodern over modern Sharīʿa. Given that the modern evolution of Sharīʿa has already been judged to be acceptable to the majority of its stakeholders, the answer to the initial question is that the Sharīʿa as understood by most of its proponents in Egypt, for instance, has already been partially restored.

If the Sharīʿa can be restored, then the question remains as to whether pragmatic eclecticism would continue to inform legislators after the Arab Spring. We have seen thus far that the content of Islamic substantive law is vast and that this very fact has enabled it to deal with many social and historical changes brought about by the hegemonic discourses of modernity. The partial modern codification of personal status laws in Egypt is a good example of the pragmatic eclectic methods used to accommodate modern discourses. An example of this diversity in contemporary Egypt is Abū al-Futūḥ's view that women and non-Muslims should not be excluded from senior positions in the state. This view contradicts the declared Muslim Brotherhood's draft party platform.[82] It is these debates that will shape the efforts to search for an Islamic modernity and determine how different it will be from Western modernity.[83]

It is highly unlikely that a comprehensive modernist Islamic legal code will be written in its entirety and pushed through the legislative process for enactment. The creation of a substantive legal system inspired by the modernist project will likely continue to be piecemeal, a fact that I do not see as a sign of incoherence or weakness. In this process, al-Azhar will likely play an important role in the potential operationalization of Article II of Egypt's 1971 constitution (which was kept intact in Egypt's 2012 and 2014 constitutions) stipulating that the principles of Sharīʿa are the main source of legislation. Since al-Azhar has been the point of reference for most political activists in Egypt today, it is important to outline its main trends toward legal reform in post–2011 Revolution Egypt.

Al-Azhar's Position

We have already discussed different approaches to legal reform in the contemporary period, namely the modernist, purist, and liberalist camps. These approaches are all represented within al-Azhar, although Islamic modernism has always prevailed within the institution. As the birthplace of modernism in Egypt, most scholars at al-Azhar have focused their reform efforts on the utilization of *taqlīd* and to a lesser degree on *ijtihād*, but within the well-established premodern hermeneutic and methodological parameters. Al-Azhar's towering figures of modernism such as 'Abduh, al-Marāghī, Shaltūt, Muḥammad al-Ghazālī, and al-Qaraḍāwī have been, generally speaking, diametrically opposed to liberalist hermeneutics. They rejected the challenges liberalists posed to the hadith literature and the latter's attempts to devise revolutionary hermeneutics. The success of modernism within al-Azhar is partly owing to the conservative approach of modernists to legal codification, especially through pragmatic eclecticism, which is viewed by many within the institution as a traditional tool.

Since Egypt's 2011 Revolution, al-Azhar has returned to the scene with renewed vigor. The institution's leadership took a clear position against the purist tendency, with the shaykh of al-Azhar, Aḥmad al-Ṭayyib, calling purists "modern-day Khārijites," a reference to a violent group that was responsible for much bloodshed in the early years of Islam. He also severely criticized the attacks in March and April 2011 against shrines, blamed on purist "Salafī" elements.[84]

Al-Azhar's leadership went further in taking a modernist position on the debates that have been taking place in Egypt. Top leaders within al-Azhar participated in the drafting of a document, with the full backing of the institution, that was created by both Egyptian intellectuals from different ideological backgrounds and Azharī scholars. The document calls for middle-of-the-road Islamic thought (*al-fikr al-Islāmī al-wasaṭī*). It explains that the participants were keen on seeking inspiration from the famous figures of reform in al-Azhar, starting with Ḥasan al-ʿAṭṭār and his student Rifāʿa al-Ṭahṭāwī, as well as Muḥammad ʿAbduh and his students, al-Marāghī, Muḥammad ʿAbd Allāh Dirāz, Muṣṭafā ʿAbd al-Razzāq, Shaltūt, and others. According to the document, those in attendance also received inspiration from non-Azharī Egyptian intellectuals who had contributed to the epistemological and human evolution of Egypt and the Arab world, including philosophers, lawyers, and artists. The objective of the document was to determine the principles regulating the relationship between Islam and the state. It calls for the establishment of a "modern state" (*dawla ʿaṣriyya*) and a "democratic transformation" (*al-taḥawwul al-dīmuqrāṭī*) and to protect Islamic principles from extremism (*ghulūw*), misinterpretation (*sūʾ al-tafsīr*), and extremist currents (*al-tayyārāt al-munḥarifa*) that rely on sectarian and immoderate religious rhetoric.[85]

The document supports the establishment of a modern, constitutional democratic nation-state, which guarantees the separation of powers, and grants the people's representatives the right to legislate in accordance with the precepts of "true Islam," a religion that has never throughout its history experienced a theocratic state, the document emphasizes.[86] Although the document supports the decisions of a legislature elected by the people and gives al-Azhar no powers in this domain, it circumscribes legislative freedom with the broad statement "provided that the general principles of Islamic Sharīʿa are the main source of legislation."[87]

By referring to the "general principles," the document drafters took a position on the debate between purists and their opponents from the entire political spectrum, including the Muslim Brotherhood, over the wording of the constitution. Many purist leaders called for changing "general principles" to the "rulings of Islamic Sharīʿa" (*aḥkām*). According to them, general principles can be a way to avoid instituting Islamic substantive law by relying on an interpretation that refers to general values such as equality and justice.[88] This concern over the meaning of "principles of Islamic Sharīʿa" was motivated by the Egyptian Supreme Constitutional Court's (SCC) interpretation, which mirrored the view of the modernist pioneer Muḥammad Rashīd Riḍā. The SCC justices argued that the state should only respect rules that are considered apodictic with respect to both their authenticity and their meaning. This approach guaranteed that only a few rules may be ultimately incorporated into state law.[89] In a manner similar to the interpretation of the SCC, the signatories to al-Azhar's document agreed on the principle that "Islamic reference" (*marjiʿiyya*) refers to "a number of comprehensive issues, derived from Sharʿī texts that are apodictic in their authenticity and meaning."[90]

One of the most important aspects of the document is that it calls for al-Azhar's independence from the state through the creation of a new statute regulating the institution, which would enable it to elect its own grand shaykh. It also preserves al-Azhar's status as the only institution that may be legitimately consulted on all things Islamic, without confiscating people's right to express their views, "provided that they meet necessary scholarly conditions."[91]

Al-Azhar's document is, in some ways, similar to the Muslim Brotherhood's 2007 party platform, wherein it calls for the establishment of an elected council of religious scholars whose decisions on legislative matters of religious law are binding.[92] After the revolution, as noted, the MB's approach was tested when the *khulʿ* law was challenged by some members of the People's Assembly. The Assembly, which was more than 70 percent controlled by the MB and Salafīs, consulted al-Azhar on the matter, and al-Azhar's decision that the *khulʿ* law was fully in accordance with the Sharīʿa led lawmakers to keep the law intact. As we saw in chapter 5, the *khulʿ* law represents a clear modernist approach to women's divorce rights.

Because of al-Azhar's confirmation of the *khulʿ* law, as well as the efforts of the rector of al-Azhar and the grand mufti in countering purist rhetoric, al-Azhar has been touted by the overwhelming majority of the political spectrum as the voice of moderation.[93] This image of al-Azhar, albeit a trope that goes back at least to the nineteenth century, was reinforced by the resurgence of purist Salafism. Even Egyptian Christians, who were concerned about their freedoms in a state dominated by political Islam, have largely echoed the same discourse, which represents al-Azhar as the voice of "real" and moderate Islam.[94]

Against this backdrop, most political forces declared their support for the independence of the institution. The rector of al-Azhar, Aḥmad al-Ṭayyib, wasted no time. He, along with members of al-Azhar's leadership, drafted a new bill to regulate the medieval institution, amending Law

103 of 1961, which gave Egypt's president the power to appoint the rector of al-Azhar. In 2012 the Supreme Council of the Armed Forces (SCAF), which had legislative powers after the fall of Mubarak and his parliament, passed the law only four days before Egypt's first freely elected People's Assembly convened. The law, which guarantees the institution's financial independence, also revived the Supreme Council of 'Ulamā' (SCU) (Hay'at Kibār al-'Ulamā')—abolished by Nasser in 1961—stipulating that its members must be drawn from the four Sunnī *madhāhib*. This council was also charged with electing the mufti and the rector of al-Azhar.[95]

According to the new law, the current rector of al-Azhar will choose the members of the first council. The elected members, who are not to exceed forty individuals, will then elect both the mufti and the rector of al-Azhar when these positions become vacant. The council will also issue decisions regarding matters of juristic disagreement, after examining the opinion of the Islamic Research Academy (Majma' al-Buḥūth al-Islāmiyya). One of the conditions for membership in this new influential organization is that the member must abide by al-Azhar's approach, that is, the approach of the people of the Sunna and the orthodox community (*ahl al-sunna wa'l-jamā'a*), in the realms of legal methodology and substantive law in the four schools.[96] This reference to the four schools clearly weeds out some purist elements that abandon the schools in both legal methodology and substantive law. The reference to legal methodology would also exclude liberalists who reject premodern hermeneutics. The speed with which SCAF issued the law, only a few days before an Islamist-dominated parliament had convened, was seen as springing from anxiety among members of SCAF that a law issued by the purist Salafīs, who controlled 25 percent of the postrevolutionary parliament, and the MB may lead to the new government's selecting a hard-line rector or mufti. This newly won independence means that the current rector would have greater impact on the future of the institution.[97] Under the law, the current rector will set al-Azhar's agenda for decades to come through the selection of the committee that will, in turn, choose his successor.

Given the toppling of Morsi in 2013 and the designation of the Muslim Brotherhood as a terrorist organization by both Egypt and Saudi Arabia, as well as the wide support that al-Sisi's regime enjoys among the top echelons of the institution, al-Azhar will most likely continue to play a decisive role in the legal landscape of Egypt. Given al-Azhar's current leadership, the modernist approach will likely continue to be the dominant strand of legal thought in Egypt for decades to come. Al-Azhar's role as a source of guidance on matters of Sharīʿa appeared in Article IV of Egypt's 2012 constitution, which states that "the opinion of al-Azhar's Supreme Council of ʿUlamāʾ must be taken in matters related to Islamic Sharīʿa."[98] The interpretation of the article has caused some confusion among different political parties, with purist Salafīs supporting a reading that obligates the legislature to take the opinion of al-Azhar, and the Muslim Brotherhood supporting the interpretation that the institution's role is merely consultative and that its opinion does not have to be solicited.[99] My reading of the article is that al-Azhar's opinion must be solicited, since the Arabic present tense for "must be taken" (*yuʾkhadh raʾy*) is used in modern legal writing to signify obligation, but the implication from the use of "opinion" is that it is, nevertheless, not binding. In other words, the legislature is indeed under an obligation to listen to al-Azhar's opinion without having to actually follow it. The 2014 constitution removed this article completely, reversing an important gain of al-Azhar under the 2012 constitution.

Despite the current modernist tendencies of the leadership of al-Azhar, the institution is not immune from the purist tendency, even though it historically managed to keep it at bay. A major change in the orientation of the institution nonetheless will most likely take a long time to materialize. That does not mean that all decisions coming out of the institution's various bodies follow a modernist agenda. In reality, al-Azhar has enough complex internal structures that have guaranteed it some level of independence, even under Mubarak's dictatorship.[100]

Conclusion

We have seen in this chapter that the reign of Mehmed Ali and his successors in the nineteenth century witnessed a process of Ḥanafization, departing from seventeenth- and eighteenth-century legal pluralism. Legal homogenization, a desideratum in the nineteenth century, was later reversed in the partial codification of personal status laws, in which the

Mālikī school, for instance, was utilized to grant women greater access to divorce rights. The Ḥanafī school in twentieth-century legislation retained its default status, since in the absence of statutes, judges were required to follow the preponderant view of the Ḥanafī School. The twentieth-century partial codification of family law represented a return to the pluralistic system that existed in Ottoman Egypt before the rise of Mehmed Ali.

Feminist demands for greater rights for women were partially served through pragmatic eclecticism. Sometimes legislators went beyond the dominant views within the four Sunnī schools to include opinions of the Companions of the Prophet where necessary. *Tatabbuʿ al-rukhaṣ* was nevertheless drawn upon more often than *talfīq*. We can even sense a certain level of aversion to *talfīq* among Egyptian judges in the practice of twentieth-century courts.

The partial codification of family law, which was more similar to eighteenth-century than to nineteenth-century Egypt, represents an evolutionary process rather than an abrupt rupture. This is not to say that codification itself has not changed Islamic law. On the contrary, Islamic law will never be the same again. One major difference is that while in the Mamluk and Ottoman periods legal subjects selected the forum of adjudication on a case-by-case basis, in the modern period that prerogative is precluded as the various school rules are already built into the system's court proceedings by the modern state legislature.[101] Although the reformers had a conception of the welfare of society in mind when they wrote these laws, in a limited sense they have placed greater restrictions on the leeway that legal subjects enjoyed in the Ottoman period.

Conclusion

> When the traditional authorities had to be manipulated in this fashion to yield the required rule, any claim that this process constituted *taqlīd* had become nothing more than a thin veil of pretense, a purely formal and superficial adherence to the established principles of jurisprudence, which masked the reality of an attempt to fashion the terms of the law to meet the needs of society as objectively determined.[1]

THE ABOVE is a commonly held view about the utilization of pragmatic eclecticism in the modern period. There is an assumption that employing legal pluralism to meet the needs of society is a novelty of modern legislation, a manipulation of pure *taqlīd*. This claim assumes that *taqlīd* was not fashioned to meet the needs of society in the premodern period. While many historians such as Coulson supported these "modern" developments because of the greater rights they granted women, among other marginalized groups, they assumed that these changes have no roots in the discourse and practice of Islamic law in the premodern period.[2] The reason for Coulson's assessment of a rupture partly springs from a perception that Islamic law prior to modern codification was not responsive to social change.[3] I hope that this study has succeeded in challenging this narrative.

Prior to the thirteenth century, there was no mention of the term *talfīq* since the more general type of pragmatic eclecticism, known as *tatabbuʿ al-rukhaṣ*, was itself forbidden by almost all jurists. The strong opposition to *tatabbuʿ al-rukhaṣ*, which dominated juristic discourse until the thirteenth century, was followed by increasingly permissive attitudes after the stabilization of the Sunnī schools and the institutionalization of *taqlīd*. This shift was occasioned by the desire on the part of some jurists to adjust legal discourse to the reality of the practice of pragmatic eclecticism of which they were fully aware, leading to the rise of a pro-pragmatic eclecticism camp in the thirteenth century. Notwithstanding the large divisions among jurists of the thirteenth century over the validity of *tatabbuʿ al-rukhaṣ*, the Mamluk authorities chose one side of the debate. In 1265 Baybars appointed four chief judges in Cairo, thus formalizing pragmatic eclecticism in court practice. With the growing acceptance of *tatabbuʿ al-rukhaṣ* in the thirteenth century, some jurists created a semantic split of *tatabbuʿ al-rukhaṣ*, singling out *talfīq* as the only type of pragmatic eclecticism that ought to be forbidden. It was used as a foil for *tatabbuʿ al-rukhaṣ*, with almost unanimous agreement that *talfīq* was prohibited.

The rise of *tatabbuʿ al-rukhaṣ* can be situated squarely within the context of the *longue durée* evolution of *taqlīd* and *ijtihād*, with *taqlīd* serving the social function of creating a more stable and predictable legal system. With the maturation of *taqlīd* and its emergence as the dominant practice, the flexibility that *ijtihād* afforded to the legal process was no longer available. This necessitated an opening in the legal system to allow for greater maneuverability in the repertoire of available rules. The narrower interpretive powers granted to judges and muftis under the regime of *taqlīd* motivated the legal establishment to engineer a system of legal pluralistic pragmatism.

In juristic discourse, the voices supporting pragmatic eclecticism grew stronger over the course of the Mamluk and Ottoman periods. The chief contribution of these increasingly dissenting voices was that they challenged the consensus claimed by jurists of the formative and classical periods over the subject, thus negating the earlier accusation of sin leveled against those practicing pragmatic eclecticism. Despite the efforts of many jurists to bridge the gap between court practice and juristic discourse on pragmatic eclecticism, no consensus permitting pragmatic eclecticism was reached. It was hard for juristic discourse to completely turn its back on the opposition of jurists of the formative and classical periods, resulting in the persistence of disagreement over the issue into the modern period.

The late Mamluk and Ottoman periods saw the rise of a strand of thought within juristic discourse, which permitted muftis not only to choose weaker legal opinions from within their schools, but also to cross school boundaries in pursuit of less stringent juristic views. Some tried to circumvent the strong opposition to muftis crossing school boundaries by claiming a difference between giving a formal fatwa, which must be restricted to the mufti's school, and the mere transmission (*riwāya*) of other schools' views. In contrast to the formal fatwa, a transmission is simply legal advice given to a layperson on the authority of another school. This distinction effectively gave muftis some of the functions of modern lawyers. It enabled them to provide legal advice on the vast body of juristic views within the four schools with the help of a new Ottoman *ikhtilāf* genre, which focused on narrow topics of disagreement among the schools. This new genre was succinct. It was even sometimes versified for greater ease of memorization by legal professionals.

The new *ikhtilāf* genre, which started in the Mamluk period, became very popular in the Ottoman period. Ottoman jurists were increasingly explicit about the motivation behind writing *ikhtilāf* manuals, to wit, to help residents of cities and minor religious figures in rural areas navigate legal pluralism. The proliferation of these manuals and the explicit references to the jurists' interest in the legal result, rather than in the process of legal reasoning, point to a shift from the process of the law to its content, which is inherent in school boundary-crossing. This is not to say that legal methodology (*uṣūl al-fiqh*) disappeared, but it is to say that jurists at the interface between court practice and legal discourse were more focused on the content of the law to accommodate people's needs than on the methodological coherence of abiding by the doctrines of one school. Discussions in juristic discourse regarding whether or not muftis may be paid for their legal advice, as well as the fear of manipulation that can result from providing them with remuneration for the production of legal opinions, should be read in the context of these functions of the mufti as a navigator of legal pluralism.

The newer, revisionist view, which permitted pragmatic eclecticism, especially *tatabbuʿ al-rukhaṣ*, prevailed over time, partly because jurists gave more weight to later layers of juristic interpretation. This phenomenon of preferring the views of later authorities over earlier ones was clear in the selection of varying authoritative texts in different periods, as epitomized by the commentary tradition. Authoritative legal doctrine was to be found in recent works, as evidenced by the preference for Ottoman manuals of substantive law over their Mamluk counterparts in the court records we examined. Specific Ottoman authorities and works were being consistently invoked. One finds works such as *Ghāyat al-Wuṣūl Sharḥ Lubb al-Uṣūl* of the Shāfiʿī Zakariyyā al-Anṣārī (d. 926/1520),[4] *al-Baḥr al-Rāʾiq* or *al-Ashbāh waʾl-Naẓāʾir* of the Ḥanafī Ibn Nujaym (d. 970/1563), and *Nihāyat al-Muḥtāj ilā Sharḥ al-Minhāj* of the Shāfiʿī Shams al-Dīn al-Ramlī (d. 1004/1595) being repeatedly mentioned in the courts,[5] to the extent that it becomes clear that judges had regular access to these texts. It would not be far-fetched to speculate that these texts may have been readily available for consultation in the courts, serving in a sense as proto-codes.

There was even an awareness of this growing phenomenon of giving later authorities greater priority over their earlier counterparts. Thus the views of Ibn Ḥajar al-Haytamī, Shams al-Dīn al-Ramlī (d. 1004/1595), and Zakariyyā al-Anṣārī began to be preferred to the opinions of al-Nawāwī and al-Rāfiʿī. Earlier on, the works of al-Nawāwī and al-Rāfiʿī had enjoyed priority over *al-Umm* of al-Shāfiʿī himself. The justification was that they were more knowledgeable about the texts of al-Shāfiʿī. Some jurists even argued that there must have been a good, albeit unknown, reason for whenever their works contradicted *al-Umm*.[6] This invocation of the views of the *mutaʾakhkhirīn* (jurists active after roughly 950 CE) over those of earlier authorities is ironic, since earlier generations are often perceived as more pious and knowledgeable owing to their temporal proximity to the Prophet.[7] But these works were more responsive to social needs through their vertical and horizontal eclecticism. This historical change of the locus of authority helped later jurists contribute to the evolution of substantive law. Even the commentators among the later jurists (*arbāb al-ḥawāshī ʿalā kutub al-mutaʾakhkhirīn*), who came after Shams al-Dīn al-Ramlī and Ibn Ḥajar, were adjudged acceptable as sources of fatwas because they followed them in most of their views.[8] This ability of Islamic law to update its authorities was one of the main mechanisms that allowed for a change in juristic attitudes toward pragmatic eclecticism to take hold.

In the Ottoman period, voices supporting *talfīq* began to emerge, mostly in order to legitimize people's rituals. By the seventeenth century, the issue became the subject of a very heated debate, causing discord among jurists. This debate led to an acknowledgment of *talfīq* as an issue of disagreement in which no consensus had been reached, in contrast to the prevailing perspective of the thirteenth century.

The Mamluk and later the Ottoman authorities (as indicated by the seventeenth- and eighteenth-century courts) permitted people to cross school boundaries in their transactions in order to serve the interests of elite groups for the most part. However, a subaltern woman like Riḍā benefited from this system of pluralism when she needed an annulment of her marriage, just in the same way members of elite groups drew upon pragmatic eclecticism to facilitate their sale of endowment (*waqf*) properties. To achieve such flexibility, the Ḥanbalī school, which had the least following in Egypt, completely monopolized the sale of endowment properties known as *istibdāl*. The economic and social significance of such a move cannot be overemphasized since the role of endowments in the overall economy was comparatively large. Afaf Lutfi Sayyid-Marsot, for instance, estimated that 20 percent of all arable land in eighteenth-century Egypt was in the form of *waqf*. Owing to pragmatic eclecticism's ability to circumvent the stringent conditions imposed on the sale of endowments, we need to reevaluate our view of the role this system played in the economic decline of the Middle East. Through legal pluralism, endowment properties functioned, for all intents and purposes, like private property.

On the practical level, both pragmatic strategies were used in the Ottoman and modern periods in somewhat similar ways. Thus a seventeenth-century Ottoman woman such as Riḍā, who belonged to the subaltern classes of Miṣr al-Qadīma in Cairo, would end up before a judge whose school could best facilitate her legal transaction. She would choose to go before a Shāfiʿī judge in order to avoid an irrevocable divorce, as we saw in chapter 3, even though her marriage had been concluded under Ḥanafī law. But if she were to engage in the sale of an endowment, a procedure known as *istibdāl*, she would most certainly go to a Ḥanbalī judge. In this manner, if we were to investigate each individual's litigation history, we would end up with something resembling a code, with a high correlation between types of cases and the school affiliation of presiding judges. This consistency was achieved in the modern period by codifying specific legal rules into modern state legislation, whereas in the Ottoman period, it was performed through a complex negotiation between legal subjects, judges, muftis, and author-jurists. This negotiation involved instances of doctrinal eclecticism performed by author-jurists who compiled legal manuals, as well as the selection of forum, which was orchestrated by legal subjects, judges, and muftis. In the activities of legal subjects, judges, muftis, and author-jurists, a balance between stability and flexibility was achieved through pragmatic eclectic *taqlīd*, where change took place within the school when the *rājiḥ* was abandoned for pragmatic reasons, or through the utilization of pragmatic eclecticism across school boundaries.

In the nineteenth century, Mehmed Ali undertook a process of Ḥanafization, which saw systematic restrictions on the other three schools. This process created new legal problems that did not exist in the seventeenth and eighteenth centuries. The attempts of twentieth-century legislators to draw upon Islamic legal pluralism in their new legal codes through existing Sharīʿa tools such as *tatabbuʿ al-rukhaṣ* and *talfīq* created a rupture. Ironically, this rupture was not between the twentieth and eighteenth centuries, but rather between the nineteenth and twentieth centuries. The utilization of pragmatic eclecticism in the codification of the Sharīʿa in the modern period does not, therefore, represent a break with the juristic past as far as codification strategies are concerned. This is not to argue that the act of codification itself was a neutral move that did not change the way the law functioned in Islamic societies. It is simply to show that modern legislators tapped into an existing system of *taqlīd* to accommodate their modern needs.

In light of these newly studied sources, it becomes clear that pragmatic eclecticism, whether in the form of *tatabbuʿ al-rukhaṣ* or *talfīq*, was as much a part of premodern *taqlīd* as it was a part of *taqlīd* in the modern period. Contrary to the views of Layish and Hallaq, *talfīq* was not outright forbidden in the premodern period, but was, on the contrary, highly contested. This very fact of its contestation enabled its incorporation in the legal system in premodern legal practice. There was a clear line of continuity in this aspect of legal modernization, with pragmatic eclecticism having a far greater impact on the modern codification of Sharīʿa in Egypt than *ijtihād*. We saw that jurists such as the eighteenth-century al-Dasūqī permitted pragmatic eclecticism and that his student Ḥasan al-ʿAṭṭār (himself a teacher of Rifāʿa al-Ṭahṭāwī) followed his teacher. It is not surprising that this line of continuity that goes right to the heart of the modern Arab renaissance came with a pragmatic eclectic ethos. Throughout the modern period, jurists from the nineteenth and twentieth centuries were divided over pragmatic eclecticism in the same way Ottoman jurists were. They invoked the same Ottoman authorities in these discussions, illustrating a striking level of discursive continuity.

In the modern period, the debate over legal reform did not center on the codification process,[9] that is, on the mechanics of the legislature setting down a uniform legal code, but it mostly focused on how selections in that code were made. The points of contention in traditional scholarly circles were mostly related to an older discussion with which jurists were already familiar. What is striking is not only the continuity in the discourse about pragmatic eclecticism before and after the nineteenth century but also the continuity in juristic attitudes in the age of modern codes up to the present time.

Rashīd Riḍā, who died in 1935, outlined five major approaches to legal reform in his time. The same approaches can still be seen even today, decades after his passing. The proponents of these approaches to legal reform continue to compete over the definition of Islamic law in post-Mubarak and post-Morsi Egypt. One of the important developments of the last few decades has been the emergence of novel attempts at creating new hermeneutic approaches to religious source texts that do not correspond to premodern hermeneutics. These new hermeneutic approaches were given momentum by the rise of human rights discourse and its articulation in several treaty obligations in the second half of the twentieth century. The challenges posed by these discourses to Islamic law gave rise to the hermeneutics of Fazlur Rahman, Amina Wadud, Asma Barlas, and Jamāl al-Bannā. Such attempts have thus far remained largely intellectual ventures, failing to gain popularity among the stakeholders of the Islamic movement.

This brings us to the last question of this study: can the Sharīʿa be restored? We have seen that there has been a thirteenth-century shift toward the law-as-content and away from an emphasis on legal methodology, as evidenced by the rise of pragmatic eclecticism and the *mukhtaṣar* (legal compendia) and *ikhtilāf* (juristic disagreements) manuals. This slow but steady evolution can be seen clearly in the ability of juristic discourse to accept the content of the law as driving the forum of adjudication, as opposed to remaining committed to the coherence of each school's legal methodology by forbidding school boundary-crossing. This situation is similar to the way Islamic law has been perceived by its stakeholders in the debate over the reinstatement of Sharīʿa in the modern period. According to them, what is meant by Sharīʿa is its content, rather than its process. They do not seem disturbed by the fact that modern Islamic law lost its endowment infrastructure and its premodern modes of knowledge production. They see the Sharīʿa as a body of rules, rather than as a process of knowledge production and legal reasoning, and, therefore, they call for the *reinstatement* of Islamic law by enacting Islamic legal rules in state legislation. As noted, most attempts to restore the Sharīʿa among its stakeholders—both discursive and legislative—deal with specific substantive legal issues without trying to articulate an overall legal methodology. Since enacting Islamic law into state legislation is perceived by the majority of stakeholders in the Islamic movement as Sharīʿa, then one can say with confidence that, yes, the Sharīʿa can be and is being restored.

Appendix

•

Notes

•

Glossary

•

Bibliography

•

Index

Appendix

List of Most of the Jurists Mentioned in the Book

'Abduh, Muḥammad (d. 1323/1905)	Born AD 1849 in the Nile Delta, Egypt. A renowned jurist and reformer, considered one of the key founding figures of Islamic modernism.
Abū Ḥanīfa, al-Nu'mān b. Thābit b. Zūṭā b. Marzubān (d. 150/767)	Born 80/699 in Kufa and died in Baghdad. Eponym of the Ḥanafī school.
Al-Isfrāyīnī, Abū Isḥāq (d. 418/1027)	Originally from Esfarayen in Khorasan (in modern-day northern Iran) and died in Nishapur. A Shāfi'ī scholar, theologian, and legal theoretician.
Abū Ṭālib, Ḥāmid Muḥammad	Professor and former dean of the Sharī'a faculty at al-Azhar University.
Abū Zayd, Naṣr Ḥāmid (d. 2010)	Born 1943 in Quhafa, near Tanta, Egypt and died in Cairo. An Egyptian liberal theologian and academic, whose research focus was the development of humanist Qur'anic hermeneutics. Famous for the apostasy court hearings brought against him in the 1990s.
Al-Albānī, Muḥammad Nāsir al-Dīn (d. 1999)	Born 1914 in Shkodër, Albania. An Albanian scholar of hadith criticism whose family moved to Syria at a young age, where he completed his early

	Islamic education. Widely regarded as one of the primary figures of the Salafī movement in the twentieth century.
ʿAlī al-Qārī, Mullah Nūr al-Dīn Ibn Sulṭān (d. 1014/1605)	Born in Herat, where he received his basic Islamic education. A Ḥanafī scholar and master of hadith, he also authored works on Qur'anic exegesis, Sufism, and history. He moved to Mecca, where he studied under Ibn Ḥajar al-Haytamī (973/1567) and lived and taught there until his death.
Amīr Bādshāh, Muḥammad Amīn b. Maḥmūd al-Bukhārī (d. ca. 972/1564)	Ḥanafī scholar from Bukhara. Author of a commentary on Ibn Humām's *al-Taḥrīr*, entitled *Taysīr al-Taḥrīr.*
Al-Anṣārī, Zakariyyā Yāḥyā b. Muḥammad Zayn al-Dīn al-Sunaykī (d. 926/1520)	Born ca. 823/1420 in Sharqiyya and later moved to Cairo. A renowned Shāfiʿī jurist and Sufi scholar. Though initially reluctant, he was eventually persuaded by the Mamluk sulṭān Qāyitbay to take on the role of chief judge of the Shāfiʿīs.
Al-ʿAṭṭār, Ḥasan (d. 1250/1835)	Born 1766. A prominent reformist figure at al-Azhar, where he served as rector from 1830 till his death in 1835.
Al-Bānī, Muḥammad Saʿīd (d. 1351/1933)	Modern Syrian jurist.
Al-Bannā, Jamāl (d. 2013)	Born 1920 in Muhmudiyya, Egypt. The youngest brother of the founder of the Muslim Brotherhood, Ḥasan al-Bannā. He was a liberal scholar, known particularly for his critical approach to the hadith.
Al-Baṣrī, ʿUmar (d. unknown)	Late Ottoman Shāfiʿī jurist and contemporary of Ibn Mullah Farrūkh al-Makkī (d. 1061/1650).

Al-Bayhaqī, Abū Bakr Aḥmad b. al-Ḥusayn b. ʿAlī (d. 458/1066)	Born 994/384 in Khorasan. A famous hadith scholar and Shāfiʿī jurist, who was considered the foremost pupil of al-Ḥākim al-Nīsābūrī (d. 403/1012).
Bayyūmī, ʿAbd al-Muʿṭī	Contemporary professor and member of the Islamic Research Academy.
Al-Bazzāzī, Muḥammad b. Muḥammad b. Shihāb b. Yūsuf al-Kurdarī (d. 827/1424)	From Kurdar, near Khwarezm. A Ḥanafī scholar. Author of *al-Fatāwā al-Bazzāziyya*.
Al-Bukhārī, Abū ʿAbd Allāh Muḥammad b. Ismāʿīl (d. 256/870)	Born 194/810 in the city of Bukhara in present day Uzbekistan. A Persian traditionalist and one of the most celebrated hadith scholars of Islamic history, whose *Ṣaḥīḥ al-Bukhārī* is widely held as the most authoritative work of hadith.
Al-Burnusī, Zarrūq al-Fāsī Shihāb al-Dīn Abū al-ʿAbbās Aḥmad b. Aḥmad b. Muḥammad b. ʿĪsā (d. 899/1493)	Born 846/1442 around Tiwilan, Morocco. A Berber, one of the prominent scholars of the Mālikī school, better known for his systematization of Sufi doctrine and as the founder of the Zarrūqī branch of the Shādhilī Sufi *ṭarīqa*. Author of the popular *Qawāʿid al-Taṣawwuf*.
Al-Būṭī, Muḥammad Saʿīd Ramaḍān (d. 2013)	Born 1929 in Ayn Diwar, Turkey. Of Kurdish background, his father fled Kamalist repression, seeking refuge in Damascus when al-Būṭī was only four. As a world-renowned traditional scholar, he was highly critical of modernist and Salafī Islam. Strongly criticized for tacitly supporting the Asad regime, he was assassinated in a bombing in Damascus in March 2013.
Al-Dimyāṭī, Abū Bakr b. al-Sayyid Muḥammad Shaṭā (d. 1310/1892)	A nineteenth-century Egyptian Shāfiʿī jurist.

Dirāz, Muḥammad ʿAbd Allāh (d. 1958)	A modernist influenced by ʿAbduh's teachings. He was the former dean of the faculty of Uṣūl al-Dīn at al-Azhar.
Al-Dukhayyil, ʿAbd al-ʿAzīz b. Ibrāhīm	A contemporary Saudi Ḥanbalī jurist.
Ebu's-Su'ud Efendi [Shaykh al-Islām] (d. AD 1574)	Born in 1490. Famous Ottoman jurist and Qur'an exegete who was promoted to grand mufti by Sulaymān the Magnificent in AD 1545.
Al-Fazārī, Tāj al-Dīn Abū Muḥammad ʿAbd al-Raḥmān b. Sibāʿ b. Ḍiyā' al-Dīn (d. 690/1291)	Born ca. 624/1226. A Shāfiʿī scholar from Damascus. Author of *Sharḥ al-Waraqāt li-Imām al-Ḥaramayn al-Juwaynī.*
Fazlur Rahman, Malik (d. 1988)	Born 1919 in the Hazara area of British India (now Pakistan). A well-known and influential Muslim liberal intellectual and academic, he graduated from Oxford and taught Islamic studies at McGill University, UCLA, and the University of Chicago.
Al-Ghannūshī, Rāshid	Born 1941, outside of al-Hamma in southern Tunisia. A Muslim intellectual and politician who founded the Nahḍa movement, currently the largest party in Tunisia. His writings on Islam, modernity, democracy, and secularism are considered highly influential in the Arab and Islamic worlds.
Al-Ghazālī, Muḥammad (d. 1996)	Born 1917 in al-Buhayra, near Alexandria. A popular modern Egyptian scholar and prolific writer.
Al-Ḥamawī, Aḥmad b. Muḥammad (d. 1098/1686)	Seventeenth-century Ḥanafī jurist.
Hāshim, Aḥmad ʿUmar	Member of Islamic Research Academy and former president of al-Azhar University from 1995 to 2003.

Al-Hāshimī, Muḥammad Munīb (d. 1334/1915)	A late eighteenth-/early nineteenth-century jurist.
Al-Haytamī, Ibn Ḥajar Abū al-ʿAbbās Aḥmad b. Muḥammad b. ʿAlī Shihāb al-Dīn (973/1567)	Born 909/1504 in Maballat, Gharbiyya, Egypt. Moved to Cairo to continue studies at al-Azhar in 924/1518, where his main teacher was Zakariyyā al-Anṣārī. A prolific Shāfiʿī scholar, he authored the commentary on al-Nawawī's *Minhāj al-Ṭalibīn*, entitled *Tuḥfat al-Muḥtāj li-Sharḥ al-Minhāj*.
Al-Ḥifnāwī, Muḥammad Ibrāhīm	A contemporary scholar.
Al-Hilālī, Saʿd al-Dīn	An influential contemporary scholar who teaches at al-Azhar's Department of Comparative Jurisprudence and trains muftis in the Dār al-Iftāʾ program.
Al-Ḥusaynī, Aḥmad (d. 1332/1914)	A late nineteenth-/early twentieth-century Shafiʿī jurist.
Ibn ʿAbd al-Barr, Yūsuf (d. 463/1071)	Born ca. 367/977 in Shatiba, in Muslim Spain. Originally a Ẓāhirī, he later switched to the Mālikī school. Author of *Jāmiʿ Bayān al-ʿIlm wa-Faḍlih*.
Ibn ʿAbd al-Salām, ʿIzz al-Dīn al-Sulamī (d. 660/1262)	Born in Damascus 577/1181. Migrated to Egypt in AH 639. An eminent and popular Shāfiʿī scholar, nicknamed *Sulṭān al-ʿUlamāʾ* for his scholarly achievements. Wrote of Shāfiʿī law and Sufism, having studied with Abū al-Ḥasan al-Shādhilī. Author of *Qawāʿid al-Aḥkām fī Iṣlāḥ al-Anām*, also known as *al-Qawāʿid al-Kubrā*.
Ibn ʿAbd al-Wahhāb, Muḥammad (d. 1206/1792)	Born 1703 in ʿUyayna, in Najd in modern Saudi Arabia. The ideological father figure of the modern purist movement, known among its detractors as Wahhābīs. He played an

instrumental role in the formation of modern Saudi Arabia.

Ibn Abī al-Damm, Abū Isḥāq Ibrāhīm b. ʿAbd Allāh b. ʿAbd al-Munʿim b. ʿAli b. Muḥammad b. Fattāk (d. 622/1244)
Born 583/1182 in Hama, Syria. A Shāfiʿī scholar who travelled to Baghdad, Aleppo, and Cairo. Author of *Sharḥ Mushkil al-Wasīṭ, Kitāb al-Tārīkh* and *Adab al-Qāḍī* among other works.

Ibn ʿĀbidīn, Muḥammad Amīn b. ʿUmar (d. 1252/1836)
Born 1198/1784 in Damascus and lived in Syria. A prominent Ḥanafī jurist and Ottoman mufti known as *Amīn al-Fatwā*. Authored the authoritative Ḥanafī work *Radd al-Muḥtār ʿalā al-Durr al-Mukhtār.*

Ibn Amīr al-Ḥājj, Abū ʿAbd Allāh Muḥammad b. Muḥammad b. Muḥammad (d. 879/1474)
Born ca. 825/1421 in Aleppo, where he also died. A Ḥanafī scholar and author of the commentary on Ibn Humām's *al-Taḥrīr*, entitled *al-Taqrīr wa'l-Taḥbīr.*

Ibn ʿArabī, Muḥyi al-Dīn Abū ʿAbd Allāh Muḥammad b. ʿAlī b. Muḥammad (d. 638/1240).
Born 560/1165 in Murcia, in Muslim Spain. A preeminent Sufi mystic, jurist, theologian, and philosopher; known as *al-Shaykh al-Akbar* among the Sufis. A highly prolific author and widely traveled, his two most celebrated works are his massive magnum opus *al-Futūḥāt al-Makkiyya* and *Fuṣūṣ al-Ḥikam.*

Ibn ʿArafa, Abū ʿAbd Allāh Muḥammad al-Warghammī (d. 803/1400)
Born 716/1316; a Berber from southeastern Tunisia, he was a major Mālikī figure and the imam and mufti of the Great Mosque of Tunis. Author of *al-Mabsūṭ*, also known as *al-Mukhtaṣar al-Kabīr.*

Ibn Bīrī, Ibrāhīm b. Ḥusayn b. Aḥmad b. Muḥammad b. Aḥmad (d. 1099/1687)
Born 1023/1614 in Medina and died in Mecca. Ḥanafī scholar who wrote on *fiqh* and hadith and became a mufti in Mecca.

Ibn al-Ḥājib, Abū ʿAmr ʿUthmān b. ʿUmar b. Abī Bakr b. Yūnus (d. 646/1249)
Born 570–71/1174–75 in Isna, Egypt and died in Alexandria. A Mālikī scholar, legal theoretician, and grammarian.

	Lived in Cairo and Damascus. Author of *Muntahā al-Sawl wa'l-Jadal* and a *Mukhtaṣar* on it.
Ibn Ḥanbal, Abū 'Abd Allāh Aḥmad b. Muḥammad (d. 241/855)	Born 164/780. A celebrated early traditionalist (the eponym of the Ḥanbalī school of Sunnī law) theologian from Baghdad.
Ibn Ḥazm, Abū Muḥammad 'Alī b. Aḥmad b. Sa'īd (d. 456/1064)	Born 384/994 in Cordova and died near Seville. An eminent Andalusian jurist, theologian, and philosopher who was the most important theoretician of the Ẓāhirī school of law. Author of *al-Muḥallā*.
Ibn al-Humām, Muḥammad b. 'Abd al-Wāḥid (d. 861/1457)	Born 788/1386 in Alexandria. Ḥanafī jurist. Moved to Cairo, where he lived and died. Author of *Fatḥ al-Qadīr*.
Ibn Jamā'a, Badr al-Dīn Abū 'Abd Allāh al-Kanānī al-Ḥamawī (d. 733/1333)	Born ca. 639/1241 in Hama, Syria. A Shāfi'ī scholar who lived and studied in Damascus, Jerusalem, Cairo, Alexandria, and Qus. He was appointed as a judge in both Egypt and Syria.
Ibn Khaldūn, Abū Zayd 'Abd al-Raḥmān b. Muḥammad (d. 808/1406)	Born 732/1332 in Tunis and died in Cairo. A philosopher and historian. Author of *al-Muqaddima* (the Prolegomena).
Ibn Mufliḥ al-Maqdisī, Shams al-Dīn Muḥammad (d. 763/1362)	Born 708/1308 in Jerusalem and died in al-Ṣāliḥiyya, Damascus. He was considered among the most distinguished Ḥanbalī scholars of his generation. Author of *al-Mubdi'*, a long commentary on Ibn Qudāma's *al-Muqni'*.
Ibn al-Najjār, Taqī al-Dīn Muḥammad b. Shihāb al-Dīn Aḥmad b. 'Abd al-'Azīz b. 'Alī al-Futūḥī (d. 972/1564)	Born ca. 898/1492 in Cairo, where he lived until his death. A Ḥanbalī scholar who taught in addition to being a judge. Author of the popular *Muntahā al-Irādāt*.

Ibn Nujaym, Sirāj al-Dīn ʿUmar b. Ibrāhīm al-Miṣrī (d. 1005/1596)	Ḥanafī jurist and younger brother of Zayn al-Dīn Ibn Nujaym al-Miṣrī. He studied under his older brother and authored *al-Nahr al-Fā'iq*, a commentary on his brother's *al-Baḥr al-Rā'iq*.
Ibn Nujaym al-Miṣrī, Zayn al-Dīn b. Ibrahīm (d. 970/1563)	Born 926/1520 in Cairo. A Ḥanafī scholar with an interest in Sufism, who kept close ties with the renowned ʿAbd al-Wahhāb al-Shaʿarānī. Author *of al-Baḥr al-Rā'iq*, a commentary on *Kanz al-Daqā'iq* of al-Nasafī.
Ibn Qayyim al-Jawziyya, Muḥammad b. Abī Bakr (d. 751/1350)	Born 691/1292 in the village of Izra' in Hawran, near Damascus. The most loyal disciple of Ibn Taymiyya (d. 728/1328), he mastered the various Islamic sciences and is known particularly for his extensive writings on human behavior and ethics.
Ibn Rushd, Abū al-Walīd Muḥammad b. Aḥmad (d. 595/1198)	Born 520/1126 in Córdoba and died in Marrakesh, Morocco. An Andalusian polymath (Latinized name: Averroes) who was a master of Aristotelian philosophy, theology, politics, Mālikī law, and the natural sciences. Author of the popular *ikhtilāf* work *Bidāyat al-Mujtahid*.
Ibn Sanad, Shams al-Dīn Abū al-ʿAbbās Muḥammad b. Mūsā b. Muḥammad al-Lakhmī (d. 792/1390)	Born 729. Lived in Cairo and Damascus. A scholar of Shāfiʿī law and hadith. Known to have lost his memory and forgotten much of his knowledge in his later years.
Ibn Taymiyya, Taqī al-Dīn Abū al-ʿAbbās Aḥmad b. ʿAbd al-Ḥalīm b. ʿAbd al-Salām b. ʿAbd Allāh (d. 728/1328)	Born 661/1263 in Harran, Turkey, and died in Damascus. A major Ḥanbalī scholar, philosopher, theologian, and logician. Teacher of the Ibn Qayyim al-Jawziyya.

Jum'a, 'Alī	Born 1952 in Bani Suwayf, Egypt. He was appointed grand mufti of Egypt by Hosni Mubarak in Sept. 2003, retiring from the position in March 2013.
Al-Karkhī, Abū al-Ḥasan 'Ubayd Allāh b. Dallāl (d. 340/952)	Born 260/873 and taught in Baghdad. Regarded as the head of the Ḥanafīs of his period. Author of *Risāla fī al-Uṣūl Allatī 'alayhā Madār Furū' al-Ḥanafiyya.*
Al-Karmī, Mar'ī b. Yūsuf b. Abī Bakr (d. 1033/1623)	Born in Tulkarm, near Nablus, Palestine. Later moved to Egypt, where he briefly taught at al-Azhar, became the shaykh of Sulṭan Ḥasan mosque, and the mufti of the Ḥanbalīs.
Al-Kharāshī, Sulaymān b. Ṣāliḥ	Contemporary Salafī Saudi scholar.
Al-Mahdī, Muḥammad al-'Abbāsī (d. 1315/1897)	Born in 1827; an Egyptian Ḥanafī jurist who served as the grand mufti of Egypt from 1848 until his death in 1897.
Al-Makkī, Ibn Mullah Farrūkh Muḥammad b. 'Abd al-'Aẓīm (d. 1061 /1650)	Born ca. 996/1587. A Ḥanafī scholar and mufti from Makkah. Author of *al-Qawl al-Sadīd fī Ba'ḍ Masā'il al-Ijtihād wa'l-Taqlīd.*
Al-Malībārī, Zayn al-Dīn b. 'Abd al-'Azīz (d. 987/1579)	A Shāfi'ī scholar and student of Ibn Ḥajar al-Haytamī (973/1567). Author of the commentary *Fatḥ al-Mu'īn bi-Sharḥ Qurrat al-'Ayn.*
Mālik, b. Anas b. Mālik b. Abī 'Āmir al-Aṣbaḥī (d. 179/795)	Born 93/711 in Medina, where he lived and died. The celebrated eponym of the Mālikī school, known as *'Ālim al-Madīna*. Author of the important *al-Muwaṭṭa'.*
Al-Maqdisī, Ibn Ghānim Nūr al-Dīn 'Alī b. Muḥammad b. 'Alī (d. 1004/1596)	Born 920/1514 in Cairo, where he also died. A Ḥanafī jurist.
Al-Marāghī, Muṣṭafā (d. 1435/1945)	Born 1881. A major twentieth-century Egyptian modernist figure and rector of al-Azhar.

Al-Marīsī, al-Bishr b. Ghiyāth (d. 218/833)	A prominent early Baghdadi theologian associated with the Muʿtazila for his belief that the Qur'an was created.
Al-Marwazī, Abū Isḥāq Ibrāhīm b. Aḥmad (d. 340/951)	Lived most of his life in Baghdad, but later moved to Egypt, where he was the head of the Shāfiʿīs and where he died. Ibn Surayj's (d. 306/918) most distinguished student.
Al-Māwardī, Abū al-Ḥasan ʿAlī b. Muḥammad b. Ḥabīb (d. 450/1058)	Born 364/974 in Basra and died in Baghdad. A famous Shāfiʿī jurist and judge, known in the Latin West as Alboacen. Author of the classic work *al-Aḥkām al-Sulṭāniyya*.
Muhannā, Muḥammad	A contemporary scholar who is a professor of law at al-Azhar University.
Mujāhid, b. Jabr (d. 104/722)	Born 21/642. A Persian scholar and major early Qur'an commentator and hadith narrator from among the generation of *Tābiʿūn* (Successors). Studied with major Companions such as ʿAlī b. Abī Ṭālib and Ibn ʿAbbās.
Al-Munāwī, Muḥammad ʿAbd al-Ra'ūf b. Tāj al-ʿĀrifīn b. ʿAlī b. Zayn al-ʿĀbidīn (d. 1029/1620)	Born ca. 952/1545 in Cairo, where he also died. A prolific Shāfiʿī scholar whose most popular work is *Fayḍ al-Qadīr*, a commentary on al-Suyūṭī's *al-Jāmiʿ al-Ṣaghīr*.
Al-Muṭīʿī, Muḥammad Bakhīt (d. 1354/1935)	Born 1271/1854 in the village of Mutiʿa in Asyut, Egypt. A Ḥanafī jurist and scholar who served as the grand mufti of Egypt from 1914 to 1921.
Al-Najjār, ʿAbd Allāh	A contemporary scholar and prominent member of al-Azhar's Islamic Research Academy.
Al-Nawawī, Abū Zakariyyā Muḥyī al-Dīn Yaḥyā b. Sharaf (d. 676/1277)	Born 631/1233 in Nawa, near Damascus. As a scholar of *fiqh* and hadith, he is

	regarded as one of the authoritative figures of the Shāfiʿī school.
Al-Qaffāl al-Shāshī, Sayf al-Dīn Abū Bakr Muḥammad b. Aḥmad (d. 507/1114)	Born in Tashkent (Shāsh), where he also died, *not to be confused with Muḥammad al-Qaffāl al-Kabīr al-Shāshī (d. 365/975)*. Sayf al-Dīn Abū Bakr al-Shāshī was a widely traveled Shāfiʿī scholar, and was considered a leading exponent of Shāfiʿī jurisprudence of his day.
Al-Qahistānī, Shams al-Dīn Muḥammad (d. 953/1546)	A Ḥanafī scholar and mufti from Bukhara. Author of *Jāmiʿ al-Rumūz*, a commentary on *al-Niqāya Mukhtaṣr al-Wiqāya* of Ṣadr al-Sharīʿa ʿUbayd Allāh b. Masʿūd.
Al-Qalhūd, Abdul-Rahman	A modern scholar writing in the 1960s.
Al-Qaraḍāwī, Yūsuf	Born 1926 in the Nile Delta. An influential contemporary Egyptian scholar who has played a prominent role in the intellectual leadership of the Muslim brotherhood. In 1977 he became the dean of the Faculty of Sharīʿa and Islamic Studies at the University of Qatar.
Al-Qarāfī, Abū al-ʿAbbās Aḥmad b. Abī al-ʿAlāʾ Idrīs b. ʿAbd al-Raḥmān b. ʿAbd Allāh b. Yallīn (d. 684/1285)	Grew up in al-Qarafa in Old Cairo. He later became the head of the Mālikī school in Cairo. Regarded by some as the greatest Mālikī legal theoretician of seventh-/thirteenth-century Egypt. Among his teachers was the renowned Shāfiʿī ʿIzz al-Dīn b. ʿAbd al-Salām (d. 660/1262).
Al-Qāsimī, Jamāl al-Dīn Muḥammad (d. 1332/1914)	Late nineteenth-/early twentieth-century jurist from Damascus, Syria.

Al-Rāfi'ī, Abū al-Qāsim Imām al-Dīn 'Abd al-Karīm b. Abī Sa'īd Muḥammad b. 'Abd al-Karīm (d. 623/1226)	Born 555/1160 in Qazwin, Iran, where he also died. A famous Shāfi'ī scholar. Al-Nawawī's renowned *Minhāj al-Ṭālibīn* is a compendium of his *Kitāb al-Muḥarrar.*
Al-Ramlī, Khayr al-Dīn b. Aḥmad b. Nūr al-Dīn 'Alī b. Zayn al-Dīn b. 'Abd al-Wahhāb al-Ayyūbī al-Fārūqī (d. 1081/1671).	Born 993/1585 in Ramla, Ottoman Palestine. A renowned Ḥanafī scholar who studied at al-Azhar. He returned to Ramla in AD 1604, where he became a major and influential scholar. Author of *al-Fatāwā al-Khayriyya li-Naf' al-Bariyya*.
Al-Ramlī, Shams al-Dīn Muḥammad b. Aḥmad b. Ḥamza al-Manūfī al-Anṣārī (d. 1004/1595)	Born 917/1511 in Cairo, where he also died. Like his father, who was a student of Zakariyyā al-Anṣārī (d. 926/1520), he was a teacher at al-Azhar and considered the leading Shāfi'ī Egyptian mufti of his time.
Riḍā, Muḥammad Rashīd (d. 1354/1935)	Born 1282/1865 near Tripoli, Ottoman Syria. He was an influential Islamic reformer who was deeply affected by Muḥammad 'Abduh's ideas. He moved to Cairo in 1897 and launched the widely read *al-Manār* journal the following year in collaboration with 'Abduh.
Al-Samhūdī, [al-Sayyid] Nūr al-Dīn 'Alī b. 'Abd Allāh b. Aḥmad al-Ḥasanī (d. 911/1505)	Born 844/1440 in Samhud, in Upper Egypt. A Shāfi'ī scholar and Ḥasanid Sayyid, he studied in Cairo and eventually settled in Medina. Author of the extant history of Medina *Wafā' al-Wafā'*, which is an abridgement of a more extended history that was lost in a fire.
El-Sanhoori, Mohammad Ahmad Farag	A modern scholar writing in the 1960s.

Al-Shabrakhītī, Burhān al-Dīn Abū Isḥāq Ibrāhīm b. Mar'ī b. 'Aṭiyya (d. 1106/1694)	A Mālikī scholar who lived in Egypt. Author of a commentary on al-Nawawī's forty hadiths entitled *al-Futūḥāt al-Wahbiyya*.
Al-Shāfi'ī, Abū 'Abd Allāh Muḥammad b. Idrīs (d. 204/820)	Born 150/767 in Gaza, Palestine. Eponym of the Shāfi'ī school and widely regarded as the founder of Islamic legal methodology. Author of *al-Umm* and *al-Risāla*.
Al-Shafshawīnī, 'Abd al-Qādir (d. 1313/1895)	A North African jurist who died in Cairo.
Al-Shahrazūrī, Ibn al-Ṣ alāḥ Taqī al-Dīn Abū 'Amr b. 'Abd al-Raḥmān (d. 643/1245)	Born 577/1181 in in Irbil (Iraq). A Shāfi'ī jurist and eminent scholar of Qur'anic exegesis, hadith, and *'ilm al-rijāl*, who settled in Damascus after some travel, where he died. His most famous work on hadith is published under the title *Muqaddimat Ibn al-Ṣalāḥ*.
Shaḥrūr, Muḥammad	Born 1938 in Damascus. A professor of civil engineering, he is known for his controversial writings on Islam and calls for radical reform through his uniquely liberal interpretation of the Qur'an. He is particularly known for his association with the Qur'anist movement, which rejects the hadith literature as unreliable.
Shaltūt, Maḥmūd (d. 1963)	Born 1893 in Buhayra, Lower Egypt. A prominent Islamic reformer, theologian, and disciple of Muḥammad 'Abduh's school of thought. Served as the rector of al-Azhar under Nasser from 1958 until his death in 1963.
Al-Sha'rānī, 'Abd al-Wahhāb b. Aḥmad (d. 973/1565)	An Egyptian Shāfi'ī scholar and Sufi mystic known for his defense of the controversial Sufi Mystic Muḥyī

al-Dīn Ibn 'Arabī, whose theories he simplified and rendered more accessible.

Al-Sharqāwī, 'Abd Allāh b. Ḥijāzī b. Ibrāhīm (d. 1227/1812)
Born AD 1737. An Egyptian eighteenth-/nineteenth-century Mālikī jurist who was also a scholar and author of the Khalwatī Sufi order.

Al-Shāṭibī, Abū Isḥāq Ibrāhīm b. Mūsā b. Muḥammad al-Lakhmī (d. 790/1388)
Born and died in Granada, in Muslim Spain. A major legal theoretician. Author of the *uṣūl* work *al-Muwāfaqāt fī Uṣūl al-Sharī'a.*

Al-Shaybānī, Muḥammad b. al-Ḥasan (d. 189/805)
Born ca. 132/750 in Wasit, grew up in Kūfa, and died in Rayy. One of the important authorities of the Ḥanafī school. He was a student of Abū Ḥanīfa and Abū Yūsuf. Author of *Kitāb al-Āthār.*

Al-Shurunbulālī, Ḥasan b. 'Alī (d. 1069/1658)
Born 994/1585 and grew up in Cairo until his death. Author of *Nūr al-Īḍāḥ* and its commentary *Marāqī al-Falāḥ.*

Al-Subkī, Tāj al-Dīn Abū al-Naṣr 'Abd al-Wahhāb b. Taqī al-Dīn 'Alī (d. 771/1370)
Born ca. 727/1326 in Cairo. Shāfi'ī scholar and author of the biographical dictionary *Ṭabaqāt al-Shāfi'iyya*, which exists in three versions (*Kubrā, Wusṭā,* and *Ṣughrā*). Son of Taqī al-Dīn al-Subkī.

Al-Subkī, Taqī al-Dīn Abū al-Ḥasan 'Alī b. 'Abd al-Kāfī b. 'Alī b. Tammām (d. 756/1355)
Born 683/1284 in the village of Subk, Egypt. A famous Shāfi'ī scholar, master of hadith and Qur'anic exegesis. He eventually settled in Syria, where he served as a chief judge of the Umayyad mosque for seventeen years, after which he was replaced by his son Tāj al-Dīn al-Subkī and returned to Cairo, where he died.

Al-Suyūṭī, Jalāl al-Dīn Abū al-Faḍl 'Abd al-Raḥmān b. Abī Bakr (d. 911/1505)
Born 849/1445 in Cairo, where he also died. One of the later authorities of the Shāfi'ī school; nicknamed *Ibn al-Kutub,* he was an unusually prolific writer and

	wrote on a wide array of Islamic topics. Two noteworthy popular works include *al-Itqān fī ʿUlūm al-Qurʾān* and his *Tafsīr al-Jalālayn*.
Al-Ṭahṭāwī, Rifāʿa Rāfiʿ (d. 1873)	Born 1801 in the Upper Egyptian town of Tahta. An educationist and author, he is recognized as the symbol of the Egyptian "Awakening" (*nahḍa*) and the leading intellectual of his generation. Taught at al-Azhar between 1820 and 1824 and was deeply influenced by his teacher Ḥasan al-ʿAṭṭār.
Ṭanṭāwī, Muḥammad Sayyid (d. 2010)	Born 1928 near Suhaj, Egypt. He served as the grand mufti of Egypt from 1986 to 1996, after which he was appointed as the rector of al-Azhar mosque by President Hosni Mubarak, a position he retained until his death. Author of a lengthy exegesis of the Qur'an.
Al-Ṭarsūsī, Najm al-Dīn b. Ibrahīm b. ʿAlī b. Aḥmad b. ʿAbd al-Wāḥid b. ʿAbd al-Munʿim (d. 758/1358)	Born 721/1321 in Damascus, where he also died. Became the Ḥanafī judge of Damascus after his father in AH 746.
Al-Taymī, Sulaymān b. Ṭarkhān al-Baṣrī (d. 143/760)	Born ca. 46/666. He was from the Successor generation (*tābiʿīn*) and a major early narrator of hadith.
Al-Ṭayyib, Aḥmad	Born 1946 in Qina, Egypt. Current rector of al-Azhar University.
Al-Timurtāshī, al-Khaṭīb Shams al-Dīn Abū ʿAbd Allāh Muḥammad b. ʿAbd Allāh al-Ghazzī (d. 1004/1595)	A Ḥanafī scholar who was born in 939/1532 in Gaza, where he also died. He visited Egypt several times and was one of the main Ḥanafī authorities in his time. Author of *al-Fatāwā al-Timurtāshiyya* and *Minaḥ al-Ghaffār bi-Sharḥ Tanwīr al-Abṣār*.
Wadud, Amina	Born 1952. An American scholar of Islam, whose research focuses on

	progressive readings of the Qur'an and gender issues. In March 2005, she controversially led a mixed congregation Friday prayer in New York.
Al-Wansharīsī, Abū al-'Abbās Aḥmad b. Yaḥyā b. Muḥammad b. 'Abd al-Wāḥid b. 'Alī (d. 914/1508)	Born ca. 834/1340 in Tlemcen, western Algeria. A Mālikī scholar. Author of *al-Mi'yār al-Mu'rib* and *Īḍāḥ al-Masālik ilā Qawā'id al-Imām Mālik*. Fled political violence to Fez, Morocco, when he was over forty, where he led the rest of his life.
Al-Zāhidī, Najm al-Dīn Abū al-Rajā' Mukhtār b. Maḥmūd b. Muḥammad al-Ghazmīnī (d. 658/1259),	A Ḥanafī scholar from Khwarezm. Author of *Qunyat al-Fatāwā*.
Al-Zahrāwī, 'Abd al-Ḥamīd (d. 1334/1915)	Born in Homs, modern Syria. A Syrian politician, journalist, Arab nationalist, and religious reformer, with a strong association with Syrian Salafī circles. In 1914, he became a member of the Ottoman senate but was publicly hanged two years later for alleged dealings with the Allies.
Al-Zarkashī, Abū 'Abd Allāh Badr al-Dīn Muḥammad b. 'Abd Allāh b. Bahādur (d. 794/1392)	Born 745/1344 in Cairo, where he also died. A prolific Shāfi'ī author, he studied hadith and *uṣūl* in Syria, before returning to Cairo for further studies. Author of *al-Baḥr al-Muḥīṭ fī Uṣūl al-Fiqh* and the famous work *al-Burhān fī 'Ulūm al-Qur'ān*.

Notes

Preface

1. For the first use of the term in the context of Islamic law, see Ahmed Fekry Ibrahim, "Al-Shaʿrānī's Response to Legal Purism: A Theory of Legal Pluralism," *Islamic Law and Society* 20:1–2 (2013): 110–40.

2. B. Z. Tamanaha, "Pragmatism in U.S. Legal Theory: Its Application to Normative Jurisprudence, Sociolegal Studies, and the Fact-Value Distinction," *American Journal of Jurisprudence* 41:1 (1996): 321–29; Christopher Hookway, *The Pragmatic Maxim: Essays on Peirce and Pragmatism* (Oxford: Oxford Univ. Press, 2012), 1–10; Richard Rorty, *Consequences of Pragmatism: Essays, 1972–1980* (Minneapolis: Univ. of Minnesota Press, 1982), xiii–xliv, 160–175; Cornel West, *The American Evasion of Philosophy: A Genealogy of Pragmatism* (Madison: Univ. of Wisconsin Press, 1989); Richard Rorty, "The Banality of Pragmatism and the Poetry of Justice," *Southern California Law Review* 63 (1990): 1813–14.

3. Tamanaha, "Pragmatism in U.S. Legal Theory," 334.

4. Ibid., 335–37; Thomas F. Cotter, "Legal Pragmatism and Intellectual Property Law," in *Intellectual Property and the Common Law*, ed. Shyamkrishna Balganesh (Cambridge, UK: Cambridge University Press, 2013); Thomas F. Cotter, "Legal Pragmatism and the Law and Economics Movement," *Georgetown Law Journal* 84:6 (1996): 2071–2142; Richard A. Posner, "Pragmatic Adjudication," *Cardozo Law Review* 18 (1996–97): 1–20; Posner, *Overcoming Law* (Cambridge, MA: Harvard Univ. Press, 1995); Posner, *The Problems of Jurisprudence* (Cambridge, MA: Harvard Univ. Press, 1990), 18–26; Joseph Singer, "Legal Realism Now," *California Law Review* 76:2 (1988): 468–70; Duncan Kennedy, "Form and Substance in Private Law Adjudication," *Harvard Law Review* 89:8 (1976): 1685–1778; Helge Dedek, "The Splendour of Form: Scholastic Jurisprudence and 'Irrational Formality,'" *Law and Humanities* 5:2 (2011): 349–83.

5. Daniel A. Farber, "The Inevitability of Practical Reason: Statutes, Formalism, and the Rule of Law," *Vanderbilt Law Review* 45 (1992): 533–34; Rorty, "The Banality of Pragmatism," 1818; Nancy Levit, "Practically Unreasonable—A Critique of Practical Reason: A Review of the Problems of Jurisprudence by Richard A. Posner," *Northwestern University Law Review* 85:2 (1991): 494–518; Ronald Dworkin, *Law's Empire* (Cambridge, MA: Belknap Press, 1986);

Tamanaha, "Pragmatism in U.S. Legal Theory," 336–38; Hart argues that any legal system requires some judicial discretion in some cases, despite the importance of predictability in the law; H. L. A. Hart, *The Concept of Law* (Oxford: Clarendon Press, 1961), 138–44.

6. Richard Warner, "Pragmatism and Legal Reasoning," in *Hilary Putnam: Pragmatism and Realism*, ed. James Contant and Urszula M. Żegleń (London and New York: Routledge, 2002), 25.

7. John Dewey, "Logical Method and Law," *Philosophical Review* 33:6 (1924): 26 (emphasis in the original).

8. Ibid.

9. Joseph Schacht, *An Introduction to Islamic Law* (Oxford [Oxfordshire]; New York: Clarendon Press, 1982), 69–75; Noel James Coulson, *A History of Islamic Law* (Edinburgh: Edinburgh Univ. Press, 1962), 7, 73, 182–201.

10. Rudolph Peters, for instance, found both pragmatic and mundane reasons for some of the choices of forum in the Dakhla Oasis. Rudolph Peters, "Body and Spirit of Islamic Law: *Madhhab* Diversity in Ottoman Documents from the Dakhla Oasis, Egypt," in *Islamic Law in Theory: Studies on Jurisprudence in Honor of Bernard Weiss*, ed. A. Kevin Reinhart and Robert Gleave (Leiden and Boston: Brill, 2014), 322–27.

11. See my monograph currently under review: *Child Custody in Islamic Law: The Best Interests of the Child in Theory and Practice.*

Introduction

1. See, for instance, Noha El-Hennawy, "Islamist Presidential Candidate Declares Conversion Permissible," *Al-Masry al-Youm Newspaper,* May 16, 2011, http://www.egyptindependent.com/news/islamist-presidential-candidate-declares-conversion-permissible; Sarah Carr, "In Platforms, Presidential Candidates Reassure on Rights and Liberties," *Egypt Independent,* May 20, 2013, http://www.egyptindependent.com/news/platforms-presidential-candidates-reassure-rights-and-liberties.

2. I use the term *purist* to refer to the strand of legal thought that attempts to purify Islamic law of nonscriptural influences, as well as most utilitarian practices. This strand of thought has existed throughout Islamic legal history, but in the modern period this purism acquired the added element of an aversion to the influence of modern discourses of human rights on Islamic law. This strand of thought is commonly referred to as "Salafī" in popular discourse, despite the fact that modern Salafism started as a project that endeavored to accommodate modernity. I will also use terms such as *textualist* and *scripturalist* interchangeably to describe purists, especially in the premodern period when they did not have to contend with the Western hegemonic discourses of modernity. It is important, however, to point out that scripturalism was used by some scholars to refer to a focus on the Qur'an as the only valid source of law, to the exclusion of the hadith literature. In this sense, scripturalism stood in opposition to *traditionalism* in the formative period of Islamic law, but as time went on, scripturalists accepted the hadith literature as part of the canon of scripture,

leading to a great overlap between the two terms. For discussions of scripturalism, traditionalism, and Salafism, see Michael Cook, *Studies in Origins of Early Islamic Culture and Tradition* (Aldershot, UK: Ashgate/Variorum, 2004), 161–82; David Vishanoff, *The Formation of Islamic Hermeneutics: How Sunni Legal Theorists Imagined a Revealed Law* (New Haven: American Oriental Society, 2011), 69–108; Robert Gleave, *Scripturalist Islam: The History and Doctrines of the Akhbārī Shīʿī School* (Leiden: Brill, 2007); Christopher Melchert, "Traditionist-Jurisprudents and the Framing of Islamic Law," *Islamic Law and Society* 8:3 (2001): 383–406, at 385–86; Ibrahim, "Al-Shaʿrānī's Response to Legal Purism," 110–40, at 126–32; Bernard Haykel, "On the Nature of Salafi Thought and Action," in *Global Salafism: Islam's New Religious Movement*, ed. Roel Meijer (New York: Columbia Univ. Press, 2009); Scott Lucas, "The Legal Principles of Muḥammad B. Ismāʿīl al-Bukhārī and Their Relationship to Classical Salafī Islam," *Islamic Law and Society* 13:3 (2006): 289–324.

3. Ehab Elbaroudy, "Al-Ḥuwaynī wa-Niẓām al-Jawārī wa'l-Sabāya Huwa al-Ḥall," *Masrawy*, May 23, 2011.

4. On the notion that Mehmed Ali's reign marked a setback for Islamic law, see further Abū al-Fatḥ Naṣr b. Ibrāhīm al-Maqdisī, *Mukhtaṣar al-Hujja ʿalā Tārik al-Maḥajja* (Riyadh, Saudi Arabia: Dār Aḍwāʾ al-Salaf, 2005).

5. I use the term *Islamist* to refer to activists who endeavor to promote a political Islamic vision, be they members of the Muslim Brotherhood, Salafī parties, or even active members of the historically less oppositional al-Azhar, who have been increasingly involved in post–Arab Spring politics. Needless to say, there is much ideological overlap among these groups, with al-Azhar particularly being home to all politico-religious currents.

6. This distinction can be seen, for instance, in Rashīd Riḍā, "Madaniyyat al-Qawānīn," ed. Muḥammad Rashīd Riḍā, *al-Manār* 23 (1898): 539.

7. On *ijtihād* and *taqlīd*, see further Sherman A. Jackson, "*Taqlīd*, Legal Scaffolding and the Scope of Legal Injunctions in Post-Formative Theory: *Muṭlaq* and *ʿĀmm* in the Jurisprudence of Shihāb al-Dīn al-Qarāfī," *Islamic Law and Society* 3:2 (1996): 165–92, at 167. This is the same definition used to refer to the independent *mujtahid* (*al-mustaqill*), for instance, in Ibn al-Ṣalāḥ al-Shahrazūrī, *Fatāwā wa-Masāʾil Ibn al-Ṣalāḥ fi'l-Tafsīr wa'l-Ḥadīth wa'l-Uṣūl wa'l-Fiqh*, ed. ʿAbd al-Muʿṭī Amīn Qalʿajī (Beirut: Dār al-Maʿrifa, 1986), 1:26. In this sense, analogy plays an important role as one of the tools through which rules are derived directly from the textual sources. See Wael B. Hallaq, *A History of Islamic Legal Theories: An Introduction to Sunnī Uṣūl al-Fiqh* (Cambridge, UK: Cambridge Univ. Press, 1997), 23; Wael B. Hallaq, "Was the Gate of Ijtihad Closed?" *International Journal of Middle East Studies* 16:1 (1984): 3–41. Calder's work should be added as a qualification to Hallaq's work: Norman Calder, "Al-Nawawī's Typology of *Muftīs* and Its Significance for a General Theory of Islamic Law," *Islamic Law and Society* 3:2 (1996): 137–64, at 155–56.

8. Some parallels can be drawn between my concept of pragmatic eclecticism in the context of Islamic law and *legal pragmatism* (and its later iteration *neopragmatism*), a concept that is tied to legal realism. Legal pragmatism is used in the Anglo-American common law

tradition to refer to an anti-formalistic and anti-foundationalist view of judicial decision-making. In the American context, legal pragmatists have criticized the classical approach to law for its excessive focus on analogical reasoning and legal precedent, as well as its overly legalistic vision, in which the law is treated as a philosophical abstraction. American legal pragmatists emphasize the practical aspects of governing societies, and therefore they reason that judges should turn their attention to consequences, context, and the contingency of laws, rather than to a timeless notion of *stare decisis*. According to legal pragmatists—whose view of the law is consequentialist—a legal system must be flexible and dynamic while paying due regard to the stability and predictability embodied in *stare decisis*. As we shall see in the rest of this study, there are some parallels between American legal pragmatists and the proponents of pragmatic eclecticism in the Islamic context. Despite these parallels, there are essential differences, which I address in a study I am currently undertaking. On legal pragmatism in the American context, see further Posner, *Overcoming Law*, 1–29, 387–405, 445–67; Cotter, "Legal Pragmatism and Intellectual Property Law," 213–16; Daniel A. Farber, "Legal Pragmatism and the Constitution," *Minnesota Law Review* 72 (1987–88): 1331–87; Cotter, "Legal Pragmatism and the Law and Economics Movement," 2071–2142; Posner, "Pragmatic Adjudication," 1–20. The term *pragmatic eclecticism* was used to describe American Protestants' picking and choosing from among different values ones that fit their own tastes and conditions. It was also used to describe picking and choosing among different programs of investigations and problems in the philosophy of science. Lee Harris, *The Next American Civil War: The Populist Revolt against the Liberal Elite* (New York: Macmillan, 2010); John H. Zammito, *A Nice Derangement of Epistemes: Post-Positivism in the Study of Science from Quine to Latour* (Chicago: Univ. of Chicago Press, 2004).

9. Abū Isḥāq Ibrāhīm b. Mūsā al-Shāṭibī, *al-Muwāfaqāt* (Riyadh, Saudi Arabia: Dār Ibn 'Affān, 1997), 5:77–78; Abū Ḥāmid al-Ghazālī, *al-Mustaṣfā min 'Ilm al-Uṣūl*, ed. Ḥamza b. Zuhayr Ḥāfiẓ (Medina: Sharikat al-Madina al-Munawwara li'l-Ṭibā'a, 1992), 4:154–55. For a good discussion of the roles played by al-Ghazālī and al-Shāṭibī in the development of the concept of *maṣlaḥa* in Islamic law, see Felicitas Opwis, *Maṣlaḥa and the Purpose of the Law: Islamic Discourse on Legal Change from the 4th/10th to 8th/14th Century* (Leiden: Brill, 2010), 65–88, 247–333; Opwis, "*Maṣlaḥa* in Contemporary Islamic Legal Methodology," *Islamic Law and Society* 12:2 (2005): 182–223, at 187–205.

10. Ibrahim, "Al-Sha'rānī's Response to Legal Purism," 110–40, at 112–13.

11. Wael B. Hallaq, "Can the Shari'a Be Restored?" in *Islamic Law and the Challenges of Modernity*, ed. Yvonne Yazbeck Haddad and Barbara Freyer Stowasser (Walnut Creek, CA: AltaMira Press, 2004), 33–34.

12. Wael B. Hallaq, *Authority, Continuity, and Change in Islamic Law* (Cambridge, UK: Cambridge Univ. Press, 2001), 147–66; Ulrich Rebstock, "A Qāḍī's Errors," *Islamic Law and Society* 6:1 (1999): 1–37, at 10–11.

13. The term *law* in the context of Islam incorporates strictly legal, ritual, and moral normativities. "Subjects of the law" refers both to laypeople and to jurists in their capacity

as consumers of the law (as litigants and fatwa-seekers on ritual and moral matters) rather than to interpreters of the law.

14. *Ijtihād* is the exercise of independent legal reasoning, whereas *taqlīd* is the opposite, as it refers to following the ruling of another authority, usually one of the four Sunnī legal schools.

15. In a forthcoming article, I discuss the utilization of different pragmatic eclectic and hermeneutic approaches to legal reform in the work of Egyptian modernist Jamāl al-Bannā. Ahmed Fekry Ibrahim, "Jamāl al-Bannā's New Jurisprudence and Post-Mubarak Egypt," *Encounters*, forthcoming.

16. The work of the Egyptian jurist ʿAbd al-Razzāq al-Sanhūrī, in which he tried to reconcile French legal concepts with Islamic law, epitomizes this balancing act between Islamic law and European discourses and laws. Oussama Arabi, "Al-Sanhūrī's Reconstruction of Islamic Law of Contract Defects," *Journal of Islamic Studies* 6:2 (1995): 153–72; Enid Hill, "Islamic Law as a Source for the Development of a Comparative Jurisprudence: Theory and Practice in the Life and Work of Sanhūrī," in *Islamic Law: Social and Historical Contexts*, ed. ʿAzīz ʿAẓmah (London: Routledge, 1988).

17. In my periodization of Islamic legal history (more on this in the section "Note on Periodization"), the formative period ends with the rise of schools by the beginning of the tenth century. The period between the tenth century and the end of the twelfth century/beginning of the thirteenth century is the classical period, during which schools stabilized (*istiqrār al-madhāhib*) and *taqlīd* was fully institutionalized. On the stabilization of schools, see further Jackson, "*Taqlīd*, Legal Scaffolding," 168.

18. Wael B. Hallaq, "Juristic Authority vs. State Power: The Legal Crises of Modern Islam," in *Islamic Law*, ed. Gavin N. Picken, Critical Concepts in Islamic Studies (London: Routledge, 2011), 257; Coulson, *A History of Islamic Law*, 201.

19. Nathan Brown, in agreement with Mitchell and Messick, juxtaposes the modern focus on content with the pre-nineteenth-century "process of deriving law," insisting that "the form of derivation and instruction of the sharīʿa cannot be divorced from its content." Brown rightly points out discontinuities with regard to the institutional transformations that gave more authority to the state in creating the content of the law and controlling the finances of the courts. Similarly, Hallaq bemoans the changes that took place in the modern period, eventually leading to his assessment that the Sharīʿa cannot be restored owing to the dismantlement of the endowment system, the *madrasa*, and the Arabicate hermeneutic. This evaluation that the Sharīʿa has been reduced to its content, thus divorcing it from its institutional habitat, builds on Brinkley Messick's insightful characterization of Sharīʿa as a "total" discourse, in which "all kinds of institutions find simultaneous expression: religious, legal, moral and economic." Nathan J. Brown, "*Shariʿa* and State in the Modern Muslim Middle East," *International Journal of Middle East Studies* 29:3 (1997): 359–76, at 359, 363–65, 370–71; Hallaq, "Can the Shariʿa Be Restored?" 21–53, at 25, 45–48; Wael B. Hallaq, *Sharīʿa: Theory, Practice, Transformations* (Cambridge, UK: Cambridge Univ. Press, 2009), 375, 401–20,

446–48; Brinkley Messick, *The Calligraphic State: Textual Domination and History in a Muslim Society* (Berkeley: Univ. of California Press, 1993), 3.

20. Prior to the nineteenth century, the link was thought to exist through what Hallaq calls "*ijtihād*ic pluralism" and the discourse of preponderance (*tarjīḥ*). Hallaq, "Can the Shari'a Be Restored?" 21–53, at 25, 28–30, 45–48; Hallaq, *Sharī'a*, 368.

21. Hallaq, "Can the Shari'a Be Restored?" 21–53, at 25, 28–30, 45–48; Hallaq, *Sharī'a*, 368.

22. Hallaq, *Sharī'a*, 448.

23. On the role of pious endowments in providing education, as well as food and medical care, to the poor in the Mamluk period, see Adam Abdelhamid Sabra, *Poverty and Charity in Medieval Islam: Mamluk Egypt, 1250–1517* (Cambridge, UK: Cambridge Univ. Press, 2000).

24. Hallaq, "Can the Shari'a Be Restored?" 24.

25. Behnam Sadeghi, *The Logic of Law Making in Islam: Women and Prayer in the Legal Tradition* (Cambridge, UK: Cambridge Univ. Press, 2013), 1–39.

26. In his outstanding work on women's prayer in the Ḥanafī tradition, Behnam Sadeghi shows a similar phenomenon in which jurists do not abide by legal methodology, opting for ad hoc decisions that can justify the specific legal problems at hand. Such ad hoc decisions include claiming abrogation of a legal rule without providing the legal methodological justification for why it is abrogated and what the abrogating text is. Sadeghi, *The Logic of Law Making in Islam*, 76–104.

27. On legal transplants, see Alan Watson, *Legal Transplants: An Approach to Comparative Law* (Athens: Univ. of Georgia Press, 1993), 21–29; Watson, *The Evolution of Law* (Baltimore: Johns Hopkins Univ. Press, 1985), 77–96, at 75; Watson, *The Nature of Law* (Edinburgh: Edinburgh Univ. Press, 1977), 99–113; Watson, *Society and Legal Change* (Edinburgh: Scottish Academic Press, 1977), 98–114.

28. Shaham conducted a study on legal forum shopping among Egyptian Christians within the pluralistic Egyptian legal system of the nineteenth century. He showed that Christians regularly maneuvered between their own family laws and those of the Islamic majority and suggested that a similar study should be conducted for the four Sunnī schools of law among Muslims. Ron Shaham, "Shopping for Legal Forums: Christians and Family Law in Modern Egypt," in *Dispensing Justice in Islam: Qadis and Their Judgements*, ed. Muhammad Khalid Masud, Rudolph Peters, and David Stephan Powers (Leiden: Brill, 2006), 468.

29. Judith E. Tucker, *Women, Family, and Gender in Islamic Law* (Cambridge, UK: Cambridge Univ. Press, 2008), 108.

30. Judith E. Tucker, *In the House of the Law: Gender and Islamic Law in Ottoman Syria and Palestine* (Berkeley: Univ. of California Press, 1998), 82–83.

31. *Ikhtilāf* refers to the body of legal literature on which jurists from the four Sunnī schools of law disagreed, be it on issues of substantive law or legal methodology.

32. "Legal pluralism" typically refers to the situation in colonial contexts where parts of the law that was applied in state courts consisted of native law and custom. Some of these

native laws and customs received official recognition from the state, while others did not receive the same formal recognition. This term has since been used outside of the colonial context to refer to the existence of more than one legal system in practice. For a discussion of legal pluralism, see John Griffiths, preface to *Legal Pluralism in the Arab World*, ed. Baudouin Dupret, Maurits Berger, and Laila al-Zwaini (The Hague: Kluwer Law International, 1999), xii.

33. For discussions of the role of *qiyās* in *ijtihād*, see J. Schacht and D. B. MacDonald, "Idjtihād," in *Encyclopaedia of Islam*, 2nd ed., ed. P. Bearman, Th. Bianquis, C. E. Bosworth, E. van Donzel, and W. P. Heinrichs (Leiden: Brill, 2011); Hallaq, "Was the Gate of Ijtihad Closed?" 30.

34. On the different types of *ijtihād* and *taqlīd* and the hierarchy of legal authorities, see further Calder, "Al-Nawawī's Typology of *Muftī*s."

35. Another activity that is utilized to generate laws around the middle of the continuum is "extrapolation" (*takhrīj*). This is a practice through which a jurist derives a legal norm on the basis of the legal methodology of the eponym of his school. On *takhrīj*, see further Sherman A. Jackson, *Islamic Law and the State: The Constitutional Jurisprudence of Shihāb al-Dīn al-Qarāfī* (Leiden: Brill, 1996), 91–96; Wael B. Hallaq, *The Origins and Evolution of Islamic Law* (Cambridge, UK: Cambridge Univ. Press, 2005), 161–63.

36. On *tashhīr*, see further Jackson, *Islamic Law and the State*, 83–89.

37. On *fasād al-zamān*, see further Haim Gerber, *Islamic Law and Culture, 1600–1840* (Leiden: Brill, 1999), 124–28.

38. In fact, some jurists even used the term *'umūm al-ḍarūra*, which combines both necessity and actual practice. Muḥammad Amīn b. 'Ābidīn, *Sharḥ al-Manẓūma al-Musammāh bi-'Uqūd Rasm al-Muftī*, 2nd ed. (Hayderabad, India: Markaz Taw'iyat al-Fiqh al-Islāmī, 2000), 39.

39. On the notion of "stagnation" under the regime of *taqlīd*, see Schacht, *Introduction to Islamic Law*, 70; Coulson, *A History of Islamic Law*, 75–85.

40. According to Jackson, *ijtihād fi'l-madhhab* is essentially a form of *taqlīd*, as there are intermediaries between the jurist and the text. He also cautions that legal conformism (*taqlīd*) and interpretive freedom (*ijtihād*) should not be viewed as binaries that could not coexist, but as competing hegemonies in which the dominance of one did not completely dispense with the other. Jackson, *Islamic Law and the State*, 77; Jackson, "*Taqlīd*, Legal Scaffolding"; Mohammad Fadel, "The Social Logic of *Taqlīd* and the Rise of the *Mukhtaṣar*," *Islamic Law and Society* 3:2 (1996): 193–233; Watson, *Society and Legal Change*, 87–97; Calder, "Al-Nawawī's Typology of *Muftī*s and Its Significance for a General Theory of Islamic Law"; Hallaq, "Was the Gate of Ijtihad Closed?" For more on *taqlīd* and *ijtihād*, see chapter 1.

41. For examples of studies examining instances of legal change, see Eyyup Said Kaya, "Continuity and Change in Islamic Law: The Concept of *madhhab* and the Dimensions of Legal Disagreements in Ḥanafī Scholarship of the Tenth Century," in *The Islamic School of*

Law: Evolution, Devolution and Progress, ed. Peri Bearman, Rudolph Peters, and Frank E. Vogel (Cambridge, MA: Harvard Univ. Press, 2005), 26–40; Maribel Fierro, "Ill-Treated Women Seeking Divorce: The Qur'anic Two Arbiters and Judicial Practice among the Mālikīs in al-Andalus and North Africa," in *Dispensing Justice in Islam: Qadis and Their Judgments*, ed. Muhammad Khalid Masud, Rudolph Peters, and David Stephan Powers (Leiden: Brill, 2006), 331–43; Wael B. Hallaq, "*Qāḍīs* Communicating: Legal Change and the Law of Documentary Evidence," *Al-Qanṭara* 20 (1999): 437–66, at 466; Baber Johansen, *The Islamic Law on Land Tax and Rent: The Peasants' Loss of Property Rights as Interpreted in the Hanafite Legal Literature of the Mamluk and Ottoman Periods* (London: Croom Helm, 1988); Johansen, "The Valorization of the Human Body in Muslim Sunni Law," in *Law and Society in Islam*, ed. Devin J. Stewart, Baber Johansen, and Amy Singer (Princeton, NJ: Markus Wiener Publishers, 1996), 71–112; Chibli Mallat, review of "The Islamic Law on Land Tax and Rent: The Peasants' Loss of Property Rights as Interpreted in the Hanafite Legal Literature of the Mamluk and Ottoman Periods," *Bulletin of the School of Oriental and African Studies* 54:1 (1991): 155–56; Haim Gerber, *State, Society, and Law in Islam: Ottoman Law in Comparative Perspective* (Albany: State Univ. of New York Press, 1994), 19–20, 98–99; Sadeghi, *The Logic of Law Making in Islam*.

42. Watson, *Society and Legal Change*, 1–11, at 8; 115–27; Watson, *The Evolution of Law*; Jean-Etienne-Marie Portalis, *Discours Préliminaire du Premier Projet de Code Civil* (Bordeaux: Ed. Confluences, 1999), 14, 27–28.

43. Jean-Etienne-Marie Portalis and Frédéric Portalis, *Discours et Rapports sur le Code Civil: Précédés de l'Éssai sur l'Utilité de la Codification, de Frédéric Portalis* (Caen: Presses Universitaires de Caen, 2010), 75. Emphasis in the original.

44. On the different levels of mufti, see further Norman Calder, "Al-Nawawī's Typology of *Muftīs* and Its Significance for a General Theory of Islamic Law," *Islamic Law and Society* 3:2 (1996): 137–64.

45. Ahmed El Shamsy, "The *Ḥāshiya* in Islamic Law: A Sketch of the Shāfiʿī Literature," *Oriens* 41:3–4 (2013): 295–99; Ahmed Fekry Ibrahim, "The Codification Episteme in Islamic Juristic Discourse Between Inertia and Change," *Islamic Law and Society*, forthcoming; Wael B. Hallaq, "From *Fatwās* to *Furūʿ*: Growth and Change in Islamic Substantive Law," *Islamic Law and Society* 1:1 (1994): 29–65.

46. Sadeghi, *Logic of Law Making in Islam*, 76–104.

47. It is important to add here that pragmatic eclecticism, an important source of flexibility in Islamic law, was not the only source. Other sources include *tarjīḥ* (the exercise of preponderance) and *istiḥsān* (juristic preference), the latter being one of the main tools of law making in the formative years of the Ḥanafī school. There are two main meanings of *istiḥsān*, as the term underwent a semantic evolution because of the attacks of traditionalists. The first is a general concept of discretionary decisions similar to *ra'y* (literally "opinion"), a particular form of legal reasoning based on juristic discretion rather than the textual sources. Al-Shāfiʿī used *istiḥsān* and *ra'y* synonymously. In this sense, it is a term that supports legal change through the jurist's own concept of justice, without a

clear link to the textual canon. The second meaning, which emerged after the devastating attacks of traditionalists, refers to setting aside an established analogy, in favor of other textual evidence or through particularizing the *ratio legis* of analogy. This meaning was the jurists' attempt to reclaim *istiḥsān* by dissociating it from the "arbitrariness" critique of traditionalists and emphasizing its link to analogy. Under the regime of *taqlīd*, *istiḥsān* in both conceptual senses continued to play a role in legal change. In its first sense, *istiḥsān* was practiced by muftis and author-jurists who continued to choose rules not owing to clear *uṣūlī* arguments but in an ad hoc manner to effect legal change. Jurists also continued to abandon analogies to refine older doctrines. This process was complementary to pragmatic eclecticism in that they were methods that pushed at the boundaries of legal inertia when necessary. Hallaq, *History of Islamic Legal Theories*, 107–11; John Makdisi, "Legal Logic and Equity in Islamic Law," *American Journal of Comparative Law* 33:1 (1985): 63–92; Gerber, *Islamic Law and Culture*, 92–97; Mohammad Hashim Kamali, *Principles of Islamic Jurisprudence*, 3rd ed. (Cambridge, UK: Islamic Texts Society, 2003), 323–50; Ahmed El Shamsy, *The Canonization of Islamic Law: A Social and Intellectual History* (Cambridge, UK: Cambridge Univ. Press, 2013), 22–34; Schacht, *Introduction to Islamic Law*, 37–48; Coulson, *A History of Islamic Law*, 40.

48. While the assertion that the gate of *ijtihād* was closed was an attempt to argue for the decline of Islamic law and society more generally, Hallaq's counter argument was meant to challenge this notion of an early decline. On this debate, see further Hallaq, "Was the Gate of Ijtihad Closed?"; Calder, "Al-Nawawī's Typology of *Muftī*s and Its Significance for a General Theory of Islamic Law"; Coulson, *A History of Islamic Law*, 75–85; Schacht, *Introduction to Islamic Law*, 70; Norman Anderson, *Law Reform in the Muslim World* (London: Athlone Press, 1976), 7.

49. Fadel, "The Social Logic of *Taqlīd* and the Rise of the *Mukhtaṣar*," 193–233, at 197.

50. On such changes of schools, see ʿIzz al-Dīn b. ʿAbd al-Salām, *al-Qawāʿid al-Kubrā: Qawāʿid al-Aḥkām fī Iṣlāḥ al-Anām*, ed. Nazīh Kamāl Ḥammād and ʿUthmān Jumʿa Ḍamīriyya (Damascus: Dār al-Qalam, 2000), 2:274–75; Taqī al-Dīn b. Taymiyya, *Mukhtaṣar al-Fatāwā al-Miṣriyya*, ed. ʿAbd al-Majīd Salīm (Beirut: Dār al-Kutub al-ʿIlmiyya, 1949), 60–61, 601–3.

51. Nūr al-Dīn al-Samhūdī, "Al-ʿIqd al-Farīd fī Aḥkām al-Taqlīd," Cairo, n.d., MS Dār al-Kutub 45 Uṣūl Taymūr, folio 14a–16b, microfilm #11397.

52. See, for instance, Shams al-Dīn Muḥammad b. ʿArafa al-Dasūqī, *Ḥāshiyat al-Dasūqī ʿalā al-Sharḥ al-Kabīr* (Cairo: Dār Iḥyāʾ al-Kutub al-ʿArabiyya, 1984), 2:349.

53. Hallaq discussed *taṣḥīḥ* within schools, which is another name for *tarjīḥ*, in which opinions within the schools were weighed evidentially to determine which one was more *ṣaḥīḥ* or *rājiḥ*. See Hallaq, *Authority, Continuity, and Change*, 147–66; Hallaq, "Can the Shariʿa Be Restored?" 35, 38; ʿAlāʾ al-Dīn ʿAlī b. Sulaymān al-Mirdāwī, *Taṣḥīḥ al-Furūʿ*, ed. ʿAbd Allāh b. ʿAbd al-Muḥsin Turkī (Riyadh, Saudi Arabia: Muʾassasat al-Risāla, 2003), 1:32.

54. On the *madhhab*-opinion and the adoption of non-preponderant views out of necessity, see Hallaq, "Can the Shariʿa Be Restored?" 38.

55. *Tamadhhub* refers to the view that every person is required to affiliate strictly with one school in all transactions. See al-Samhūdī, "Al-ʿIqd al-Farīd fī Aḥkām al-Taqlīd."

56. Abū al-Maʿālī ʿAbd al-Malik al-Juwaynī, *Maghīth al-Khalq fī Tarjīḥ al-Qawl al-Ḥaqq* (Cairo: al-Maṭbaʿa al-Miṣriyya, 1934), 13–14.

57. As cited by al-Samhūdī (d. 911/1505), see al-Samhūdī, "al-ʿIqd al-Farīd fī Aḥkām al-Taqlīd."

58. ʿIzz al-Dīn b. ʿAbd al-Salām, *al-Qawāʿid al-Kubrā: Qawāʿid al-Aḥkām fī Iṣlāḥ al-Anām* (Damascus: Dār al-Qalam, 2000), 2:274–75; Ibn Taymiyya, *Mukhtaṣar al-Fatāwā al-Miṣriyya* (Beirut: Dār al-Kutub al-ʿIlmiyya, 1949), 60–61, 601–3.

59. In *al-Fatāwā al-Miṣriyya,* Ibn Taymiyya (d. 728/1328) presents two views. The first gives preference to following one school in all transactions, and the second—his own view—is to avoid following the same eponym at all times. Ibn Taymiyya, *Mukhtaṣar al-Fatāwā al-Miṣriyya,* 60–61.

60. Al-Dasūqī, *Ḥāshiyat al-Dasūqī ʿalā al-Sharḥ al-Kabīr* (Cairo: Dār Iḥyāʾ al-Kutub al-ʿArabiyya, 1984), 1:40–47.

61. For slightly different periodization schemes, see Vishanoff, *The Formation of Islamic Hermeneutics,* xv; Hallaq, *Origins and Evolution of Islamic Law,* 2–3.

62. On the early evolution of Islamic law, see El Shamsy, *The Canonization of Islamic Law,* 17–117.

63. According to Melchert, schools were formed in the late ninth century. Other scholars placed the formation in the first half of the ninth century or in the tenth century. On the formation of schools, see further Christopher Melchert, *The Formation of the Sunni Schools of Law, 9th–10th Centuries C.E.* (Leiden: Brill, 1997), xxii–xviii; Coulson, *A History of Islamic Law,* 62–73; El Shamsy, *The Canonization of Islamic Law,* 167–93; Brannon M. Wheeler, *Applying the Canon in Islam: The Authorization and Maintenance of Interpretive Reasoning in Ḥanafī Scholarship* (Albany: State Univ. of New York Press, 1996), 1–113.

64. On authority formation within the schools, see further Wael B. Hallaq, *Authority, Continuity, and Change in Islamic Law* (Cambridge, UK: Cambridge Univ. Press, 2001), 24–120.

65. Jackson, *Islamic Law and the State,* 77.

66. For examples of substantive legal continuity and change, see Coulson, *A History of Islamic Law,* 21–35; David Stephan Powers, *Studies in Qur'an and Ḥadīth: The Formation of the Islamic Law of Inheritance* (Berkeley: Univ. of California Press, 1986), 87–188, 209–16.

67. Ibn Taymiyya, *Mukhtaṣar al-Fatāwā al-Miṣriyya,* 61.

68. On the *longue durée* and new calls for its revival, see Fernand Braudel, "Histoire et Sciences Sociales: La Longue Durée," *Réseaux* 5:27 (1987): 7–37; New calls for reviving *longue durée* historiography were made recently by David Armitage and Jo Guldi, *The History Manifesto* (Cambridge: Cambridge Univ. Press, 2014).

69. Jackson, "*Taqlīd,* Legal Scaffolding," 168. On al-Māwardī, see Noah Feldman, *Fall and Rise of the Islamic State* (Princeton, NJ: Princeton Univ. Press, 2008), 36–38; Roy Jackson, *Fifty Key Figures in Islam* (London: Routledge, 2006), 77.

70. Abū al-Wafā' b. 'Aqīl, *Kitāb al-Funūn*, ed. George Makdisi (Beirut: Dār al-Mashriq, 1970), 1:92–93; Hallaq, "Was the Gate of Ijtihad Closed?" 21; Abū Ḥāmid al-Ghazālī, *al-Wasīṭ fi'l-Madhhab*, ed. Muḥammad Muḥammad Tāmir (Cairo: Dār al-Salām, 1997), 7:289–91; 'Abd al-Ra'ūf b. Nūr al-Dīn al-Munāwī, *Fayḍ al-Qadīr*, 2nd ed. (Beirut: Dār al-Ma'rifa, 1972).

71. Rudolph Peters, "What Does It Mean to Be an Official Madhhab? Ḥanafism and the Ottoman Empire," in Bearman, Peters, and Vogel, *Islamic School of Law: Evolution, Devolution and Progress*, 149–52.

72. Jackson, *Islamic Law and the State*, 78–79.

73. For more on the regime of *taqlīd* and the stabilization of schools, see Jackson, "*Taqlīd*, Legal Scaffolding," 168; Hallaq, *Authority, Continuity, and Change*, 75–85.

74. For instances of legal change, see Hallaq, "*Qāḍīs* Communicating"; Johansen, *Islamic Law on Land Tax and Rent*; Kaya, "Continuity and Change in Islamic Law"; 'Abd al-Ra'ūf b. Nūr al-Dīn al-Munāwī, *Fayḍ al-Qadīr*, 2nd ed. (Beirut: Dār al-Ma'rifa, 1972), 1:11–12.

75. Cited by Ḍiyā' Yūnus in his introduction to Qāsim b. Qaṭlūbaghā al-Miṣrī, *al-Taṣḥīḥ wa'l-Tarjīḥ 'alā Mukhtaṣar al-Qudūrī*, ed. Ḍiyā' Yūnus (Beirut: Dār al-Kutub al-'Ilmiyya, 2002), 73–74.

76. For a discussion of the rise of the school compendium (*mukhtaṣar*), which was an important indication of the stability of *taqlīd* and the ideal of legal predictability inherent in it, see Fadel, "The Social Logic of *Taqlīd* and the Rise of the *Mukhtaṣar*"; Jackson, "*Taqlīd*, Legal Scaffolding."

77. The term "early modern" also challenges the now debunked view held by many Ottomanists that the Ottoman Empire became the "sick man of Europe" over the course of the period between the death of Suleyman I in 1566 and the reform project set in motion by Selim III in the late eighteenth century. This thesis, which is now obsolete, was partly predicated on discussions in Ottoman sources, describing the reign of Suleyman the Magnificent as a golden age in the history of the empire. The trope of the golden age of Suleyman the Magnificent, which can be found in the primary sources, was also challenged by historians. Dana Sajdi, "Decline, Its Discontents and Ottoman Cultural History: By Way of Introduction," in *Ottoman Tulips, Ottoman Coffee: Leisure and Lifestyle in the Eighteenth Century*, ed. Dana Sajdi (London: Tauris Academic Studies, 2007), 1–40.

78. Peter Gran, *Islamic Roots of Capitalism: Egypt, 1760–1840* (Syracuse, NY: Syracuse Univ. Press, 1998), 4–131; on 'Alī Bey al-Kabīr, see further Daniel Crecelius, *The Roots of Modern Egypt: A Study of the Regimes of 'Ali Bey al-Kabir and Muhammad Bey Abu al-Dhahab, 1760–1775* (Minneapolis: Bibliotheca Islamica, 1981).

79. Timothy Mitchell, *Colonising Egypt*, Cambridge Middle East Library (Cambridge, UK: Cambridge Univ. Press, 1988), 34–36.

80. Ibid., 63–69.

81. Ibid., 15–16; Khaled Fahmy, *All the Pasha's Men: Mehmed Ali, His Army, and the Making of Modern Egypt* (Cairo: American Univ. in Cairo Press, 2002), 9–12, 112–59, 313.

82. Mitchell, *Colonising Egypt*, 15–16; Fahmy, *All the Pasha's Men*, 9–12.

83. Roger Owen, *Cotton and the Egyptian Economy, 1820–1914: A Study in Trade and Development* (Oxford, UK: Clarendon Press, 1969), 3–160; Patrick O'Brien, "The Long-Term Growth of Agricultural Production in Egypt: 1821–1962," in *Political and Social Change in Modern Egypt: Historical Studies from the Ottoman Conquest to the United Arab Republic*, ed. Peter Malcolm Holt (London: Oxford Univ. Press, 1968), 162–95.

84. Mitchell, *Colonising Egypt*, 15–18; Fahmy, *All the Pasha's Men*, 11–12.

85. Mitchell, *Colonising Egypt*, 69–71; Owen, *Cotton and the Egyptian Economy*, 55–56.

86. Rudolph Peters, "The Codification of Criminal Law in Nineteenth Century Egypt: Tradition or Modernization?" in *Law, Society and National Identity*, ed. J. M. Abun-Nasr, U. Wanitzek, and U. Spellenberg (Hamburg: Buske, 1991), 211–25.

87. Rudolph Peters, *Crime and Punishment in Islamic Law: Theory and Practice from the Sixteenth to the Twenty-First Century* (Cambridge, UK: Cambridge Univ. Press, 2005), 133–36. In the case of criminal law, Mehmed Ali issued the first criminal legislation that complemented Sharīʿa rules; see Rudolph Peters, "'For His Correction and as a Deterrent Example for Others': Meḥmed ʿAlī's First Criminal Legislation (1829–1830)," *Islamic Law and Society* 6:2 (1999): 164–92; Rudolph Peters, "1829–1871 or 1876–1883? The Significance of Nineteenth-Century Pre-Colonial Legal Reform in Egypt" (presented at the New Approaches to Egyptian Legal History: Late Ottoman Period to the Present, Cairo, June 11, 2009).

88. Peter Gran, "'Passive Revolution' as a Possible Model for Nineteenth-Century Egyptian History," in *Money, Land and Trade: An Economic History of the Muslim Mediterranean*, ed. Nelly Hanna (London: I. B. Tauris, 2002), 85–87, 87.

1. The Codification Episteme and the Multiplicity of Truth

1. On the distinction between common law and civil law systems, see Joseph Dainow, "The Civil Law and the Common Law: Some Points of Comparison," *American Journal of Comparative Law* 15:3 (1966): 419–35. On the positivist view of codes in eighteenth-century France, see Jean-Louis Carra, *Systeme de la Raison: ou le Prophete philosophe* (London: Kearby, 1782), 171.

2. Alan Watson, *Making of the Civil Law* (Cambridge, MA: Harvard Univ. Press, 1981), 39–41.

3. Lawrence Rosen, *The Justice of Islam: Comparative Perspectives on Islamic Law and Society* (Oxford: Oxford Univ. Press, 2000), 38.

4. Ibid., 46.

5. Ibid., 48.

6. Ibid., 40, 49.

7. Watson, *Making of the Civil Law*, 2–4, at 4.

8. Dainow, "The Civil Law and the Common Law"; Rémy Cabrillac, *Les codifications* (Paris: Presses Universitaires de France, 2002), 65–96, 136–69. On common laws generally, see further H. Patrick Glenn, *On Common Laws* (Oxford, UK: Oxford Univ. Press, 2005). Precedent can also be rhetorically manipulated to accommodate cultural change when there is

such need. For an example from the nineteenth-century United States, see Leslie J. Harris, "The Court, Child Custody, and Social Change: The Rhetorical Role of Precedent in a 19th Century Child Custody Decision," *Rhetoric Society Quarterly* 34:1 (2004): 29–45.

9. Cabrillac, *Les codifications*, 68–69; Portalis, *Discours Préliminaire*, 28; Portalis and Portalis, *Discours et rapports sur le code civil*, 68, 93, 119.

10. Cabrillac, *Les codifications*, 67–135; Portalis, *Discours Préliminaire*, 64–66.

11. Noel James Coulson, "Muslim Custom and Case-Law," *Die Welt Des Islams* 6:1–2 (1959): 13–24, at 20.

12. Joseph Schacht, "Problems of Modern Islamic Legislation," *Studia Islamica* 12 (1960): 99–129, at 108; Ann Mayer, "The *Sharī'ah*: A Methodology or a Body of Substantive Rules?" in *Islamic Law and Jurisprudence*, ed. Nicholas Heer and Farhat Jacob Ziadeh (Seattle: Univ. of Washington Press, 1990), 177–98.

13. Drawing on Edward Levi, Rosen adds that in common law systems, each court has the ability to "regroup the facts of present and past cases in such a way as to shift or extend prior categories to meet current instances. This is, however, accomplished with such linkages to the terms of the prior set of categories as to give a restrained sense of continuity even where significant departure may be present." Rosen, *Justice of Islam*, 38–68, at 40. For a similar view of Islamic law prior to the nineteenth century, see Feldman, *Fall and Rise of the Islamic State*, 61–68.

14. Rosen, *Justice of Islam*, 50–58.

15. On the flexibility of the legal hermeneutic of al-Shāfi'ī and other law-oriented hermeneutists, see Vishanoff, *The Formation of Islamic Hermeneutics*, 15–65.

16. The comparison between a Muslim jurisconsult and a Roman jurist was made by H. Patrick Glenn, *Legal Traditions of the World: Sustainable Diversity in Law* (Oxford, UK: Oxford Univ. Press, 2000), 165.

17. Ibid., 177.

18. 'Abd Allāh b. al-Muqaffa', *Risāla fi'l-Ṣaḥāba*, vol. 1 (Beirut: Dār al-Kutub al-'Ilmiyya, 1989), 316–18.

19. Abū Bakr Aḥmad b. al-Ḥusayn b. 'Alī al-Bayhaqī, *al-Sunan al-Kubrā*, ed. Muḥammad 'Abd al-Qādir 'Atā, 3rd ed. (Beirut: Dār al-Kutub al-'Ilmiyya, 2003), 10:356–57.

20. Dimitri Gutas, *Greek Thought, Arabic Culture, the Graeco-Arabic Translation Movement in Baghdad and Early 'Abbāsid Society (2nd–4th/8th–10th Centuries)* (London: Routledge, 1998), 75–104.

21. Feldman, *Fall and Rise of the Islamic State*, 27–55.

22. For an excellent account of the effect of the Inquisition on Egypt, see El Shamsy, *The Canonization of Islamic Law*, 126–32.

23. Al-Ghazālī says that if a judge's decision changes every time he comes up with a new interpretation, this would erode people's confidence in legal rulings (*la-iḍṭarabat al-aḥkām wa lam yūthaq bihā*). See al-Ghazālī, *al-Mustaṣfā min 'Ilm al-Uṣūl*, 4:123.

24. For an excellent discussion of the canonization and standardization of legal methodology, as opposed to substantive law, see El Shamsy, *The Canonization of Islamic Law.*

25. For a discussion of the rise of the school compendium (*mukhtaṣar*), which was an important indication of the stability of *taqlīd* and the ideal of legal predictability inherent in it, see Fadel, "The Social Logic of *Taqlīd* and the Rise of the *Mukhtaṣar*"; Jackson, "*Taqlīd*, Legal Scaffolding."

26. Jackson, *Islamic Law and the State*, 78–79; Hallaq, *Authority, Continuity, and Change*, 75–85. On the hegemony of the *taqlīd* episteme in juristic discourse in the postclassical period, see Ahmed Fekry Ibrahim, "Personal Conviction versus *Madhhab* Interpretation: A Fourteenth-Century Court Ruling," under review.

27. Similarly, in seventeenth- and eighteenth-century Syria and Palestine, the Ottoman Ḥanafī jurist Khayr al-Dīn al-Ramlī (d. 1081/1671) expressed the common view that Ḥanafī muftis and judges should not follow the doctrines of other schools. Tucker, *In the House of the Law*, 81–84.

28. Yūsuf b. ʿAbd al-Barr, *Jāmiʿ Bayān al-ʿIlm wa-Faḍlih* (Cairo: Idārat al-Ṭibāʿa al-Munīriyya, n.d.), 2:927.

29. Al-Ḥāfiẓ al-Dhahabī (d. 748/1374), *Siyar Aʿlām al-Nubalāʾ* (Beirut: Muʾassasat al-Risāla, 1988), 7:125.

30. For a critique of drawing a clear line between law and morality, see Wael Hallaq, "Groundwork of the Moral Law: A New Look at the Qurʾān and the Genesis of Sharīʿa," *Islamic Law and Society* 16:3/4 (2009): 239–79.

31. El Shamsy, *The Canonization of Islamic Law*, 126–44.

32. Clifford Edmund Bosworth, *The New Islamic Dynasties: A Chronological and Genealogical Manual* (New York: Columbia Univ. Press, 1996), 61–63.

33. Nezar AlSayyad, *Cairo Histories of a City* (Cambridge, MA: Belknap Press of Harvard Univ. Press, 2011), 50–70; Marshall G. S. Hodgson, *The Venture of Islam: Conscience and History in a World Civilization*, vol. 2 (Chicago: Univ. of Chicago Press, 1974), 21–36; Subhi Labib, "Egyptian Commercial Policy in the Middle Ages," in *Studies in the Economic History of the Middle East: From the Rise of Islam to the Present Day*, ed. Michael Cook (London: Oxford Univ. Press, 1970), 64–77; Janet L. Abu-Lughod, *Before European Hegemony: The World System A.D. 1250–1350* (New York: Oxford Univ. Press, 1989), 212–44.

34. El Shamsy, *The Canonization of Islamic Law*, 126–44.

35. On the history of Mālikism, Shāfiʿism, and Ḥanafism in Egypt in the eighth and ninth centuries, see ibid., 91–144.

36. For a discussion of the political motivations behind this Fatimid decision, see Adel Allouche, "The Establishment of Four Chief Judgeships in Fatimid Egypt," *Journal of the American Oriental Society* 105:2 (1985): 317–20.

37. According to Melchert, schools were formed in the late ninth century. Other scholars placed the formation in the first half of the ninth century or in the tenth century.

Christopher Melchert, *The Formation of the Sunnī Schools of Law, 9th–10th Centuries C.E.* (Leiden: Brill, 1997), xxii–xviii; Coulson, *A History of Islamic Law*, 62–73; El Shamsy, *The Canonization of Islamic Law*, 167–93.

38. Walter J. Fischel, "The Spice Trade in Mamluk Egypt," in *Spices in the Indian Ocean World*, ed. M. N. Pearson (Aldershot, UK: Variorum, 1996), 51–62.

39. Joseph H. Escovitz, "The Establishment of Four Chief Judgeships in the Mamlūk Empire," *Journal of the American Oriental Society* 102:3 (1982): 529–31.

40. Labib, "Egyptian Commercial Policy in the Middle Ages," 64–77; Fischel, "Spice Trade in Mamluk Egypt," 51–68.

41. André Raymond, *Cairo* (Cambridge, MA: Harvard Univ. Press, 2000), 96.

42. Yossef Rapoport, "Legal Diversity in the Age of *Taqlīd*: The Four Chief *Qāḍī*s under the Mamluks," *Islamic Law and Society* 10:2 (2003): 210–28; Escovitz, "Establishment of Four Chief Judgeships in the Mamlūk Empire"; Allouche, "Establishment of Four Chief Judgeships in Fatimid Egypt."

43. Abū al-ʿAbbās Aḥmad al-Qalqashandī, *Ṣubḥ al-Aʿshā fī Ṣināʿat al-Inshāʾ*, 14 vols. (Cairo: Dār al-Kutub al-Miṣriyya, 1922), 12:55–57.

44. Muḥammad b. Aḥmad b. Iyās, *Badāʾiʿ al-Zuhūr fī Waqāʾiʿ al-Duhūr*, ed. Muḥammad Muṣṭafā (Mecca: Maktabat Dār al-Bāz, 1984), 5:203.

45. Ibid., 5:208.

46. Ibid., 5:161–62, 208–12.

47. Jane Hathaway, *The Politics of Households in Ottoman Egypt: The Rise of the Qazdağlis* (New York: Cambridge Univ. Press, 1997), 8–14; Crecelius, *Roots of Modern Egypt*, 104–8.

48. Benjamin Lellouch, *Les Ottomans en Egypte: historiens et conquérants au XVIe siècle* (Paris: Peeters, 2006), 85–88.

49. On the Mamluks under the Ottomans, see further ibid., 39–46, 51–53; Michael Winter, *Egyptian Society Under Ottoman Rule, 1517–1798* (London: Routledge, 1992), 60–71; Afaf Lutfi Sayyid-Marsot, *A History of Egypt: From the Arab Conquest to the Present* (Cambridge, UK: Cambridge Univ. Press, 2007), 48–53.

50. Reem Meshal, "Antagonistic Sharīʿas and the Construction of Orthodoxy in Sixteenth-Century Ottoman Cairo," *Journal of Islamic Studies* 21:2 (2010): 183–212, at 183–85; Cornell H. Fleischer, "The Lawgiver as Messiah: The Making of the Imperial Image in the Reign of Süleymân," in *Soliman Le Magnifique et Son Temps* (Paris: Ecole du Louvre, 1992), 159–77, at 165–71.

51. Ibn Iyās, *Badāʾiʿ al-Zuhūr fī Waqāʾiʿ al-Duhūr*, 5:165–66.

52. Ibid., 5:162–65.

53. Aḥmad b. Aḥmad al-Damīrī, *Quḍāt Miṣr*, ed. ʿAbd al-Rāziq ʿAbd al-Rāziq ʿĪsā and Yūsuf Muṣṭafā Maḥmūdī (Cairo: Al-ʿArabī li'l-Nashr, 2000), 307. On the tension between Mamluk legal pluralism and Ottoman Ḥanafization, see further Ibrahim, "Al-Shaʿrānī's Response to Legal Purism," 110–40, at 115–19.

54. Ibrahim, "Al-Shaʿrānī's Response to Legal Purism," 110–40, at 115–35.

55. Halil İnalcık and Donald Quataert, *An Economic and Social History of the Ottoman Empire, 1300–1914* (Cambridge, UK: Cambridge Univ. Press, 1994), 2:584–85.

56. Ibid., 2:507–9.

57. On the importance of endowments and the concentration of endowment deeds in the Mamluk period in the hands of the Mamluk families and the shift to merchants in the Ottoman period, see Sylvie Denoix, "Pour une Exploitation d'Ensemble d'un Corpus: Les Waqfs Mamelouks du Caire," in *Le Waqf dans l'Espace Islamique: Outil de Pouvoir Socio-Politique*, ed. Randi Deguilhem (Damascus: Institut Français de Damas, 1995), 38–39.

58. Sayyid-Marsot, *History of Egypt*, 56.

59. Lellouch, *Les Ottomans en Egypte*, 85–88.

60. İnalcık and Quataert, *Economic and Social History*, 2:596, 674–76; Hathaway, *Politics of Households in Ottoman Egypt*, 109–10; Afaf Lutfi Sayyid-Marsot, *Women and Men in Late Eighteenth-Century Egypt* (Austin: Univ. of Texas Press, 1995), 7–8, 35–36.

61. Sayyid-Marsot, *Women and Men*, 53.

62. Ibid., 8.

63. Ibid., 33.

64. Ibrahim, "Al-Shaʿrānī's Response to Legal Purism," 110–40, at 115–35.

65. On the formation of the Ottoman elite in Egypt, see Lellouch, *Les Ottomans en Egypte*, 85–88.

66. Jackson, *Islamic Law and the State*, 65–66.

67. Ibid., 103.

68. For a general discussion of the debate about the infallibility of *mujtahid*s, see Bernard G. Weiss, *The Spirit of Islamic Law*, (Athens: Univ. of Georgia Press, 1998), 88–126; Aron Zysow, *The Economy of Certainty: An Introduction to the Typology of Islamic Legal Theory* (Atlanta: Lockwood Press, 2013), 259–78.

69. El Shamsy, *The Canonization of Islamic Law*, 55–63; Vishanoff, *The Formation of Islamic Hermeneutics*, 68–88.

70. The two contradictory positions of *taṣwīb* and *takhṭīʾa* were attributed to the eponyms of the four schools, according to Ibn al-Ḥājib. See Shams al-Dīn al-Iṣfahānī, *Bayān al-Mukhtaṣar Sharḥ Mukhtaṣar Ibn al-Ḥājib*, ed. Muḥammad Maẓhar Baqā (Jiddah: Dār al-Madanī, 1986), 3:310.

71. Abī al-Maʿālī ʿAbd al-Malik al-Juwaynī, *al-Burhān fī Uṣūl al-Fiqh*, ed. ʿAbd al-ʿAẓīm al-Dīb (Doha, Qatar: N.p., 1978), 2:1319–22.

72. Al-Juwaynī, *Maghīth al-Khalq fī Tarjīḥ al-Qawl al-Ḥaqq*, 8–19.

73. Al-Ghazālī, *al-Mustaṣfā min ʿIlm al-Uṣūl*, 4:50.

74. Al-Iṣfahānī, *Bayān al-Mukhtaṣar Sharḥ Mukhtaṣar Ibn al-Ḥājib*, 3:320–21.

75. Ibid., 3:307–11.

76. Al-Ghazālī, *al-Mustaṣfā min ʿIlm al-Uṣūl*, 4:32–44; al-Iṣfahānī, *Bayān al-Mukhtaṣar Sharḥ Mukhtaṣar Ibn al-Ḥājib*, 3:307–11; Taqī al-Dīn b. Taymiyya, *Kitāb Bayān al-Dalīl ʿalā Buṭlān al-Taḥlīl*, ed. Ḥamdī ʿAbd al-Majīd al-Salafī (Beirut: al-Maktab al-Islāmī, 1988), 322–24.

Al-Marīsī and al-Aṣamm were important figures of the Muʿtazila scripturalism of the formative period; see Vishanoff, *The Formation of Islamic Hermeneutics*, 73–78.

77. Al-Juwaynī, *al-Burhān fī Uṣūl al-Fiqh*, 2:1319–22.

78. Al-Ghazālī, *al-Mustaṣfā min ʿIlm al-Uṣūl*, 4:42–43.

79. Al-Iṣfahānī, *Bayān al-Mukhtaṣar Sharḥ Mukhtaṣar Ibn al-Ḥājib*, 3:316–19; al-Ghazālī, *al-Mustaṣfā min ʿIlm al-Uṣūl*, 4:112.

80. Another argument forwarded by those who believe that the divine ruling is always knowable is that the *mujtahid* in a disputation is a seeker of the correct ruling (*ṭālib*), which means that there must necessarily be something sought (*maṭlūb*). According to them, the thing sought must necessarily have existed prior to the act of seeking, which means that there can only be one *truth* that is known beforehand, and whoever does not attain it must thus be in error (*mukhṭiʾ*). Ibn al-Ḥājib responds by noting that even then, the *maṭlūb* is what the *mujtahid* believes to be the truth, even if it is not so in reality. See al-Iṣfahānī, *Bayān al-Mukhtaṣar Sharḥ Mukhtaṣar Ibn al-Ḥājib*, 3:316–20.

81. Ibid., 3:321–26.

82. Ibid., 3:310.

83. Some jurists held the view that *ijtihād* has become easier for later generations owing to the efforts of earlier scholars. While the predecessors had to travel to distant lands to collect traditions, later jurists already had at their disposal many works of authentic traditions. See, for example, Aḥmad b. Yaḥyā al-Wansharīsī, *al-Miʿyār al-Muʿrib wa'l-Jāmiʿ al-Mughrib ʿan Fatāwā Ahl Ifrīqiya wa'l-Andalus wa'l-Maghrib*, ed. Muḥammad Ḥajjī (Rabat: Wizārat al-Awqāf wa'l-Shu'ūn al-Islāmiyya li'l-Mamlaka al-Maghribiyya, 1981), 6:363–64; For a discussion of scripturalism, see Vishanoff, *The Formation of Islamic Hermeneutics*, 66–108; Gleave, *Scripturalist Islam*.

84. Ibn Taymiyya, *Kitāb Bayān al-Dalīl ʿalā Buṭlān al-Taḥlīl*, 322–24.

85. Ibid., 145–46.

86. Ibid., 318–22.

87. Ibid.

88. Ibn Qayyim al-Jawziyya, *al-Ṣawāʿiq al-Mursala ʿalā al-Jahmiyya wa'l-Muʿaṭṭila*, ed. Sayyid Ibrāhīm. (Cairo: Dār al-Ḥadīth, 1992), 563–69.

89. Ibn Qayyim al-Jawziyya, *Iʿlām al-Muwaqqiʿīn ʿan Rabb al-ʿĀlamīn*, ed. Abū ʿUbayda Mashhūr b. Ḥasan Āl Salmān and Abū ʿUmar Aḥmad ʿAbd Allāh Aḥmad (Riyadh, Saudi Arabia: Dār Ibn al-Jawzī, 2002), 3:525–26.

90. Abū Muḥammad al-Ḥasan b. ʿAlī b. Khalaf al-Barbahārī, *Sharḥ al-Sunna*, ed. ʿAbd al-Raḥmān b. Aḥmad al-Jumayzī (Riyadh, Saudi Arabia: Dār al-Minhāj, 2005), 91.

91. Ibid., 69, 111.

92. Ibid., 116.

93. Ibn Taymiyya, *Kitāb Bayān al-Dalīl ʿalā Buṭlān al-Taḥlīl*, 145–46.

94. Al-Ghazālī, *al-Mustaṣfā min ʿIlm al-Uṣūl*, 4:59–64.

95. Al-Iṣfahānī, *Bayān al-Mukhtaṣar Sharḥ Mukhtaṣar Ibn al-Ḥājib*, 3:316–19.

96. This explanation of the dictum "Every *mujtahid* is correct" can be seen in later juristic works as well. See Ibn Mullah Farrūkh al-Mawrawī al-Makkī, "Taʿlīqa fi'l-Ijtihād wa'l-Taqlīd," Cairo, n.d., MS Dār al-Kutub 166 Uṣūl Taymūr, folio 3a; al-Iṣfahānī, *Bayān al-Mukhtaṣar Sharḥ Mukhtaṣar Ibn al-Ḥājib*, 3:316–19.

97. Al-Juwaynī, *al-Burhān fī Uṣūl al-Fiqh*, 2:1322.

98. Ibn Taymiyya, *Kitāb Bayān al-Dalīl ʿalā Buṭlān al-Taḥlīl*, 319–25.

99. In some ways, this distinction resembles the distinction made by the Akhbārī Muḥammad Amīn al-Astarābādī (d. 1033/1623–24 or 1036/1626) between knowledge of the actions with which the believer is charged and God's knowledge of the law. See Gleave, *Scripturalist Islam*, 66–67.

2. *Tatabbuʿ al-Rukhaṣ* in Juristic Discourse Prior to the Nineteenth Century

1. *Tatabbuʿ al-rukhaṣ* refers to following the less stringent juristic views.

2. Hallaq, *Sharīʿa*, 448; Tucker, *In the House of the Law*, 82–83, 108.

3. Rudolph Peters, J. G. J. Ter Haar, "Rukhṣa," in *Encyclopaedia of Islam*, 2nd ed., ed. P. Bearman, Th. Bianquis, C. E. Bosworth, E. van Donzel, and W. P. Heinrichs (Leiden: Brill, 2010).

4. ʿAbd al-Wahhāb al-Shaʿrānī, *al-Mīzān al-Shaʿrāniyya al-Mudkhala*, Cairo, n.d., MS Dār al-Kutub 77 Fiqh Madhāhib, folio 8a, 8b, 15a, microfilm #48209.

5. This is the definition of *tatabbuʿ al-rukhaṣ* in *taqlīd*. There is also another less common type, known as *tatabbuʿ al-rukhaṣ* in *ijtihād*, which simply refers to when the same ruling of another school is reached coincidentally through one's independent *ijtihād* as opposed to *taqlīd*.

6. "Judge between them in the light of what has been revealed by God, and do not follow their whims." Q. 5:49; Aḥmad Alī, *al- Qur'an: A Contemporary Translation* (Princeton, NJ: Princeton Univ. Press, 1993).

7. See for example, Muḥammad al-Baghdādī, *Risāla fi'l-Taqlīd*, Cairo, n.d., MS Dār al-Kutub 125 Uṣūl Taymūr, folio 3a-5b, microfilm #23855; ʿAbd al-Ghanī al-Nābulsī, *al-Ajwiba ʿan al-As'ila al-Sitta*, Cairo, n.d., MS Dār al-Kutub 365 Uṣūl Fiqh, folio 5a-5b, microfilm #16703.

8. Ibn ʿAbd al-Barr, *Jāmiʿ Bayān al-ʿIlm Wa-Faḍlih*, 2:927.

9. Al-Ḥāfiẓ al-Dhahabī (d. 748/1374), *Siyar Aʿlām al-Nubalā'* (Beirut: Mu'assasat al-Risāla, 1988), 7:125.

10. Nūr al-Dīn Mullah ʿAlī al-Qārī, *al-Asrār al-Marfūʿa fi'l-Akhbār al-Mawḍūʿa*, ed. Muḥammad b. Luṭfī al-Ṣabbāgh, 2nd ed. (Riyadh, Saudi Arabia: al-Maktab al-Islāmī, 1986), 108–10; Muḥammad Nāṣir al-Dīn al-Albānī, *Silsilat al-Aḥādīth al-Ḍaʿīfa wa'l-Mawḍūʿa wa-Atharihā al-Sayyi' fi'l-Umma* (Riyadh, Saudi Arabia: Maktabat al-Maʿārif, 1992), 1:141–48.

11. See al-Nuʿmān b. Thābit Abū Ḥanīfa, *Sharḥ al-Fiqh al-Akbar*, ed. ʿAbd Allāh b. Ibrāhīm al-Anṣārī (Hayderabad, India: Majlis Dā'irat al-Maʿārif al-Niẓāmiyya, 1903), 10–11.

12. Al-Barbahārī, *Sharḥ al-Sunna*, 56.

13. Muḥammad b. Idrīs al-Shāfiʿī, *al-Risāla*, ed. Aḥmad Muḥammad Shākir (Beirut: Dār al-Kutub al-ʿIlmiyya, 1939), 560–98.

14. For more on al-Shāfiʿī's approach, see Ahmed Fekry Ibrahim, "Rethinking the *Taqlīd-Ijtihād* Dichotomy: A Conceptual-Historical Approach," *Journal of the American Oriental Society*, forthcoming.

15. Al-Shāfiʿī, *al-Risāla*, 560–98.

16. Al-Shahrazūrī, *Fatāwā wa Masāʾil Ibn al-Ṣalāḥ fi'l-Tafsīr wa'l-Ḥadīth wa'l-Uṣūl wa'l-Fiqh*, 1:63–64.

17. Abū Bakr al-Khallāl, *Kitāb al-Amr bi'l-Maʿrūf wa'l-Nahī ʿan al-Munkar*, ed. Mashhūr Ḥasan Maḥmūd Salmān and Hishām b. Ismāʿīl al-Saqqā (Beirut: al-Maktab al-Islāmī, 1990), 87; Aḥmad b. Ḥanbal, *Masāʾil al-Imām Aḥmad Ibn Ḥanbal Riwāyatu Ibnihi ʿAbd Allāh Ibn Aḥmad*, ed. Zuhayr al-Shāwīsh (Beirut: al-Maktab al-Islāmī, 1981), 449.

18. Cited in Nimrod Hurvitz, *The Formation of Hanbalism: Piety into Power* (London: RoutledgeCurzon, 2002), 105.

19. Opponents of *tatabbuʿ al-rukhaṣ* frequently cited a hypothetical situation in which a woman is married without the different conditions of a marriage, which they described as fornication. The assumption is that *tatabbuʿ al-rukhaṣ* can lead to *zinā* since a woman who is married with no legal guardian (*walī*) nor witnesses is not in fact in a marriage. Ibn Ḥazm, *al-Muḥallā* (Beirut: Dār al-Āfāq al-Jadīda, n.d.), 11:250–52. See also Ḥasan b. ʿAmmār b. ʿAlī al-Shurunbulālī, *al-ʿIqd al-Farīd li-Bayān al-Rājiḥ min al-Khilāf fi'l-Taqlīd*, Cairo, n.d., MS Dār al-Kutub 367 Uṣūl Fiqh, folio 8b, microfilm #38391.

20. Ibn Ḥazm al-Andalusī, *al-Iḥkām fī Uṣūl al-Aḥkām* (Cairo: Maṭbaʿat ʿĀṭif, 1978), 6:1130–39.

21. ʿAlī b. Aḥmad b. Ḥazm, *Marātib al-Ijmāʿ fi'l-ʿIbādāt wa'l-Muʿāmalāt wa'l-Iʿtiqādāt*, 3rd ed. (Beirut: Dār al-Āfāq al-Jadīda, 1982), 196.

22. Ibn ʿAbd al-Barr, *Jāmiʿ Bayān al-ʿIlm wa-Faḍlih*, 2:927.

23. Al-Juwaynī, *Maghīth al-Khalq fī Tarjīḥ al-Qawl al-Ḥaqq*, 8–19.

24. Al-Ghazālī, *al-Mustaṣfā min ʿIlm al-Uṣūl*, 4:88, 112–14.

25. Ibid., 4:154–55.

26. Ibid.

27. Al-Shahrazūrī, *Fatāwā wa Masāʾil Ibn al-Ṣalāḥ fi'l-Tafsīr wa'l-Ḥadīth wa'l-Uṣūl wa'l-Fiqh*, 1:47, 60, 63–64.

28. Ibid., 1:88–90.

29. Daniella Talmon-Heller, "Fidelty, Cohesion and Conformity within Madhhabs in Zangid and Ayyubid Syria," in *The Islamic School of Law: Evolution, Devolution, and Progress*, ed. Peri Bearman, Rudolph Peters, and Frank E. Vogel (Cambridge, MA: Harvard Univ. Press, 2005), 106.

30. Richard W. Bulliet, *The Patricians of Nishapur: A Study in Medieval Islamic Social History* (Cambridge, MA: Harvard Univ. Press, 1972); Talmon-Heller, "Fidelty, Cohesion and Conformity within Madhhabs in Zangid and Ayyubid Syria," 108–10.

31. Ibn Taymiyya, *Kitāb Bayān al-Dalīl 'alā Buṭlān al-Taḥlīl*, 140–44.

32. Taqī al-Dīn b. Taymiyya, *al-Ikhtiyārāt al-Fiqhiyya min Fatāwā Shaykh al-Islām Ibn Taymiyya*, ed. Muḥammad Ḥāmid al-Fiqī (Cairo: Maṭba'at al-Sunnah al-Muḥammadiyya, n.d.), 332–36. Ibn Taymiyya also rejected the view supporting the incumbency of abiding by one school in all transactions (*tamadhhub*). According to him, if someone were to argue that it is incumbent upon people to follow one specific imam, he should be asked to repent, and if he does not, he should be killed. He encouraged people who usually follow a specific imam to switch to the opinions of another based on the strength of their evidence or because of their greater knowledge or piety. He juxtaposed this approach with following the less stringent opinions (*al-akhdh bi'l-rukhaṣ*) and only permitted the selection of opinions based on an assessment of evidence. According to him, a judge can delegate another to preside over a case if he thinks the other school's opinion is more preponderant, but he may never do so for pragmatic considerations.

33. Ibn Qayyim al-Jawziyya, *I'lām al-Muwaqqi'īn 'an Rabb al-'Ālamīn*, 2:55.

34. Ibid., 3:453–59. The prominent calls to *ijtihād* sounded by modern purists, usually inspired by Ibn Taymiyya and Ibn Qayyim, are ultimately a call for the exercise of *tarjīḥ*, which is in the middle of the continuum of *ijtihād-taqlīd* and known in the primary sources as *ijtihād fi'l-madhhab*.

35. On *ittibā'* and *taqlīd*, see further Ahmed Fekry Ibrahim, "Rethinking the *Taqlīd-Ijtihād* Dichotomy: A Conceptual Historical Approach," *Journal of the American Oriental Society*, forthcoming. For examples of a yes or no response to fatwas, see al-Shahrazūrī, *Fatāwā wa-Masā'il Ibn al-Ṣalāḥ fi'l-Tafsīr wa'l-Ḥadīth wa'l-Uṣūl wa'l-Fiqh*, 1:77–80.

36. Ibn 'Abd al-Barr, *Jāmi' Bayān al-'Ilm wa-Faḍlih*, 2:117.

37. Al-Ghazālī, who supported the traditional definition of *taqlīd*—accepting an opinion without evidence (*ḥujja*)—did not draw a distinction between *taqlīd* and *ittibā'*. In fact, he used the two terms synonymously, arguing, for instance, that *ittibā'* consists of relying on ignorance (*fa'l-ittibā'u fīhī i'timādun 'alā jahl*). See al-Khaṭīb al-Baghdādī, *Kitāb al-Faqīh wa'l-Mutafaqqih* (Riyadh, Saudi Arabia: Dār Ibn al-Jawzī, 1996), 2:127–33; al-Ghazālī, *al-Mustaṣfā min 'Ilm al-Uṣūl*, 4:140, 147–48.

38. Al-Ghazālī, *al-Mustaṣfā min 'Ilm al-Uṣūl*, 4:140; Muḥammad Amīn al-Ḥusaynī al-Ḥanafī Amīr Bādshāh, *Taysīr al-Taḥrīr 'Alā Kitāb al-Taḥrīr* (Cairo: Muṣṭafā al-Bābī al-Ḥalabī, 1834), 4:241–42.

39. See, for instance, al-Wansharīsī, *al-Mi'yār al-Mu'rib wa'l-Jāmi' al-Mughrib 'an Fatāwā Ahl Ifrīqiya wa'l-Andalus wa'l-Maghrib*, 6:363–64. On this notion that *ijtihād* should be exercised by everyone, see further Ibrahim, "Rethinking the *Taqlīd-Ijtihād* Dichotomy."

40. Ibn Taymiyya, *al-Ikhtiyārāt al-Fiqhiyya min Fatāwā Shaykh al-Islām Ibn Taymiyya*, 332–66.

41. The obligation to follow the same school in all transactions does not extend to judicial matters since the legal subject might not have a say on the choice of judge in the court context. Thus he or she may have to occasionally obey the ruling of a judge from another

school. Ibrāhīm b. Ḥusayn b. Aḥmad b. Muḥammad b. Aḥmad Ibn Bīrī, "Al-Kashf wa'l-Tadqīq li-Sharḥ Ghāyat al-Taḥqīq," Cairo, n.d., MS Dār al-Kutub 403 Uṣūl Fiqh, folio 5a–6b.

42. Ibid., 6a–7b.

43. Al-Samhūdī, "Al-ʿIqd al-Farīd fī Aḥkām al-Taqlīd," folio 13b–14a.

44. The opposite of pursuing the more stringent rulings (*tatabbuʿ al-ʿazāʾim*) is not necessarily more acceptable than *tatabbuʿ al-rukhaṣ*. When the Mālikī jurist Ibn ʿArafa (d. 803/1401) was asked by the jurists of Grenada whether it is better to avoid jurisprudential differences, as al-Ghazālī and Ibn Rushd had urged people to do, he replied that neither *tatabbuʿ al-rukhaṣ* nor *tatabbuʿ al-ʿazāʾim* is praiseworthy. Al-Samhūdī disagreed with Ibn ʿArafa, arguing that following the more stringent opinion is better. According to him, wiping the entire head in ritual ablution is better than wiping only part of it. See ibid., 17a–19a; al-Wansharīsī, *al-Miʿyār al-Muʿrib wa'l-Jāmiʿ al-Mughrib ʿan Fatāwā Ahl Ifrīqiya wa'l-Andalus wa'l-Maghrib*, 6:369.

45. Al-Samhūdī, "Al-ʿIqd al-Farīd fī Aḥkām al-Taqlīd," 11b, 12a, 16a.

46. There are some references to al-Marwazī's disagreement with the dominant paradigm against pragmatic eclecticism, but it is difficult to authenticate this claim. See, for instance, Tāj al-Dīn al-Subkī, *Jamʿ al-Jawāmiʿ fī Uṣūl al-Fiqh*, ed. ʿAbd al-Munʿim Khalīl Ibrāhīm, 2nd ed. (Beirut: Dār al-Kutub al-ʿIlmiyya, 2003), 123; Ḥasan al-ʿAṭṭār, *Ḥāshiyat al-ʿAṭṭār ʿalā Sharḥ al-Jalāl al-Maḥallī ʿalā Jamʿ al-Jawāmiʿ* (Beirut: Dār al-Kutub al-ʿIlmiyya, n.d.), 2:441.

47. This example also illustrates that despite the widely held view that the laity have no *madhhab*, some people had a school affiliation, most likely based on geography and family history.

48. Muḥyī al-Dīn b. ʿArabī, *al-Futūḥāt al-Makkiyya* (Cairo: Dār al-Kutub al-ʿArabiyya, n.d.), 1:392, 2:685.

49. Al-Ghazālī, *al-Mustaṣfā min ʿIlm al-Uṣūl*, 4:154–55.

50. ʿIzz al-Dīn b. ʿAbd al-Salām, *Kitāb al-Fatāwā*, ed. ʿAbd al-Raḥmān b. ʿAbd al-Fattāḥ (Beirut: Dār al-Maʿrifa, 1986), 150–54.

51. As we have seen, determining what constitutes a clear textual source was subject to debate. For some jurists, all school opinions are legitimate areas of *khilāf*. For others, who narrow the areas of *khilāf* by challenging well-established school doctrines that are deemed to contradict clear textual evidence, some controversial decisions, especially the Ḥanafī opinions on drinking date wine and the possibility of capital punishment for a Muslim who unjustly kills a non-Muslim, for example, are not considered valid areas of *khilāf*. There is only one correct opinion that is objectively knowable in such cases. Ibn ʿAbd al-Salām, *al-Qawāʿid al-Kubrā: Qawāʿid al-Aḥkām fī Iṣlāḥ al-Anām*, 2:274–75.

52. Shihāb al-Dīn al-Qarāfī, *Sharḥ Tanqīḥ al-Fuṣūl fī Ikhtiṣār al-Maḥṣūl fi'l-Uṣūl* (Beirut, Lebanon: Dār al-Fikr, 2004), 339.

53. Ibid.

54. For a good study of the image of Ibn ʿArabī in the later Islamic tradition, see generally Alexander D. Knysh, *Ibn ʿArabī in the Later Islamic Tradition: The Making of a Polemical Image in Medieval Islam* (Albany: State Univ. of New York Press, 1999).

55. It is clear that the attribution is to the Syro-Egyptian Shāfi'ī 'Izz al-Dīn b. 'Abd al-Salām al-Sulamī rather than to the Egyptian al-'Izz b. 'Abd al-Salām al-Mālikī. There is a reference to his renowned knowledge and piety, a formula that would more likely be used with the Shāfi'ī scholar (*al-muttafaq 'alā 'ilmihi wa-ṣalāḥih*). In addition, al-Wansharīsī cited his *fatāwā* collection, which is conclusive evidence that it is the Shāfi'ī Ibn 'Abd al-Salām who dealt with this issue in his *fatāwā*. See Ibn 'Abd al-Salām, *Kitāb al-Fatāwā*, 150–54.

56. Al-Wansharīsī, *al-Mi'yār al-Mu'rib wa'l-Jāmi' al-Mughrib 'an Fatāwā Ahl Ifrīqiya wa'l-Andalus wa'l-Maghrib*, 6:382.

57. Al-Samhūdī, *al-'Iqd*, folio 17a–19b.

58. 'Abd al-Ra'ūf b. Nūr al-Dīn al-Munāwī, *Fayḍ al-Qadīr*, 2nd ed. (Beirut: Dār al-Ma'rifa, 1972), 1:210.

59. The restriction related to not following a different opinion on a preceding similar case is a precaution against *talfīq* as we shall see in the next chapter. Ibn Amīr al-Ḥājj, *al-Taqrīr wa'l-Taḥbīr*, 2nd ed. (Beirut: Dār al-Kutub al-'Ilmiyya, 1983), 3:351–52.

60. One of the ways that supporters of *tatabbu' al-rukhaṣ* used to explain away the prohibition is to argue that it does not refer to *taqlīd*. The implication is that such pragmatism is used in the exercise of *ijtihād*. Ibid.

61. Badr al-Dīn Muḥammad al-Zarkashī, *al-Baḥr al-Muḥīṭ fī Uṣūl al-Fiqh*, ed. 'Abd al-Qādir al-'Āfī and 'Umar Sulaymān al-Ashqar, 2nd ed. (Kuwait: Wizārat al-Awqāf wa'l-Shu'ūn al-Islāmiyya, 1992), 5:319.

62. Ibn al-Humām was quoted extensively by both Mamluk and Ottoman jurists from the four schools. The Shāfi'ī al-Samhūdī (d. 911/1505) and the Ḥanafī al-Shurunbulālī (d. 1069/1658) cited his views and repeated the Prophet's tradition that differences of opinion among his *umma* are a blessing (*raḥma*). They both cited Companions and traditions related to *ikhtilāf*. Amīr Bādshāh's view (d. 972/1564), discussed below, was also cited by al-Shurunbulālī. Ḥasan b. 'Ammār b. 'Alī Shurunbulālī, "Al-'Iqd al-Farīd li-Bayān al-Rājiḥ Min al-Khilāf fi'l-Taqlīd," n.d., MS Dār al-Kutub 367 Uṣūl Fiqh, folio 11a–b; al-Samhūdī, "Al-'Iqd al-Farīd fī Aḥkām al-Taqlīd," folio 17a–b.

63. Al-Samhūdī, "Al-'Iqd al-Farīd fī Aḥkām al-Taqlīd," folio 16a–17a.

64. Amīr Bādshāh, *Taysīr al-Taḥrīr 'alā Kitāb al-Taḥrīr*, 4:254–55.

65. See, for instance, al-Shahrazūrī, *Fatāwā wa-Masā'il Ibn al-Ṣalāḥ fi'l-Tafsīr wa'l-Ḥadīth wa'l-Uṣūl wa'l-Fiqh*, 1:43–45; Muḥammad al-Fiqhī, "Risāla fīmā Yata'allaq bi-Aḥwāl al-Muftī," Cairo, n.d., MS Dār al-Kutub 198 Uṣūl Fiqh, folio 3a–4a; Amīr Bādshāh, *Taysīr al-Taḥrīr 'alā Kitāb al-Taḥrīr*, 4:183.

66. Sayyid 'Alawī b. Aḥmad al-Saqqāf, *Majmū'at Sab'at Kutub Mufīda* (Cairo: Maṭba'at Muṣṭafā al-Bābī al-Ḥalabī, 1983), 51.

67. Unlike the Ḥanafīs, the Shāfi'īs consider the testimony of one witness and an oath sufficient for the claimant to establish his claim.

68. The text of Ibn Nujaym's *fatāwā* is in the margin of the *Fatāwā al-Ghiyāthiyya*, Zayn al-Dīn b. Nujaym, *Fatāwā Ibn Nujaym al-Ḥanafī* (Cairo: al-Maṭba'a al-Amīriyya, 1903), 140.

69. See for example David Stephan Powers, "*Kadijustiz* or *Qāḍī*-Justice? A Paternity Dispute from Fourteenth-Century Morocco," *Islamic Law and Society* 1:3 (1994): 345.

70. Nūr al-Dīn Mullah 'Alī al-Qārī, "Tawḍīḥ al-Mabānī 'alā Mukhtaṣar al-Manār," Cairo, n.d., MS Dār al-Kutub 367 Uṣūl Fiqh, folio 163a–b.

71. *'Azīma* is the opposite of *rukhṣa*, that is to say, following a more stringent view.

72. Al-Qārī, "Tawḍīḥ al-Mabānī 'alā Mukhtaṣar al-Manār," folio 163a–b.

73. Al-Munāwī, *Fayḍ al-Qadīr*, 1:210.

74. Al-Shurunbulālī, "Al-'Iqd al-Farīd li-Bayān al-Rājiḥ min al-Khilāf fi'l-Taqlīd," folio 2a–4b.

75. Ibid., folio 6a.

76. Aḥmad b. Muḥammad al-Ḥamawī, "Al-Durr al-Farīd fī Bayān Ḥukm al-Taqlīd," Cairo, n.d., Dār al-Kutub 569 Uṣūl Taymūr, folio 5a–b.

77. Muḥammad b. Sulaymān al-Madanī al-Shāfi'ī al-Kurdī, *al-Fawā'id al-Madaniyya fī Bayān Ikhtilāf al-'Ulamā' Min al-Shāfi'iyya* (Diyār Bakr, Turkey: Al-Maktaba al-Islāmiyya, n.d.), 232–41.

78. Al-Dasūqī, *Ḥāshiyat al-Dasūqī 'alā al-Sharḥ al-Kabīr*, 1:20.

79. Ibid., 4:130.

80. Ibid., 1:20–30.

81. Al-'Aṭṭār, *Ḥāshiyat al-'Aṭṭār 'alā Sharḥ al-Jalāl al-Maḥallī 'alā Jam' al-Jawāmi'*, 2:440–42.

82. Ibid., 2:440.

83. Hallaq, *Sharī'a*, 448.

84. Lutz Wiederhold, "Legal Doctrines in Conflict: The Relevance of *Madhhab* Boundaries to Legal Reasoning in the Light of an Unpublished Treatise on *Taqlīd* and *Ijtihād*," *Islamic Law and Society* 3:2 (1996): 234–304, at 256–57.

85. Ibn Ḥajar al-'Asqalānī, *Inbā' al-Ghumr bi Abnā' al-'Umr*, ed. Ḥasan Ḥabashī (Egypt: Al-Majlis al-A'lā li'l-Shu'ūn al-Islāmiyya, 1969), 1:106, 410.

86. Khayr al-Dīn al-Ramlī, for instance, uses the term *ṣaḥḥaḥahu* to refer to the activities of some jurists who correct juristic opinions on the basis of people's changing conditions over time. Khayr al-Dīn al-Ramlī, *al-Fatāwā al-Khayriyya li-Naf' al-Bariyya* (Būlāq: al-Maṭba'a al-Kubrā al-Mīriyya, 1882), 1:2.

87. Taqī al-Dīn Muḥammad b. Aḥmad al-Futūḥī b. al-Najjār, *Muntahā al-Irādāt fī Jam' al-Muqni' ma'a al-Tanqīḥ wa Ziyādāt*, ed. 'Abd Allāh b. 'Abd al-Muḥsin Turkī (Beirut: Mu'assasat al-Risāla, 1999), 1:6.

88. Hallaq, "*Qāḍīs* Communicating."

89. Al-Bazzāzī is also known as al-Kurdarī. Muḥammad b. Muḥammad b. Shihāb b. Yūsuf al-Kurdarī al-Bazzāzī, *al-Fatāwā al-Bazzāziyya*; it is printed on the margin of *al-Fatāwā al-Hindiyya*; see Niẓām al-Dīn Balkhī, *al-Fatāwā al-Hindiyya*, 2nd ed. (Beirut: Dār Ṣādir, 1893), 5:183; Hallaq, "*Qāḍīs* Communicating," 438.

90. For a discussion of *madhhab*-opinion, see Hallaq, "Can the Shari'a Be Restored?" 37–38.

91. Hallaq, "*Qāḍīs* Communicating," 437–66, at 466; Abū Qāsim ʿAlī b. Muḥammad b. Aḥmad al-Raḥbī al-Simnānī, *Rawḍat al-Quḍāh wa Ṭarīq al-Najāh*, ed. Ṣalāḥ al-Dīn Nāhī, 2nd ed. (Beirut: Mu'assasat al-Risāla, 1984), 1:332–33.

92. Al-Simnānī, *Rawḍat al-Quḍāh wa Ṭarīq al-Najāh*, 1:332–33.

93. Aḥmad b. Ḥijāzī b. Budayr Shihāb al-Dīn Fishnī, "Kifāyat al-Mustafīd fī Aḥkām al-Taqlīd," Cairo, n.d., MS Dār al-Kutub 367 Uṣūl Fiqh, folio 5a.

94. The practice of tailoring legal opinions to people's individual needs may have contributed to the general aversion to issuing legal advice for hypothetical events, since in such cases the mufti would not know the individual circumstances of the people to whom they are issued. Al-Ḥājj, *al-Taqrīr wa'l-Taḥbīr*, 3:341–42.

95. Al-Kurdī, *al-Fawā'id al-Madaniyya fī Bayān Ikhtilāf al-ʿUlamā' min al-Shāfiʿiyya*, 220; Ibn Ḥajar al-Haytamī, *al-Fatāwā al-Kubrā al-Fiqhiyya* (Cairo: Multazim al-Ṭabʿ wa'l-Nashr ʿAbd al-Ḥamīd Aḥmad Ḥanafī, 1938), 4:317–18.

96. This anonymous jurist most likely lived between the sixteenth and the eighteenth centuries since he mentioned Ibn Ḥajar al-Haytamī (d. 973/1567) in his treatise.

97. Anonymous, "Risāla Jalīla fi'l-Taqlīd," Cairo, n.d., MS Dār al-Kutub 94 Uṣūl Taymūr, folio 3b; al-Fiqhī, "Risāla fīmā Yataʿallaq bi Aḥwāl al-Muftī," folio 7a–b.

98. Al-Ḥājj, *al-Taqrīr wa'l-Taḥbīr*, 3:347; al-Kurdī, *al-Fawā'id al-Madaniyya fī Bayān Ikhtilāf al-ʿUlamā' min al-Shāfiʿiyya*, 220.

99. Al-Ḥājj, *al-Taqrīr wa'l-Taḥbīr*, 3:348–49; al-Ghazālī, *al-Mustaṣfā min ʿIlm al-Uṣūl*, 4:136–37.

100. Wiederhold, "Legal Doctrines in Conflict," 234–304, at 252.

101. Hallaq argues that the connection between fatwa practice and the term "*madhhab*-opinion" appeared among the *muta'akhkhirīn*, namely, after the tenth century when the *madhhab*-opinion gained its authoritative status from its use as the basis for issuing legal opinions. Hallaq, "Can the Shariʿa Be Restored?" 36–38.

102. Rudolph Peters, "What Does It Mean to Be an Official Madhhab?" in Bearman, Peters, and Vogel, *Islamic School of Law: Evolution, Devolution, and Progress*, 150–54.

103. A similar process took place in the Shāfiʿī school in the Ottoman period, whereby there was an assumption that jurists were no longer able to exercise *tarjīḥ* and a hierarchy of later authorities was created. This process revolved around specific commentaries (*ḥawāshī*) to be consulted in a specific hierarchical order that sometimes varied by region. See al-Saqqāf, *Majmūʿat Sabʿat Kutub Mufīda*, 37–38. On the institutionalization of the *taqlīd* hegemony and the widespread view that most jurists were believed to be *muqallids* by the thirteenth century, see further Ahmed Fekry Ibrahim, "Personal Conviction versus *Madhhab* Interpretation: A Fourteenth-Century Court Ruling," currently under review.

104. See my forthcoming article, Ibrahim, "The Codification Episteme."

105. Whether the opinion selected was based on evidentiary grounds or on a hierarchy of juristic authority, neither legal method, at least in theory, was directly tied to the needs of society. There were also at least thirty-two cases in which the Ottomans

imposed their own legal choices, a process that was neither based on the exercise of preponderance (*tarjīḥ*) nor on the hierarchy of juristic authority, but on political expedience (*siyāsa shar'iyya*). See Peters, "What Does It Mean to Be an Official Madhhab?" 150–54; Colin Imber, *Ebu's-Su'ud: The Islamic Legal Tradition* (Redwood City, CA: Stanford Univ. Press, 1997), 169.

106. Muḥammad b. Muḥammad b. Shihāb b. Yūsuf al-Kurdarī al-Bazzāzī, "al-Fatāwā al-Bazzāziyya," Cairo, n.d., MS Dār al-Kutub 66 Fiqh Ḥanafī Khalīl Aghā, folio 163a–65a, microfilm #55712.

107. Ibid., folio 163–65a.

108. Although there was an implication that these juristic choices were pragmatic, there was no explicit reference to this and neither was the term *tatabbu' al-rukhaṣ* used here. Al-Wansharīsī, *al-Mi'yār al-Mu'rib wa'l-Jāmi' al-Mughrib 'an Fatāwā Ahl Ifrīqiya wa'l-Andalus wa'l-Maghrib*, 6:364–66.

109. A note on translation: I simplified the original Arabic by omitting the frequent repetitions of the original, as well as titles, which are not necessary for understanding the text. Words in square brackets are my own and are added to facilitate the reading of the text.

110. Al-Samhūdī, "Al-'Iqd al-Farīd fī Aḥkām al-Taqlīd," folio 17a–19b.

111. Ibid.

112. This is a type of divorce in which the woman pays the husband a sum of money, usually equivalent to the amount she received in dower, in exchange for a divorce. For a brief overview of the Ḥanbalī position on *khul'*, see Mar'ī b. Yūsuf al-Karmī, *Dalīl al-Ṭalib li-Nayl al-Maṭālib*, ed. Abū Qutayba Naẓar Muḥammad Fāryābī, 3rd ed. (Riyadh, Saudi Arabia: Dār Ṭība, 2008), 301–2.

113. Al-Fiqhī, "Risāla fīmā Yata'allaq bi-Aḥwāl al-Muftī," 9a–10b.

114. Ibid., folio 7a–b.

115. Ibid., folio 9a–10b.

116. Ibid., folio 3b–5b.

117. Wiederhold, "Legal Doctrines in Conflict," 234–304, at 250.

118. Not to be confused with the famous al-Suyūtī (d. 911/1505), who was also a Shāfi'ī.

119. Shams al-Dīn Muḥammad b. Aḥmad al-Minhājī al-Asyūṭī, *Jawāhir al-'Uqūd wa-Mu'īn al-Quḍāh wa'l-Muwwaqi'īn wa'l-Shuhūd*, ed. Mus'ad 'Abd al-Ḥamīd Muḥammad Sa'danī (Beirut: Dār al-Kutub al-'Ilmiyya, 1996), 1:100–103.

120. Wiederhold read Ibn Ḥajar al-Haytamī's reference to practical consensus as referring to the layperson's selection of the less stringent juristic opinions, which is not the case since al-Haytamī stated that the Shāfi'ī judge delegates the Ḥanafī on issues whose desired legal results are not acceptable in the Shāfi'ī school (*anna al-Shāfi'ī yuwallī al-Ḥanafī . . . fī masā'il 'āmma wa-khāṣṣa lā yarāhā al-muwallī*). This delegation was common in the court records I examine in chapter 4. Al-Haytamī then explained that the Shāfi'ī judge is not guilty of aiding and abetting an error, namely the Ḥanafī opinion that contradicts his

school affiliation (*wa-annahū lā i'āna fī dhālika 'alā ma'ṣiya al-batta*). Wiederhold, "Legal Doctrines in Conflict," 234–304, at 253; al-Haytamī, *al-Fatāwā al-Kubrā al-Fiqhiyya*, 4:314.

121. Muḥammad b. 'Abd Allāh 'Alī Zādah, "Tuḥfat al-Ḥukkam fī Malja' al-Qaḍā'," Cairo, n.d., MS Dār al-Kutub 446 Fiqh Ḥanafī Ṭal'at, folio 22b, microfilm #8509.

122. Ibid.

123. It is not clear when al-Baṣrī died, but he was a contemporary of Ibn Mullah Farrūkh al-Makkī (d. 1061 /1650), since the latter wished al-Baṣrī a long life (*aṭāl Allāhu baqā'ah*) in his treatise. See Ibn 'Alān al-Makkī, "Al-Talaṭṭuf fi'l-Wuṣūl ilā al-Ta'arruf," Cairo, n.d., MS Dār al-Kutub Uṣūl Fiqh 144, folio 9a, microfilm #40314.

124. Al-Saqqāf, *Majmū'at Sab'at Kutub Mufīda*, 37–38.

125. See, for instance, al-Kurdī, *al-Fawā'id al-Madaniyya fī Bayān Ikhtilāf al-'Ulamā' min al-Shāfi'iyya*, 232–46.

126. Taqī al-Dīn al-Subkī, *Fatāwā al-Subkī* (Beirut: Dār al-Ma'rifa, n.d.), 1:146–48; al-Samhūdī, "Al-'Iqd al-Farīd fī Aḥkām al-Taqlīd," folio 24a–25a.

127. Al-Zarkashī, *al-Baḥr al-Muḥīṭ fī Uṣūl al-Fiqh*, 6:319–27.

128. Al-Subkī, *Fatāwā al-Subkī*, 1:146–48.

129. Al-Ghazālī, *al-Mustaṣfā min 'Ilm al-Uṣūl*, 2:478–506.

130. See al-Subki, *Fatāwā al-Subkī*, 1:147; al-Samhūdī, *al-'Iqd al-Farīd fī Aḥkām al-Taqlīd*, folio 24a–25a.

131. Interestingly, the contemporary Turkish scholar Fethullah Gulen has a similar approach to *ḍarūra*. To him, the determination of what constitutes *ḍarūra* is not governed by formal criteria but is left to the individual Muslim to assess. See Ihsan Yilmaz, "Inter-Madhhab Surfing, Neo-Ijtihad, and Faith-Based Movement Leaders," in Bearman, Peters, and Vogel, *Islamic School of Law: Evolution, Devolution, and Progress*, 201.

132. 'Abd al-Wahhāb al-Sha'rānī, *al-Mīzān*, 2 vols. (Cairo: al-Maṭābi' al-Amīriyya, 1900), 1:10–12.

133. Ibid., 2:64–75, 185.

134. Ibid., 1:3, 12.

135. Ibid., 1:14, 60.

136. 'Abd al-Raḥmān al-Nasā'ī, *Ṣaḥīḥ al-Nasā'ī* (Riyadh, Saudi Arabia: Maktabat al-Ma'ārif li'l-Nashr wa'l-Tawzī', 1998), 188, hadith No. 5695.

137. Al-Sha'rānī, *al-Mīzān*, 1:88.

138. Ibid., 1:13.

139. Ibid., 1:7.

140. Ibid., 1:4–6.

141. 'Abd al-Wahhāb al-Sha'rānī, *Kashf al-Ghumma 'an Jamī' al-Umma* (Cairo: al-Maṭba'a al-Maymaniyya, n.d.), 8.

142. Al-Samhūdī, "Al-'Iqd al-Farīd fī Aḥkām al-Taqlīd," folio 17b; Ibn Bīrī, "Al-Kashf wa'l-Tadqīq li-Sharḥ Ghāyat al-Taḥqīq," folio 6a–7b.

143. Al-Sha'rānī, *al-Mīzān*, 1:28–29.

144. Ibid., 1:18.

145. Ibid.

146. Al-Sha'rānī, *Kashf al-Ghumma 'an Jamī' al-Umma*, 2–5.

147. Ibid.

148. Ibid.

149. This idea can be seen, for instance, in the writings of the eighteenth-century Yemeni revivalist al-Shawkānī, who emphasized the necessity of laypeople's demanding evidence from the mufti. According to al-Shawkānī, people should not follow the opinions of *mujtahids*, but they should rather follow their transmission (*riwāya*). This can be seen as an attempt at combating non-scripturally-based opinions of some of the schools. Muḥammad b. 'Alī b. Muḥammad al-Shawkānī, *Irshād al-Fuḥūl Ilā Taḥqīq al-Ḥaqq Min 'Ilm al-Uṣūl*, ed. Abū Ḥafṣ Sāmī b. al-'Arabī al-Atharī (Riyadh, Saudi Arabia: Dār al-Faḍīla, 2000), 245–70.

150. Al-Sha'rānī's theory is ambiguous about whether the scales of strictness and leniency are to be restricted to the opinions of the eponyms or are inclusive of later opinions. On several occasions, he explicitly included the contradictory opinions within each school in the continuum of leniency and stringence. This seems to be the tenor of his argument, although on one occasion, he narrowly defined the eponym's doctrine as those opinions he held until his death, as opposed to what was understood by his disciples. See Ibrahim, "Al-Sha'rānī's Response to Legal Purism," 110–40, at 135–37.

151. Ibn 'Arabī, *al-Futūḥāt al-Makkiyya*, 1:392.

152. Al-Sha'rānī, *al-Mīzān*, 1:27.

153. Ibid., 1:3, 5.

154. Purists were hostile to school loyalty (*tamadhhub*). Ibn Amīr al-Ḥājj, for instance, pointed to the attitude attributed to some Ḥanbalīs that following a school in all legal matters amounts to obeying someone other than the Prophet. Al-Ḥājj, *al-Taqrīr wa'l-Taḥbīr*, 3:345.

155. For a discussion of Ottoman Ḥanafization, which was associated with the *tamadhhub* position, see Ibrahim, "Al-Sha'rānī's Response to Legal Purism," 110–40, at 126–35.

156. Zayn al-Dīn b. 'Abd al-'Azīz al-Malībārī, *Fatḥ al-Mu'īn bi-Sharḥ Qurrat al-'Ayn* (Cairo: Maṭba'at Muḥammad 'Alī Ṣubayḥ, 1928), 138.

157. 'Umar Muḥammad al-Fāraskūrī, "Kitāb al-Bahja al-Muraṣṣa'a bi-Durar Yanābī' Ikhtilāf al-A'imma al-Arba'a," Cairo, n.d., MS Dār al-Kutub 66 Fiqh Madhāhib 'Arabī, folio 2b.

158. Ibid.

159. For a discussion of *maqāṣid al-Sharī'a*, see al-Ghazālī, *al-Mustaṣfā min 'Ilm al-Uṣūl*, 2:478–506.

160. Al-Fiqhī, "Risāla Fīmā Yata'allaq bi-Aḥwāl al-Muftī," folio 5b–6b.

161. Al-Kurdī, *al-Fawā'id al-Madaniyya fī Bayān Ikhtilāf al-'Ulamā' min al-Shāfi'iyya*, 233; al-Haytamī, *al-Fatāwā al-Kubrā al-Fiqhiyya*, 4:317.

162. Al-Kurdī also cited al-Samhūdī as stating that his teacher the Shāfi'ī Walī al-Dīn Aḥmad al-Ashīṭī often issued *fatāwā* based on the school of Mālik concerning a pilgrim who

wears stitched clothes on more than one occasion. According to the Mālikīs, one is only subject to paying the expiation (*fidya*) once, but for the Shāfiʿīs, the expiation is repeated each time one wears the stitched clothes. He explained that the Mālikī opinion is selected here because the Shāfiʿī view is more stringent (*limā fī madhhabinā min al-mashaqqa fī dhālik*). This discussion was taken verbatim from al-Haytamī's *al-Fatāwā al-Kubrā*. Al-Kurdī, *al-Fawā'id al-Madaniyya fī Bayān Ikhtilāf al-ʿUlamā' min al-Shāfiʿiyya*, 233; al-Haytamī, *al-Fatāwā al-Kubrā al-Fiqhiyya*, 4:317.

163. Ibn ʿĀbidīn, *Sharḥ al-Manẓūma al-Musammāh bi-ʿUqūd Rasm al-Muftī*, 39.

164. Ibid., 41.

165. George Makdisi, *Ibn ʿAqil: Religion and Culture in Classical Islam* (Edinburgh: Edinburgh Univ. Press, 1997), 5–6.

166. ʿAbd al-Raḥmān al-Dimashqī, *Raḥmat al-Umma fī Ikhtilāf al-A'imma* (Cairo: al-Maṭābiʿ al-Amīriyya, 1900), 1:1–3. This book is printed on the margin of al-Shaʿrānī's *al-Mīzān*.

167. On the Ottoman *ikhtilāf* genre, see further Ibrahim, "The Codification Episteme."

168. Sayf al-Dīn Abū Bakr Muḥammad b. Aḥmad al-Shāshī al-Qaffāl, *Ḥilyat al-ʿUlamā' fī maʿrifat Madhāhib al-Fuqahā'*, ed. Yāsīn Aḥmad Ibrāhīm Darādkah, 8 vols. (Amman: Maktabat al-Risāla al-Dīniyya, 1988).

169. See, for instance, Abū Muḥammad ʿAlī b. Aḥmad b. Saʿīd Ibn Ḥazm, *al-Muḥallā*, ed. Muḥammad Munīr Dimashqī, 11 vols. (Cairo: Idārat al-Ṭibāʿa al-Munīriyya, 1933); Muḥammad b. Naṣr Abū ʿAbd Allāh al-Marwazī, *Ikhtilāf al-ʿUlamā'*, ed. Ṣubḥī Sāmrā'ī, 2nd ed. (Beirut: ʿĀlam al-Kutub, 1985); Muḥammad b. Jarīr al-Ṭabarī, *Ikhtilāf al-Fuqahā'* (Beirut: Dār al-Kutub al-ʿIlmiyya, 1980).

170. Maribel Fierro, "The Legal Policies of Almohad Caliphs and Ibn Rushd's *Bidāyat al-Mujtahid*," *Journal of Islamic Studies* 10:3 (1999): 226–48; Yasin Dutton, "The Introduction to Ibn Rushd's *Bidāyat al-Mujtahid*," *Islamic Law and Society* 1:2 (1994): 188–205.

171. In his discussion of *khilāf*, the Shāfiʿī jurist Tāj al-Dīn al-Fazārī (d. 690/1291) explained that what he means by *khilāf* is not what was usually understood by the term in his time, namely the differences between al-Shāfiʿī and Abū Ḥanīfa. According to him, such an understanding would be insufficient for any jurist wishing to attain the status of a *mujtahid*. Tāj al-Dīn Fazārī and Abū al-Maʿālī al-Juwaynī, *Sharḥ al-Waraqāt li-Imām al-Ḥaramayn al-Juwaynī*, ed. Sāra Shāfī Ḥājirī (Beirut: Dār al-Bashā'ir al-Islāmiyya, 2001), 358.

172. Al-Fāraskūrī, "Kitāb al-Bahja al-Muraṣṣaʿa bi-Durar Yanābīʿ Ikhtilāf al-A'imma al-Arbaʿa," folio 2b–3b.

173. Nūr al-Dīn ʿAlī b. Ibrāhīm, "Mabāhij al-Umma fī Manāhij al-A'imma al-Arbaʿa," Cairo, n.d., MS Dār al-Kutub 63 Fiqh Madhāhib Ṭalʿat, folio 2b.

174. Abū al-ʿAbbās Aḥmad b.ʿUmar al-Dayrabī, *Ghāyat al-Maqṣūd li-Man Yataʿāṭā al-ʿUqūd ʿalā al-Madhāhib al-Arbaʿa*, 2nd ed. (Cairo: Maktabat Muṣṭafā al-Bābī al-Ḥalabī, 1956), 2–3.

175. ʿAbd al-Muʿṭī al-Samalāwī, "Al-Qawl al-Murabbaʿ fī Ḥukm al-ʿAqd ʿalā al-Madhāhib al-Arbaʿ," Cairo, n.d., MS Dār al-Kutub 226 Fiqh Taymūr, folio 2a.

176. ʿAbd Allāh b. Ḥijāzī al-Sharqāwī, "Sharḥ ʿalā al-Jawhar al-ʿAzīz," Cairo, n.d., MS Dār al-Kutub 68 Fiqh Madhāhib, folio 33b–34a.

177. Ibid., folio 49a.

178. Nelly Hanna, "The Administration of Courts in Ottoman Cairo," in *The State and Its Servants: Administration in Egypt from Ottoman Times to the Present*, ed. Nelly Hanna (Cairo: American Univ. in Cairo Press, 1995), 53–54.

179. Al-Samalāwī, "Al-Qawl al-Murabbaʿ fī Ḥukm al-ʿAqd ʿalā al-Madhāhib al-Arbaʿ," folio 2a.

180. On the written culture of Mamluk Egypt and Syria, see Konrad Hirschler, *The Written Word in the Medieval Arabic Lands: A Social and Cultural History of Reading Practices* (Edinburgh: Edinburgh Univ. Press, 2012), 82–201, at 172.

181. Ludovic Lalanne, *Curiosités Littéraires* (Paris: Paulin, 1845), 99–102; Paul Ackermann, *Dictionnaire Biographique Universel et Pittoresque* (N.p.: Aimé André, 1834), 475; Joseph Thomas, *The Universal Dictionary of Biography and Mythology* (Philadelphia: Lippincott, 1915), 1016.

182. Joseph-Henri Flacon-Rochelle, *Code Civil des Français Mis En Vers avec le Texte en Regard* (Paris: Theodore le Clerc, 1805), vii.

183. See Muḥammad al-Fiqhī, *Risāla fī mā Yataʿallaq bi-Aḥwāl al-Muftī*, Cairo, n.d., MS Dār al-Kutub 198 Uṣūl Fiqh, folio 3b–5b, microfilm #23027.

3. *Talfīq* in Juristic Discourse Prior to the Nineteenth Century

1. See, for example, al-Samhūdī, *al-ʿIqd al-Farīd fī Aḥkām al-Taqlīd*, Cairo, n.d., MS Dār al-Kutub 45 Uṣūl Taymūr, folio 21a, microfilm #11397.

2. See Ibn Manẓūr, *Lisān al-ʿArab*, http://www.baheth.info/web/all.jsp?select=all&search=%D8%B5%D9%8E%D9%81%D9%8E%D9%82%D9%8E#12 (accessed Aug. 31, 2010).

3. Wael B. Hallaq and Aharon Layish, "Talfīḳ," in *Encyclopaedia of Islam*, ed. P. Bearman, Th. Bianquis, C. E. Bosworth, E. van Donzel, and W. P. Heinrichs (Leiden: Brill, 2008).

4. Coulson, *A History of Islamic Law*, 182–217; Anderson, *Law Reform in the Muslim World*, 34–80; Norman Anderson, "Modern Trends in Islam: Legal Reform and Modernisation in the Middle East," *International and Comparative Law Quarterly* 20:1 (1971): 1–21.

5. Wael B. Hallaq and Aharon Layish, "Talfīḳ," in *Encyclopaedia of Islam*, ed. P. Bearman, Th. Bianquis, C. E. Bosworth, E. van Donzel, and W. P. Heinrichs (Leiden: Brill, 2008).

6. Aharon Layish, "The Transformation of the *Sharīʿa* from Jurists' Law to Statutory Law in the Contemporary Muslim World," *Die Welt Des Islams* 44:1 (2004): 85–113, at 197–201.

7. Wiederhold, "Legal Doctrines in Conflict."

8. Birgit Krawietz, "Cut and Paste in Legal Rules: Designing Islamic Norms with *Talfīq*," *Die Welt Des Islams* 42:1 (2002): 3–40.

9. Except for a polemical work such as Muḥammad Saʿīd al-Bānī, *ʿUmdat al-Taḥqīq fiʾl-Taqlīd waʾl-Talfīq* (Damascus: Maṭbaʿat Ḥukūmat Dimashq, 1923), 14–38.

10. On legal scaffolding, see further Jackson, "*Taqlīd*, Legal Scaffolding"; Watson, *Society and Legal Change*, 87–97.

11. Sadeghi, *Logic of Law Making in Islam*, 80–81, 120–24.

12. Al-Qarāfī, *Sharḥ Tanqīḥ al-Fuṣūl fī Ikhtiṣār al-Maḥṣūl fi'l-Uṣūl*, 339.

13. Krawietz, "Cut and Paste in Legal Rules," 3–40, at 13.

14. Ṭarsūsī (d. 758/1358) mentions that a judge in 681/1282 had issued a ruling that was made up of two opinions, namely Abū Ḥanīfa's and Abū Yūsuf's. Ṭarsūsī objected to the ruling, but then saw a similar form of it in *Munyat al-Muftī* where it was permitted. One of the examples that were permitted by the *Munyat al-Muftī* is when a judge issues a ruling against an absent person based on the testimony of a sinner. This ruling combines two elements, each of which is only acceptable to one of the schools. The Shāfi'īs permit issuing rulings in absentia, whereas the Ḥanafīs allow the testimony of sinners. Shurunbulālī, "Al-'Iqd al-Farīd li-Bayān al-Rājiḥ min al-Khilāf fi'l-Taqlīd," folio 14a–15b.

15. For a discussion of these two types of *talfīq*, see below in this chapter.

16. Al-Makkī, "Al-Talaṭṭuf fi'l-Wuṣūl ilā al-Ta'arruf," folio 125a.

17. Al-Dayrabī, *Ghāyat al-Maqṣūd li-Man Yata'āṭā al-'Uqūd 'alā al-Madhāhib al-Arba'a*, 2–3.

18. Al-Kurdī, *al-Fawā'id al-Madaniyya fī Bayān Ikhtilāf al-'Ulamā' Min al-Shāfi'iyya*, 244–45.

19. Al-Samhūdī, "Al-'Iqd al-Farīd fī Aḥkām al-Taqlīd," folio 12a–18a; al-Shurunbulālī, "Al-'Iqd al-Farīd Li-Bayān al-Rājiḥ Min al-Khilāf fi'l-Taqlīd," folio 2a–4b, 15b–16b; al-'Aṭṭār, *Ḥāshiyat al-'Aṭṭār 'alā Sharḥ al-Jalāl al-Maḥallī 'alā Jam' al-Jawāmi'*, 2:440–42.

20. Ibn Bīrī, "Al-Kashf wa'l-Tadqīq li-Sharḥ Ghāyat al-Taḥqīq," folio 2a–5b.

21. Amīr Bādshāh, *Taysīr al-Taḥrīr 'Alā Kitāb al-Taḥrīr*, 4:254–55.

22. Mar'ī b. Yūsuf b. Abī Bakr al-Karmī and Abū al-'Awn Muḥammad b. Aḥmad Saffārīnī, *al-Taḥqīq fī Buṭlān al-Talfīq Naṣṣ 'alā Futyā li'l-Shaykh Mar'ī al-Ḥanbalī*, ed. 'Abd al-'Azīz b. Ibrāhīm Dukhayyil (Riyadh, Saudi Arabia: Dār al-Ṣumay'ī, 1998), 178–81. For a discussion of these two *fatāwā*, see Krawietz, "Cut and Paste in Legal Rules."

23. Al-Makkī, "Ta'līqa fi'l-Ijtihād wa'l-Taqlīd," folio 4b–5a.

24. Ibn Bīrī, "Al-Kashf wa'l-Tadqīq li-Sharḥ Ghāyat al-Taḥqīq," folio 2a.

25. Al-Makkī, "Ta'līqa fi'l-Ijtihād wa'l-Taqlīd," folio 7b; Ibn Mullah Farrūkh al-Mawrawī al-Makkī, *al-Qawl al-Sadīd fī Ba'ḍ Masā'il al-Ijtihād wa'l-Taqlīd*, ed. Jāsim b. Muḥammad b. Muhalhal Yāsīn and 'Adnān b. Sālim b. Muḥammad Rūmī, 2nd ed. (al-Manṣūra, Egypt: Dār al-Wafā', 1992), 46–49.

26. Ibn Bīrī, "Al-Kashf wa'l-Tadqīq li-Sharḥ Ghāyat al-Taḥqīq," folio 10b.

27. 'Abd al-Ghanī al-Nābulsī, "Al-Ajwiba 'an al-As'ila al-Sitta," Cairo, n.d., MS Dār al-Kutub Uṣūl Fiqh 365, folio 14b.

28. Ibn Mullah Farrūkh al-Mawrawī al-Makkī, *al-Qawl al-Sadīd fī Ba'ḍ Masā'il al-Ijtihād wa'l-Taqlīd*, ed. Jāsim b. Muḥammad b. Muhalhal Yāsīn and 'Adnān b. Sālim b. Muḥammad Rūmī, 2nd ed. (al-Manṣūra, Egypt: Dār al-Wafā', 1992), 14.

29. Al-Makkī, "Ta'līqa fi'l-Ijtihād wa'l-Taqlīd," folio 4b; al-Bānī, *'Umdat al-Taḥqīq fi'l-Taqlīd wa'l-Talfīq*, 93.

30. There is disagreement over how much water is in a *qulla* (a type of jug), with most views ranging from 100 to 500 pounds. See, for example, Yaḥyā al-Zaḥlī b. Hubayra, "Ma'īn

al-Umma ʿalā Maʿrifat al-Wifāq wa'l-Khilāf Bayna al-A'imma," Cairo, n.d., MS Dār al-Kutub Fiqh Madhāhib Ṭalʿat 51, folio 7a–b.

31. Ibn Bīrī, "Al-Kashf wa'l-Tadqīq li-Sharḥ Ghāyat al-Taḥqīq," folio 8a; Amīr Bādshāh, *Taysīr al-Taḥrīr ʿalā Kitāb al-Taḥrīr*, 4:227–28; Shurunbulālī, "Al-ʿIqd al-Farīd li-Bayān al-Rājiḥ min al-Khilāf fi'l-Taqlīd," folio 20a.

32. Al-Nābulsī, "Al-Ajwiba ʿan al-As'ila al-Sitta," folio 9a–b.

33. Al-Makkī, *al-Qawl al-Sadīd fī Baʿḍ Masā'il al-Ijtihād wa'l-Taqlīd*, 107.

34. Ibn Bīrī, "Al-Kashf wa'l-Tadqīq li-Sharḥ Ghāyat al-Taḥqīq," folio 8a.

35. A *waqf* is a source of revenue set aside as either a charitable endowment (*waqf khayrī*) or as a civil endowment (*waqf ahlī*). Most instances of *waqf* in the Ottoman period were of the latter type, in which the beneficiaries were members of the endower's family.

36. This example was rejected by some opponents of *talfīq*, who argued that combining the doctrines of authorities in the same school does not constitute *talfīq*. Al-Makkī, "Taʿlīqa fi'l-Ijtihād wa'l-Taqlīd," folio 5a–b; al-Nābulsī, "Al-Ajwiba ʿan al-As'ila al-Sitta," folio 9b–13b.

37. Al-Dasūqī, *Ḥāshiyat al-Dasūqī ʿalā al-Sharḥ al-Kabīr*, 1:20.

38. Chibli Mallat, "From Islamic to Middle Eastern Law, a Restatement of the Field (Part II)," *American Journal of Comparative Law* 52:1 (2004): 209–86, at 257–62.

39. Ibn Bīrī, "Al-Kashf wa'l-Tadqīq li-Sharḥ Ghāyat al-Taḥqīq," folio 4a.

40. Shurunbulālī, "Al-ʿIqd al-Farīd li-Bayān al-Rājiḥ Min al-Khilāf fi'l-Taqlīd," folio 13b–14a; Qāsim b. Qaṭlūbaghā al-Miṣrī, *al-Taṣḥīḥ wa'l-Tarjīḥ ʿalā Mukhtaṣar al-Qudūrī*, 123–24.

41. Al-Makkī, "Taʿlīqa fi'l-Ijtihād wa'l-Taqlīd," folio 4b–5a.

42. Ibid., folio 4a.

43. Ibid.

44. Al-Karmī and al-Saffārīnī, *al-Taḥqīq fī Buṭlān al-Talfīq Naṣṣ ʿalā Futyā li'l-Shaykh Marʿī al-Ḥanbalī*, 178–81.

45. Al-Makkī, "Taʿlīqa fi'l-Ijtihād wa'l-Taqlīd," folio 7b; al-Makkī, *al-Qawl al-Sadīd fī Baʿḍ Masā'il al-Ijtihād wa'l-Taqlīd*, 46–51, 113.

46. Coulson, *A History of Islamic Law*, 147.

47. See Zayn al-Dīn b. ʿAbd al-ʿAzīz al-Malībārī, *Fatḥ al-Muʿīn bi-Sharḥ Qurrat al-ʿAyn* (Cairo: Maṭbaʿat Muḥammad ʿAlī Ṣubayḥ, 1928), 138.

48. Anonymous, "Risāla Jalīla fi'l-Taqlīd," folio 5a–b. In all four Sunnī schools, when a woman is divorced three times, she cannot remarry her first husband unless she marries another man and obtains a divorce. This man is called a *muḥallil*.

49. Al-Khaṭīb Muḥammad b. ʿAbd Allāh al-Ghazzī al-Ḥanafī al-Timurtāshī, "Al-Fatāwā al-Timurtāshiyya," Cairo, n.d., MS Dār al-Kutub Fiqh Ḥanafī Ṭalʿat 520, folio 96b, microfilm #8558.

50. Fishnī, "Kifāyat al-Mustafīd fī Aḥkām al-Taqlīd," folio 8b.

51. Ibn Bīrī, "Al-Kashf wa'l-Tadqīq li-Sharḥ Ghāyat al-Taḥqīq," folio 4a.

52. Al-Makkī, *al-Qawl al-Sadīd fī Baʿḍ Masā'il al-Ijtihād wa'l-Taqlīd*, 100–102.

53. Al-Makkī, "Taʿlīqa fi'l-Ijtihād wa'l-Taqlīd," folio 5a–b; al-Makkī, *al-Qawl al-Sadīd fī Baʿḍ Masā'il al-Ijtihād wa'l-Taqlīd*, 100–113.

54. Sadeghi, *Logic of Law Making in Islam*, 40.

55. Al-Shurunbulālī explicitly stated that the view that considers the validity of the prayer from the *ma'mūm*'s perspective is against *talfīq*. Ḥasan b. ʿAmmār b. ʿAlī Shurunbulālī, *Marāqī al-Falāḥ Sharḥ Nūr al-Īḍāḥ* (Cairo: Al-Maṭbaʿa al-ʿIlmiyya, 1897), 48; al-Shurunbulālī, "Al-ʿIqd al-Farīd li-Bayān al-Rājiḥ min al-Khilāf fi'l-Taqlīd," folio 13a.

56. It is difficult to establish the identity of this author al-Sindī. He cannot be Muḥammad ʿUmar al-Sindī (d. 978/1570) since the introduction states that he is a student of Ibn al-Humām (d. 861/1457). "Bayān al-Iqtidā' bi'l-Shāfiʿiyya," Cairo, n.d., MS Dār al-Kutub Uṣūl Taymūr 233, folio 3b; al-Nābulsī, "Al-Ajwiba ʿan al-As'ila al-Sitta," fol. 7b.

57. On another occasion (folio 7a), he did not demote the prohibition to detestability, arguing instead that if someone knows that an imam does not avoid the areas of disagreement, it is not permissible for a Ḥanafī to follow him in prayer (*idhā ʿarafa min ḥālihi annahū lam yaḥtaṭ mawḍiʿ al-khilāf lā yajūzu al-iqtidāʾu bihi*). Nūr al-Dīn Mullah ʿAlī al-Qārī, "Al-Ihtidā' fi'l-Iqtidā'," Cairo, n.d., MS Dār al-Kutub Uṣūl Taymūr 172, folio 5b–6a, 7a.

58. Al-Makkī, "Taʿlīqa fi'l-Ijtihād wa'l-Taqlīd," folio 3b.

59. Al-Makkī, *al-Qawl al-Sadīd fī Baʿḍ Masā'il al-Ijtihād wa'l-Taqlīd*, 44–63.

60. Al-Iṣfahānī, *Bayān al-Mukhtaṣar Sharḥ Mukhtaṣar Ibn al-Ḥājib*, 1:694–95.

61. Al-Qarāfī held that jurists are in agreement that rulings contradicting consensus must be overruled, but there is disagreement among jurists over violating *fiqh* rules (*qawāʿid*), the textual sources (*naṣṣ*), or an obvious case of analogy (*al-qiyās al-Jalī*). See Shihāb al-Dīn Qarāfī, *al-Iḥkām fī Tamyīz al-Fatāwā ʿan al-Aḥkām wa-Taṣarrufāt al-Qāḍī wa'l-Imām*, ed. ʿAbd al-Fattāḥ Abū Ghudda, 2nd ed. (Beirut: Maktabat al-Maṭbūʿāt al-Islāmiyya bi-Ḥalab, 1995), 88.

62. A *dhimmī* is a term that refers to non-Muslim Christians, Jews, and Zoroastrians living under Muslim rule.

63. Al-Saqqāf, *Majmūʿat Sabʿat Kutub Mufīda*, 59.

64. Ibn Ḥajar al-ʿAsqalānī, *Fatḥ al-Bārī bi-Sharḥ Ṣaḥīḥ al-Bukhārī* (Cairo: Maktabat al-Kulliyyāt al-Azhariyya, 1978), Hadith No. 6517.

65. Al-Samhūdī, "Al-ʿIqd al-Farīd fī Aḥkām al-Taqlīd," folio 31b–32a.

66. Ibid.

67. Shams al-Dīn Muḥammad b. Mufliḥ al-Maqdisī, *al-Mubdiʿ Sharḥ al-Muqniʿ*, ed. Muḥammad Ḥasan Muḥammad Ḥasan Ismāʿīl al-Shāfiʿī (Beirut: Dār al-Kutub al-ʿIlmiyya, 1997), 8:176–77.

68. Although the reasons for rejecting or accepting these decisions are framed in the language of evidence, it is possible (or perhaps likely) that there are other considerations on which it is difficult to speculate. Yūsuf b. Ibrāhīm Ardabīlī, *al-Anwār li-Aʿmāl al-Abrār*, ed. Khalaf Mufḍī al-Muṭliq and Ḥusayn ʿAbd Allāh al-ʿAllī, (Kuwait: Dār al-Ḍiyā', 2006), 3:492–93.

69. Al-Haytamī, *al-Fatāwā al-Kubrā al-Fiqhiyya*, 2:211–12.

70. Al-Bazzāzī, "Al-Fatāwā al-Bazzāziyya," folio 163b.

71. Al-Fāraskūrī, "Kitāb al-Bahja al-Muraṣṣaʿa bi-Durar Yanābīʿ Ikhtilāf al-A'imma al-Arbaʿa," folio 2b.

72. James Baldwin, "Islamic Law in an Ottoman Context: Resolving Disputes in Late 17th/Early 18th-Century Cairo" (PhD diss., New York Univ., 2010), 120, 152, 274.

73. Wael B. Hallaq and Aharon Layish, "Talfīḳ," in *Encyclopaedia of Islam*, ed. P. Bearman, Th. Bianquis, C. E. Bosworth, E. van Donzel, and W. P. Heinrichs (Leiden: Brill, 2008).

74. See, for instance, Ibrāhīm b. Ḥusayn b. Aḥmad b. Muḥammad b. Aḥmad b. Bīrī, *al-Kashf wa'l-Tadqīq li-Sharḥ Ghāyat al-Taḥqīq*, Cairo, n.d., MS Dār al-Kutub Uṣūl Fiqh 403, folio 6a–7b, microfilm #38418; al-Bazzāzī, "al-Fatāwā al-Bazzāziyya," folio 163a–65a, microfilm #55712.

75. This phenomenon was bemoaned, for instance, by the Ḥanbalī Ḥamad b. Nāṣir b. Muʿammar (d. 1225/1810), who stated that many jurists in his day preferred the opinions of later authorities (*muta'akhkhirīn*) over those of earlier ones (*mutaqaddimīn*). Similarly, he argued that Ḥanbalīs neglected the *ijtihād* of Ibn Ḥanbal in favor of such jurists as Ibn al-Najjār (d. 972/1564) and al-Ḥajjawī (d. 960/1553), while later Shāfiʿīs began deferring to Ibn Ḥajar al-Haytamī (d. 973/1567) over al-Shāfiʿī, and later Mālikīs were increasingly turning to Khalīl (d. 776/1365) over Mālik. See the commentary of ʿAbd al-ʿAzīz b. Ibrāhīm al-Dukhayyil about the debate between Al-Karmī and Saffārīnī in *al-Taḥqīq fī Buṭlān al-Talfīq Naṣṣ ʿalā Futyā li'l-Shaykh Marʿī al-Ḥanbalī* (Riyadh, Saudi Arabia: Dār al-Ṣumayʿī, 1998), 91–94.

4. Pragmatic Eclecticism in Court Practice: A Thousand and One Cases

1. For more on early Ottoman Ḥanafization efforts, see Ibrahim, "Al-Shaʿrānī's Response to Legal Purism," at 115–19.

2. See, for instance, al-Haytamī, *al-Fatāwā al-Kubrā al-Fiqhiyya*, 4:314; Wiederhold, "Legal Doctrines in Conflict," 234–304, at 253.

3. George Makdisi, *The Rise of Colleges: Institutions of Learning in Islam and the West* (Edinburgh: Edinburgh Univ. Press, 1981), 6; Rapoport, "Legal Diversity in the Age of *Taqlīd*," 210–28, at 212.

4. Cited in al-Kurdī, *al-Fawā'id al-Madaniyya fī Bayān Ikhtilāf al-ʿUlamā' Min al-Shāfiʿiyya*, 237.

5. Jackson, *Islamic Law and the State*, 52–55.

6. Jackson, "*Taqlīd*, Legal Scaffolding," 165–92, at 168; Fadel, "The Social Logic of *Taqlīd* and the Rise of the *Mukhtaṣar*"; Rapoport, "Legal Diversity in the Age of *Taqlīd*," 210–28, at 221; Allouche, "Establishment of Four Chief Judgeships in Fatimid Egypt."

7. Tāj al-Dīn al-Subkī (d. 771/1370), for example, approved of the Mamluk practice of referring cases requiring *taʿzīr* (discretionary punishment) to Mālikī judges because, under Mālikī law, the judge has unrestricted powers in determining the punishment, which may include the administration of the death penalty. Tāj al-Dīn al-Subkī, *Muʿīd al-Niʿam*

wa-Mubīd al-Niqam, ed. David M. Myhrman (Leiden: Brill, 1908), 36; Rapoport, "Legal Diversity in the Age of *Taqlīd*," 210–28, at 221.

8. Rapoport, "Legal Diversity in the Age of *Taqlīd*," 221–27, at 221–27.

9. Al-Subkī, *Fatāwā al-Subkī*, 2:445–46.

10. Al-Bazzāzī, "al-Fatāwā al-Bazzāziyya," folio 163–5a.

11. In one example, the Ḥanafī chief judge referred the case to his Ḥanbalī deputy to officiate a long rental contract on a *waqf* property lasting ninety years. "Sijill 105," n.d., doc. 98, the Court of Miṣr al-Qadīma (Rabīʿ al-Awwal 1092/Mar. 1681), Dār al-Wathāʾiq al-Qawmiyya (Cairo).

12. Jackson, *Islamic Law and the State*, 111–15.

13. In a similar vein, al-Bazzāzī cited the view of al-Ḥalawānī that in cases in which there are differences among the schools, the judge should ask the claimant whether the ruling corresponds to his personal belief. If it does not, he should not issue a ruling in this case. See al-Bazzāzī, "al-Fatāwā al-Bazzāziyya," folio 163b.

14. Al-Asyūṭī, *Jawāhir al-ʿUqūd wa-Muʿīn al-Quḍāh wa'l-Muwwaqiʿīn wa'l-Shuhūd*, 2:194–95. Names were added to make the quote more readable.

15. Ibid.

16. Ibid.

17. Ibid., 2:194–97.

18. Peters, "What Does It Mean to Be an Official Madhhab?" 154–55.

19. In the Ottoman period, the Ḥanafī jurist Shaykhul Islām Ebu's-su'ud, supported the dominant opinion by siding with al-Shaybānī. Abdurrahman Atcil, "Procedure in the Ottoman Court and the Duties of Kadis" (MA Thesis, Dept. of History, Bilkent Univ., 2002), 42–43; Peters, "What Does It Mean to Be an Official Madhhab?" 154–56.

20. Al-Dasūqī, *Ḥāshiyat al-Dasūqī ʿalā al-Sharḥ al-Kabīr*, 4:130.

21. On the evolution of *ikhtilāf* manuals in the Ottoman period, see further Ibrahim, "The Codification Episteme."

22. Consider, for instance, the Ḥanafī jurist Muḥammad al-Fiqhī's (d. 1147/1734) negative view of the practice of some muftis among his contemporaries who relied on some peripheral jurisprudential opinions to issue the fatwa that *khul*ʿ is not a final divorce (*bāʾin*), the aim being to help their fatwa-seekers avoid a final dissolution of marriage. Al-Fiqhī, "Risāla fīmā Yataʿallaq bi-Aḥwāl al-Muftī," 9a–10b.

23. On Shāfiʿism and Mālikism in Egypt, see El Shamsy, *The Canonization of Islamic Law*, 118–66; Shaham, "Shopping for Legal Forums," 454.

24. As we saw in chapter 1, the Fatimid experiment with a quadruple judicial system consisted only of Shāfiʿī and Mālikī judges from the Sunnī schools, as well as Ismāʿīlī and Imāmī judges. See Allouche, "Establishment of Four Chief Judgeships in Fatimid Egypt"; Rapoport, "Legal Diversity in the Age of *Taqlīd*," 210–28, at 210–13.

25. Although most jurists assumed that laypeople do not have a school affiliation, the discussions of al-Qarāfī and others regarding a person's designation of a school as

his *madhhab* must refer to some level of school consciousness among the laity, most likely shaped by geography. This possibility is particularly true for laypeople issuing from learned families and/or for people in certain regions where only one school dominated such as North Africa or Upper Egypt.

26. The sample was collected from four different registers in three Egyptian courts from the seventeenth and eighteenth centuries as follows: Miṣr al-Qadīma (251 cases dated from Shawwāl 20, 1091, to Dhū al-Qiʿda 14, 1092 / Nov. 27, 1680, to Nov. 25, 1681); Miṣr al-Qadīma (250 cases dated from Dhū al-Qiʿda 1121 to Jumādā al-Awwal 6, 1124 / Jan. 15, 1710, to June 11, 1712); Būlāq (250 cases dated from Dhū al-Ḥijja 4, 1139, to Rabīʿ Awwal 22, 1141 / July 23, 1727, to Oct. 28, 1728); and al-Bāb al-ʿĀlī (250 cases dated from Muḥarram 8, 1172, to Dhū al-Qiʿda 26, 1172 / Sept. 11, 1758, to Nov. 27, 1758). I have randomly examined the first 251 cases of the first register and the first 250 cases of the following three registers.

27. Cases from register #105 include the first 259 cases of that register. Entries 70, 89, 104, 119, 140, and 147 were excluded because they were decrees or administrative announcements, as were cases 152 and 165 because they were illegible. From register #106 of the same court, a total of 27 entries were excluded as 18 of them were official correspondences in the form of official decrees or announcements, while a total of 9 entries, mostly in the first two pages, were damaged. An equivalent 27 entries were added to the first 250 entries to make up for those lost entries. "Sijill 105."

28. "Sijill 66," n.d., the Court of Būlāq (AD 1139–AD 1143), Dār al-Wathāʾiq al-Qawmiyya (Cairo).

29. See ʿAbd al-Rāziq Ibrāhīm ʿĪsā, *Tārīkh al-Qaḍāʾ fī Miṣr al-ʿUthmāniyya 1798–1517* (Cairo: al-Hayʾa al-Miṣriyya al-ʿĀmma liʾl-Kitāb, 1998), 92.

30. "Sijill 361," n.d., doc. 2, the Court of Jāmiʿ al-Ṣāliḥ, Dār al-Wathāʾiq al-Qawmiyya (Cairo).

31. *Istibdāl* is the exchange of a derelict endowment property for another property that is productive. This was meant as a way of maintaining the profitability of an endowment. Despite the intention of the permission of *istibdāl* in the law, it was used as a way to effectively sell the endowment, even when it was not derelict. According to the practice of Ottoman Egypt, there was often no replacement of the endowment after the initial sale.

32. See Document 1, Register 424, the Court of Bāb al-Saʿāda, Dār al-Wathāʾiq al-Qawmiyya (Cairo), reproduced in Salwā ʿAlī Mīlād, *al-Wathāʾiq al-ʿUthmāniyya: Dirāsa Arshīfiyya Wathāʾiqiyya li-Sijillāt Maḥkamat al-Bāb al-ʿĀlī* (Alexandria: Dār al-Thaqāfa al-ʿIlmiyya, 2004), 116.

33. "Sijill 66," p. 1.

34. This feeling was widespread in the Ottoman period; see Muḥammad ʿAfīfī, *al-Awqāf waʾl-Ḥayāh al-Iqtiṣādiyya fī Miṣr fiʾl-ʿAṣr al-ʿUthmānī* (Cairo: al-Hayʾa al-Miṣriyya al-ʿĀmma liʾl-Kitāb, 1991), 151–82. One representative example of such corruption involved a long rental contract on an endowment that did not meet the necessary conditions. The judge nullified the contract because the rules were not observed. The long rental contract

of ninety-nine years, issued by Shaykh ʿAbd al-Wahhāb Abū al-Surūr below the fair value (*ujrat al-mithl*), was also invalidated because there was no justification for the long rent (*musawwigh*) in the first place, i.e., there was no evidence that it was in ruins. "Sijill 254," n.d., doc. 137, the Court of al-Bāb al-ʿĀlī, Dār al-Wathāʾiq al-Qawmiyya (Cairo).

35. See, for instance, ʿĪsā, *Tārīkh al-Qaḍāʾ fī Miṣr al-ʿUthmāniyya 1798–1517*, 134.

36. An example of the justification for *istibdāl* is as follows: "He bought (*istabdala*) from himself for himself . . . and he has the authority to sell that in the *sharʿī* manner as there is a *sharʿī* justification . . . namely that it [the building] is in ruins and is of no use to the aforementioned endowment beneficiaries." "Sijill 254," doc. 17.

37. On seventeenth- and eighteenth-century alienation of endowments and long rental contracts, see Nelly Hanna, "Guild *Waqf*: Between Religious Law and Common Law," in *Held in Trust: Waqf in the Islamic World*, ed. Pascale Ghazaleh (Cairo: American Univ. in Cairo Press, 2011); Nelly Hanna, *The State and Its Servants: Administration in Egypt from Ottoman Times to the Present* (Cairo: American Univ. in Cairo Press, 1995), 52–53; Nelly Hanna, *Habiter au Caire: la maison moyenne et ses habitants aux XVIIe et XVIIIe Siècles* (Cairo: Institut français d'archéologie orientale du Caire, 1991), 30–36; Daniel Crecelius, "The Waqf of Muhammad Bey Abu al-Dhahab in Historical Perspective," *International Journal of Middle East Studies* 23:1 (1991): 57–81; Daniel Crecelius, "Incidences of *Waqf* Cases in Three Cairo Courts: 1640–1802," *Journal of the Economic and Social History of the Orient* 29:2 (1986): 176–89.

38. Out of the first 254 cases of this register, document 176 was excluded because it is not a court case but is rather an administrative order sent by the chief judge. Documents 38, 68, and 179 were also excluded owing to their illegibility.

39. For a discussion of the Ottoman policy of Ḥanafization, see Ibrahim, "Al-Shaʿrānī's Response to Legal Purism," 110–40, at 115–19.

40. Jamāl Khūlī, *al-Istibdāl wa-Ightiṣāb al-Awqāf: Dirāsa Wathāʾiqiyya* (Alexandria: Dār al-Thaqāfa al-ʿIlmiyya, 2000), 54, 77.

41. Muḥammad Amīn b. ʿUmar b. ʿĀbidīn, *Radd al-Muḥtār ʿalā al-Durr al-Mukhtār Sharḥ Tanwīr al-Abṣār* (Beirut: Dār al-Kutub al-ʿIlmiyya, 2003), 6:583–84.

42. For a discussion of the rules of *istibdāl* and some of the later Ḥanafī restrictions introduced by jurists such as Ibn Nujaym and al-Ṭarsūsī, see Muḥammad Abū Zahra, *Muḥāḍarāt fi'l-Waqf* (Cairo: Maʿhad al-Dirāsāt al-ʿArabiyya al-ʿĀliya, 1959), 183–210.

43. For similar observations that no properties were purchased to replace the sold *waqf* property, see Khūlī, *al-Istibdāl wa-Ightiṣāb al-Awqāf: Dirāsa Wathāʾiqiyya*, 55.

44. "Sijill 254," doc. 74, p. 37.

45. Khūlī, *al-Istibdāl wa-Ightiṣāb al-Awqāf: Dirāsa Wathāʾiqiyya*; ʿAfīfī, *al-Awqāf wa'l-Ḥayāh al-Iqtiṣādiyya fī Miṣr fi'l-ʿAṣr al-ʿUthmānī*.

46. In a charitable endowment (*al-waqf al-khayrī*), since the intention of the founder is to establish a charity, calling the sale of such properties, in contradiction to the founder's wish, "corrupt" is more warranted.

47. "Sijill 254," doc. 132, p. 67.

48. Timur Kuran, "Why the Middle East Is Economically Underdeveloped: Historical Mechanisms of Institutional Stagnation," *Journal of Economic Perspectives* 18:3 (2004): 71–90; Timur Kuran, *The Long Divergence: How Islamic Law Held Back the Middle East* (Princeton, NJ: Princeton Univ. Press, 2010); ʿAfīfī, *al-Awqāf wa'l-Ḥayāh al-Iqtiṣādiyya fī Miṣr fi'l-ʿAṣr al-ʿUthmānī*; Max Weber, *Economy and Society: An Outline of Interpretive Sociology*, ed. Guenther Roth and Claus Wittich (Berkeley: Univ. of California Press, 1978), 2:806, 2:896; 3:976–78; Weber, *Max Weber on Law in Economy and Society*, trans. Max Rheinstein and Edward A. Shils (Cambridge, MA: Harvard Univ. Press, 1954); Bryan S. Turner, "Islam, Capitalism and the Weber Theses," *British Journal of Sociology* 25:2 (1974): 230–43, Ahmed Fekry Ibrahim, "Review of Timur Kuran, The Long Divergence: How Islamic Law Held Back the Middle East," *New Middle Eastern Studies* 1:1 (2011), http://www.brismes.ac.uk/nmes/archives/XXX.

49. Cited in Johansen, *Islamic Law on Land Tax and Rent*, 82.

50. Abū Zahra, *Muḥāḍarāt fi'l-Waqf*, 179. For a discussion of the Mālikī permission of sale of *manfaʿa*, see ʿAfīfī, *al-Awqāf wa'l-Ḥayāh al-Iqtiṣādiyya fī Miṣr fi'l-ʿAṣr al-ʿUthmānī*, 168–69.

51. "Sijill 66," docs. 21, 70, 72, 82, 83, 96, 127, 130, 153, 160, 174, 177, 183, 192, 193, 217, 229, 244, 118, 206, 210, 239, 3, 224.

52. "Sijill 254."

53. "Sijill 66," docs. 135, 173, 182, pp. 52, 65, 70.

54. Ibid., doc. 186, p. 70.

55. "Sijill 254," doc. 211, p. 112.

56. Ibid., doc. 92.

57. Rental contracts are considered long if they exceed three years. The majority of long contracts tended to be close to a hundred years.

58. Some Ḥanafī jurists tried to restrict the period of tenancy in *waqf* lands to three years, others to a year. See Johansen, *Islamic Law on Land Tax and Rent*, 34.

59. The case continues as follows: "He rented from him with his own money for his pure self all the land . . . and he has the legal authority until this date to rent this and receive its rental revenues on behalf of the aforementioned *waqf* . . . for 30 *ʿiqdan*, or 90 years, each *ʿiqd* being three full consecutive lunar years . . . This was witnessed in front of our master, the aforementioned *sharʿī* judge with the testimony of his witnesses in the *sharʿī* manner. He ruled in the aforementioned rental contract according to his revered school and his elevated doctrine, the school of the great and honorable Imām Aḥmad b. Ḥanbal al-Shaybānī . . . who forbids increase in the aforementioned rented property and the nullification of the rental contract at the death of one of the two parties to the contract or with the transfer of the guardianship [of the endowment] . . . issued on the first of Rabīʿ in 1092." "Sijill 105," doc. 98.

60. "Sijill 66," docs. 47, 53, 56, pp. 18, 21, 22.

61. See for instance, Hilāl b. Yaḥyā b. Muslim Baṣrī, *Kitāb Aḥkām al-Waqf* (Hyderabad, India: Majlis Dā'irat al-Maʿārif al-ʿUthmāniyya, 1936), 206–7.

62. "Sijill 66," doc. 47.

63. See Abdul-Karim Rafeq, "The Application of Islamic Law in the Ottoman Courts in Damascus: The Case of the Rental of *Waqf* Land," in *Dispensing Justice in Islam: Qadis and Their Judgments*, ed. Muhammad Khalid Masud, Rudolph Peters, and David Stephan Powers (Leiden: Brill, 2006), 413–18.

64. Ibid.

65. "Sijill 254," doc. 58; "Sijill 105," doc. 15.

66. "Sijill 66," docs. 67, 179, 216.

67. The case goes as follows: "Before the Shāfiʿī, the honorable, venerable Ḥājj Muḥammad, known as al-Farghalī . . . testified that he owes . . . the woman Badawiyya . . . the sum of ten gold dinars . . . which is the amount he owes her through a *sharʿī* loan that he received from her before this date . . . After binding himself to this, the aforementioned Ḥājj Muḥammad al-Farghalī made a consensual *sharʿī* votive offering to God obligating himself that, God willing, he would pay the aforementioned woman Badawiyya one *dīwānī* silver piece for every day that passes starting from the first of Dhū al-Qiʿda al-Ḥarām of the year of the date below, so long as he owes [her] the aforementioned amount or part of it. The aforementioned woman Badawiyya accepted that from him for herself in the described manner . . . It was issued on the 28th of Shawwāl, in the year 1140." Ibid., 179.

68. See Coulson, *A History of Islamic Law*, 140–42.

69. ʿAbd al-Raḥmān Muḥammad ʿAbd al-Qādir, "Naẓariyyat al-Isqāṭ fi'l-Sharīʿa al-Islāmiyya" (PhD diss., al-Azhar Univ., 1977), 283; Muḥammad Zayn Ibyānī Bek, *Sharḥ al-Aḥkām al-Sharʿīyya fi'l-Aḥwāl al-Shakhṣiyya* (Cairo: Maṭbaʿat al-Nahḍa, 1919), 432–40.

70. *Murābaḥa* is a type of sale, in which the seller accrues a known percentage of profit in addition to the price of the commodity. See Gerber, *State, Society, and Law in Islam*, 74–75.

71. "Sijill 106," n.d., docs. 178, 186, 235, the Court of Miṣr al-Qadīma, Dār al-Wathā'iq al-Qawmiyya (Cairo); "Sijill 66," docs. 81, 242. Document 242 will be handled in the discussion on *talfīq* since the Ḥanafī judge in this case was adjudicating along with the Shāfiʿī judge in the same transaction.

72. For a discussion of the differences among the Sunnī schools over the issue of physical control, see Ḥasan al-ʿIdwī Ḥamzāwī, *Tabṣirat al-Quḍāh wa'l-Ikhwān* (Cairo: Dār al-Ṭibāʿa al-Mīriyya al-Miṣriyya, 1859); "Sijill 254," doc. 254.

73. "Sijill 66," doc. 81, p. 30.

74. Ibid.

75. "Sijill 106," n.d., docs. 114, 213, 255, the Court of Miṣr al-Qadīma, Dār al-Wathā'iq al-Qawmiyya (Cairo); "Sijill 66," docs. 134, 175.

76. For a discussion of conditional sales, see ʿAbd al-Raḥmān al-Jazīrī, *al-Fiqh ʿalā al-Madhāhib al-Arbaʿa*, 2nd ed. (Beirut: Dār al-Kutub al-ʿIlmiyya, 2003), 2:203–8.

77. "Sijill 106," doc. 213, p. 55.

78. "Sijill 105," doc. 220, p. 78.

79. "Sijill 106," doc. 115, p. 29.

80. "Sijill 254," docs. 141, 193.

81. For a discussion of the marriage of minors in the four schools, see al-Jazīrī, *al-Fiqh ʿalā al-Madhāhib al-Arbaʿa*, 4:17–39.

82. The case goes as follows: "Before the Mālikī judge, the revered Ḥājj ʿAbd al-Jawwād, son of the late Ḥājj Aḥmad al-Madābighī in Miṣr al-Maḥrūsa gave a dower to the fiancée of his son Ibrāhīm, who is below the age of puberty . . . [his fiancée] is a virgin who is also below the age of puberty, the daughter of Shaykh Muḥammad Salīm . . . And according to this, the aforementioned father married her off to him, with his legal authority over her, [rendering this] a legal marriage. The aforementioned father accepted this on behalf of the aforementioned husband with his authority over him as well . . . The aforementioned marriage contract will be effective according to the rules to which our aforementioned master the *sharʿī* Mālikī judge adheres . . . This took place on the first of Shawwāl 1092." "Sijill 105," doc. 220.

83. Ibid., doc. 203.

84. For Ḥanafī and Shāfiʿī views on the husband's inability to provide for his wife and whether or not she can seek a divorce on such grounds, see al-Jazīrī, *al-Fiqh ʿalā al-Madhāhib al-Arbaʿa*, 4:172, 508–10; Wizārat al-Awqāf wa'l-Shu'ūn al-Islāmiyya, *al-Mawsūʿa al-Fiqhiyya al-Kuwaytiyya*, 2nd ed. (Kuwait: Dhāt al-Salāsil, 1983), 41:66–67.

85. "Sijill 106," docs. 139, 143, pp. 36–37.

86. "Sijill 105," docs. 41, 66, 76, 91.

87. ʿAfīfī, *al-Awqāf wa'l-Ḥayāh al-Iqtiṣādiyya fī Miṣr fi'l-ʿAṣr al-ʿUthmānī*, 146–52.

88. See for instance the opening paragraphs of Sijills 127, 131, 140, 141, 148, 164, 169, Dār al-Wathā'iq al-Qawmiyya (Cairo), the Court of al-Bāb al-ʿĀlī.

89. Shaham, "Shopping for Legal Forums," 454.

90. "Sijill 254," doc. 3, p. 2.

91. "Sijill 66," doc. 3, p. 2.

92. Ibid., doc. 103; "Sijill 254," doc. 53, p. 27.

93. This exact wording is used in "Sijill 254," docs. 9, 16, 17, 18, 25, 26, 27, 28.

94. Ibid., docs. 31, 32, 34, 35, 41, 48.

95. Ibid., doc. 163.

96. "Sijill 105," docs. 40, 121, 199, 203, 225, 261, 259.

97. Ibid., doc. 199.

98. All four schools of Sunnī Islamic law agree that after being divorced three times, a couple may not remarry without the wife first marrying and then divorcing someone else. The second husband, who makes remarriage to the first permissible, or *ḥalāl*, is called a *muḥallil*.

99. Al-Jazīrī, *al-Fiqh ʿalā al-Madhāhib al-Arbaʿa*, 4:28.

100. This is the Shāfiʿī jurist Muḥammad b. Aḥmad Shams al-Dīn al-Ramlī (d. 1004/1595), not to be confused with the Ḥanafī Khayr al-Dīn al-Ramlī (d. 1081/1671).

101. The *mithl* dower is determined by the dower paid for a woman of the same socio-economic status, usually based on another relative's dower.

102. "Sijill 105," doc. 199.

103. This case is reminiscent of the Bombay case of Muḥammad Ibrāhīm v. Gulām Aḥmad (1864), in which the woman was brought up as a Shāfi'ī, but had married without her father's consent, which contradicts Shāfi'ī law. The court recognized her marriage after she claimed that she had become a Ḥanafī. Riḍā's case is more complex though because it has two judges in the same transaction. On the Bombay case, see further Coulson, *A History of Islamic Law*, 183.

104. "Sijill 105," doc. 199.

105. Ibid.

106. Amira Sonbol has argued that the entire spectrum of juristic doctrines regarding the prerogative of adult virgin women to approve their own marriages can be found in Ottoman Egyptian courts. Amira El Azhary Sonbol, "Adults and Minors in Ottoman Shari'a Courts," in *Women, the Family, and Divorce Laws in Islamic History*, ed. Amira El Azhary Sonbol (Syracuse, NY: Syracuse Univ. Press, 1996), 242–50.

107. Gerber, *State, Society, and Law in Islam*, 90.

108. "Sijill 254," doc. 6, p. 2.

109. "Sijill 105," docs. 41, 66, 76, 91.

110. Ibid., doc. 203.

111. A payment that is dependent upon the consummation of the marriage.

112. This is the waiting period after divorce during which a woman cannot be married to avoid confusion over the father of her child if she discovers she is pregnant. According to some jurists, the husband is required to support the wife during this period following divorce.

113. "Sijill 105," doc. 40; al-Jazīrī, *al-Fiqh 'alā al-Madhāhib al-Arba'a*, 4:485–510; Wizārat al-Awqāf wa'l-Shu'ūn al-Islāmiyya, *al-Mawsū'a al-Fiqhiyya al-Kuwaytiyya*, 41:34–100.

114. For a discussion of *khul'*, see 'Abd al-Qādir, "Naẓariyyat al-Isqāṭ fi'l-Sharī'a al-Islāmiyya," 283; Ibyānī Bek, *Sharḥ al-Aḥkām al-Shar'iyya fi'l-Aḥwāl al-Shakhṣiyya*, 252–69; al-Jazīrī, *al-Fiqh 'alā al-Madhāhib al-arba'a*, 4:342–66; Wizārat al-Awqāf wa'l-Shu'ūn al-Islāmiyya, *al-Mawsū'a al-Fiqhiyya al-Kuwaytiyya*, 19:234–59.

115. For a discussion of maintenance during the *'idda* period, see Wizārat al-Awqāf wa'l-Shu'ūn al-Islāmiyya, *al-Mawsū'a al-Fiqhiyya al-Kuwaytiyya*, 41:57–60; Ibyānī Bek, *Sharḥ al-Aḥkām al-Shar'iyya fi'l-Aḥwāl al-Shakhṣiyya*, 252–73.

116. Ibyānī Bek, *Sharḥ al-Aḥkām al-Shar'iyya fi'l-Aḥwāl al-Shakhṣiyya*, 258–59.

117. The other cases contain similar language. Consider the following example: "In front of the Ḥanafī *shar'ī* judge and the Mālikī *shar'ī* judge a person asked . . . the venerable 'Atā Allāh, son of the late Manṣūr al-Zaydānī in Miṣr al-Qadīma, to divorce his wife, the woman Umm al-Khayr, daughter of the venerable Yaḥyā al-Qulalī from his matrimonial authority, one first divorce utterance for one dirham that he owes her . . . He agreed to divorce her from his matrimonial authority the requested divorce utterance for the aforementioned compensation, having admitted that he consummated the marriage with her . . .

Each one of them [the two judges] ruled according to what is acceptable to him [his school], which for our master the Ḥanafī *shar'ī* judge means losing any past *kiswa* and maintenance money owed to the mentioned divorcée and to our master the aforementioned Mālikī *shar'ī* judge means losing the *mut'a* and *'idda* money owed to the aforementioned divorcée, so long as she is not legitimately pregnant . . . on the sixth of the blessed month of Shawwāl, in the year 1092." "Sijill 105," doc. 225.

118. "Sijill 66," docs. 91, 257; "Sijill 254," doc. 42.

119. The eponym of the Ḥanafī school, Abū Ḥanīfa, believed that an endowment is not binding, meaning that one may change his or her mind and retract it. His disciples Abū Yūsuf and Muḥammad al-Shaybānī ruled against the founder that it is in fact binding. Since a judge has issued a ruling establishing that the endowment is binding, this cannot be challenged in the future, following the jurisprudential rule that the judge's decision negates juristic views contradicting it (*ḥukm al-qāḍī yarfa'u al-khilāf*). This ruling means that it is not possible in the future to seek a Ḥanafī judge who would permit the repeal of the *waqf* on the authority of Abū Ḥanīfa. This practice was a strategy to avoid the subsequent repealing of *waqf*.

120. In the same document, 'Umar, a prominent merchant from Bulaq, established another *waqf*, with one of the beneficiaries being the mausoleum of the Imam al-Shāfi'ī. He sensed no irony in the fact that he had established a *waqf* to a Shāfi'ī institution without relying on the Shāfi'ī school for that transaction! "Sijill 66," doc. 91.

121. The case goes as follows: "He handed over the aforementioned properties that he owns to a *shar'ī* guardian . . . then the endower decided to retract the endowment of the aforementioned properties that he [once] owned to return them to his ownership as they were before . . . following the opinion of the great Imām and early *mujtahid* Abū Ḥanīfa al-Nu'mān . . . whose view is that establishing a *waqf* to oneself is permitted but not binding. The guardian of the *waqf* challenged him . . . stating that the endowment is sound and binding . . . referring to the view of the two honorable companions, namely Imām Abū 'Abd Allāh Muḥammad b. al-Ḥasan and Imām Ya'qūb b. Yūsuf, may God be pleased with them, that endowments are binding as soon as they are issued, even if designated to oneself. They [the founder and the guardian] disagreed, until the issue was taken to our master, the aforementioned Ḥanafī judge . . . The establishment of the *waqf* on the usufruct of the building, which is mentioned above, was approved by our master the aforementioned Ḥanbalī judge . . . Then our master the aforementioned Ḥanafī judge looked closely into this disputed issue and considered it thoroughly, until he found that the view of the two companions [of Abū Ḥanīfa] had a stronger proof. It is also what is used for *fatwā* and [legal] practice . . . he then judged that the *waqf* is valid." "Sijill 66," doc. 91.

122. Ibid., doc. 257.

123. "Sijill 254," doc. 42.

124. "Sijill 66," docs. 118, 206, 210, 239.

125. Ibid., docs. 154, 155.

126. Ibid., doc. 134.

127. "Sijill 254," doc. 205.

128. Ibid., doc. 177.

129. Ibid., doc. 3.

130. For this and more examples, see ibid., docs. 49, 68, 79, 80, 136.

131. In one of the documents of the court of al-Bāb al-ʿĀlī, after a case had been transcribed, the names of some people in attendance were later added above the opening line, where they would have normally been mentioned. This could be either because the scribe forgot to mention their names or because they appeared after the proceedings had already started. Although there were already two undersigned witnesses, these two prominent figures were also mentioned as witnesses. See ibid., doc. 186, p. 99.

132. Ibid., doc. 92, p. 42.

133. For a discussion of the socioeconomic history of eighteenth-century Egypt and the ascendancy of the Mamluk Shaykh al-Balad ʿAlī Bey al-Kabīr, see Gran, *Islamic Roots of Capitalism*, 11–34.

134. Kuran, "Why the Middle East Is Economically Underdeveloped."

135. "Sijill 254," doc. 92, p. 42.

136. Certainly Weber's views were not informed by any extensive study of Islamic law in practice or knowledge of Arabic. Yet they were perpetuated by some scholars. For instance, building on Weber's thesis, Rosen discusses the role of the judge in the contemporary Moroccan town of Sefrou. He argues that the judge was not bound by fixed legal rules, thereby making the legal process one of fluid bargaining. Other scholars reached different conclusions. Gerber's study of Ottoman courts shows that Ottoman judges applied laws that were known in advance to litigants, with the legal outcomes being completely predictable. Similarly, Chibli Mallat demonstrates through a study of seventeenth-century courts in Tripoli that the court system was not arbitrary but rather grounded in consistent rules. He shows that the single judge directed the administration of evidence systematically and efficiently. "The flexibility, predictability and consistency of the system are notable for the modern reader," he adds. For both sides of the debate, see Weber, *Economy and Society*, 2:806, 896; 3:976–78; Turner, "Islam, Capitalism and the Weber Theses," 230–43, at 234–38; Lawrence Rosen, *The Anthropology of Justice: Law as Culture in Islamic Society*, Lewis Henry Morgan Lectures 1985 (Cambridge, UK: Cambridge Univ. Press, 1989), 11–19; Gerber, *State, Society, and Law in Islam*, 1–2, 177; Mallat, "From Islamic to Middle Eastern Law," 209–86, at 230; Abraham L. Udovitch, *Partnership and Profit in Medieval Islam* (Princeton, NJ: Princeton Univ. Press, 1970), 3–12; Schacht, *Introduction to Islamic Law*, 75.

5. Juristic Discourse on Pragmatic Eclecticism in Modern Egypt

1. Hallaq and Layish, "Talfīḳ."

2. Coulson, *A History of Islamic Law*, 197; Albert Hourani, *Arabic Thought in the Liberal Age, 1798–1939* (Cambridge, UK: Cambridge Univ. Press, 1983), 152–53; Anderson, *Law*

Reform in the Muslim World, 52; Norman Anderson, "The Shari'a Today," *Journal of Comparative Legislation and International Law*, 31:3/4 (1949): 18–25, at 22; Anderson, "Modern Trends in Islam," 1–21, at 13–14.

3. Coulson cites an example of *talfīq* in modern Egyptian law that creates a mixture of Ḥanafī and Mālikī laws with regard to inheritance among non-Muslims. Ḥanafī law stipulates that non-Muslims have no rights of inheritance when one of the parties to the inheritance is the subject of a Muslim state and the other is the subject of a non-Muslim state, whereas Mālikī law does not bar inheritance based on the place of domicile. Egyptian law sets no bar on inheritance when there is a difference of domicile, provided the laws of the non-Muslim state in question permit reciprocal treatment, but if these laws do not provide the same treatment, the Ḥanafī prohibition comes into effect. To pre-nineteenth-century Muslims, whether or not the above example can be called *talfīq* would have depended on the adjudication of the case rather than the discrete statute. The test that jurists used to determine whether a case involves synchronic *talfīq* was to determine whether the resulting ruling would be unacceptable to all the schools owing to the presence of an illegitimate element from their different perspectives. Thus, in the above example, in which a subject of a different country comes before an Egyptian court to claim her or his inheritance from a relative, the claim would only be brought before a Mālikī judge if the individual's country of domicile permits reciprocal treatment. But since the resulting ruling is accepted in the Mālikī school, no synchronic *talfīq* has taken place. Rather, this would be an example of *tatabbuʿ al-rukhaṣ*, unless, of course, that person had conducted a related transaction under another school, which would render it diachronic *talfīq*. In other words, viewing it from the standpoint of a discrete, written law, some modern historians felt justified in calling this combination of two doctrines within the same law an instance of *talfīq*. A jurist living before the nineteenth century would have described it as an instance of *tatabbuʿ al-rukhaṣ*, viewing the case from the judicial perspective as a single legal transaction, not as a hybrid code. Another example that Coulson cited is the application of the Ḥanbalī doctrine of allowing for stipulations in marriage contracts preventing the husband from taking a second wife. Again, a premodern Muslim jurist would have called this an instance of *talfīq* had the same contract contained elements of other schools besides the Ḥanbalī school or had there been two related transactions under two different schools. But if the couple had entered into a marriage contract under Ḥanbalī law only, this would not constitute *talfīq* but rather *tatabbuʿ al-rukhaṣ*. Coulson, *A History of Islamic Law*, 197–99.

4. Coulson also rightly cites a case of synchronic *talfīq* relating to inheritance among non-Muslims. Egyptian law allows a Jewish person domiciled in a non-Muslim state to inherit from a Christian relative living in a Muslim state. This would not, however, be possible under Ḥanafī law because of the different domiciles of the relatives, nor would it be allowed under Mālikī law because of the relative's different religion, which is considered sufficient to bar the inheritance. This is a clear example of synchronic *talfīq*, as neither the Mālikīs nor the Ḥanafīs would allow this one case to be adjudicated in this manner. Ibid., 197–99.

5. Hourani, *Arabic Thought in the Liberal Age, 1798–1939*, 152–53.

6. Malcolm H. Kerr, *Islamic Reform: The Political and Legal Theories of Muḥammad ʿAbduh and Rashīd Riḍā* (Berkeley: Univ. of California Press, 1966), 216–17.

7. Al-Bayhaqī, *al-Sunan al-Kubrā*, 10:356–57.

8. Al-Bānī, *ʿUmdat al-Taḥqīq fi'l-Taqlīd wa'l-Talfīq*, 47.

9. Muḥammad Rashīd Riḍā, *Fatāwā al-Imām Muḥammad Rashīd Riḍā*, ed. Ṣalāḥ al-Dīn Munjid (Beirut: Dār al-Kitāb al-Jadīd, 1970), 1:69–70.

10. Ibid.

11. Ibid., 1:239.

12. Muḥammad Rashīd Riḍā, ed., "Al-Muḥāwara al-Tāsiʿa Bayna al-Muṣliḥ wa'l-Muqallid," *al-Manār* 4:10 (1901): 361–400, at 374.

13. Muḥammad Rashīd Riḍā, "Al-Ṭalāq ʿalā al-Ghā'ib wa'l-Muʿsir fi'l-Sūdān," *al-Manār* 6:6 (1903): 233–36, at 235.

14. Abdul-Rahman al-Qalhūd, "Al-Talfeek and Its Rules in Jurisprudence," in *The First Conference of the Academy of Islamic Research* (Cairo: Al-Azhar Academy of Islamic Research, 1964), 75; Mohammad Ahmad Farag El Sanhoori, "Eclecticism in Rules of Rites," in *The First Conference of the Academy of Islamic Research* (Cairo: Al-Azhar Academy of Islamic Research, 1964), 57–71.

15. Muḥammad Ibrāhīm Ḥifnāwī, *Tabṣīr al-Nujabā' bi-Ḥaqīqat al-Ijtihād wa'l-Taqlīd wa'l-Talfīq wa'l-Iftā'* (Cairo: Dār al-Ḥadīth, 1995), 218, 262.

16. Ibid., 282–83.

17. The Ḥanafī view is to wait until he is unlikely to be alive, which is estimated by some in the Ḥanafī school to be around the age of ninety.

18. Muḥammad Amīn b. ʿUmar b. ʿĀbidīn, *Radd al-Muḥtār ʿalā al-Durr al-Mukhtār* (Riyadh, Saudi Arabia: Dār ʿĀlam al-Kutub, 2003), 6:460–61.

19. Al-Bānī, *ʿUmdat al-Taḥqīq fi'l-Taqlīd wa'l-Talfīq*, 83.

20. Abū Bakr b. al-Sayyid Muḥammad Shaṭā al-Dimyāṭī, *Iʿānat al-Ṭālibīn ʿalā Fatḥ al-Muʿīn bi-Sharḥ Qurrat al-ʿAyn*, 5th ed. (Cairo: al-Maṭbaʿa al-Maymaniyya, n.d.), 4:218–19.

21. The *ḥarām* formula in cases of divorce refers to when the husband verbally expresses to his wife that she is henceforth forbidden (*ḥarām*) upon him, which the Shāfiʿīs consider a mere *kināya* (metonymy) for *ṭalāq*, and, therefore, allows the person to return to the marriage, if he had intended it to be a revocable repudiation. The Ḥanafīs, on the other hand, do not allow the husband that option. They consider this repudiation irrevocable regardless of his intention, as they base its meaning on common practice (*ʿurf*). See al-Jazīrī, *al-Fiqh ʿalā al-Madhāhib al-Arbaʿa*, 4:300–302.

22. Muḥammad al-ʿAbbāsī al-Mahdī, *al-Fatāwā al-Mahdiyya fi'l-Waqā'iʿ al-Miṣriyya* (Cairo: al-Maṭbaʿa al-Azhariyya al-Miṣriyya, 1883), 1:216.

23. Ibid.

24. The second change would be, for instance, to take the view of Ibn Taymiyya that counts the triple *ṭalāq* formula as one instance of *ṭalāq*. Ibid.

25. Rudolph Peters, "Muḥammad al-'Abbāsī al-Mahdī (d. 1897), Grand Muftī of Egypt, and His 'al-Fatāwā al-Mahdiyya,'" *Islamic Law and Society* 1:1 66–82, at 80.

26. Ibid., 66–82, at 79–80.

27. A drink that is brewed until two-thirds of its volume evaporate and that can lead to intoxication when concentrated in this manner.

28. Aḥmad al-Ḥusaynī, "Al-Qawl al-Sadīd fī Ḥukm al-Ijtihād wa'l-Taqlīd," Cairo, n.d., MS Dār al-Kutub 507 Uṣūl Fiqh, folio 23.

29. Ibid., folio 25–27.

30. Muḥammad Munīb al-Hāshimī, "Al-Qawl al-Sadīd fī Aḥkām al-Taqlīd," Cairo, n.d., MS Dār al-Kutub 197 Uṣūl Taymūr, folio 4a–6b,

31. Muḥammad Bakhīt Muṭī'ī, "Al-Talfīq fi'l-'Ibāda," *Fatāwā al-Azhar wa-Dār al-Iftā' fī Mi'at 'Ām* (Cairo: Kalimāt), accessed Apr. 30, 2012, http://www.kl28.com/fat1r.php?search=3169.

32. Al-Bānī, *'Umdat al-Taḥqīq fi'l-Taqlīd wa'l-Talfīq*, 14–38.

33. Leila Hudson, "Reading al-Sha'rānī: The Sufi Genealogy of Islamic Modernism in Late Ottoman Damascus," *Journal of Islamic Studies* 15:1 (2004): 39–68.

34. Ibrahim, "Al-Sha'rānī's Response to Legal Purism."

35. For a detailed discussion of those episodes mobilized in support of *talfīq*, see chapter 3.

36. Al-Bānī, *'Umdat al-Taḥqīq fi'l-Taqlīd wa'l-Talfīq*, 91–106.

37. On al-Qāsimī, see Muḥammad b. Nāṣir al-'Ajmī, *al-Rasā'il al-Mutabādala Bayna Jamāl al-Dīn al-Qāsimī wa-Maḥmūd Shukrī al-Alūsī* (Beirut: Dār al-Bashā'ir al-Islāmiyya, 2001), 17–25.

38. Al-Bānī, *'Umdat al-Taḥqīq fi'l-Taqlīd wa'l-Talfīq*, 94–97.

39. This is a reference to Law 25 of 1920, Law 31 of 1910, and perhaps also to Law 56 of 1923.

40. Al-Bānī, *'Umdat al-Taḥqīq fi'l-Taqlīd wa'l-Talfīq*, 44–70.

41. Ibid., 85–90.

42. Maḥmūd Dīnarī, Muḥammad 'Anānī, and Ḥusayn Bayyūmī, *Mudhakkira bi'l-Radd 'alā Mashrū' al-Qānūn al-Khāṣṣ bi-Ba'ḍ Aḥkām al-Aḥwāl al-Shakhṣiyya* (Cairo: Maṭba'at al-Taḍāmun al-Akhawī, 1929), 6–7.

43. Ibid., 56.

44. Ibid., 33; al-Ardabīlī, *al-Anwār li-A'māl al-Abrār*, 2:609.

45. Feldman, *Fall and Rise of the Islamic State*, 64–68; Brown, "*Shari'a* and State in the Modern Muslim Middle East."

46. On codification, see further Sami Zubaida, *Law and Power in the Islamic World* (London: I. B. Tauris, 2003), 133–35.

47. The pioneers of the *Salafiyya* movement in the nineteenth century did not shy away from the use of *talfīq*, even in matters of theology. Muḥammad 'Abduh (1849–1905), for instance, not only incorporates some of the positions of Maturidism in his predominantly

Ash'arī theology, but he also draws on Mu'tazilism. Muḥammad 'Abduh, *Risālat al-Tawḥīd* (Cairo: Dār al-Hilāl, 1980); Louis Gardet, "'Ilm al-Kalām," in *Encyclopaedia of Islam*, ed. P. Bearman, Th. Bianquis, C. E. Bosworth, E. van Donzel, and W. P. Heinrichs (Leiden: Brill, 2008).

48. Riḍā, *Fatāwā al-Imām Muḥammad Rashīd Riḍā*, 1:239.

49. Ibid., 1:69–70.

50.Ibid., 3:385.

51. Al-Karmī and al-Saffārīnī, *al-Taḥqīq fī Buṭlān al-Talfīq Naṣṣ 'alā Futyā li'l-Shaykh Mar'ī al-Ḥanbalī*, 7–9, 136.

52. Ibid., 8, 57.

53. The debate continues in many corners of the Muslim World. For instance, the contemporary Turkish scholar Fethullah Gulen permitted *tatabbu' al-rukhaṣ* but not *talfīq*, whereas the contemporary Saudi jurist 'Abd al-'Azīz 'Abd Allāh al-Rājiḥī cited the two views on *tatabbu' al-rukhaṣ*, siding with its opponents. He extensively quoted Ibn Taymiyya's opposition to it, but he added that some later scholars (*muta'akhkhirīn*) permitted it. Despite his personal opposition to the practice, he admitted that it is subject to disagreement. Yilmaz, "Inter-Madhhab Surfing, Neo-Ijtihad, and Faith-Based Movement Leaders," 201; 'Abd al-'Azīz 'Abd Allāh al-Rājiḥī, *al-Taqlīd wa'l-Iftā' wa'l-Istiftā'* (Riyadh, Saudi Arabia: Kunūz Ishbīliya, 2007), 114–23.

54. Abū Ḥāmid al-Ghazālī, *al-Mankhūl min Ta'līqāt al-Uṣūl*, ed. Muḥammad Ḥasan Haytū, 2nd ed. (Damascus: Dār al-Fikr, 1980), 483–95.

55. Al-Juwaynī, *al-Burhān fī Uṣūl al-Fiqh*, 2:1350–51.

56. Al-Shahrazūrī, *Fatāwā wa-Masā'il Ibn al-Ṣalāḥ fi'l-Tafsīr wa'l-Ḥadīth wa'l-Uṣūl wa'l-Fiqh*, 1:60–64; al-Iṣfahānī, *Bayān al-Mukhtaṣar Sharḥ Mukhtaṣar Ibn al-Ḥājib*, 3:277.

57. Al-Qarāfī, *Sharḥ Tanqīḥ al-Fuṣūl fī Ikhtiṣār al-Maḥṣūl fi'l-Uṣūl*, 326–29.

58. Ibid.

59. Al-Subkī, *Fatāwā al-Subkī*, 2:433.

60. Al-Subkī, *Jam' al-Jawāmi' fī Uṣūl al-Fiqh*, 123.

61. Ibn 'Ābidīn, *Radd al-Muḥtār 'alā al-Durr al-Mukhtār* (Riyadh, Saudi Arabia: Dār 'Ālam al-Kutub, 2003) 8:32–33.

62. Muṣṭafā al-Marāghī, "Khuṭbat al-Ustādh al-Akbar Shaykh al-Jāmi' al-Azhar," *al-Manār* 35:3 (1935): 180–87, at 187.

63. For discussions of *takhayyur*, see, for instance, John L. Esposito, *Women in Muslim Family Law*, 2nd ed. (Syracuse, NY: Syracuse Univ. Press, 2001), 95–101; Krawietz, "Cut and Paste in Legal Rules," 4; Coulson, A *History of Islamic Law*; Wiederhold, "Legal Doctrines in Conflict," 247; Aharon Layish and Ron Shaham, "Tashrī'," in *Encyclopaedia of Islam*, ed. P. Bearman, Th. Bianquis, C. E. Bosworth, E. van Donzel, and W. P. Heinrichs (Leiden: Brill, 2008).

64. Muḥammad Rashīd Riḍā, *Yusr al-Islām wa-Uṣūl al-Tashrī' al-'Āmm fī Nahy Allāh wa-Rasūlihi 'an Kathrat al-Su'āl* (Cairo: Maktabat al-Salām al-'Ālamiyya, 1984), 9–16.

65. Ibid., 15–16.

66. I prefer to use the term *modernist,* for although a large part of the solution for the perceived challenge of the encounter between modernity and tradition—whether in the form of reviving the Ḥanbalī debates about *ijtihād* or utilizing pragmatic eclecticism on a large scale—appears to have been traditional in basis, the problems posed were modern. Modernist scholars decided to accommodate and engage with modernity, rather than to renounce it in exchange for some notion of legal purity. Although I recognize the impossibility of ridding ourselves of all unwanted connotations in whatever term we choose, this term does not have as wide a range of connotations as, let us say, the term *moderate.* Similarly, the term *purist* is useful in singling out the *textualist* strand of *Salaf*ism that attempts to purify Islam, not only of juristic accretions—which was the primary concern of the premodern proto-*salafī*s—but also of modern discourses and pragmatic eclecticism. This purist tendency arises from a prevailing sense of alienation with modernity and is informed by a reaction to Western encroachment on Islamic societies, which has typically led to calls for greater cultural isolationism. Other scholars used terms such as *puritan.* For example, Hashemi draws comparisons between the rise of Islamic fundamentalism and the English Puritans of the seventeenth century. See Nader Hashemi, *Islam, Secularism, and Liberal Democracy: Toward a Democratic Theory for Muslim Societies* (Oxford, UK: Oxford Univ. Press, 2009), 15–18.

67. Hallaq has a different characterization of the actors on the legal scene, as he divides them into: the state, "secular" modernists, the *'ulamā',* and Islamists. Hallaq, *Sharī'a,* 474; Hallaq, "Can the Shari'a Be Restored?"

68. For a discussion of overlapping consensus, see John Rawls, *Political Liberalism* (New York: Columbia Univ. Press, 1993). For a discussion of overlapping consensus in the Muslim context, see Andrew F. March, "Islamic Foundations for a Social Contract in Non-Muslim Liberal Democracies," *American Political Science Review* 101:2 (2007): 235–53; March, *Islam and Liberal Citizenship the Search for an Overlapping Consensus* (Oxford, UK: Oxford Univ. Press, 2009).

69. For an example of a project that was clearly inspired by political liberalism, see Ibrahim, "Jamāl al-Bannā's New Jurisprudence."

70. Khaled Abou El Fadl, "The Ugly Modern and the Modern Ugly: Reclaiming the Beautiful in Islam," in *Progressive Muslims: On Justice, Gender and Pluralism,* ed. Omid Safi (Oxford, UK: Oneworld, 2003), 60.

71. Henri Lauzière, "The Construction of *Salafiyya*: Reconsidering Salafism from the Perspective of Conceptual History," *International Journal of Middle East Studies* 42:3 (2010): 369–89.

72. Ibn Ḥanbal's definition of Sunna includes abiding by the conduct of the Companions of the Prophet. Aḥmad b. Ḥanbal, *Sharḥ Uṣūl al-Sunna li-Aḥmad Ibn Ḥanbal,* ed. 'Abd Allāh b. 'Abd al-Raḥmān Jabrayn and 'Alī b. Ḥusayn b. Lawz (Riyadh, Saudi Arabia: Dār al-Musayyir, 1999), 35. For an insightful discussion of scripturalism that converged with traditionalism in the later part of its evolution, see Vishanoff, *The Formation of Islamic*

Hermeneutics, 66–108; Melchert, "Traditionist-Jurisprudents," 383–406, at 384–87; Haykel, "On the Nature of Salafi Thought and Action," 35–45. References to *al-salaf al-ṣāliḥ* abound in juristic discourse. For instance, al-Shaʿrānī in his *al-Mīzān* said that the *salaf al-ṣāliḥ* did not use *ta'wīl* (metaphorical interpretation) or analogy in understanding the textual sources. See al-Shaʿrānī, *al-Mīzān*, 1:16; Similarly, Maqdisī compared the approach of *muta'akhkhirīn* with that of the *salaf*. He said that some scholars tried to explore issues that were never tapped before by the *salaf* and urged his readers, instead, to follow the way of the *salaf*. See al-Maqdisī, *Mukhtaṣar al-Hujja ʿalā Tārik al-Maḥajja*, 2:537.

73. It is precisely because of the appropriation of the term in various Islamic discourses in the modern period that it has ceased to be useful in demarcating the lines between different approaches to legal reform. In this mayhem of a terminological indeterminacy, Abou El Fadl opted for using the terms "puritanical" and "moderate" to describe the two poles of the modern Islamic reform movement (Riḍā's third and fourth camps). Khaled Abou El Fadl, *The Great Theft: Wrestling Islam from the Extremists* (New York: HarperSanFrancisco, 2005).

74. For a discussion of multiple modernities, see S. N. Eisenstadt, "Multiple Modernities," *Daedalus* 129:1 (2000): 1–29.

75. Hallaq also speaks of the *liberalists* who try to develop more sophisticated and systematic approaches to hermeneutics and the *utilitarianists* (our modernists); Hallaq, "Can the Shariʿa Be Restored?" 45–48.

76. However, even some jurists who were not necessarily purist in their legal approach opposed the practice of pragmatic eclecticism, such as al-Ghazālī and al-Shāṭibī. As such, the most important characteristic setting purists apart from other jurists was their strict adherence to the divine source texts. Thus, while the overwhelming majority of textualists were opposed to pragmatic eclecticism, there was more diversity of opinion among nontextualist jurists. See al-Shāṭibī, *al-Muwāfaqāt*, 5:77–78; al-Ghazālī, *al-Mustaṣfā min ʿIlm al-Uṣūl*, 4:154–55.

77. Ibn Taymiyya, *Kitāb Bayān al-Dalīl ʿalā Buṭlān al-Taḥlīl*, 318–22.

78. For more on traditionist jurisprudence, see Christopher Melchert, "Traditionist-Jurisprudents and the Framing of Islamic Law," in *Islamic Law*, ed. Gavin N. Picken, Critical Concepts in Islamic Studies (London: Routledge, 2011); Susan A. Spectorsky, "Aḥmad Ibn Ḥanbal's Fiqh," *Journal of the American Oriental Society* 102:3 (1982): 461–65. On the relaxation of the rules of hadith criticism regarding the existence of traditions attributed to both the Prophet and the Companions, see Jonathan A. C. Brown, "Critical Rigor vs. Juridical Pragmatism: How Legal Theorists and Ḥadīth Scholars Approached the Backgrowth of *Isnād*s in the Genre of *ʿIlal al-Ḥadīth*," *Islamic Law and Society* 14:1 (2007): 1–41.

79. In discussions of following the Companions of the Prophet as opposed to the four schools, most jurists gave preference to observing the rules of the four schools, with orthodoxy itself being largely restricted to these schools. See, for instance, al-Zarkashī, *al-Baḥr al-Muḥīṭ fī Uṣūl al-Fiqh*, 6:288–90.

80. Ahmad Dallal, "The Origins and Objectives of Islamic Revivalist Thought, 1750–1850," *Journal of the American Oriental Society* 113:3 (1993): 341–59.

81. On al-Shāfiʿī's role in creating a middle ground between traditionalists and rationalists, see El Shamsy, *The Canonization of Islamic Law*, 1–117; Melchert, "Traditionist-Jurisprudents"; Joseph E. Lowry, *Early Islamic Legal Theory: The Risāla of Muḥammad Ibn Idrīs al-Shāfiʿī* (Leiden: Brill, 2007); Wael B. Hallaq, "Was al-Shāfiʿī the Master Architect of Islamic Jurisprudence?" *International Journal of Middle East Studies* 25:4 (1993): 587–605.

82. On the characteristics of the early proto-Salafī approach to law, see further Lucas, "The Legal Principles of Muḥammad B. Ismāʿīl al-Bukhārī."

83. For a discussion of traditionist jurists and Ibn Ḥazm's scripturalism, as well as its convergence with traditionalism in the later part of its evolution, see Vishanoff, *The Formation of Islamic Hermeneutics*, 66–108. For an account of traditionalism, see Melchert, "Traditionist-Jurisprudents," 383–406, at 384–87.

84. Raymond William Baker, *Islam without Fear: Egypt and the New Islamists* (Cambridge, MA: Harvard Univ. Press, 2003), 106.

85. Muḥammad Sulṭān al-Maʿṣūmī Khājandī, *Hal al-Muslim Mulzam bi-Ittibāʿ Madhhab Muʿayyan min al-Madhāhib al-Arbaʿa?* (N.p.: Jamʿiyyat Iḥyāʾ al-Turāth al-Islāmī, 1939), 7.

86. Abou El Fadl, *The Great Theft*, 47–49.

87. Nājiḥ Ibrāhīm ʿAbd Allāh and ʿAlī Muḥammad ʿAlī Sharīf, *Ḥurmat al-Ghulūw fi'l-Dīn wa-Takfīr al-Muslimīn*, ed. Karam Muḥammad Zuhdī et al. (ʿĀbidīn, Cairo: Maktabat al-Turāth al-Islāmī, 2002), 11, 19, 79–83.

88. Ibn Taymiyya, *Kitāb Bayān al-Dalīl ʿalā Buṭlān al-Taḥlīl*, 140–44.

89. ʿAbd Allāh and Sharīf, *Ḥurmat al-Ghulūw fi'l-Dīn wa-Takfīr al-Muslimīn*, 19.

90. Ibid., 64–65.

91. See, for instance, Ḥamdī ʿAbd al-Raḥmān ʿAbd al-ʿAẓīm, *Taslīṭ al-Aḍwāʾ ʿalā mā Waqaʿa fi'l-Jihād min Akhṭāʾ* (ʿĀbidīn, Cairo: Maktabat al-Turāth al-Islāmī, 2002), 19–71; Riḍā, *Yusr al-Islām wa-Uṣūl al-Tashrīʿ al-ʿĀmm fī Nahy Allāh wa-Rasūlihi ʿan Kathrat al-Suʾāl*, 50–100, 141.

92. ʿAlī Muḥammad ʿAlī Sharīf, *al-Nuṣḥ wa'l-Tabyīn fī Taṣḥīḥ Mafāhīm al-Muḥtasibīn* (Cairo: Maktabat al-Turāth al-Islāmī, 2002), 167–68.

93. Mawqiʿ al-Shaykh Muḥammad Nāṣir al-Dīn al-Albānī, "Al-Taṣfiya wa'l-Tarbiya," *Mawqiʿ al-Shaykh Muḥammad Nāṣir al-Dīn al-Albānī*, May 22, 2012, http://www.alalbany.net/misc006.php.

94. School loyalty, referred to as *tamadhhub* in premodern juristic discourse and *madhhabiyya* in the modern period, was rejected by many jurists such as Ibn Taymiyya; see Ibn Taymiyya, *Mukhtaṣar al-Fatāwā al-Miṣriyya*, 60–61; Ibrahim, "Al-Shaʿrānī's Response to Legal Purism."

95. The purist emphasis on *ijtihād* and *tarjīḥ* explains the controversy that was generated after the announcement of the Saudi government's plan to codify Islamic law in the form of a compendium of legal rules. There was a concern that such a move would

lead to the implementation of *tatabbuʿ al-rukhaṣ* and the end of *ijtihād*. By freeing the Muslim community from the schools, the modern proponents of this view believed that they were removing the accretions of juristic preference (*istiḥsān*), *tatabbuʿ al-rukhaṣ*, *talfīq*, and *qiyās* from Islamic law. Khājandī, *Hal al-Muslim Mulzam bi-Ittibāʿ Madhhab Muʿayyan min al-Madhāhib al-Arbaʿa?* 7–10.

96. Ibid., 6–10. For a discussion in which juristic views are rejected because they are viewed as contradictory to the Prophetic tradition literature, see Ashraf b. ʿAbd al-Raḥīm, *Jināyat al-Shaykh Muḥammad al-Ghazālī ʿalā al-Ḥadīth wa-Ahlih: Maʿa Mulḥaq li'l-Radd ʿalā Mā Jāʾa min Rudūd wa-Taʿqībāt bi'l-Ṭabʿah al-Sādisah li-Kitāb al-Sunnah al-Nabawīyya* (al-Ismāʿīliyya, Egypt: Maktabat al-Imām al-Bukhārī, 1989), 153–54.

97. Khājandī, *Hal al-Muslim Mulzam bi-Ittibāʿ Madhhab Muʿayyan min al-Madhāhib al-Arbaʿa?*, 6–10.

98. Muḥammad Nāṣir al-Dīn al-Albānī, *Maʿālim al-Manhaj al-Salafī fi'l-Taghyīr*, ed. Salīm b. ʿĪd al-Hilālī al-Salafī al-Atharī (Cairo: Dār al-Imām Aḥmad, 2006), 17.

99. Muḥammad Nāṣir al-Dīn al-Albānī, *Taḥrīm Ālāt al-Ṭarab: Aw al-Radd bi'l-Waḥyayn wa-Aqwāl A'immatinā ʿalā Ibn Ḥazm wa-Muqallidīhi al-Mubīḥīna li'l-Maʿāzif wa'l-Ghināʾ wa-ʿalā al-Ṣūfiyyīn Alladhīna Ittakhadhūhu Qurbatan wa-Dīnan*, 2nd ed. (al-Jubayl, Saudi Arabia: Maktabat al-Dalīl, 1997), 18–19.

100. Al-Albānī, *Maʿālim al-Manhaj al-Salafī fi'l-Taghyīr*, 5–18.

101. Ibid., 37–41.

102. Ibid., 12–15.

103. Ibid., 18–19.

104. Al-Albānī, *Taḥrīm Ālāt al-Ṭarab*, 5–20.

105. ʿAlī b. Aḥmad Ibn Ḥazm, *Rasāʾil Ibn Ḥazm al-Andalusī*, ed. Iḥsān ʿAbbās, 2nd ed. (Beirut: al-Muʾassasa al-Arabiyya li'l-Dirāsāt wa'l-Nashr, 1987), 1:419–39.

106. Al-Albānī, *Taḥrīm Ālāt al-Ṭarab*, 5–20.

107. Sulaymān b. Ṣāliḥ al-Kharāshī, "Tadarrujāt Rāshid al-Ghannūshī wa-Ahamm Inḥirāfātih," *Islamway.com*, Apr. 2005, 3–5, http://ar.islamway.com/book/825.

108. Ibid., 16–19.

109. ʿAbd al-Raḥmān b. Saʿd al-Shithrī, *Taqnīn al-Sharīʿa Bayna al-Taḥlīl wa'l-Taḥrīm* (Riyadh, Saudi Arabia: Dār al-Faḍīla, 2005), 10–15.

110. Ibn ʿAbd al-Raḥīm, *Jināyat al-Shaykh Muḥammad al-Ghazālī ʿalā al-Ḥadīth wa-Ahlih*, 82–83.

111. The two discourses for and against codification can also be seen in Saudi Arabia, long thought to be immune from Islamic legal codification. The calls of reformers and businesspeople—exasperated by the unpredictability of the uncodified legal system and its restrictions on personal freedoms—prompted King Abdullah in 2005 to charge the Supreme Judiciary Council (SJC) with looking into the possibility of codification. After much controversy, the SJC agreed in May 2010 to codify Islamic law in the form of a compendium (*majallah*) of published laws. It is not clear at this point what types of reforms

will be introduced and whether such reforms would veer away from the legal doctrines of the Ḥanbalī school. Such efforts have already faced serious opposition from some jurists, whose concerns ranged from misgivings about their future ability to exercise *ijtihād* in the new fixed system to worries about the state drawing upon the other schools in a utilitarian manner to better appeal to modern mores. Oxford Analytica, "Saudi Arabia: Codified Sharia Could Benefit Business," *Zawya*, Aug. 26, 2010, http://www.zawya.com/story/ZAWYA20100826075952/Benefiting%20Business/; al-Shithrī, *Taqnīn al-Sharī'a Bayna al-Taḥlīl wa'l-Taḥrīm*, 10–15; "The Codification of Islamic Sharia," *Asharq Alawsat*, Apr. 28, 2006, http://www.asharq-e.com/news.asp?section=2&id=4740.

112. 'Abd al-Ḥamīd al-Zahrāwī, *al-A'māl al-Kāmila*, ed. 'Abd al-Ilāh Nabhān (Damascus: Wizārat al-Thaqāfa fi'l-Jumhūriyya al-'Arabiyya al-Sūriyya, 1995), 2:261–66.

113. Riḍā, *Yusr al-Islām wa-Uṣūl al-Tashrī' al-'Āmm fī Nahy Allāh wa-Rasūlihi 'an Kathrat al-Su'āl*, 10.

114. Ibid., 16–19.

115. Dawoud S. El Alami, "Law No. 100 of 1985 Amending Certain Provisions of Egypt's Personal Status Laws," *Islamic Law and Society* 1:1 (1994): 130.

116. Al-Albānī, *Taḥrīm Ālāt al-Ṭarab*, 18–19.

117. Yūsuf al-Qaraḍāwī, *Fī Fiqh al-Aqalliyyāt al-Muslima* (Cairo: Dār al-Shurūq, 2001), 57–60.

118. Al-Ghannūshī even tried to save the term *salafī* from any association with the anti-school position by arguing that the term does not necessarily entail a war against the schools of jurisprudence and theology. According to him, such a war would be undesirable because, at the very least, it would lead to further fragmentation of the Muslim community. Rāshid al-Ghannūshī, *al-Ḥaraka al-Islāmiyya wa-Mas'alat al-Taghyīr* (London: al-Markaz al-Maghāribī li'l-Buḥūth wa'l-Tarjama, 2000), 121–22.

119. For a discussion of *Maṣlaḥa*, see Opwis, *Maṣlaḥa and the Purpose of the Law: Islamic Discourse on Legal Change from the 4th/10th to 8th/14th Century*, 259–67; Opwis, "*Maṣlaḥa* in Contemporary Islamic Legal Methodology."

120. Rāshid al-Ghannūshī, *al-Ḥurriyyāt al-'Āmma fi'l-Dawla al-Islāmiyya* (Beirut: Markaz Dirāsāt al-Waḥdah al-'Arabiyya, 1993), 46.

121. Ibid., 48–51.

122. Ibid., 125–33.

123. Ibid., 18–19, 65, 88.

124. Ibid., 46.

125. Ibid., 155–57.

126. The eclecticism that we have seen in the works of the above modernists is emblematic of the preferred methods of legal reform in the modern period. This approach appears clearly in the discourse of the jurists of the influential International Islamic Fiqh Academy (*Majma' al-Fiqh al-Islāmī*), which does not even mention the different opinions on *tatabbu' al-rukhaṣ* and *talfīq*, but it stipulates decisively that following the more lenient juristic opinions

is permitted, so long as they are not anomalous (*shādhdh*) and as long as there is a need. The conditions for *talfīq* are more stringent, practically excluding synchronic and only permitting diachronic *talfīq*. This attitude of the *Majma'* is reminiscent of the dominant strand in Ottoman juristic discourse that we saw above. Muḥammad 'Alī Taskhīrī, *Ma'a Mu'tamarāt Majma' al-Fiqh al-Islāmī* (Beirut: Dār Iḥyā' al-Turāth al-'Arabī, 2003), 2:230–73.

127. Riḍā, *Yusr al-Islām wa-Uṣūl al-Tashrī' al-'Āmm fī Nahy Allāh wa-Rasūlihi 'an Kathrat al-Su'āl*, 50–54.

128. Ibid., 9–16.

129. For a discussion of approaches that challenge the Prophetic tradition literature in the modern period, see G. H. A. Juynboll, *The Authenticity of the Tradition Literature: Discussions in Modern Egypt* (Leiden: Brill, 1969), 22–44; al-Zahrāwī, *al-A'māl al-Kāmila*, 2:271–74; Andrew Rippin, *Muslims: Their Religious Beliefs and Practices* (London: Routledge, 1990), 80.

130. Ibrahim, "Jamāl al-Bannā's New Jurisprudence"; Jamāl al-Bannā, *Naḥwa Fiqh Jadīd: Al-Sunna wa-Dawruhā fi'l-Fiqh al-Jadīd* (Cairo: Dār al-Fikr al-Islāmī, 1997).

131. Kilian Bälz, "Submitting Faith to Judicial Scrutiny through the Family Trial: The 'Abu Zayd Case,'" *Die Welt Des Islams* 37:2 (1997): 135–55.

132. For a good discussion of early hadith *matn* criticism, see Jonathan A. C. Brown, "How We Know Early Ḥadīth Critics Did *Matn* Criticism and Why It's So Hard to Find," *Islamic Law and Society* 15 (2008): 160–70.

133. Ibn Qayyim listed examples of traditions rejected by jurists because they were perceived to contradict the Qur'an, such as the tradition "A Muslim should not be killed for killing an infidel" (*Lā yuqtalu mu'minun bi-kāfir*), because it appears to contradict the plain meaning of Qur'an 5:45: "And We ordained for them therein a life for a life, an eye for an eye, a nose for a nose, an ear for an ear, a tooth for a tooth, and for wounds is legal retribution." The group to which Ibn Qayyim is referring would have included the Ḥanafīs, who rejected the tradition disallowing the death penalty when a Muslim murders a non-Muslim. For a discussion of the early *matn*-critical approach, which reemerged in the modern period, see Ibn Qayyim al-Jawziyya, *al-Ṣawā'iq al-Mursala 'alā al-Jahmiyya wa'l-Mu'aṭṭila*, 578–83; Ibn 'Abd al-Raḥīm, *Jināyat al-Shaykh Muḥammad al-Ghazālī 'alā al-Ḥadīth wa-Ahlih*, 119–20.

134. Al-Bannā, *Naḥwa Fiqh Jadīd II*, 77–109; Jamāl al-Bannā, *Naḥwa Fiqh Jadīd III* (Cairo: Dār al-Fikr al-Islāmī, 1999), 14–25. For a polemical critique of al-Bannā's work, see Ḥasan Abū al-Ashbāl Zuhayrī, "al-Difā' 'an Allāh wa-Rasūlihi wa-Shar'ih: al-Radd 'alā Jamāl al-Bannā," *Islamweb.net*, May 24, 2012, http://audio.islamweb.net/audio/index.php?page=FullContent&audioid=153079.

135. Hallaq calls reformers who abandon the Arabicate hermeneutics in search of a new legal methodology "liberalists." He includes in this group figures such as Fazlur Rahman and Shahrur. Hallaq realizes that this group has very little appeal in Muslim societies. Thus he believes that Islamic law has reached an impasse in the twenty-first century. Hallaq, "Can the Shari'a Be Restored?" 45–48.

136. Fazlur Rahman, *Islam and Modernity: Transformation of an Intellectual Tradition* (Chicago: Univ. of Chicago Press, 1982), 2–25, 144; Asma Barlas, *Believing Women in Islam: Unreading Patriarchal Interpretations of the Qur'ān* (Austin: Univ. of Texas Press, 2002).

137. Al-Ghannūshī, *al-Ḥurriyyāt al-ʿĀmma fi'l-Dawla al-Islāmiyya*, 11–19.

6. Codification and the Arab Spring: Can the Sharīʿa Be Restored?

1. Amira El Azhary Sonbol, "The Genesis of Family Law: How *Shariʿah*, Custom and Colonial Laws Influenced the Development of Personal Status Codes," in *Wanted: Equality and Justice in the Muslim Family*, ed. Zainah Anwar (Kuala Lumpur: Musawah, 2009), 179–207; Amira El Azhary Sonbol, "Law and Gender Violence in Ottoman and Modern Egypt," in *Women, the Family, and Divorce Laws in Islamic History*, ed. Amira El Azhary Sonbol (Syracuse, NY: Syracuse Univ. Press, 1996), 280–89.

2. Middle Eastern modernity refers to dramatic social, economic, and political changes that took place in nineteenth-century Egypt under Mehmed Ali and European colonialism. For more on the processes of colonizing, modernizing, and centralizing Egypt, see the introduction.

3. The question of whether there was a hierarchical structure in Islamic legal practice prior to the process of legal modernization in the nineteenth and twentieth centuries is subject to debate. The common wisdom is that the strict rules of Sharīʿa do not allow for a judge's decisions to be appealed. For a discussion of judicial hierarchies in Islamic law, see David Stephan Powers, "On Judicial Review in Islamic Law," *Law & Society Review* 26:2 (1992): 315–41, at 315–16; Emile Tyan, "Judicial Organization," in *Law in the Middle East*, ed. Majid Khadduri and H. J. Liebesny (Washington, DC: Middle East Institute, 1995), 236–78; Martin Shapiro, *Courts: A Comparative and Political Analysis* (Chicago: Univ. of Chicago Press, 1981), 52, 209–22; Baber Johansen, "Le Jugement Comme Preuve: Preuve Juridique et Vérité Religieuse Dans Le Droit Islamique Hanéfite," *Studia Islamica* 72 (1990): 5–17; Rudolph Peters, "Islamic and Secular Criminal Law in Nineteenth Century Egypt: The Role and Function of the Qadi," *Islamic Law and Society* 4:1 (1997): 70–90.

4. Peters, *Crime and Punishment in Islamic Law*, 133–36.

5. For different views on the periodization of Egyptian legal modernization, see Laṭīfa M. Sālim, *al-Niẓām al-Qaḍā'ī al-Miṣrī al-Ḥadīth* (Cairo: al-Hay'a al-Miṣriyya al-ʿĀmma li'l-Kitāb, 2001), 1:51–96; Nathan J. Brown, *The Rule of Law in the Arab World: Courts in Egypt and the Gulf* (Cambridge, UK: Cambridge Univ. Press, 1997), 26–29; For the British colonial view of the Egyptian legal system, see Evelyn Baring Cromer, *Modern Egypt* (London: Macmillan, 1908), 2:514–23.

6. Ibid. In the case of criminal law, Mehmed Ali issued the first criminal legislation that complemented Sharīʿa rules. See Rudolph Peters, "'For His Correction and as a Deterrent Example for Others': Meḥmed ʿAlī's First Criminal Legislation (1829–1830)," *Islamic Law and Society* 6:2 (1999): 164–92; Peters, "1829–1871 or 1876–1883? The Significance of Nineteenth-Century

Pre-Colonial Legal Reform in Egypt" (presented at the New Approaches to Egyptian Legal History: Late Ottoman Period to the Present, Cairo, June 11, 2009).

7. Zeinab A. Abul-Magd, "Empire and Its Discontents: Modernity and Subaltern Revolt in Upper Egypt 1700–1920" (PhD diss., Georgetown Univ., 2008), 132–33. The centralization efforts of Mehmed Ali included reforming the army and education, and codifying some of the laws, as well as placing the state in the personal lives of individuals by surveilling (the panoptican) and controlling their movement; see Fahmy, *All the Pasha's Men*; Mitchell, *Colonising Egypt*, 24–62.

8. For a discussion of how reforming the army, through different laws, regulations, and manuals, was part of the modernizing ethos, see Fahmy, *All the Pasha's Men*; Mine Ener, "Prohibitions on Begging and Loitering in Nineteenth-Century Egypt," *Die Welt Des Islams*, n.s., 39:3 (Nov. 1999): 319–39.

9. The term "Ḥanafization" was used by Amira Sonbol to refer to the wide utilization of Ḥanafī law in modern Egyptian personal status and family laws in the twentieth century. Kenneth Cuno of the University of Illinois has extended this term, in private conversations, to refer to Mehmed Ali's efforts in the nineteenth century. I believe that the term is better suited for Mehmed Ali's process of homogenization, but not to the modern codification of personal status law because the term implies: (1) moving closer toward the Ḥanafī school, as compared to the prior period, and (2) minimizing the role of the other schools in the new system. Neither of these processes is true for the codification of Islamic law in twentieth-century Egypt. As I show in the rest of this chapter, the twentieth century saw a return to Ottoman legal pluralism following Mehmed Ali's experiment with Ḥanafization. See Amira Sonbol, "Women in Shariʿah Courts: A Historical and Methodological Discussion," *Fordham International Law Journal* 27:1 (2003): 225–53, at 238.

10. For a discussion of this tendency, see Baber Johansen, "The Constitution and the Principles of Islamic Normativity Against the Rules of *Fiqh*: A Judgement of the Supreme Constitutional Court of Egypt," in *Dispensing Justice in Islam: Qadis and Their Judgments*, ed. Muhammad Khalid Masud, Rudolph Peters, and David Stephan Powers (Leiden: Brill, 2006), 171; Shaham, "Shopping for Legal Forums: Christians and Family Law in Modern Egypt," 454–57.

11. Abul-Magd, "Empire and Its Discontents: Modernity and Subaltern Revolt in Upper Egypt, 1700–1920," 133–34. But even as early as 1802, after the expulsion of the French troops from Egypt, non-Ḥanafī judges were said to have been removed from courts in Egypt. See Peters, "What Does It Mean to Be an Official Madhhab?" 157.

12. For a discussion of sixteenth-century Ottoman attempts at Ḥanafization, see Ibrahim, "Al-Shaʿrānī's Response to Legal Purism," 110–40, at 115–19, 134–35; al-Ḥamzāwī, *Tabṣirat al-Quḍāh wa'l-Ikhwān*.

13. Peters, "For His Correction and as a Deterrent Example for Others"; Ener, "Prohibitions on Begging and Loitering in Nineteenth-Century Egypt."

14. Mitchell, *Colonising Egypt*, 100–102.

15. David Bonderman, "Modernization and Changing Perceptions of Islamic Law," *Harvard Law Review* 81:6 (Apr. 1968): 1169–93, at 1177.

16. Hallaq, *Sharīʿa*, 420–25; Bonderman, "Modernization and Changing Perceptions of Islamic Law," 1169–93, at 1182; Sonbol, "Women in Shariʿah Courts: A Historical and Methodological Discussion," 225–53, at 230.

17. Layish, "The Transformation of the Sharīʿa from Jurists' Law to Statutory Law in the Contemporary Muslim World," 85–113, at 89–92.

18. Johansen, "The Constitution and the Principles of Islamic Normativity Against the Rules of *Fiqh*," 171; Shaham, "Shopping for Legal Forums," 454–57.

19. Fāṭima al-Zahrāʾ ʿAbbās Aḥmad and Ḥilmī ʿAbd al-ʿAẓīm Ḥasan, *Qānūn al-Aḥwāl al-Shakhṣiyya li'l-Muslimīn wa'l-Qarārāt al-Munaffidha li-Aḥkāmih wa-Baʿḍ Aḥkām al-Maḥkama al-Dustūriyya al-ʿUlyā al-Ṣādira bi-Sha'nih* (Cairo: al-Maṭābiʿ al-Amīriyya, 2009), 23; Aḥmad Naṣr al-Jundī, *Mabādi' al-Qaḍā' al-Sharʿī fī Khamsīna ʿĀman* (Cairo: Dār al-Fikr al-ʿArabī, 1978), 378, 770.

20. Aḥmad and Ḥasan, *Qānūn al-Aḥwāl al-Shakhṣiyya li'l-Muslimīn wa'l-Qarārāt al-Munaffidha li-Aḥkāmih wa-Baʿḍ Aḥkām al-Maḥkama al-Dustūriyya al-ʿUlyā al-Ṣādira bi-Sha'nih*, 23.

21. Al-Zahrāwī, *al-Aʿmāl al-Kāmila*, 2:271–74.

22. Conditional divorce is a type of divorce in which the husband makes the divorce conditional upon a certain action or state. An example is when a man tells his wife that if she leaves the house, she is divorced. Aḥmad and Ḥasan, *Qānūn al-Aḥwāl al-Shakhṣiyya li'l-Muslimīn wa'l-Qarārāt al-Munaffidha li-Aḥkāmih wa-Baʿḍ Aḥkām al-Maḥkama al-Dustūriyya al-ʿUlyā al-Ṣādira bi-Sha'nih*, 4–5, 16–17.

23. Ibid., 17; al-Jundī, *Mabādi' al-Qaḍā' al-Sharʿī fī Khamsīna ʿĀman*, 662.

24. Aḥmad and Ḥasan, *Qānūn al-Aḥwāl al-Shakhṣiyya li'l-Muslimīn wa'l-Qarārāt al-Munaffidha li-Aḥkāmih wa-Baʿḍ Aḥkām al-Maḥkama al-Dustūriyya al-ʿUlyā al-Ṣādira bi-Sha'nih*, 16.

25. Al-Jundī, *Mabādi' al-Qaḍā' al-Sharʿī fī Khamsīna ʿĀman*, 189–96.

26. For actual court cases from twentieth-century Egypt, in which the concept of "harm" (*ḍarar*) is applied in Egyptian courts, see ibid., 190–98.

27. Ibid., 202–5.

28. Ibid., 215–16; Aḥmad and Ḥasan, *Qānūn al-Aḥwāl al-Shakhṣiyya li'l-Muslimīn wa'l-Qarārāt al-Munaffidha li-Aḥkāmih wa-Baʿḍ Aḥkām al-Maḥkama al-Dustūriyya al-ʿUlyā al-Ṣādira bi-Sha'nih*, 18–19.

29. El Alami, "Law No. 100 of 1985 Amending Certain Provisions of Egypt's Personal Status Laws," 116–36, at 116–18.

30. Ibid.

31. Aḥmad and Ḥasan, *Qānūn al-Aḥwāl al-Shakhṣiyya li'l-Muslimīn wa'l-Qarārāt al-Munaffidha li-Aḥkāmih wa-Baʿḍ Aḥkām al-Maḥkama al-Dustūriyya al-ʿUlyā al-Ṣādira bi-Sha'nih*, 32–33.

32. Modern legislators did not only use the Mālikī school, but also the Shāfiʿī and even Shīʿī Zaydism. Article 18, Law 100 of 1985 also stipulates that a woman is entitled

to a *mut'a* payment if she is divorced against her will. This payment was estimated at the equivalent of two years' maintenance. This was explicitly based on the Shāfi'ī view, as well as the view of Aḥmad b. Ḥanbal. The exercise of *tatabbu' al-rukhaṣ* also went beyond the four schools of Sunnī law to draw on Zaydism. Legislators, for instance, added doctor fees and the cost of medicines to the maintenance of the wife, departing from all four Sunnī schools. Ibid., 34–35, 49.

33. *Khul'* is a type of divorce that is usually, but not always, initiated by the wife and according to which she makes a payment to the husband (usually the dower amount) in exchange for a repudiation (*ṭalāq*).

34. Aḥmad and Ḥasan, *Qānūn al-Aḥwāl al-Shakhṣiyya li'l-Muslimīn wa'l-Qarārāt al-Munaffidha li-Aḥkāmih wa-Ba'ḍ Aḥkām al-Maḥkama al-Dustūriyya al-'Ulyā al-Ṣādira bi-Sha'nih,* 201.

35. Ibid., 71–72.

36. Oussama Arabi, "The Dawning of the Third Millennium on Shari'a: Egypt's Law No. 1 of 2000, or Women May Divorce at Will," *Arab Law Quarterly* 16:1 (2001): 2–21, at 5.

37. Aḥmad and Ḥasan, *Qānūn al-Aḥwāl al-Shakhṣiyya li'l-Muslimīn wa'l-Qarārāt al-Munaffidha li-Aḥkāmih wa-Ba'ḍ Aḥkām al-Maḥkama al-Dustūriyya al-'Ulyā al-Ṣādira bi-Sha'nih,* 193–202.

38. Ibid., 198–99.

39. Ibid., 202.

40. For the debate about whether the imperative implies obligation (*wujūb*), see, for instance, al-Ghazālī, *al-Mustaṣfā min 'Ilm al-Uṣūl,* 4:125–26.

41. 'Abd al-Qādir, "Naẓariyyat al-Isqāṭ fi'l-Sharī'a al-Islāmiyya," 283; Ibyānī Bek, *Sharḥ al-Aḥkām al-Shar'īyya fi'l-Aḥwāl al-Shakhṣiyya,* 252–69; al-Jazīrī, *al-Fiqh 'alā al-Madhāhib al-Arba'a,* 4:342–66; Wizārat al-Awqāf wa'l-Shu'ūn al-Islāmiyya, *al-Mawsū'a al-Fiqhiyya al-Kuwaytiyya,* 19:234–59.

42. Arabi, "The Dawning of the Third Millennium on Shari'a," 2–21, at 4.

43. Ibid., 2–21, at 5, 8, 20.

44. Muḥammad Muhanna, "Qanūn al-Aḥwāl al-Shakhṣiyya," *Al-Muslim Magazine,* Mar. 2000.

45. Ibid.

46. Marwa Bashīr, "Ḥall Shar'ī wa-Qanūnī lil-Khilāfāt al-Zawjiyya: 'Ulamā' al-Azhar: Qanūn al-Khul' Muṭābiq li'l-Sharī'a al-Islāmiyya," *Al-Ahram Newspaper,* Apr. 10, 2012.

47. "Sijill 105," doc. 56.

48. Abdal-Rahman Abdal-Rehim, "The Family and Gender Laws in Egypt During the Ottoman Period," in *Women, the Family, and Divorce Laws in Islamic History,* ed. Amira El Azhary Sonbol (Syracuse, NY: Syracuse Univ. Press, 1996), 105.

49. Aḥmad and Ḥasan, *Qānūn al-Aḥwāl al-Shakhṣiyya li'l-Muslimīn wa'l-Qarārāt al-Munaffidha li-Aḥkāmih wa-Ba'ḍ Aḥkām al-Maḥkama al-Dustūriyya al-'Ulyā al-Ṣādira bi-Sha'nih,* 24.

50. For a translation of the law, see El Alami, "Law No. 100 of 1985 Amending Certain Provisions of Egypt's Personal Status Laws."

51. Aḥmad and Ḥasan, *Qānūn al-Aḥwāl al-Shakhṣiyya li'l-Muslimīn wa'l-Qarārāt al-Munaffidha li-Aḥkāmih wa-Ba'ḍ Aḥkām al-Maḥkama al-Dustūriyya al-'Ulyā al-Ṣādira bi-Sha'nih*, 11–24.

52. To get an idea of the diversity of views on the matter, let us consider the dominant opinions within the four Sunnī schools, to say nothing of their less dominant views. The Mālikī school gives custody to women until the boy reaches puberty and the girl consummates a marriage. The Shāfi'īs have no specific age for custody and base it completely on the will of the child. The Ḥanbalī dominant view is that the age of female custody is until seven for both girls and boys. For boys, the child is given the choice after seven, but if the judge feels that the choice of the child is not in his interest, he may overrule it. Al-Jazīrī, *al-Fiqh 'alā al-Madhāhib al-Arba'a*, 4:523–25.

53. Islām Naḥrāwī and Lu'ai 'Alī, "Al-Muftī Yata'ahhad bi-I'ādat al-Naẓar fī Qawānīn al-Usra," *al-Yawm al-Sābi' Newspaper*, Apr. 18, 2001, http://www.youm7.com/News.asp?NewsID=393950.

54. Āya Nabīl, "Ba'd Ta'ahhud al-Muftī bi-Taghyīr Qawānīn Suzanne Mubarak Ḥuqūqiyyūn Yarfuḍūna al-Misās bi-Qawānīn al-Usra wa'l-Ṭifl Ḥattā Tashkīl Majlis al-Sha'b," *al-Yawm al-Sābi' Newspaper*, Apr. 20, 2011, http://www.youm7.com/News.asp?NewsID=394822.

55. Al-Jazīrī, *al-Fiqh 'alā al-Madhāhib al-Arba'a*, 4:520–22.

56. Al-Jundī, *Mabādi' al-Qaḍā' al-Shar'ī fī Khamsīna 'Āman*, 666–68.

57. Abū Zahra, *Muḥāḍarāt fi'l-Waqf*, 98–102.

58. Al-Jundī, *Mabādi' al-Qaḍā' al-Shar'ī fī Khamsīna 'Āman*, 212, 219–20.

59. Ibid., 221–22.

60. Ibid., 378.

61. For a discussion of examples of equally valid views within a single school, see Hallaq, *Authority, Continuity, and Change*, 91–93.

62. Al-Jundī, *Mabādi' al-Qaḍā' al-Shar'ī fī Khamsīna 'Āman*, 88–91.

63. Ibid.

64. Ibid., 337–39.

65. Ibid.

66. Aḥmad and Ḥasan, *Qānūn al-Aḥwāl al-Shakhṣiyya li'l-Muslimīn wa'l-Qarārāt al-Munaffidha li-Aḥkāmih wa-Ba'ḍ Aḥkām al-Maḥkama al-Dustūriyya al-'Ulyā al-Ṣādira bi-Sha'nih*, 214–18.

67. Layish, "The Transformation of the Sharī'a from Jurists' Law to Statutory Law in the Contemporary Muslim World," 85–113, at 94; Coulson, *A History of Islamic Law*, 197–201; Bonderman, "Modernization and Changing Perceptions of Islamic Law," 1169–93, at 1177.

68. Coulson, *A History of Islamic Law*, 201.

69. Hallaq, "Can the Shari'a Be Restored?" 24.

70. In addition to his specific critiques of modern Sharī'a, Hallaq has a larger argument about the incompatibility of the nation-state itself with the ethos of Sharī'a. But this critique is not directly linked to pragmatic eclecticism and therefore does not concern us here. Wael

B. Hallaq, *The Impossible State: Islam, Politics, and Modernity's Moral Predicament* (New York: Columbia Univ. Press, 2013); Hallaq, "Can the Shari'a Be Restored?" 24.

71. "Sharī'a" as used by Hallaq consists of *fiqh* (substantive law proper and ritual law), *uṣūl al-fiqh* (legal methodology), and the process of Sharī'a, which subsumes its institutions such as the *waqf* (endowments), its teaching institution the *madrasa*, the court, and the relationship between lawmakers and the state. According to him, the Sharī'a can never be restored and neither can its substantive laws (*fiqh*) because they have been uprooted from their traditional context. He contends that the institutional bearers, namely the *waqf* and *madrasa*, were dismantled by the nation state, thus severing personal status law from its "indigenous jural *system*, its own ecological environment." Hallaq, *Sharī'a*, 446–47; Hallaq, "Can the Shari'a Be Restored?" 42.

72. Hallaq, *Sharī'a*, 447.

73. Al-Subkī, *Fatāwā al-Subkī*, 1:146–48.

74. Hallaq, "Can the Shari'a Be Restored?" 42.

75. Hallaq, *Sharī'a*, 501.

76. Hallaq, "Can the Shari'a Be Restored?" 45.

77. Hallaq, *A History of Islamic Legal Theories*, 214–55; Hallaq, "Can the Shari'a Be Restored?" 45–48.

78. Brown, "*Shari'a* and State in the Modern Muslim Middle East," 359–76, at 359.

79. Ibrahim, "The Codification Episteme."

80. Brown, "*Shari'a* and State in the Modern Muslim Middle East." See also Muḥammad Rashīd Riḍā's reference in *al-Manār* to the silence of the Azharī *'ulamā'* to the proposals put forward by those whom he calls "geographical Muslims": Riḍā, Madaniyyat al-Qawānīn, *al-Manār* 23:539.

81. For a discussion of "liberalists" such as Soroush, 'Ashmāwī, Fazlur Rahman, and Shaḥrūr, see Hallaq, *Sharī'a*, 519–35. For al-Bannā's new jurisprudence, see Jamāl al-Bannā, *Naḥwa Fiqh Jadīd I* (Cairo: Dār al-Fikr al-Islāmī, 1996); al-Bannā, *Naḥwa Fiqh Jadīd II*; al-Bannā, *Naḥwa Fiqh Jadīd III*.

82. For a discussion of the MB's stance on this issue, see Nathan J. Brown and Amr Hamzawy, "The Draft Party Platform of the Egyptian Muslim Brotherhood: Foray into Political Integration or Retreat into Old Positions?" *Carnegie Endowment for International Peace*, Middle East Series, 89 (2008): 5. For Abū al-Futūḥ's view, which he held before he resigned from the MB to run for presidential elections in 2012, see Aḥmad Khaṭīb and Usāma Ṣalāḥ, "Khilāf Jadīd Dākhil Maktab Irshād al-Ikhwān," *al-Masry al-Youm Newspaper*, Nov. 1, 2007, http://today.almasryalyoum.com/article2.aspx?ArticleID=81393.

83. For a discussion of multiple modernities, see Eisenstadt, "Multiple Modernities."

84. Muḥammad 'Abd al-Khāliq, "Shaykh al-Azhar: Al-Salafiyyūn al-Judud Khawārij Najjasū Madhhab al-Ḥanābila," *Al-Ahram Newspaper*, May 11, 2011, http://gate.ahram.org.eg/News/56957.aspx.

85. Al-Azhar, "Naṣṣ Wathīqat al-Azhar Ḥawla Mustaqbal Miṣr," *Onislam*, June 20, 2011, http://www.onislam.net/arabic/newsanalysis/documents-data/131244-2011-06-20-10-01-45.html.

86. Ibid.

87. Ibid.

88. Ṣalāḥ al-Dīn Ḥasan, Muḥammad Kāmil, and Sa'īd Ḥijāzī, "Intihā' Azmat al-Sharī'a: Al-Salafiyyūn Yaqbalūn bi-Naṣṣ al-Māda al-Thāniya fi'l-Dustūr," *al-Watan*, Dec. 7, 2012, http://www.elwatannews.com/news/details/26091.

89. Clark B. Lombardi and Nathan J. Brown, "Do Constitutions Requiring Adherence to Shari'a Threaten Human Rights? How Egypt's Constitutional Court Reconciles Islamic Law with the Liberal Rule of Law," *American University International Law Review* 21:3 (2006): 379–45, especially at 392–434.

90. Al-Azhar, "Naṣṣ Wathīqat al-Azhar Ḥawla Mustaqbal Miṣr."

91. Al-Azhar's document also supports freedom of expression, respect for human rights, and respect for all heavenly religions: a reference to Islam, Christianity, and Judaism. No similar respect is afforded other religious communities in Egypt, despite the reference in the following line to citizenship as the source of responsibility. Ibid.

92. Brown and Hamzawy, "Draft Party Platform of the Egyptian Muslim Brotherhood," 4.

93. Al-Azhar also rejected the call made by some Muslim preachers for the reinstatement of slavery, an institution that was accepted by premodern Muslim legists. See "Majma' al-Buḥūth bi'l-Azhar: Milk al-Yamīn Da'wa li-'Ilāqa Jinsiyya Āthima," *CNNArabic*, June 7, 2012, http://arabic.cnn.com/2012/middle_east/7/6/index.html.

94. Sāra Rashād and Riḥāb Aḥmad, "Aqbāṭ Yuraḥḥibūn bi-Iqtirāḥ al-Azhar fi'l-Ta'sīsiyya wa-Ya'tabirūnahū al-Marji'iyya al-Wasaṭiyya li'l-Miṣriyyīn," *almesryoon*, Cairo, June 7, 2012, http://www.almesryoon.com/permalink/15611.html.

95. Noha El-Hennawy, "SCAF Issued Laws Ahead of Parliament Induction," *Egypt Independent*, Cairo, Jan. 30, 2012, http://www.egyptindependent.com/news/scaf-issued-laws-ahead-parliament-induction; Haytham Sa'd al-Dīn, "Ta'dīlāt Qanūn I'ādat Tanẓīm al-Azhar," *Al-Ahram Newspaper*, Cairo, Jan. 30, 2012, http://gate.ahram.org.eg/News/166452.aspx.

96. El-Hennawy, "SCAF Issued Laws Ahead of Parliament Induction"; Sa'd al-Dīn, "Ta'dīlāt Qanūn I'ādat Tanẓīm al-Azhar."

97. Ibid.

98. This article was removed from the subsequent constitution of 2014, under the Sisi regime.

99. Muḥammad Fatḥī, "Ḥizb al-Nūr: Sa-Nalja' li'l-Dustūriyya li-Ibṭāl Qānūn al-Ṣukūk," *Almesryoon*, Jan. 25, 2013, http://www.almesryoon.com/permalink/112826.html; al-Masry al-Youm, "FJP Leader Criticizes Salafi Nour Party over Sukuk Draft Law," *Egypt*

Independent, Apr. 14, 2013, http://www.egyptindependent.com/news/fjp-leader-criticizes-salafi-nour-party-over-sukuk-draft-law.

100. For a discussion of the complexity of al-Azhar, see Luisa Orelli, "Islam Institutionnel Égyptien et Modernité: Aperçu Du Débat À Travers Les Fatâwâ D'al-Azhar et de Dâr al-Iftâ'," *Studia Islamica*, no. 95 (2002): 109–33, at 110–18.

101. In the case of criminal law, Mehmed Ali issued the first criminal legislation that complemented Sharīʿa rules. See Rudolph Peters, "'For His Correction and as a Deterrent Example for Others'," 164–92.

Conclusion

1. Coulson, A *History of Islamic Law*, 201.

2. Ibid., 201.

3. See also David Bonderman, "Modernization and Changing Perceptions of Islamic Law," *Harvard Law Review* 81:6 (1968): 1177.

4. For a good overview of al-Anṣarī's life, see Matthew B. Ingalls, "Subtle Innovation within Networks of Convention: The Life, Thought, and Intellectual Legacy of Zakariyyā al-Anṣārī (d. 926/1520)" (New Haven: Yale Univ. Press, 2011), 32–121.

5. "Sijill 105," doc. 199.

6. Muḥammad b. Sulaymān al-Madanī al-Shāfiʿī al-Kurdī, *al-Fawāʾid al-Madaniyya fī Bayān Ikhtilāf al-ʿUlamāʾ min al-Shāfiʿiyya* (Diyār Bakr, Turkey: al-Maktaba al-Islāmiyya, n.d.), 14–22, 220.

7. For a discussion of the competition between different generations of authority, see Hallaq, *Authority, Continuity, and Change in Islamic Law*, 24–56, 149–51.

8. Al-Kurdī, *al-Fawāʾid al-Madaniyya fī Bayān Ikhtilāf al-ʿUlamāʾ min al-Shāfiʿiyya*, 232.

9. Nathan Brown, "Shariʿa and State in the Modern Muslim Middle East," 359–76.

Glossary of Key Terms

ḍarūra: Necessity
fatwa, pl. ***fatāwā***: A nonbinding legal opinion issued by a mufti
furū': Substantive law
ḥāja: Need
Ijtihād: The exercise of individual legal reasoning
Ikhtilāf: Juristic disagreement
istibdāl: The exchange and sale of *waqf*
madhhab: Sunnī legal school
mufti: Jurisconsult
mujtahid: A jurist exercising *ijtihād*
muqallid: The jurist exercising *taqlīd*
pragmatic eclecticism: The eclectic utilization of legal pluralism to achieve pragmatic objectives
simple pragmatic eclecticism: see *tatabbu' al-rukhaṣ*
complex pragmatic eclecticism: see *talfīq*
rājiḥ: Preponderant
rukhaṣ: Less stringent opinions
takhayyur: The process of selecting the least stringent juristic opinion
takhrīj: Extrapolation
talfīq: The process of combining two juristic opinions in the same legal transaction
tamadhhub: School loyalty
taqlīd: Legal conformism
tarjīḥ: The exercise of preponderance
tatabbu' al-rukhaṣ: The process of selecting the least stringent juristic opinion
uṣūl al-fiqh: Legal methodology
waqf: Endowment

Bibliography

‘Abd al-‘Aẓīm, Ḥamdī ‘Abd al-Raḥmān. *Taslīṭ al-Aḍwā’ ‘alā mā Waqa‘a fi’l-Jihād min Akhṭā’*. ‘Ābidīn, al-Qāhirah: Maktabat al-Turāth al-Islāmī, 2002.

‘Abd al-Ghanī al-Nābulsī, *al-Ajwiba ‘an al-As’ila al-Sitta*, MS Dār al-Kutub 365 Uṣūl Fiqh, folio 5a-5b, microfilm #16703.

‘Abd al-Khāliq, Muḥammad. “Shaykh al-Azhar: al-Salafiyyūn al-Judud Khawārij Najjasū Madhhab al-Ḥanābila.” *Al-Ahram Newspaper*, May 11, 2011. http://gate.ahram.org.eg/News/56957.aspx.

‘Abd Allāh, Nājiḥ Ibrāhīm, and ‘Alī Muḥammad ‘Alī Sharīf. *Ḥurmat al-Ghulūw fi’l-Dīn wa-Takfīr al-Muslimīn*. Edited by Karam Muḥammad Zuhdī, Usāma Ibrāhīm Ḥāfiẓ, Fu’ād Maḥmūd Dawālībī, Ḥamdī ‘Abd al-Raḥmān ‘Abd al-‘Aẓīm, Muḥammad ‘Iṣām al-Dīn Dirbāla, and ‘Āṣim ‘Abd al-Majīd Muḥammad. Cairo: Maktabat al-Turāth al-Islāmī, 2002.

‘Abd al-Qādir, ‘Abd al-Raḥmān Muḥammad. “Naẓariyyat al-Isqāṭ fi’l-Sharī‘a al-Islāmiyya.” PhD diss., Faculty of Sharī‘a, al-Azhar Univ., 1977.

Abdal-Rehim, Abdal-Rahman. “The Family and Gender Laws in Egypt During the Ottoman Period.” In *Women, the Family, and Divorce Laws in Islamic History*, edited by Amira El Azhary Sonbol. Contemporary Issues in the Middle East. Syracuse, NY: Syracuse Univ. Press, 1996.

‘Abduh, Muḥammad. *Risālat al-Tawḥīd*. Cairo: Dār al-Hilāl, 1980.

Abou El Fadl, Khaled. *The Great Theft: Wrestling Islam from the Extremists*. New York: Harper San Francisco, 2005.

———. “The Ugly Modern and the Modern Ugly: Reclaiming the Beautiful in Islam.” In *Progressive Muslims: On Justice, Gender and Pluralism*, edited by Omid Safi. Oxford, UK: Oneworld, 2003.

Abū Ḥanīfa, al-Nu‘mān b. Thābit. *Sharḥ al-Fiqh al-Akbar*. Edited by ‘Abd Allāh b. Ibrāhīm al-Anṣārī. Hayderabad, India: Majlis Dā’irat al-Ma‘ārif al-Niẓāmiyya, 1903.

Abu-Lughod, Janet L. *Before European Hegemony: The World System A.D. 1250–1350.* New York: Oxford Univ. Press, 1989.

Abū Zahra, Muḥammad. *Muḥāḍarāt fi'l-Waqf.* Cairo: Ma'had al-Dirāsāt al-'Arabiyya al-'Āliya, 1959.

Abul-Magd, Zeinab A. "Empire and Its Discontents: Modernity and Subaltern Revolt in Upper Egypt, 1700–1920." PhD diss., Georgetown Univ., 2008.

Ackermann, Paul. *Dictionnaire Biographique Universel et Pittoresque.* N.p.: Aimé André, 1834.

'Afīfī, Muḥammad. *al-Awqāf wa'l-Ḥayāh al-Iqtiṣādiyya fī Miṣr fi'l-'Aṣr al-'Uthmānī.* Cairo: al-Hay'a al-Miṣriyya al-'Āmma li'l-Kitāb, 1991.

Aḥmad, Fāṭima al-Zahrā' 'Abbās, and Ḥilmī 'Abd al-'Aẓīm Ḥasan. *Qānūn al-Aḥwāl al-Shakhṣiyya li'l-Muslimīn wa'l-Qarārāt al-Munaffidha li-Aḥkāmih wa-Ba'ḍ Aḥkām al-Maḥkama al-Dustūriyya al-'Ulyā al-Ṣādira bi-Sha'nih.* Cairo: al-Maṭābi' al-Amīriyya, 2009.

Al-'Ajmī, Muḥammad b. Nāṣir. *al-Rasā'il al-Mutabādala Bayna Jamāl al-Dīn al-Qāsimī wa-Maḥmūd Shukrī al-Alūsī.* Beirut: Dār al-Bashā'ir al-Islāmiyya, 2001.

Al-Albānī, Muḥammad Nāṣir al-Dīn. *Silsilat al-Aḥādīth al-Ḍa'īfa wa'l-Mawḍū'a wa-Atharihā al-Sayyi' fi'l-Umma.* 14 vols. Riyadh, Saudi Arabia: Maktabat al-Ma'ārif, 1992.

———. *Ma'ālim al-Manhaj al-Salafī fi'l-Taghyīr.* Edited by Salīm b. 'Īd al-Hilālī al-Salafī al-Atharī. Cairo: Dār al-Imām Aḥmad, 2006.

———. *Taḥrīm Ālāt al-Ṭarab aw-al-Radd bi'l-Waḥyayn wa-Aqwāl A'immatinā 'alā Ibn Ḥazm wa-Muqallidīhi al-Mubīḥīna li'l-Ma'āzif wa'l-Ghinā' wa-'alā al-Ṣūfiyyīn Alladhīna Ittakhadhūhu Qurbatan wa-Dīnan.* 2nd ed. al-Jubayl, Saudi Arabia: Maktabat al-Dalīl, 1997.

———. "Al-Taṣfiya wa'l-Tarbiya." *Mawqi' al-Shaykh Muḥammad Nāṣir al-Dīn al-Albānī.* May 22, 2012. http://www.alalbany.net/misc006.php.

'Alī Zādah, Muḥammad b. 'Abd Allāh. "Tuḥfat al-Ḥukkam fī Malja' al-Qaḍā'." Cairo, n.d., MS Dār al-Kutub 446 Fiqh Ḥanafī Ṭal'at, Microfilm #8509.

Allouche, Adel. "The Establishment of Four Chief Judgeships in Fāṭimid Egypt." *Journal of the American Oriental Society* 105:2 (1985): 317–20.

Al-'Asqalānī, Ibn Ḥajar. *Inbā' al-Ghumr bi-Abnā' al-'Umr.* Edited by Ḥasan Ḥabashī. 4 vols. Egypt: Al-Majlis al-A'lā li'l Shu'ūn al-Islāmiyya, 1969.

———. *Fatḥ al-Bārī bi-Sharḥ Ṣaḥīḥ al-Bukhārī.* Hadith No. 6517. Cairo: Maktabat al-Kulliyyāt al-Azhariyya, 1978.

AlSayyad, Nezar. *Cairo: Histories of a City.* Cambridge, MA: Belknap Press of Harvard Univ. Press, 2011.

Amīr Bādshāh, Muḥammad Amīn b. Maḥmūd al-Bukhārī. *Taysīr al-Taḥrīr ʿalā Kitāb al-Taḥrīr*. 4 vols. Cairo: Muṣṭafā al-Bābī al-Ḥalabī, 1834.

Anderson, Norman. "Modern Trends in Islam: Legal Reform and Modernisation in the Middle East." *International and Comparative Law Quarterly* 20:1 (1971): 1–21.

———. "The Shari'a Today." *Journal of Comparative Legislation and International Law* 31:3/4 (1949): 18–25.

———. *Law Reform in the Muslim World*. London: Athlone Press, 1976.

Anonymous. "Risāla Jalīla fi'l-Taqlīd." Cairo, n.d., MS Dār al-Kutub 94 Uṣūl Taymūr.

Arabi, Oussama. "Al-Sanhūrī's Reconstruction of Islamic Law of Contract Defects." *Journal of Islamic Studies* 6:2 (1995): 153–72.

———. "The Dawning of the Third Millennium on Shari'a: Egypt's Law No. 1 of 2000, or Women May Divorce at Will." *Arab Law Quarterly* 16:1 (2001): 2–21.

Ardabīlī, Yūsuf b. Ibrāhīm. *Al-Anwār li-Aʿmāl al-Abrār*. Edited by Khalaf Mufḍī al-Muṭliq and Ḥusayn ʿAbd Allāh al-ʿAllī. 3 vols. Kuwait: Dār al-Ḍiyāʾ, 2006.

Armitage, David and Jo Guldi. *The History Manifesto* (Cambridge, UK: Cambridge Univ. Press, 2014).

Al-Asyūṭī, Shams al-Dīn Muḥammad b. Aḥmad al-Minhājī. *Jawāhir al-ʿUqūd wa-Muʿīn al-Quḍāh wa'l-Muwwaqiʿīn wa'l-Shuhūd*. Edited by Musʿad ʿAbd al-Ḥamīd Muḥammad Saʿdanī. 2 vols. Beirut: Dār al-Kutub al-ʿIlmiyya, 1996.

Atcil, Abdurrahman. "Procedure in the Ottoman Court and the Duties of Kadis." MA thesis, Bilkent Univ., 2002.

Al-ʿAṭṭār, Ḥasan. *Ḥāshiyat al-ʿAṭṭār ʿalā Sharḥ al-Jalāl al-Maḥallī ʿalā Jamʿ al-Jawāmiʿ*. 2 vols. Beirut: Dār al-Kutub al-ʿIlmiyya, n.d.

Al-Azhar. "Naṣṣ Wathīqat al-Azhar Ḥawla Mustaqbal Miṣr." *Onislam*. June 20, 2011. http://www.onislam.net/arabic/newsanalysis/documents-data/131244-2011-06-20-10-01-45.html.

Al-Baghdādī, al-Khaṭīb. *Kitāb al-Faqīh wa'l-Mutafaqqih*. 2 vols. Riyadh, Saudi Arabia: Dār Ibn al-Jawzī, 1996.

Al-Baghdādī, Muḥammad. *Risāla fi'l-Taqlīd*. Cairo, n.d., MS Dār al-Kutub 125 Uṣūl Taymūr, folio 3a-5b, microfilm #23855.

Baker, Raymond William. *Islam without Fear: Egypt and the New Islamists*. Cambridge, MA: Harvard Univ. Press, 2003.

Baldwin, James. "Islamic Law in an Ottoman Context: Resolving Disputes in Late 17th/Early 18th-Century Cairo." PhD diss., New York Univ., 2010.

Balkhī, Niẓām al-Dīn. *Al-Fatāwā al-Hindiyya*. 2nd ed. Beirut: Dār Ṣādir, 1893.

Bälz, Kilian. "Submitting Faith to Judicial Scrutiny through the Family Trial: The Abu Zayd Case." *Die Welt Des Islams*, n.s., 37:2 (1997): 135–55.

Al-Bānī, Muḥammad Saʿīd. *ʿUmdat al-Taḥqīq fi'l-Taqlīd wa'l-Talfīq*. Damascus: Maṭbaʿat Ḥukūmat Dimashq, 1923.

Al-Bannā, Jamāl. *Naḥwa Fiqh Jadīd: al-Sunna wa-Dawruhā fi'l-Fiqh al-Jadīd*. Cairo: Dār al-Fikr al-Islāmī, 1997.

Al-Barbahārī, Abū Muḥammad al-Ḥasan b. ʿAlī b. Khalaf. *Sharḥ al-Sunna*. Edited by ʿAbd al-Raḥmān b. Aḥmad al-Jumayzī. Riyadh, Saudi Arabia: Dār al-Minhāj, 2005.

Barlas, Asma. *Believing Women in Islam: Unreading Patriarchal Interpretations of the Qur'an*. Austin: Univ. of Texas Press, 2002.

Bashīr, Marwa. "Ḥall Sharʿī wa-Qanūnī li'l-Khilāfāt al-Zawjiyya: ʿUlamā' al-Azhar: Qanūn al-Khulʿ Muṭābiq li'l-Sharīʿa al-Islāmiyya." *Al-Ahram Newspaper*, Apr. 10, 2012.

Baṣrī, Hilāl b. Yaḥyā b. Muslim. *Kitāb Aḥkām al-Waqf*. Hyderabad: Majlis Dā'irat al-Maʿārif al-ʿUthmāniyya, 1936.

Al-Bayhaqī, Abū Bakr Aḥmad b. al-Ḥusayn b. ʿAlī. *Al-Sunan al-Kubrā*. Edited by Muḥammad ʿAbd al-Qādir ʿAtā. 3rd ed. 11 vols. Beirut: Dār al-Kutub al-ʿIlmiyya, 2003.

Al-Bazzāzī, Muḥammad b. Shihāb b. Yūsuf al-Kurdarī. "Al-Fatāwā al-Bazzāziyya." Cairo, n.d., MS Dār al-Kutub Fiqh Ḥanafī Khalīl Aghā 66.

Bonderman, David. "Modernization and Changing Perceptions of Islamic Law." *Harvard Law Review* 81:6 (Apr. 1968): 1169–93.

Bosworth, Clifford Edmund. *The New Islamic Dynasties: A Chronological and Genealogical Manual*. New York: Columbia Univ. Press, 1996.

Braudel, Fernand. "Histoire et Sciences Sociales: La Longue Durée." *Réseaux* 5:27 (1987).

Brown, Jonathan A. C. "Critical Rigor vs. Juridical Pragmatism: How Legal Theorists and Ḥadīth Scholars Approached the Backgrowth of *Isnād*s in the Genre of *ʿIlal al-Ḥadīth*." *Islamic Law and Society* 14:1 (2007).

———. "How We Know Early Ḥadīth Critics Did *Matn* Criticism and Why It's So Hard to Find." *Islamic Law and Society* 15 (2008): 143–84.

Brown, Nathan J. "*Shariʿa* and State in the Modern Muslim Middle East." *International Journal of Middle East Studies* 29:3 (1997): 359–76.

———. *The Rule of Law in the Arab World: Courts in Egypt and the Gulf*. Cambridge, UK: Cambridge Univ. Press, 1997.

Brown, Nathan J., and Amr Hamzawy. "The Draft Party Platform of the Egyptian Muslim Brotherhood: Foray into Political Integration or Retreat into Old

Positions?" Middle East Series 89, 1–24. Washington, DC: Carnegie Endowment for International Peace, 2008.

Bulliet, Richard W. *The Patricians of Nishapur: A Study in Medieval Islamic Social History*. Cambridge, MA: Harvard Univ. Press, 1972.

Cabrillac, Rémy. *Les codifications*. Paris: Presses Universitaires de France, 2002.

Calder, Norman. "Al-Nawawī's Typology of *Muftīs* and Its Significance for a General Theory of Islamic Law." *Islamic Law and Society* 3:2 (1996): 137–64.

Carr, Sarah. "In Platforms, Presidential Candidates Reassure on Rights and Liberties." *Egypt Independent*, May 20, 2013. http://www.egyptindependent.com/news/platforms-presidential-candidates-reassure-rights-and-liberties.

Carra, Jean-Louis. *Systeme de la Raison: ou le Prophete philosophe*. London: Kearby, 1782.

Cook, Michael. *Studies in Origins of Early Islamic Culture and Tradition*. Aldershot, UK: Ashgate/Variorum, 2004.

Cotter, Thomas F. "Legal Pragmatism and Intellectual Property Law." In *Intellectual Property and the Common Law*, ed. Shyamkrishna Balganesh, 213–16. Cambridge, UK: Cambridge Univ. Press, 2013.

———. "Legal Pragmatism and the Law and Economics Movement." *Georgetown Law Journal* 84:6 (1996): 2071–2142.

Coulson, Noel J. *A History of Islamic Law*. Edinburgh: Edinburgh Univ. Press, 1962.

———. "Muslim Custom and Case-Law." *Die Welt Des Islams* 6:1–2 (1959): 13–24.

Crecelius, Daniel. "Incidences of *Waqf* Cases in Three Cairo Courts: 1640–1802." *Journal of the Economic and Social History of the Orient* 29:2 (1986): 176–89.

———. *The Roots of Modern Egypt: A Study of the Regimes of ʿAli Bey al-Kabir and Muhammad Bey Abu al-Dhahab, 1760–1775*. Minneapolis: Bibliotheca Islamica, 1981.

———. "The Waqf of Muhammad Bey Abu al-Dhahab in Historical Perspective." *International Journal of Middle East Studies* 23:1 (1991): 57–81.

Cromer, Evelyn Baring. *Modern Egypt*. London: Macmillan, 1908.

Al-Dhahabī, al-Ḥāfiẓ. *Siyar Aʿlām al-Nubalāʾ*, 7:125. Beirut: Muʾassasat al-Risāla, 1988.

Dainow, Joseph. "The Civil Law and the Common Law: Some Points of Comparison." *American Journal of Comparative Law* 15:3 (1966): 419–35.

Dallal, Ahmad. "The Origins and Objectives of Islamic Revivalist Thought, 1750–1850." *Journal of the American Oriental Society* 113:3 (1993): 341–59.

Al-Damīrī, Aḥmad b. Aḥmad. *Quḍāt Miṣr*. Edited by ʿAbd al-Rāziq ʿAbd al-Rāziq ʿĪsā and Yūsuf Muṣṭafā Maḥmūdī. Cairo: Al-ʿArabī li'l-Nashr, 2000.

Al-Dasūqī, Shams al-Dīn Muḥammad b. 'Arafa. *Ḥāshiyat al-Dasūqī 'alā al-Sharḥ al-Kabīr*. 4 vols. Cairo: Dār Iḥyā' al-Kutub al-'Arabiyya, 1984.

Al-Dayrabī, Abū al-'Abbās Aḥmad b.'Umar. *Ghāyat al-Maqṣūd li-Man Yata'āṭā al-'Uqūd 'alā al-Madhāhib al-Arba'a*. 2nd ed. Cairo: Maktabat Muṣṭafā al-Bābī al-Ḥalabī, 1956.

Dedek, Helge. "The Splendour of Form: Scholastic Jurisprudence and 'Irrational Formality.'" *Law and Humanities* 5:2 (2011): 349–83.

Denoix, Sylvie. "Pour Une Exploitation d'Ensemble D'un Corpus: Les Waqfs Mamelouks Du Caire." In *Le Waqf Dans l'Espace Islamique: Outil de Pouvoir Socio-Politique*, edited by Randi Deguilhem. Damascus: Institut Français de Damas, 1995.

Dewey, John. "Logical Method and Law." *Philosophical Review* 33:6 (1924): 26.

Al-Dimashqī, 'Abd al-Raḥmān. *Raḥmat al-Umma fī Ikhtilāf al-A'imma*. 2 vols. Cairo: al-Maṭābi' al-Amīriyya, 1900.

Al-Dimyāṭī, Abū Bakr b. al-Sayyid Muḥammad Shaṭā. *I'ānat al-Ṭālibīn 'alā Fatḥ al-Mu'īn bi-Sharḥ Qurrat al-'Ayn*. 5th ed. 4 vols. Cairo: al-Maṭba'a al-Maymaniyya, n.d.

Dīnarī, Maḥmūd, Muḥammad 'Anānī, and Ḥusayn Bayyūmī. *Mudhakkira bi'l-Radd 'alā Mashrū' al-Qānūn al-Khāṣṣ bi-Ba'ḍ Aḥkām al-Aḥwāl al-Shakhṣiyya*. Cairo: Maṭba'at al-Taḍāmun al-Akhawī, 1929.

Dutton, Yasin. "The Introduction to Ibn Rushd's *Bidāyat al-Mujtahid*." *Islamic Law and Society* 1:2 (1994): 188–205.

Dworkin, Ronald. *Law's Empire*. Cambridge, MA: Belknap Press, 1986.

Eisenstadt, S. N. "Multiple Modernities." *Daedalus* 129:1 (2000): 1–29.

El Alami, Dawoud S. "Law No. 100 of 1985 Amending Certain Provisions of Egypt's Personal Status Laws." *Islamic Law and Society* 1:1 (Jan. 1994): 116–36.

El Sanhoori, Mohammad Ahmad Farag. "Eclecticism in Rules of Rites." In *The First Conference of the Academy of Islamic Research*, 57–70. Cairo: Al-Azhar Academy of Islamic Research, 1964.

El Shamsy, Ahmed. *The Canonization of Islamic Law: A Social and Intellectual History*. Cambridge, UK: Cambridge Univ. Press, 2013.

———. "The *Ḥāshiya* in Islamic Law: A Sketch of the Shāfi'ī Literature." *Oriens* 41:3–4 (2013): 289–315.

Elbaroudy, Ehab. "Al-Ḥuwaynī wa-Niẓām al-Jawārī wa'l-Sabāya Huwa al-Ḥall." *Masrawy*, May 23, 2011.

El-Hennawy, Noha. "Islamist Presidential Candidate Declares Conversion Permissible." *Al-Masry Al-Youm Newspaper*, May 16, 2011. http://www.egyptin

dependent.com/news/islamist-presidential-candidate-declares-conversion-permissible.

Ener, Mine. "Prohibitions on Begging and Loitering in Nineteenth-Century Egypt." *Die Welt Des Islams*, 39:3 (1999): 319–39.

Escovitz, Joseph H. "The Establishment of Four Chief Judgeships in the Mamlūk Empire." *Journal of the American Oriental Society* 102:3 (1982): 529–31.

Esposito, John L. *Women in Muslim Family Law*. 2nd ed. Contemporary Issues in the Middle East. Syracuse, NY: Syracuse Univ. Press, 2001.

Fadel, Mohammad. "The Social Logic of *Taqlīd* and the Rise of the *Mukhtaṣar*." *Islamic Law and Society* 3:2 (1996): 193–233.

Fahmy, Khaled. *All the Pasha's Men: Mehmed Ali, His Army, and the Making of Modern Egypt*. Cairo: American Univ. in Cairo Press, 2002.

Al-Fāraskūrī, ʿUmar Muḥammad. "Kitāb al-Bahja al-Muraṣṣaʿa bi-Durar Yanābīʿ Ikhtilāf al-A'imma al-Arbaʿa." Cairo, n.d., MS Dār al-Kutub 66 Fiqh Madhāhib ʿArabī.

Farber, Daniel A. "The Inevitability of Practical Reason: Statutes, Formalism, and the Rule of Law." *Vanderbilt Law Review* 45 (1992): 533–34.

———. "Legal Pragmatism and the Constitution." *Minnesota Law Review* 72 (1987–88).

Fatḥī, Muḥammad. "Ḥizb al-Nūr: Sa-Nalja' li'l-Dustūriyya li-Ibṭāl Qānūn al-Ṣukūk." *Almesryoon*, Jan. 25, 2013. http://www.almesryoon.com/permalink/112826.html.

Fazārī, Tāj al-Dīn, and Abū al-Maʿālī Juwaynī. *Sharḥ al-Waraqāt Li Imām al-Ḥaramayn al-Juwaynī*. Edited by Sāra Shāfī Ḥājirī. Beirut: Dār al-Bashā'ir al-Islāmiyya, 2001.

Feldman, Noah. *The Fall and Rise of the Islamic State*. Princeton, NJ: Princeton Univ. Press, 2008.

Fierro, Maribel. "Ill-Treated Women Seeking Divorce: The Qur'anic Two Arbiters and Judicial Practice Among the Mālikīs in al-Andalus and North Africa." In *Dispensing Justice in Islam: Qadis and Their Judgments*, edited by Muhammad Khalid Masud, Rudolph Peters, and David Stephan Powers. Leiden: Brill, 2006.

———. "The Legal Policies of Almohad Caliphs and Ibn Rushd's *Bidāyat al-Mujtahid*." *Journal of Islamic Studies* 10:3 (1999): 226–48.

Al-Fiqhī, Muḥammad. "Risāla fīmā Yataʿallaq bi-Aḥwāl al-Muftī." Cairo, n.d., MS Dār al-Kutub 198 Uṣūl Fiqh.

Fischel, Walter J. "The Spice Trade in Mamluk Egypt." In *Spices in the Indian Ocean World*, edited by M. N. Pearson. Aldershot, UK: Variorum, 1996.

Fishnī, Aḥmad b. Ḥijāzī b. Budayr Shihāb al-Dīn. "Kifāyat al-Mustafīd fī-Aḥkām al-Taqlīd." Cairo, n.d., MS Dār al-Kutub 367 Uṣūl Fiqh.

Flacon-Rochelle, Joseph-Henri. *Code Civil des Français Mis en Vers avec le Texte en Regard*. Paris: Theodore le Clerc, 1805.

Fleischer, Cornell H. "The Lawgiver as Messiah: The Making of the Imperial Image in the Reign of Süleymân." In *Soliman Le Magnifique et Son Temps*, 159–77. Paris: Ecole du Louvre, 1992.

Gardet, Louis. "'Ilm Al-Kalām." In *Encyclopaedia of Islam*, edited by Peri Bearman, Th. Bianquis, C. E. Bosworth, E. Van Donzel, and W. P. Heinrichs. Leiden: Brill, 2008.

Gerber, Haim. *Islamic Law and Culture, 1600–1840*. Leiden: Brill, 1999.

———. *State, Society, and Law in Islam: Ottoman Law in Comparative Perspective*. Albany: State Univ. of New York Press, 1994.

Al-Ghannūshī, Rāshid. *al-Ḥaraka al-Islāmiyya wa-Mas'alat al-Taghyīr*. London: al-Markaz al-Maghāribī li'l-Buḥūth wa'l-Tarjama, 2000.

———. *Al-Ḥurriyyāt al-'Āmma fi'l-Dawla al-Islāmiyya*. Beirut: Markaz Dirāsāt al-Wiḥdah al-'Arabiyya, 1993.

Al-Ghazālī, Abū Ḥāmid. *Al-Mankhūl min Ta'līqāt al-Uṣūl*. Edited by Muḥammad Ḥasan Haytū. 2nd ed. Damascus: Dār al-Fikr, 1980.

———. *al-Mustaṣfā min 'Ilm al-Uṣūl*. Edited by Ḥamza b. Zuhayr Ḥāfiẓ, 4 vols. Medina: Sharikat al-Madīna al-Munawwara li'l-Ṭibā'a, 1992.

———. *al-Wasīṭ fi'l-Madhhab*, ed. Muḥammad Muḥammad Tāmir, 7:289–91. Cairo: Dār al-Salām, 1997.

Gleave, Robert. *Scripturalist Islam: The History and Doctrines of the Akhbārī Shī'ī School*. Leiden: Brill, 2007.

Glenn, H. Patrick. *Legal Traditions of the World: Sustainable Diversity in Law*. Oxford, UK: Oxford Univ. Press, 2000.

———. *On Common Laws*. Oxford, UK: Oxford Univ. Press, 2005.

Gran, Peter. *Islamic Roots of Capitalism: Egypt, 1760–1840*. Syracuse, NY: Syracuse Univ. Press, 1998.

———. "'Passive Revolution' as a Possible Model for Nineteenth-Century Egyptian History." In *Money, Land and Trade: An Economic History of the Muslim Mediterranean*, edited by Nelly Hanna. London: I. B. Tauris, 2002.

Griffiths, John. Preface to *Legal Pluralism in the Arab World*, edited by Baudouin Dupret, Maurits Berger, and Laila al-Zwaini. The Hague: Kluwer Law International, 1999.

Gutas, Dimitri. *Greek Thought, Arabic Culture the Graeco-Arabic Translation Movement in Baghdad and Early 'Abbāsid Society (2nd–4th/8th–10th Centuries).* London: Routledge, 1998.

Al-Hājj, Ibn Amīr. *Al-Taqrīr wa'l-Taḥbīr.* 2nd ed. Beirut: Dār al-Kutub al-'Ilmiyya, 1983.

Hallaq, Wael B. "Groundwork of the Moral Law: A New Look at the Qur'ān and the Genesis of Sharī'a." *Islamic Law and Society* 16:3/4 (2009): 239–79.

———. *A History of Islamic Legal Theories: An Introduction to Sunnī Uṣūl al-Fiqh.* Cambridge, UK: Cambridge Univ. Press, 1997.

———. *Authority, Continuity, and Change in Islamic Law.* Cambridge, UK: Cambridge Univ. Press, 2001.

———. "Can the Shari'a Be Restored?" In *Islamic Law and the Challenges of Modernity*, edited by Yvonne Yazbeck Haddad and Barbara Freyer Stowasser, 21–53. Walnut Creek, CA: AltaMira Press, 2004.

———. "From *Fatwās* to *Furū'*: Growth and Change in Islamic Substantive Law." *Islamic Law and Society* 1:1 (1994): 29–65.

———. "Juristic Authority vs. State Power: The Legal Crises of Modern Islam." In *Islamic Law*, edited by Gavin N. Picken. Critical Concepts in Islamic Studies. London: Routledge, 2011.

———. "*Qāḍīs* Communicating: Legal Change and the Law of Documentary Evidence." *Al-Qanṭara* 20 (1999): 437–66.

———. *Sharī'a: Theory, Practice, Transformations.* Cambridge, UK: Cambridge Univ. Press, 2009.

———. *The Impossible State: Islam, Politics, and Modernity's Moral Predicament.* New York: Columbia Univ. Press, 2013.

———. *The Origins and Evolution of Islamic Law.* Cambridge, UK: Cambridge Univ. Press, 2005.

———. "Was the Gate of *Ijtihād* Closed?" *International Journal of Middle East Studies* 16:1 (1984): 3–41.

———. "Was al-Shāfi'ī the Master Architect of Islamic Jurisprudence?" *International Journal of Middle East Studies* 25:4 (1993): 587–605.

Hallaq, Wael B., and Aharon Layish. "Talfīḳ." In *Encyclopaedia of Islam*, edited by Peri Bearman, Th. Bianquis, C. E. Bosworth, E. Van Donzel, and W. P. Heinrichs. Leiden: Brill, 2008.

Al-Ḥamawī, Aḥmad b. Muḥammad. "Al-Durr al-Farīd fī Bayān Ḥukm al-Taqlīd." Cairo, n.d., MS Dār al-Kutub 569 Uṣūl Taymūr.

Ḥamzāwī, Ḥasan al-'Idwī. *Tabṣirat al-Quḍāh wa'l-Ikhwān.* Cairo: Dār al-Ṭibā'a al-Mīriyya al-Miṣriyya, 1859.

Hanna, Nelly. "Guild Waqf: Between Religious Law and Common Law." In *Held in Trust: Waqf in the Islamic World*, edited by Pascale Ghazaleh. Cairo: American Univ. in Cairo Press, 2011.

———. *Habiter au Caire: la maison moyenne et ses habitants aux XVIIe et XVIIIe Siècles.* Cairo: Institut français d'archéologie orientale du Caire, 1991.

———. "The Administration of Courts in Ottoman Cairo." In *The State and Its Servants: Administration in Egypt from Ottoman Times to the Present*, edited by Nelly Hanna. Cairo: American Univ. in Cairo Press, 1995.

———. *The State and Its Servants: Administration in Egypt from Ottoman Times to the Present*. Cairo: American Univ. in Cairo Press, 1995.

Harris, Lee. *The Next American Civil War: The Populist Revolt against the Liberal Elite.* New York: Palgrave Macmillan, 2010.

Harris, Leslie J. "The Court, Child Custody, and Social Change: The Rhetorical Role of Precedent in a 19th Century Child Custody Decision." *Rhetoric Society Quarterly* 34:1 (2004): 29–45.

Hart, H. L. A. *The Concept of Law.* Oxford: Clarendon Press, 1961.

Hashemi, Nader. *Islam, Secularism, and Liberal Democracy: Toward a Democratic Theory for Muslim Societies.* Oxford, UK: Oxford Univ. Press, 2009.

Ḥasan, Ṣalāḥ al-Dīn, Muḥammad Kāmil, and Sa'īd Ḥijāzī. "Intihā' Azmat al-Sharī'a: Al-Salafiyyūn Yaqbalūn bi-Naṣṣ al-Māda al-Thāniya fi'l-Dustūr." *Al-Watan*, Dec. 7, 2012.

Hāshimī, Muḥammad Munīb. "Al-Qawl al-Sadīd fī Aḥkām al-Taqlīd." Cairo, n.d., MS Dār al-Kutub 197 Uṣūl Taymūr.

Hathaway, Jane. *The Politics of Households in Ottoman Egypt: The Rise of the Qazdağlis.* New York: Cambridge Univ. Press, 1997.

Haykel, Bernard. "On the Nature of Salafi Thought and Action." In *Global Salafism: Islam's New Religious Movement*, edited by Roel Meijer. New York: Columbia Univ. Press, 2009.

Al-Haytamī, b. Ḥajar. *Al-Fatāwā al-Kubrā al-Fiqhiyya.* 4 vols. Cairo: Multazim al-Ṭab' wa'l-Nashr 'Abd al-Ḥamīd Aḥmad Ḥanafī, 1938.

Ḥifnāwī, Muḥammad Ibrāhīm. *Tabṣīr al-Nujabā' bi-Ḥaqīqat al-Ijtihād wa'l-Taqlīd wa'l-Talfīq wa'l-Iftā'.* Cairo: Dār al-Ḥadīth, 1995.

Hill, Enid. "Islamic Law as a Source for the Development of a Comparative Jurisprudence: Theory and Practice in the Life and Work of Sanhūrī." In *Islamic Law: Social and Historical Contexts*, edited by 'Azīz 'Aẓmah. London: Routledge, 1988.

Hirschler, Konrad. *The Written Word in the Medieval Arabic Lands: A Social and Cultural History of Reading Practices.* Edinburgh: Edinburgh Univ. Press, 2012.

Hodgson, Marshall G. S. *The Venture of Islam: Conscience and History in a World Civilization*. 3 vols. Chicago: Univ. of Chicago Press, 1974.

Hookway, Christopher. *The Pragmatic Maxim: Essays on Peirce and Pragmatism*. Oxford: Oxford Univ. Press, 2012.

Hourani, Albert. *Arabic Thought in the Liberal Age, 1798–1939*. Cambridge, UK: Cambridge Univ. Press, 1983.

Hudson, Leila. "Reading al-Sha'rānī: The Sufi Genealogy of Islamic Modernism in Late Ottoman Damascus." *Journal of Islamic Studies* 15:1 (2004): 39–68.

Hurvitz, Nimrod. *The Formation of Hanbalism: Piety into Power* (London: RoutledgeCurzon, 2002).

Ḥusaynī, Aḥmad. "Al-Qawl al-Sadīd fī Ḥukm al-Ijtihād wa'l-Taqlīd." Cairo, n.d., MS Dār al-Kutub 507 Uṣūl Fiqh.

Ibn 'Abd al-Barr, Yūsuf. *Jāmi' Bayān al-'Ilm Wa-Faḍlih*. 2 vols. Cairo: Idārat al-Ṭibā'a al-Munīriyya, n.d.

Ibn 'Abd al-Raḥīm, Ashraf. *Jināyat al-Shaykh Muḥammad al-Ghazālī 'alā al-Ḥadīth wa-Ahlih: Ma'a Mulḥaq li'l-Radd 'alā mā Jā'a min Rudūd wa-Ta'qībāt bi'l-Ṭab'ah al-Sādisah li-Kitāb al-Sunnah al-Nabawiyya*. Silsilat al-Difā' 'an al-Sunnah. Al-Ismā'īliyya, Egypt: Maktabat al-Imām al-Bukhārī, 1989.

Ibn 'Abd al-Salām, 'Izz al-Dīn. *Al-Qawā'id al-Kubrā: Qawā'id al-Aḥkām fī Iṣlāḥ al-Anām*. Edited by Nazīh Kamāl Ḥammād and 'Uthmān Jum'a Ḍamīriyya. 2 vols. Damascus: Dār al-Qalam, 2000.

———. *Kitāb al-Fatāwā*. Edited by 'Abd al-Raḥmān b. 'Abd al-Fattāḥ. Beirut: Dār al-Ma'rifa, 1986.

Ibn 'Ābidīn, Muḥammad Amīn b. 'Umar. *Sharḥ al-Manẓūma al-Musammāh bi-'Uqūd Rasm al-Muftī*. 2nd ed. Hayderabad, India: Markaz Taw'iyat al-Fiqh al-Islāmī, 2000.

———. *Radd al-Muḥtār 'alā al-Durr al-Mukhtār*. Beirut: Dār al-Kutub al-'Ilmiyya, 2003.

Ibn al-Muqaffa', 'Abd Allāh. *Risāla fi'l-Ṣaḥāba*. Beirut: Dār al-Kutub al-'Ilmiyya, 1989.

Ibn al-Najjār, Taqī al-Dīn Muḥammad b. Aḥmad al-Futūḥī. *Muntahā al-Irādāt fī Jam' al-Muqni' ma'a al-Tanqīḥ wa-Ziyādāt*. Edited by 'Abd Allāh Ibn 'Abd al-Muḥsin Turkī. 5 vols. Beirut: Mu'assasat al-Risāla, 1999.

Ibn 'Arabī, Muḥyī al-Dīn. *Al-Futūḥāt al-Makkiyya*. 4 vols. Cairo: Dār al-Kutub al-'Arabiyya, n.d.

Ibn Bīrī, Ibrāhīm b. Ḥusayn b. Aḥmad b. Muḥammad b. Aḥmad. "Al-Kashf wa'l-Tadqīq li-Sharḥ Ghāyat al-Taḥqīq." Cairo, n.d., MS Dār al-Kutub 403 Uṣūl Fiqh.

Ibn Ḥanbal, Aḥmad. *Masā'il al-Imām Aḥmad Ibn Ḥanbal Riwāyatu Ibnihi 'Abd Allāh Ibn Aḥmad*. Edited by Zuhayr al-Shāwīsh. Beirut: al-Maktab al-Islāmī, 1981.

———. *Sharḥ Uṣūl al-Sunna li-Aḥmad Ibn Ḥanbal*. Edited by 'Abd Allāh b. 'Abd al-Raḥmān Jabrayn and 'Alī b. Ḥusayn Ibn Lawz. Riyadh, Saudi Arabia: Dār al-Musayyir, 1999.

Ibn Ḥazm, Abū Muḥammad 'Alī b. Aḥmad b. Sa'īd. *Al-Muḥallā*. Edited by Muḥammad Munīr Dimashqī. 11 vols. Cairo: Idārat al-Ṭibā'a al-Munīriyya, 1933.

———. *Marātib al-Ijmā' fi'l-'Ibādāt wa'l- Mu'āmalāt wa'l-I'tiqādāt*. 3rd ed. Beirut: Dār al-Āfāq al-Jadīda, 1982.

———. *al-Iḥkām fī Uṣūl al-Aḥkām*. Cairo: Maṭba'at 'Āṭif, 1978.

———. *Rasā'il Ibn Ḥazm al-Andalusī*, ed. Iḥsān 'Abbās, 2nd ed. Beirut: al-Mu'assasa al-Arabiyya li'l-Dirāsāt wa'l-Nashr, 1987.

Ibn Hubayra, Yaḥyā al-Zaḥlī. "Ma'īn al-Umma 'alā Ma'rifat al-Wifāq wa'l-Khilāf Bayna al-A'imma." Cairo, n.d., MS Dār al-Kutub Fiqh Madhāhib Ṭal'at 51.

Ibn Ibrāhīm, Nūr al-Dīn 'Alī. "Mabāhij al-Umma fī Manāhij al-A'imma al-Arba'a." Cairo, n.d., MS Dār al-Kutub 63 Fiqh Madhāhib Ṭal'at.

Ibn Iyās, Muḥammad b. Aḥmad. *Badā'i' al-Zuhūr fī Waqā'i' al-Duhūr*. Edited by Muḥammad Muṣṭafā. 5 vols. Mecca: Maktabat Dār al-Bāz, 1984.

Ibn Manẓūr *Lisān al-'Arab*. Accessed Aug. 31, 2010. http://www.baheth.info/web/all.jsp?select=all&search=%D8%B5%D9%8E%D9%81%D9%8E%D9%82%D9%8E#12.

Ibn Mufliḥ al-Maqdisī, Shams al-Dīn Muḥammad. *Al-Mubdi' Sharḥ al-Muqni'*. Edited by Muḥammad Ḥasan Muḥammad Ḥasan Ismā'īl al-Shāfi'ī. 8 vols. Beirut: Dār al-Kutub al-'Ilmiyya, 1997.

Ibn Nujaym, Zayn al-Dīn. *Fatāwā Ibn Nujaym al-Ḥanafī*. Cairo: al-Maṭba'a al-Amīriyya, 1903.

Ibn Taymiyya, Taqī al-Dīn. *Al-Ikhtiyārāt al-Fiqhiyya min Fatāwā Shaykh al-Islām Ibn Taymiyya*. Edited by Muḥammad Ḥāmid al-Fiqī. Cairo: Maṭba'at al-Sunnah al-Muḥammadiyya, n.d.

———. *Kitāb Bayān al-Dalīl 'alā Buṭlān al-Taḥlīl*. Edited by Ḥamdī 'Abd al-Majīd al-Salafī. Beirut: al-Maktab al-Islāmī, 1988.

———. *Mukhtaṣar al-Fatāwā al-Miṣriyya*. Edited by 'Abd al-Majīd Salīm. Beirut: Dār al-Kutub al-'Ilmiyya, 1949.

Ibrahim, Ahmed Fekry. *Child Custody in Islamic Law: The Best Interests of the Child in Theory and Practice*. Under review.

——. "The Codification Episteme in Islamic Juristic Discourse between Inertia and Change." *Islamic Law and Society*, forthcoming.

———. "Jamāl al-Bannā's New Jurisprudence and Post-Mubarak Egypt." *Encounters.* Forthcoming.

———. "Personal Conviction versus *Madhhab* Interpretation: A Fourteenth-Century Court Ruling." Under review.

———. "Rethinking the *Taqlīd-Ijtihād* Dichotomy: A Conceptual-Historical Approach." Under review.

———. "Review of Timur Kuran, The Long Divergence: How Islamic Law Held Back the Middle East." *New Middle Eastern Studies* 1:1 (2011). <http://www.brismes.ac.uk/nmes/archives/XXX>.

———. "School Boundaries and Social Utility in Islamic Law: The Theory and Practice of *Talfīq* and *Tatabbu' al-Rukhaṣ* in Egypt." PhD diss., Georgetown Univ., 2011.

———. "Al-Sha'rānī's Response to Legal Purism: A Theory of Legal Pluralism." *Islamic Law and Society* 20:1–2 (2013): 110–40.

Ibyānī Bek, Muḥammad Zayn. *Sharḥ al-Aḥkām al-Shar'iyya fi'l-Aḥwāl al-Shakhṣiyya.* Cairo: Maṭba'at al-Nahḍa, 1919.

Imber, Colin. *Ebu's-Su'ud: The Islamic Legal Tradition.* Redwood City: Stanford Univ. Press, 1997.

İnalcık, Halil, and Donald Quataert. *An Economic and Social History of the Ottoman Empire, 1300–1914.* 2 vols. Cambridge, UK: Cambridge Univ. Press, 1994.

Ingalls, Matthew B. "Subtle Innovation within Networks of Convention: The Life, Thought, and Intellectual Legacy of Zakariyyā al-Anṣārī (d. 926/1520)." PhD diss., Yale Univ., 2011.

'Īsā, 'Abd al-Rāziq Ibrāhīm. *Tārīkh al-Qaḍā' fī Miṣr al-'Uthmāniyya 1798–1517.* Cairo: al-Hay'a al-Miṣriyya al-'Āmma li'l-Kitāb, 1998.

Al-Iṣfahānī, Shams al-Dīn. *Bayān al-Mukhtaṣar Sharḥ Mukhtaṣar Ibn al-Ḥājib.* Edited by Muḥammad Maẓhar Baqā. 3 vols. Jeddah: Dār al-Madanī, 1986.

Jackson, Roy. *Fifty Key Figures in Islam.* London: Routledge, 2006.

Jackson, Sherman A. *Islamic Law and the State: The Constitutional Jurisprudence of Shihāb al-Dīn al-Qarāfī.* Leiden: Brill, 1996.

———. "*Taqlīd*, Legal Scaffolding and the Scope of Legal Injunctions in Post-Formative Theory: *Muṭlaq* and *'Āmm* in the Jurisprudence of Shihāb al-Dīn al-Qarāfī." *Islamic Law and Society* 3:2 (1996): 165–92.

Al-Jawziyya, Ibn Qayyim. *Al-Ṣawā'iq al-Mursala 'alā al-Jahmiyya wa'l-Mu'aṭṭila.* Edited by Sayyid Ibrāhīm. Cairo: Dār al-Ḥadīth, 1992.

———. *I'lām al-Muwaqqi'īn 'an Rabb al-'Ālamīn.* Edited by Abū 'Ubayda Mashhūr b. Ḥasan Āl Salmān and Abū 'Umar Aḥmad 'Abd Allāh Aḥmad. 7 vols. Riyadh, Saudi Arabia: Dār Ibn al-Jawzī, 2002.

Al-Jazīrī, ʿAbd al-Raḥmān. *Al-Fiqh ʿalā al-Madhāhib al-Arbaʿa*. 2nd ed. 5 vols. Beirut: Dār al-Kutub al-ʿIlmiyya, 2003.

Johansen, Baber. "Le Jugement Comme Preuve. Preuve Juridique et Vérité Religieuse Dans Le Droit Islamique Hanéfite." *Studia Islamica* 72 (1990): 5–17.

———. "The Constitution and the Principles of Islamic Normativity Against the Rules of Fiqh: A Judgement of the Supreme Constitutional Court of Egypt." In *Dispensing Justice in Islam: Qadis and Their Judgments*, edited by Muhammad Khalid Masud, Rudolph Peters, and David Stephan Powers. Leiden: Brill, 2006.

———. *The Islamic Law on Land Tax and Rent: The Peasants' Loss of Property Rights as Interpreted in the Hanafite Legal Literature of the Mamluk and Ottoman Periods*. London: Croom Helm, 1988.

———. "The Valorization of the Human Body in Muslim Sunni Law." In *Law and Society in Islam*, edited by Devin J. Stewart, Baber Johansen, and Amy Singer. Princeton, NJ: Markus Wiener Publishers, 1996.

Al-Jundī, Aḥmad Naṣr. *Mabādi' al-Qaḍā' al-Sharʿī fī Khamsīna ʿĀman*. Cairo: Dār al-Fikr al-ʿArabī, 1978.

Al-Juwaynī, Abū al-Maʿālī ʿAbd al-Malik. *Al-Burhān fī Uṣūl al-Fiqh*. Edited by ʿAbd al-ʿAẓīm al-Dīb. 2 vols. Doha, Qatar: N.p., 1978.

———. *Maghīth al-Khalq fī Tarjīḥ al-Qawl al-Ḥaqq*. Cairo: al-Maṭbaʿa al-Miṣriyya, 1934.

Juynboll, G. H. A. The Authenticity of the Tradition Literature: Discussions in Modern Egypt. Leiden: Brill, 1969.

Kamali, Mohammad Hashim. *Principles of Islamic Jurisprudence*. 3rd ed. Cambridge, UK: Islamic Texts Society, 2003.

Al-Karmī, Marʿī b. Yūsuf. *Dalīl al-Ṭalib li-Nayl al-Maṭālib*. Edited by Abū Qutayba Naẓar Muḥammad Fāryābī. 3rd ed. Riyadh, Saudi Arabia: Dār Ṭība, 2008.

Al-Karmī, Marʿī b. Yūsuf, and Abī al-ʿAwn Muḥammad b. Aḥmad Saffārīnī. *Al-Taḥqīq fī Buṭlān al-Talfīq Naṣṣ ʿalā Futyā li'l-Shaykh Marʿī al-Ḥanbalī*. Edited by ʿAbd al-ʿAzīz b. Ibrāhīm Dukhayyil. Riyadh, Saudi Arabia: Dār al-Ṣumayʿī, 1998.

Kaya, Eyyup Said. "Continuity and Change in Islamic Law: The Concept of *madhhab* and the Dimensions of Legal Disagreements in Ḥanafī Scholarship of the Tenth Century." In *The Islamic School of Law: Evolution, Devolution and Progress*, edited by Peri Bearman, Rudolph Peters, and Frank E. Vogel. Cambridge, MA: Harvard Univ. Press, 2005.

Kennedy, Duncan. "Form and Substance in Private Law Adjudication." *Harvard Law Review* 89:8 (1976): 1685–1778.

Kerr, Malcolm H. *Islamic Reform: The Political and Legal Theories of Muḥammad 'Abduh and Rashīd Riḍā*. Berkeley: Univ. of California Press, 1966.

Al-Khājandī, Muḥammad Sulṭān al-Ma'ṣūmī. *Hal al-Muslim Mulzam bi-Ittibā' Madhhab Mu'ayyan min al-Madhāhib al-Arba'a?* N.p.: Jam'iyyat Iḥyā' al-Turāth al-Islāmī, 1939.

Al-Khallāl, Abū Bakr. *Kitāb al-Amr bi'l-Ma'rūf wa'l-Nahī 'an al-Munkar*. Edited by Mashhūr Ḥasan Maḥmūd Salmān and Hishām b. Ismā'īl al-Saqqā. Beirut: al-Maktab al-Islāmī, 1990.

Al-Kharāshī, Sulaymān b. Ṣāliḥ. "Tadarrujāt Rāshid al-Ghannūshī wa-Ahamm Inḥirāfātih." *Islamway.com*, Apr. 2005. http://ar.islamway.com/book/825.

Khaṭīb, Aḥmad, and Usāma Ṣalāḥ. "Khilāf Jadīd Dākhil Maktab Irshād al-Ikhwān." *Al-Masry al-Youm Newspaper*, Nov. 1, 2007. http://today.almasryal youm.com/article2.aspx?ArticleID=81393.

Khūlī, Jamāl. *Al-Istibdāl wa-Ightiṣāb al-Awqāf: Dirāsa Wathā'iqiyya*. Alexandria: Dār al-Thaqāfa al-'Ilmiyya, 2000.

Knysh, Alexander D. *Ibn 'Arabī in the Later Islamic Tradition: The Making of a Polemical Image in Medieval Islam*. Albany: State Univ. of New York Press, 1999.

Krawietz, Birgit. "Cut and Paste in Legal Rules: Designing Islamic Norms with Talfiq." *Die Welt Des Islams* 42:1 (2002): 3–40.

Kuran, Timur. *The Long Divergence: How Islamic Law Held Back the Middle East*. Princeton, NJ: Princeton Univ. Press, 2010.

———. "Why the Middle East Is Economically Underdeveloped: Historical Mechanisms of Institutional Stagnation." *Journal of Economic Perspectives* 18:3 (July 1, 2004): 71–90.

Al-Kurdī, Muḥammad b. Sulaymān al-Madanī al-Shāfi'ī. *Al-Fawā'id al-Madaniyya fī Bayān Ikhtilāf al-'Ulamā' min al-Shāfi'iyya*. Diyār Bakr, Turkey: Al-Maktaba al-Islāmiyya, n.d.

Labib, Subhi. "Egyptian Commercial Policy in the Middle Ages." In *Studies in the Economic History of the Middle East: From the Rise of Islam to the Present Day*, edited by Michael Cook. London: Oxford Univ. Press, 1970.

Lalanne, Ludovic. *Curiosités Littéraires*. Paris: Paulin, 1845.

Lauzière, Henri. "The Construction of *Salafiyya*: Reconsidering Salafism from the Perspective of Conceptual History." *International Journal of Middle East Studies* 42:3 (2010): 369–89.

Layish, Aharon. "The Transformation of the Sharī'a from Jurists' Law to Statutory Law in the Contemporary Muslim World." *Die Welt Des Islams*, n.s., 44:1 (2004): 85–113.

Layish, Aharon, and Ron Shaham. "Tashrīʿ." In *Encyclopaedia of Islam*, edited by Peri Bearman, Th. Bianquis, C. E. Bosworth, E. Van Donzel, and W. P. Heinrichs. Leiden: Brill, 2008.

Lellouch, Benjamin. *Les Ottomans en Egypte: historiens et conquérants au XVIe siècle*. Paris: Peeters, 2006.

Levit, Nancy. "Practically Unreasonable—A Critique of Practical Reason: A Review of the Problems of Jurisprudence by Richard A. Posner." *Northwestern University Law Review* 85:2 (1991): 494–518.

Lombardi, Clark B, and Nathan J Brown. "Do Constitutions Requiring Adherence to Shariʿa Threaten Human Rights—How Egypt's Constitutional Court Reconciles Islamic Law with the Liberal Rule of Law." *American University International Law Review* 21 (2006): 379.

Lowry, Joseph E. *Early Islamic Legal Theory the Risāla of Muḥammad Ibn Idrīs al-Shāfiʿī*. Leiden: Brill, 2007.

Lucas, Scott. "The Legal Principles of Muḥammad B. Ismāʿīl al-Bukhārī and Their Relationship to Classical Salafī Islam." *Islamic Law and Society* 13:3 (2006): 289–324.

Al-Mahdī, Muḥammad al-ʿAbbāsī. *Al-Fatāwā al-Mahdiyya fi'l-Waqā'iʿal-Miṣriyya*. Cairo: al-Maṭbaʿa al-Azhariyya al-Miṣriyya, 1883.

Makdisi, George. *Ibn ʿAqil: Religion and Culture in Classical Islam*. Edinburgh: Edinburgh Univ. Press, 1997.

———. *The Rise of Colleges: Institutions of Learning in Islam and the West*. Edinburgh: Edinburgh Univ. Press, 1981.

Makdisi, John. "Legal Logic and Equity in Islamic Law." *American Journal of Comparative Law* 33:1 (1985): 63–92.

Al-Makkī, Ibn ʿAlān. "Al-Talaṭṭuf fi'l-Wuṣūl ilā al-Taʿarruf." Cairo, n.d., MS Dār al-Kutub 144 Uṣūl Fiqh, Microfilm #40314.

Al-Makkī, Ibn Mullah Farrūkh al-Mawrawī. *Al-Qawl al-Sadīd fī Baʿḍ Masā'il al-Ijtihād wa'l-Taqlīd*. Edited by Jāsim b. Muḥammad b. Muhalhal Yāsīn and ʿAdnān b. Sālim b. Muḥammad Rūmī. 2nd ed. al-Mansura, Egypt: Dār al-Wafā', 1992.

———. "Taʿlīqa fi'l-Ijtihād wa'l-Taqlīd." Cairo, n.d., MS Dār al-Kutub 166 Uṣūl Taymūr.

Al-Malībārī, Zayn al-Dīn b. ʿAbd al-ʿAzīz. *Fatḥ al-Muʿīn bi-Sharḥ Qurrat al-ʿAyn*. Cairo: Maṭbaʿat Muḥammad ʿAlī Ṣubayḥ, 1928.

Mallat, Chibli. "From Islamic to Middle Eastern Law a Restatement of the Field (Part II)." *American Journal of Comparative Law* 52:1 (2004): 209–86.

———. Review of "The Islamic Law on Land Tax and Rent: The Peasants' Loss of Property Rights as Interpreted in the Hanafite Legal Literature of the Mamluk and Ottoman Periods." *Bulletin of the School of Oriental and African Studies, University of London* 54:1 (1991): 155–56.

Al-Maqdisī, Abū al-Fatḥ Naṣr b. Ibrāhīm. *Mukhtaṣar al-Hujja 'alā Tārik al-Maḥajja*. Riyadh, Saudi Arabia: Dār Aḍwā' al-Salaf, 2005.

Al-Marāghī, Muṣṭafā. "Khuṭbat al-Ustādh al-Akbar Shaykh al-Jāmi' al-Azhar." *Al-Manār* 35:3 (1935): 186–88.

March, Andrew F. "Islamic Foundations for a Social Contract in Non-Muslim Liberal Democracies." *American Political Science Review* 101:2 (2007): 235–53.

———. *Islam and Liberal Citizenship: The Search for an Overlapping Consensus*. Oxford, UK: Oxford Univ. Press, 2009.

Al-Marwazī, Muḥammad b. Naṣr Abū 'Abd Allāh. *Ikhtilāf al-'Ulamā'*. Edited by Ṣubḥī Sāmrā'ī. 2nd ed. Beirut: 'Ālam al-Kutub 1985.

Al-Masry al-Youm. "FJP Leader Criticizes Salafi Nour Party over Sukuk Draft Law." *Egypt Independent*. Apr. 14, 2013. http://www.egyptindependent.com/news/fjp-leader-criticizes-salafi-nour-party-over-sukuk-draft-law.

Mayer, Ann. "The *Sharī'ah*: A Methodology or a Body of Substantive Rules?" In *Islamic Law and Jurisprudence*, edited by Nicholas Heer and Farhat Jacob Ziadeh, 177–98. Seattle: Univ. of Washington Press, 1990.

Melchert, Christopher. *The Formation of the Sunni Schools of Law, 9th–10th Centuries C.E.* Leiden: Brill, 1997.

———. "Traditionist-Jurisprudents and the Framing of Islamic Law." *Islamic Law and Society* 8:3 (2001): 383–406.

Meshal, Reem. "Antagonistic Sharī'as and the Construction of Orthodoxy in Sixteenth-Century Ottoman Cairo." *Journal of Islamic Studies* 21:2 (July 2010): 183–212.

Messick, Brinkley. *The Calligraphic State: Textual Domination and History in a Muslim Society*. Berkeley: Univ. of California Press, 1993.

Mīlād, Salwā 'Alī. *Al-Wathā'iq al-'Uthmāniyya: Dirāsa Arshīfiyya Wathā'iqiyya li-Sijillāt Maḥkamat al-Bāb al-'Ālī*. Alexandria: Dār al-Thaqāfa al-'Ilmiyya, 2004.

Al-Mirdāwī, 'Alā' al-Dīn 'Alī b. Sulaymān. *Taṣḥīḥ al-Furū'*. Edited by 'Abd Allāh b. 'Abd al-Muḥsin Turkī. Riyadh, Saudi Arabia: Mu'assasat al-Risāla, 2003.

Al-Miṣrī, Qāsim b. Qaṭlūbaghā. *Al-Taṣḥīḥ wa'l-Tarjīḥ 'alā Mukhtaṣar al-Qudūrī*. Edited by Ḍiyā' Yūnus. Beirut: Dār al-Kutub al-'Ilmiyya, 2002.

Mitchell, Timothy. *Colonising Egypt*. Cambridge Middle East Library. Cambridge, UK: Cambridge Univ. Press, 1988.

Muhanna, Muḥammad. "Qanūn al-Aḥwāl al-Shakhṣiyya." *Al-Muslim Magazine*, Mar. 2000.

Al-Munāwī, 'Abd al-Ra'ūf b. Nūr al-Dīn. *Fayḍ al-Qadīr*. 2nd ed. 6 vols. Beirut: Dār al-Ma'rifa, 1972.

Muṭī'ī, Muḥammad Bakhīt. "Al-Talfīq fi'l-'Ibāda." *Fatāwā al-Azhar wa-Dār al-Iftā' fī Mi'at 'Ām*. Cairo: Kalimāt. Accessed Apr. 30, 2012. http://www.kl28.com/fat1r.php?search=3169.

N.A. "Majma' al-Buḥūth bi'l-Azhar: Milk al-Yamīn Da'wa li-'Ilāqa Jinsiyya Āthima," *CNNArabic*, June 7, 2012. http://arabic.cnn.com/2012/middle_east/7/6/index.html.

Nabīl, Āya. "Ba'd Ta'ahhud al-Muftī bi-Taghyīr Qawānīn Suzanne Mubarak Ḥuqūqiyyūn Yarfuḍūna al-Misās bi-Qawānīn al-Usra wa'l-Ṭifl Ḥattā Tashkīl Majlis al-Sha'b." *al-Yawm Al-Sābi' Newspaper*, Apr. 20, 2011. http://www.youm7.com/News.asp?NewsID=394822.

Al-Nābulsī, 'Abd al-Ghanī. "Al-Ajwiba 'an al-As'ila al-Sitta." Cairo, n.d., MS Dār al-Kutub 365 Uṣūl Fiqh.

Naḥrāwī, Islām, and Lu'ai 'Alī. "Al-Muftī Yata'ahhad bi-I'ādat al-Naẓar fī Qawānīn al-Usra." *Al-Yawm al-Sābi' Newspaper*, Apr. 18, 2001. http://www.youm7.com/News.asp?NewsID=393950.

Al-Nasā'ī, 'Abd al-Raḥmān. *Ṣaḥīḥ al-Nasā'ī*, 188, Ḥadīth No. 5695. Riyadh, Saudi Arabia: Maktabat al-Ma'ārif li'l-Nashr wa'l-Tawzī', 1998.

O'Brien, Patrick. "The Long-Term Growth of Agricultural Production in Egypt: 1821–1962." In *Political and Social Change in Modern Egypt: Historical Studies from the Ottoman Conquest to the United Arab Republic*, edited by Peter Malcolm Holt, 162–95. London: Oxford Univ. Press, 1968.

Al-Obeikan, Sheikh Abdul Mohsen. "The Codification of Islamic Sharia." *Asharq Al-awsat*, Apr. 28, 2006. http://www.asharq-e.com/news.asp?section=2&id=4740.

Opwis, Felicitas. *Maṣlaḥa and the Purpose of the Law: Islamic Discourse on Legal Change from the 4th/10th to 8th/14th Century*. Leiden: Brill, 2010.

———. "*Maṣlaḥa* in Contemporary Islamic Legal Theory." *Islamic Law and Society* 12:2 (2005): 182–223.

Orelli, Luisa. "Islam Institutionnel Égyptien et Modernité: Aperçu Du Débat À Travers Les Fatâwâ D'al-Azhar et de Dâr Al-Iftâ'." *Studia Islamica*, no. 95 (Jan. 1, 2002): 109–33.

Owen, Roger. *Cotton and the Egyptian Economy, 1820–1914: A Study in Trade and Development*. Oxford, UK: Clarendon Press, 1969.

Oxford Analytica. "Saudi Arabia: Codified Sharia Could Benefit Business." *Zawya,* Aug. 26, 2010. http://www.zawya.com/story/ZAWYA20100826075952/Benefiting%20Business/.

Peters, Rudolph. "1829–1871 or 1876–1883? The Significance of Nineteenth-Century Pre-Colonial Legal Reform in Egypt." Presented at New Approaches to Egyptian Legal History: Late Ottoman Period to the Present, Cairo, June 11, 2009.

———. "Body and Spirit of Islamic Law: *Madhhab* Diversity in Ottoman Documents from the Dakhla Oasis, Egypt." In *Islamic Law in Theory: Studies on Jurisprudence in Honor of Bernard Weiss,* ed. A. Kevin Reinhart and Robert Gleave, 322–27. Leiden and Boston: Brill, 2014.

———. "The Codification of Criminal Law in Nineteenth-Century Egypt: Tradition or Modernization?" In *Law, Society and National Identity,* edited by J. M. Abun-Nasr, U. Wanitzek, and U. Spellenberg, 211–25. Hamburg: Buske, 1991.

———. *Crime and Punishment in Islamic Law: Theory and Practice from the Sixteenth to the Twenty-First Century.* Cambridge, UK: Cambridge Univ. Press, 2005.

———. "'For His Correction and as a Deterrent Example for Others': Meḥmed ʿAlī's First Criminal Legislation (1829–1830)." *Islamic Law and Society* 6:2 (1999): 164–92.

———. "Islamic and Secular Criminal Law in Nineteenth-Century Egypt: The Role and Function of the Qadi." *Islamic Law and Society* 4:1 (Jan. 1, 1997): 70–90.

———. "Muḥammad al-ʿAbbāsī al-Mahdī (D. 1897), Grand Muftī of Egypt, and His 'al-Fatāwā al-Mahdiyya.'" *Islamic Law and Society* 1:1 (Jan. 1994): 66–82.

———. "What Does It Mean to Be an Official Madhhab? Ḥanafism and the Ottoman Empire." In *The Islamic School of Law: Evolution, Devolution, and Progress,* edited by Peri Bearman, Rudolph Peters, and Frank E. Vogel. Cambridge, MA: Harvard Univ. Press, 2005.

Peters, Rudolph, and J. G. J. Ter Haar. "Rukhṣa." In *Encyclopaedia of Islam,* 2nd ed., ed. P. Bearman, Th. Bianquis, C. E. Bosworth, E. van Donzel, and W. P. Heinrichs. Leiden: Brill, 2010.

Portalis, Jean-Etienne-Marie. *Discours Préliminaire du Premier Projet de Code Civil.* Bordeaux: Ed. confluences, 1999.

Portalis, Jean-Etienne-Marie, and Frédéric Portalis. *Discours et Rapports sur le Code Civil: Précédés de l'Éssai sur l'Utilité de la Codification, de Frédéric Portalis.* Caen: Presses Universitaires de Caen, 2010.

Posner, Richard A. *Overcoming Law.* Cambridge, MA: Harvard Univ. Press, 1995.

———. "Pragmatic Adjudication." *Cardozo Law Review* 18 (1996–97): 1–20.

———. *The Problems of Jurisprudence.* Cambridge, MA: Harvard Univ. Press, 1990.

Powers, David Stephan. "*Kadijustiz* or *Qāḍī*-Justice? A Paternity Dispute from Fourteenth-Century Morocco." *Islamic Law and Society* 1:3 (1994): 332–66.

———. "On Judicial Review in Islamic Law." *Law & Society Review* 26:2 (1992): 315–41.

———. *Studies in Qur'an and Ḥadīth: The Formation of the Islamic Law of Inheritance.* Berkeley: Univ. of California Press, 1986.

Al-Qaffāl, Sayf al-Dīn Abū Bakr Muḥammad b. Aḥmad al-Shāshī. *Ḥilyat al-'Ulamā' fī Ma'rifat Madhāhib al-Fuqahā'.* Edited by Yāsīn Aḥmad Ibrāhīm Darādikah. 8 vols. Amman: Maktabat al-Risāla al-Dīniyya, 1988.

Al-Qalhūd, Abdul-Rahman. "Al-Talfeek and Its Rule in Jurisprudence." In *The First Conference of the Academy of Islamic Research.* Cairo: Al-Azhar Academy of Islamic Research, 1964.

Al-Qalqashandī, Abū al-'Abbās Aḥmad. *Ṣubḥ al-A'shā fī Ṣinā'at al-Inshā'.* 14 vols. Cairo: Dār al-Kutub al-Miṣriyya, 1922.

Al-Qaraḍāwī, Yūsuf. *Fī Fiqh al-Aqalliyyāt al-Muslima.* Cairo: Dār al-Shurūq, 2001.

Al-Qarāfī, Shihāb al-Dīn. *Al-Iḥkām fī Tamyīz al-Fatāwā 'an al-Aḥkām wa-Taṣarrufāt al-Qāḍī wa'l-Imām.* Edited by 'Abd al-Fattāḥ Abū Ghudda. 2nd ed. Beirut: Maktabat al-Maṭbū'āt al-Islāmiyya bi-Ḥalab, 1995.

———. *Sharḥ Tanqīḥ al-Fuṣūl fī Ikhtiṣār al-Maḥṣūl fi'l-Uṣūl.* Beirut: Dār al-Fikr, 2004.

Al-Qārī, Nūr al-Dīn al-Mullah 'Alī. *Al-Asrār al-Marfū'a fi'l-Akhbār al-Mawḍū'a.* Edited by Muḥammad b. Luṭfī al-Ṣabbāgh. 2nd ed. Riyadh, Saudi Arabia: al-Maktab al-Islāmī, 1986.

———. "Al-Ihtidā' fi'l-Iqtidā'." Cairo, n.d., MS Dār al-Kutub 172 Uṣūl Taymūr.

———. "Tawḍīḥ al-Mabānī 'alā Mukhtaṣar al-Manār." Cairo, n.d., MS Dār al-Kutub 367 Uṣūl Fiqh.

Rafeq, Abdul-Karim. "The Application of Islamic Law in the Ottoman Courts in Damascus: The Case of the Rental of Waqf Land." In *Dispensing Justice in Islam: Qadis and Their Judgments,* edited by Muhammad Khalid Masud, Rudolph Peters, and David Stephan Powers. Leiden: Brill, 2006.

Al-Rājiḥī, 'Abd al-'Azīz 'Abd Allāh. *Al-Taqlīd wa'l-Iftā' wa'l-Istiftā'.* Riyadh, Saudi Arabia: Kunūz Ishbīliyā, 2007.

Rahman, Fazlur. *Islam and Modernity: Transformation of an Intellectual Tradition.* Chicago: Univ. of Chicago Press, 1982.

Al-Ramlī, Khayr al-Dīn. *Al-Fatāwā al-Khayriyya li-Naf' al-Bariyya.* Bulaq, Egypt: al-Maṭba'a al-Kubrā al-Mīriyya, 1882.

Rapoport, Yossef. "Legal Diversity in the Age of *Taqlīd*: The Four Chief *Qāḍīs* under the Mamluks." *Islamic Law and Society* 10:2 (2003): 210–28.

Rashād, Sāra, and Riḥāb Aḥmad. "Aqbāṭ Yuraḥḥibūn bi-Iqtirāḥ al-Azhar fi'l-Ta'sīsiyya wa-Ya'tabirūnahū al-Marji'iyya al-Wasaṭiyya li'l-Miṣriyyīn." *almesryoon*, Cairo, June 7, 2012. http://www.almesryoon.com/permalink/15611.html.

Rawls, John. *Political Liberalism*. New York: Columbia Univ. Press, 1993.

Raymond, André. *Cairo*. Cambridge, MA: Harvard Univ. Press, 2000.

Rebstock, Ulrich. "A Qāḍī's Errors." *Islamic Law and Society* 6:1 (1999): 1–37.

Riḍā, Muḥammad Rashīd. "Al-Muḥāwara al-Tāsi'a Bayna al-Muṣliḥ wa'l-Muqallid." Edited by Muḥammad Rashīd Riḍā. *Al-Manār* 4:10 (1901).

———. "Al-Ṭalāq 'alā al-Ghā'ib wa'l-Mu'sir fi'l-Sūdān." *Al-Manār* 6:6 (1903).

———. *Fatāwā al-Imām Muḥammad Rashīd Riḍā*. Edited by Ṣalāḥ al-Dīn Munjid. 6 vols. Beirut: Dār al-Kitāb al-Jadīd, 1970.

———. *Yusr al-Islām wa-Uṣūl al-Tashrī' al-'Āmm fī Nahy Allāh wa-Rasūlihi 'an Kathrat al-Su'āl*. Cairo: Maktabat al-Salām al- 'Ālamiyya, 1984.

———. "Madaniyyat al-Qawānīn." Edited by Rashīd Riḍā. *Al-Manār* 23 (1898).

Rippin, Andrew. *Muslims: Their Religious Beliefs and Practices*. London: Routledge, 1990.

Rorty, Richard. "The Banality of Pragmatism and the Poetry of Justice." *Southern California Law Review* 63 (1990): 1811–19.

———. *Consequences of Pragmatism: Essays, 1972–1980*. Minneapolis: Univ. of Minnesota Press, 1982.

Rosen, Lawrence. *The Anthropology of Justice: Law as Culture in Islamic Society*. The Lewis Henry Morgan Lectures 1985. Cambridge, UK: Cambridge Univ. Press, 1989.

———. *The Justice of Islam: Comparative Perspectives on Islamic Law and Society*. Oxford, UK: Oxford Univ. Press, 2000.

Sabra, Adam Abdelhamid. *Poverty and Charity in Medieval Islam: Mamluk Egypt, 1250–1517*. Cambridge, UK: Cambridge Univ. Press, 2000.

Sadeghi, Behnam. *The Logic of Law Making in Islam: Women and Prayer in the Legal Tradition*. Cambridge, UK: Cambridge Univ. Press, 2013.

Sajdi, Dana. "Decline, Its Discontents and Ottoman Cultural History: By Way of Introduction." In *Ottoman Tulips, Ottoman Coffee: Leisure and Lifestyle in the Eighteenth Century*, edited by Dana Sajdi. London: Tauris Academic Studies, 2007.

Sālim, Laṭīfa M. *Al-Niẓām al-Qaḍā'ī al-Miṣrī al-Ḥadīth*. Cairo: al-Hay'a al-Miṣriyya al-'Āmma li'l-Kitāb, 2001.

Al-Samalāwī, 'Abd al-Mu'ṭī. "Al-Qawl al-Murabba' fī Ḥukm al-'Aqd 'alā al-Madhāhib al-Arba'." Cairo, n.d., MS Dār al-Kutub 226 Fiqh Taymūr.

Al-Saqqāf, Sayyid ʿAlawī b. Aḥmad. *Majmūʿat Sabʿat Kutub Mufīda*. Cairo: Maṭbaʿat Muṣṭafā al-Bābī al-Ḥalabī, 1983.

Sayyid-Marsot, Afaf Lutfi. *A History of Egypt: From the Arab Conquest to the Present*. Cambridge, UK: Cambridge Univ. Press, 2007.

———. *Women and Men in Late Eighteenth-Century Egypt*. Austin: Univ. of Texas Press, 1995.

Schacht, Joseph. *An Introduction to Islamic Law*. Oxford, UK: Clarendon Press, 1982.

———. "Problems of Modern Islamic Legislation." *Studia Islamica* 12 (1960): 99–129.

Schacht, J., and D. B. MacDonald. "Idjtihād." In *Encyclopaedia of Islam*, edited by P. Bearman, Th. Bianquis, C. E. Bosworth, E. van Donzel, and W. P. Heinrichs. 2nd ed. Leiden: Brill, 2010.

Al-Samhūdī, Nūr al-Dīn. "Al-ʿIqd al-Farīd fī Aḥkām al-Taqlīd." Cairo, n.d., MS Dār al-Kutub 45 Uṣūl Taymūr.

Al-Shāfiʿī, Muḥammad b. Idrīs. *Al-Risāla*. Edited by Aḥmad Muḥammad Shākir. Beirut: Dār al-Kutub al-ʿIlmiyya, 1939.

Shaham, Ron. "Shopping for Legal Forums: Christians and Family Law in Modern Egypt." In *Dispensing Justice in Islam: Qadis and Their Judgements*, edited by Muhammad Khalid Masud, Rudolph Peters, and David Stephan Powers. Leiden: Brill, 2006.

Shapiro, Martin. *Courts: A Comparative and Political Analysis*. Chicago: Univ. of Chicago Press, 1981.

Sharīf, ʿAlī Muḥammad ʿAlī. *Al-Nuṣḥ wa'l-Tabyīn fī Taṣḥīḥ Mafāhīm al-Muḥtasibīn*. Cairo: Maktabat al-Turāth al-Islāmī, 2002.

Al-Shithrī, ʿAbd al-Raḥmān b. Saʿd. *Taqnīn al-Sharīʿa bayna al-Taḥlīl wa'l-Taḥrīm*. Riyadh, Saudi Arabia: Dār al-Faḍīla, 2005.

Al-Shahrazūrī, Ibn al-Ṣalāḥ. *Fatāwā wa-Masā'il Ibn al-Ṣalāḥ fi'l-Tafsīr wa'l-Ḥadīth wa'l-Uṣūl wa'l-Fiqh*. Edited by ʿAbd al-Muʿṭī Amīn Qalʿajī. 2 vols. Beirut: Dār al-Maʿrifa, 1986.

Al-Shaʿrānī, ʿAbd al-Wahhāb. *Kashf al-Ghumma ʿan Jamīʿ al-Umma*. Cairo: al-Maṭbaʿa al-Maymaniyya, n.d.

———. *Al-Mīzān al-Shaʿrāniyya al-Mudkhala*. 2 vols. Cairo: al-Maṭābiʿ al-Amīriyya, 1900.

Al-Sharqāwī, ʿAbd Allāh b. Ḥijāzī. "Sharḥ ʿalā al-Jawhar al-ʿAzīz." Cairo, n.d., MS Dār al-Kutub 68 Fiqh Madhāhib.

Al-Shāṭibī, Abū Isḥāq Ibrāhīm b. Mūsā. *al-Muwāfaqāt*. 6 vols. Riyadh, Saudi Arabia: Dār Ibn ʿAffān, 1997.

Al-Shawkānī, Muḥammad b. ʿAlī b. Muḥammad. *Irshād al-Fuḥūl ilā Taḥqīq al-Ḥaqq min ʿIlm al-Uṣūl*. Edited by Abū Ḥafṣ Sāmī b. al-ʿArabī al-Atharī. 2 vols. Riyadh, Saudi Arabia: Dār al-Faḍīla, 2000.

Al-Shurunbulālī, Ḥasan b. ʿAmmār b. ʿAlī. "Al-ʿIqd al-Farīd li-Bayān al-Rājiḥ min al-Khilāf fi'l-Taqlīd." Cairo, n.d., MS Dār al-Kutub 367 Uṣūl Fiqh.

———. *Marāqī al-Falāḥ Sharḥ Nūr al-Īḍāḥ*. Cairo: Al-Maṭbaʿa al-ʿIlmiyya, 1897.

"Sijill 105." n.d. The Court of Miṣr al-Qadīma (Rabīʿ al-Awwal 1092/Mar. 1681), Dār al-Wathā'iq al-Qawmiyya (Cairo).

"Sijill 106." n.d. The Court of Miṣr al-Qadīma, Dār al-Wathā'iq al-Qawmiyya (Cairo).

"Sijill 254." n.d. The Court of al-Bāb al-ʿĀlī, Dār al-Wathā'iq al-Qawmiyya (Cairo).

"Sijill 361." n.d. The Court of Jāmiʿ al-Ṣāliḥ, Dār al-Wathā'iq al-Qawmiyya (Cairo).

"Sijill 66." n.d. The Court of Būlāq (AD 1139–AD 1143), Dār al-Wathā'iq al-Qawmiyya (Cairo).

Al-Simnānī, Abū Qāsim ʿAlī b. Muḥammad b. Aḥmad al-Raḥbī. *Rawḍat al-Quḍāh wa Ṭarīq al-Najāh*. Edited by Ṣalāḥ al-Dīn Nāhī. 2nd ed. 4 vols. Beirut: Mu'assasat al-Risāla, 1984.

Al-Sindī, ʿAlī. "Risāla fī Bayān al-Iqtidā' bi'l-Shāfiʿiyya." Cairo, n.d., MS Dār al-Kutub 233 Uṣūl Taymūr.

Singer, Joseph. "Legal Realism Now." *California Law Review* 76:2 (1988): 468–70.

Sonbol, Amira. "Women in Shariʿah Courts: A Historical and Methodological Discussion." *Fordham International Law Journal* 27:1 (2003): 225–53.

Sonbol, Amira El Azhary. "Adults and Minors in Ottoman Shariʿa Courts." In *Women, the Family, and Divorce Laws in Islamic History*, edited by Amira El Azhary Sonbol. Syracuse, NY: Syracuse Univ. Press, 1996.

———. "Law and Gender Violence in Ottoman and Modern Egypt." In Sonbol, *Women, the Family, and Divorce Laws in Islamic History*.

———. "The Genesis of Family Law: How *Shariʿah*, Custom and Colonial Laws Influenced the Development of Personal Status Codes." In *Wanted: Equality and Justice in the Muslim Family*, edited by Zainah Anwar. Kuala Lumpur: Musawah, 2009.

Spectorsky, Susan A. "Aḥmad Ibn Ḥanbal's Fiqh." *Journal of the American Oriental Society* 102:3 (July 1, 1982).

Al-Subkī, Tāj al-Dīn. *Jamʿ al-Jawāmiʿ fī Uṣūl al-Fiqh*. Edited by ʿAbd al-Munʿim Khalīl Ibrāhīm. 2nd ed. Beirut: Dār al-Kutub al-ʿIlmiyya, 2003.

———. *Muʿīd al-Niʿam wa-Mubīd al-Niqam*. Edited by David M. Myhrman. Leiden: Brill, 1908.

Al-Subkī, Taqī al-Dīn. *Fatāwā al-Subkī*. 2 vols. Beirut: Dār al-Maʿrifa, n.d.

Al-Ṭabarī, Muḥammad b. Jarīr. *Ikhtilāf al-Fuqahā'*. Beirut: Dār al-Kutub al-'Ilmiyya, 1980.

Talmon-Heller, Daniella. "Fidelty, Cohesion and Conformity within Madhhabs in Zangid and Ayyubid Syria." In *The Islamic School of Law: Evolution, Devolution, and Progress*, edited by Peri Bearman, Rudolph Peters, and Frank E. Vogel. Cambridge, MA: Harvard Univ. Press, 2005.

Tamanaha, B. Z. "Pragmatism in U.S. Legal Theory: Its Application to Normative Jurisprudence, Sociolegal Studies, and the Fact-Value Distinction." *American Journal of Jurisprudence* 41:1 (1996): 321–29.

Taskhīrī, Muḥammad 'Alī. *Ma'a Mu'tamarāt Majma' al-Fiqh al-Islāmī*. Beirut: Dar Iḥyā' al-Turāth al-'Arabī, 2003.

Thomas, Joseph. *The Universal Dictionary of Biography and Mythology*. Philadelphia: Lippincott, 1915.

Al-Timurtāshī, al-Khaṭīb Muḥammad b. 'Abd Allāh al-Ghazzī al-Ḥanafī. "Al-Fatāwā al-Timurtāshiyya." Cairo, n.d., MS Dār al-Kutub Fiqh Ḥanafī Ṭal'at 520, Microfilm #8558.

Tucker, Judith E. *In the House of the Law: Gender and Islamic Law in Ottoman Syria and Palestine*. Berkeley: Univ. of California Press, 1998.

———. *Women, Family, and Gender in Islamic Law*. Cambridge, UK: Cambridge Univ. Press, 2008.

Turner, Bryan S. "Islam, Capitalism and the Weber Theses." *British Journal of Sociology* 25:2 (June 1, 1974): 230–43. doi:10.2307/589314.

Tyan, Emile. "Judicial Organization." In *Law in the Middle East*, edited by Majid Khadduri and H. J. Liebesny. Washington, DC: The Middle East Institute, 1995.

Udovitch, Abraham L. *Partnership and Profit in Medieval Islam*. Princeton, NJ: Princeton Univ. Press, 1970.

Vishanoff, David. *The Formation of Islamic Hermeneutics: How Sunni Legal Theorists Imagined a Revealed Law*. New Haven: American Oriental Society, 2011.

Al-Wansharīsī, Aḥmad b. Yaḥyā. *Al-Mi'yār al-Mu'rib wa'l-Jāmi' al-Mughrib 'an Fatāwā Ahl Ifrīqiya wa'l-Andalus wa'l-Maghrib*. Edited by Muḥammad Ḥajjī. 13 vols. Rabat: Wizārat al-Awqāf wa'l-Shu'ūn al-Islāmiyya li'l-Mamlaka al-Maghribiyya, 1981.

Warner, Richard. "Pragmatism and Legal Reasoning." In *Hilary Putnam: Pragmatism and Realism*, ed. James Contant and Urszula M. Żegleń. London and New York: Routledge, 2002.

Watson, Alan. *Legal Transplants: An Approach to Comparative Law*. Athens: Univ. of Georgia Press, 1993.

———. *Society and Legal Change*. Edinburgh: Scottish Academic Press, 1977.

———. *The Evolution of Law*. Baltimore: Johns Hopkins Univ. Press, 1985.

———. *The Making of the Civil Law*. Cambridge, MA: Harvard Univ. Press, 1981.

———. *The Nature of Law*. Edinburgh: Edinburgh Univ. Press, 1977.

Weber, Max. *Economy and Society: An Outline of Interpretive Sociology*. Edited by Guenther Roth and Claus Wittich. Berkeley: Univ. of California Press, 1978.

———. *Max Weber on Law in Economy and Society*. Translated by Max Rheinstein and Edward A. Shils. Cambridge, MA: Harvard Univ. Press, 1954.

Weiss, Bernard G. *The Spirit of Islamic Law*. Athens: Univ. of Georgia Press, 1998.

West, Cornel. *The American Evasion of Philosophy: A Genealogy of Pragmatism*. Madison: Univ. of Wisconsin Press, 1989.

Wheeler, Brannon M. *Applying the Canon in Islam: The Authorization and Maintenance of Interpretive Reasoning in Ḥanafī Scholarship*. Albany: State Univ. of New York Press, 1996.

Wiederhold, Lutz. "Legal Doctrines in Conflict: The Relevance of *Madhhab* Boundaries to Legal Reasoning in the Light of an Unpublished Treatise on *Taqlīd* and *Ijtihād*." *Islamic Law and Society* 3:2 (1996): 234–304.

Winter, Michael. *Egyptian Society Under Ottoman Rule, 1517–1798*. London: Routledge, 1992.

Wizārat al-Awqāf wa'l-Shu'ūn al-Islāmiyya. *Al-Mawsū'a al-Fiqhiyya al-Kuwaytiyya*. 2nd ed. 45 vols. Kuwait: Dhāt al-Salāsil, 1983.

Yilmaz, Ihsan. "Inter-Madhhab Surfing, Neo-Ijtihad, and Faith-Based Movement Leaders." In *The Islamic School of Law: Evolution, Devolution, and Progress*, edited by Peri Bearman, Rudolph Peters, and Frank E. Vogel. Cambridge, MA: Harvard Univ. Press, 2005.

Zahrāwī, Abd al-Ḥamīd. *Al-A'māl al-Kāmila*. Edited by 'Abd al-Ilāh Nabhān. Damascus: Wizārat al-Thaqāfa fi'l-Jumhūriyya al-'Arabiyya al-Sūriyya, 1995.

Zammito, John H. *A Nice Derangement of Epistemes: Post-Positivism in the Study of Science from Quine to Latour*. Chicago: Univ. of Chicago Press, 2004.

Al-Zarkashī, Badr al-Dīn Muḥammad. *Al-Baḥr al-Muḥīṭ fī Uṣūl al-Fiqh*. Edited by 'Abd al-Qādir al-'Āfī and 'Umar Sulaymān al-Ashqar. 2nd ed. 6 vols. Kuwait: Wizārat al-Awqāf wa'l-Shu'ūn al-Islāmiyya, 1992.

Zubaida, Sami. *Law and Power in the Islamic World*. London: I. B. Tauris, 2003.

Zysow, Aron. "The Economy of Certainty: An Introduction to the Typology of Islamic Legal Theory." PhD diss., Harvard Univ., 1984.

———. *The Economy of Certainty: An Introduction to the Typology of Islamic Legal Theory*. Atlanta: Lockwood Press, 2013.

Index

Italic page number denotes illustration.